CHILDREN'S ISSUES, LAWS AND PROGRAMS

CHILD WELFARE SYSTEM

TRANSITIONS

Children's Issues, Laws and Programs

Additional books in this series can be found on Nova's website
under the Series tab.

Additional E-books in this series can be found on Nova's website
under the E-book tab.

CHILDREN'S ISSUES, LAWS AND PROGRAMS

CHILD WELFARE SYSTEM

TRANSITIONS

AUBREY D. WILSON
AND
SALLY G. RYAN
EDITORS

Nova Science Publishers, Inc.
New York

For permission to use material from this book please contact us:
Telephone 631-231-7269; Fax 631-231-8175
Web Site: http://www.novapublishers.com

Additional color graphics may be available in the e-book version of this book.

Library of Congress Cataloging-in-Publication Data

Child welfare system : transitions / editors, Aubrey D. Wilson and Sally G. Ryan.
p. cm.
Includes bibliographical references and index.
ISBN 978-1-61324-713-6 (hardcover : alk. paper) 1. Child welfare--United States. I. Wilson, Aubrey D. II. Ryan, Sally G.
HV741.C53584 2011
362.70973--dc23
2011016634

Published by Nova Science Publishers, Inc. † New York

CONTENTS

PREFACE

In 1999, the Administration for Children and Families, U.S. Department of Health and Human Services, undertook the National Survey of Child and Adolescent Well-Being (NSCAW) to learn about children and families coming in contact with the child welfare system (CWS). The sample, which represents the population of children and families that entered the CWS within a 15 month period, comprises 5,501 children (aged 0 to 14 years) from 92 child welfare agencies nationwide. The NSCAW gathers information about children's safety, living-situation permanency, well-being, and services after a maltreatment investigation by child protective services. This book provides information about 962 children who were infants when they first became involved in investigations for child abuse or neglect and whose caregivers participated at the 5- to 6-year follow-up.

Chapter 1- In 1999 the Administration for Children and Families, U.S. Department of Health and Human Services, undertook the National Survey of Child and Adolescent Well-Being (NSCAW) to learn about children and families coming in contact with the child welfare system (CWS). The sample, which represents the population of children and families that entered the CWS within a 15-month period (October 1999 to December 2000), comprises 5,501 children (aged 0 to 14 years) from 92 child welfare agencies nationwide. The first national longitudinal survey of its kind, NSCAW gathers information about children's safety, living-situation permanency, wellbeing, and services after a maltreatment investigation by child protective services. NSCAW has examined the experiences of children and families with the CWS, starting approximately 4 months after the completion of a CWS maltreatment investigation and following up 1½ years, 3 years, and 5 to 6 years later (in 2005 and 2006).

Chapter 2- The National Survey of Child and Adolescent Well-Being (NSCAW) is a longitudinal study of a national probability sample of children involved with the child welfare system (CWS). NSCAW originated in the Personal Responsibility and Work Opportunity Reconciliation Act of 1996, which directed the U.S. Department of Health and Human Services to carry out a national study of children at risk for maltreatment or otherwise involved with the CWS. The sample, which represents the population of children and families who entered child protective services within a 15-month period (October 1999 through December 2000), included 5,501 children (aged zero to 14 years at the time of sampling) from 92 child welfare agencies nationwide. NSCAW gathered data on children's safety, permanency of living situation, well-being, and services at five points in time. Baseline data were collected approximately 4 months after the completion of the index CWS maltreatment investigation; follow-up data were collected 1 year (Wave 2), 1½ years (Wave 3), 3 years (Wave 4), and 6 to 7 years later (Wave 5).

Chapter 3- In 1999 the Administration on Children, Youth and Families, U.S. Department of Health and Human Services, undertook the National Survey of Child and Adolescent Well-Being (NSCAW) to learn about children and families coming in contact with the child welfare system (CWS). The sample, which represents the population of children and families who entered CWS services within a 15-month period (October 1999 through December 2000), included 5,501 children (aged 0 to 14 at the time of sampling) from 92 child welfare agencies nationwide. The first national longitudinal survey of its kind, NSCAW gathers information about children's safety, living-situation permanency, well-being, and services after a maltreatment investigation by child protective services. Baseline data were collected approximately 4 months after the completion of the index CWS maltreatment investigation; follow-up data were collected 1 year (Wave 2), 1 1/2 years (Wave 3), 3 years (Wave 4), and 6 to 7 years later (Wave 5). Wave 5 data for young adults were collected in 2006 and 2007.

In: Child Welfare System: Transitions
Editors: Aubrey D. Wilson and Sally G. Ryan
ISBN: 978-1-61324-713-6

Chapter 1

FROM EARLY INVOLVEMENT WITH CHILD WELFARE SERVICES TO SCHOOL ENTRY: A 5- TO 6-YEAR FOLLOW-UP OF INFANTS IN THE NATIONAL SURVEY OF CHILD AND ADOLESCENT WELL-BEING

United States Department of Health and Human Services

EXECUTIVE SUMMARY

In 1999 the Administration for Children and Families, U.S. Department of Health and Human Services, undertook the National Survey of Child and Adolescent Well-Being (NSCAW) to learn about children and families coming in contact with the child welfare system (CWS). The sample, which represents the population of children and families that entered the CWS within a 15-month period (October 1999 to December 2000), comprises 5,501 children (aged 0 to 14 years) from 92 child welfare agencies nationwide. The first national longitudinal survey of its kind, NSCAW gathers information about children's safety, living-situation permanency, wellbeing, and services after a maltreatment investigation by child protective services. NSCAW has examined the experiences of children and families with the CWS, starting approximately 4 months after the completion of a CWS maltreatment investigation and following up 1½ years, 3 years, and 5 to 6 years later (in 2005 and 2006).

Purpose of the Report

The current report provides information about 962 children who were infants (0 to 12 months old) when they first became involved in investigations for child abuse or neglect and whose caregivers participated at the 5- to 6-year follow-up. Some children's cases were closed after investigation; others had a case opened to child welfare services. Although the majority remained at home after investigation, others were removed from their homes. Five to 6 years after child protective services investigation, these children were 5 to 6 years old. This report is the first in a series presenting findings from the NSCAW 5- to 6-year follow-up.

Infants who were the focus of maltreatment for CWS constitute an especially vulnerable population. Many of these children have faced disruptions in their living arrangements that may have jeopardized their well-being. Many have developmental, emotional, behavioral, or physical health needs, or a combination of such needs, that may benefit from services. As 5- to 6-yearolds, these children were entering an important developmental period, beginning their school experience, and learning to negotiate lasting peer relationships. This report provides information to enhance our understanding of the needs of these youngest children entering the CWS:

- Who are the children who have had contact with the CWS during infancy? What types of maltreatment did they experience as infants? What risks did they face? What environments were these children living in by the time they were 5 to 6 years old?
- How well have these children been doing in terms of their physical, psychosocial, cognitive, peer, and academic development? How does this development compare with that of other children?
- How stable have the children's living situations been? Were they living in permanent homes by the time they were 5 to 6 years old?
- What services do these children, caregivers, and families need? What have they received?

Who Are the Children Who Had Contact with CWS during Infancy?

Children's age, sex and race/ethnicity

Almost all of these children were 5 (67.1%) or 6 (31.6%) years of age. They were evenly divided between males and females. White children made up the largest group (43.3%), followed by Black children (30.1%) and then Hispanic children (20.8%).

Type of abuse

At the time of the report of child abuse or neglect, caseworkers reported that about two thirds (63.9%) came to the attention of the CWS because of neglect. The caregiver's failure to provide for the child was reported for 34.9%; the caregiver's failure to supervise, for 29.0%; and physical abuse, for 19.2%. Emotional, moral/legal, or educational abuse, or abandonment, was reported for 4.8%. Another 10.5% were reported for reasons other than abuse or neglect (e.g., for mental health or domestic violence). More than one third (3 8.7%) of these maltreatment cases were *substantiated,* meaning the CWS decided that the allegations of child maltreatment were valid.

Living situation

At the 5- to 6-year follow-up, the majority of these children were living at home with their biological parents (61.7%). An additional 15.3% were living at home with kin or other caregivers, and another 16.7% were living in adoptive homes. In addition, 6.4% of children were living out of home. The interviewed caregivers were primarily female (92.7%) and White (54.7%); more than half were 25 to 44 years old. Only one third of caregivers had more than a high school education, and almost half lived beneath the federal poverty level. About half of caregivers were employed full or part time. Although fewer than half (43.2%) were married, the majority of caregivers (70.3%) lived with at least one other adult in the home.

What Risks Did These Children Face at the Time of CWS Investigation?

Prior CWS involvement

Caseworkers reported that 40.0% of families had been previously reported for child maltreatment. Of these families, 91.6% previously had been investigated for child abuse or neglect, and more than two thirds had previously substantiated incidents of abuse or neglect.

Caseworker risk assessment at investigation

At the first interview, when children were 0 to 12 months old, caseworkers were asked about their perceptions of caregivers' risk factors. Caseworkers reported that 14.4% of caregivers were abusing alcohol, 29.7% were abusing drugs, 20.2% recently had been arrested, 23.3% had a serious mental health problem, and 11.1% had a cognitive impairment. Caseworkers estimated that almost half (42.6%) of caregivers had poor parenting skills and that 14.8% had unrealistic expectations of their infants. About a third of caregivers themselves had a history of abuse and neglect, and 37.7% had been victims of domestic violence. At the time of the first interview, there was active domestic violence against 22.3% of caregivers.

How Well Were These Children Functioning and Behaving at 5 to 6 Years of Age?

Caregiver aggression and neglect

More than three quarters (77.5%) of caregivers reported using psychologically aggressive discipline tactics (e.g., shouting or screaming at a child), and 65.2% used corporal punishment or other minor hitting (Straus, 1996). Much lower proportions of caregivers reported any type of severe assault (3.5%) or very severe assault (0.2%). More than a tenth (12.3%) of caregivers reported the occurrence of some form of neglect in the year before the interview—primarily being so distracted by problems that they could not show or tell their child that they loved him or her (8.5%).

Physical well-being

The majority of children were in good, very good, or excellent health, according to their caregivers. Approximately a fifth (20.5%) had a serious chronic health condition, with the majority of these children suffering from asthma (13.3%). This rate of asthma is similar to that among similarly aged children in the general population. Some type of injury, accident, or poisoning that required the care of a doctor or nurse was experienced by 5.8% of children during the 12 months before the interview. The injuries themselves were most commonly cuts, scrapes, puncture wounds, or broken bones.

Disability risk

When several measures are considered, about a third of children showed patterns of functioning and behavior consistent with a variety of disabilities. Standardized assessments, together with caregiver and teacher reports, across several indicators showed risks for a cognitive disability, emotional or behavioral problems, or physical disability. Overall, 13.0% of children appeared to be at risk for a cognitive disability, 28.9% appeared to be at risk for an emotional or behavioral problem, and 5.9% showed signs of a physical disability.

Psychosocial well-being

Children in the NSCAW study had rates of externalizing behavior problems (e.g., aggression, hyperactivity, oppositional behaviors) higher than the rates for the normative sample, as indicated by reports from caregivers and teachers on the Achenbach scales (Achenbach, 1991). Caregivers' reports of externalizing behaviors were significantly more likely for girls than for boys and more likely for children who had been physically abused than for those who had not been physically abused. The rates of internalizing symptoms (e.g., anxiety, depression) reported by parents and teachers were similar to rates in normative samples.

Cognitive well-being

Overall, children's average score was within the average range on standardized measures of cognitive and language skills. These scores were, however, slightly lower than those for children in the normative population: The children's average score on the Kaufman Brief Intelligence Test was is one half of a standard deviation below the normative mean (Kaufman & Kaufman, 1990). Average scores for children on the Preschool Language Scale also were one half of a standard deviation below the mean for the normative population (Zimmerman, Steiner, & Pond, 1992).

Social functioning

Although the average total scores on the Social Skills Rating System (SSRS) were within the typical range for children of this age (Gresham & Elliot, 1990), they were lower than those observed in the normative population (for both the caregiver and teacher ratings). As rated by parents, girls showed fewer cooperative behaviors than boys on average. As rated by teachers, those who had experienced physical abuse had better SSRS Total scores than those with other types of maltreatment. As measured by the Vineland Adaptive Behavior Screener (Sparrow, Carter, & Cicchetti, 1993), more than a fifth of children had "low" daily- living skills, a rate substantially higher than in the general population. When asked about relationships with peers, children described themselves as lonelier than did children in the normative group on the Loneliness and Social Dissatisfaction Scale (Cassidy & Asher, 1992). They described a connection to school that was positive, according to responses to a school engagement scale.

Academic achievement

Average achievement test scores generally fell within the typical range (85 to 115), although at the lower end. Assessments of reading comprehension and oral mathematical skills were significantly below the normative means, however, on the Woodcock- Johnson III Tests of Cognitive Abilities (Woodcock, McGrew, & Mather, 2001). Teachers also rated children's performance in academic subjects. Although most children were described as being "at grade level," a sizable percentage were said to be performing "below" or "far below" in language arts (39.0%) and mathematics (35.1%).

How Stable Are the Children's Living Situations? Are They Living in Permanent Homes?

Living situation

By the time children were 5 to 6 years old, about a third of children had been placed out of the home at some point in their lives. Black (46.9%), Hispanic (43.2%), and "Other" children (46.7%) were more likely to be placed outside the home than White children (26.8%). Of the children who had been placed, 23.5% had two placements during their lifetime, and 27.3% had three or more placements. Parental rights were terminated in more than one third of cases that had at least one placement out of home. Of the children with out-of-home placement histories, only about a fifth were reunified with their birth parents.

Adoption

Fewer than one fifth (17.0%) of all children were adopted by age 5 to 6. The median time between placement and finalized adoption was almost 2 years. More than three quarters of those adopted had been placed outside the home before the adoption. As the number of children adopted increased over time, the number of children in foster care decreased.

What Services Do Children Receive? Do They Receive the Services That They Need?

Health services

Nearly all children (95.7%) were reported to have a pediatric (or medical) home. Most children had received preventive and routine health services (such as immunizations, dental care, and vision and hearing screening). Children with chronic health conditions were more likely to receive a well-child checkup and to report having a pediatric home than children without chronic health conditions. About one quarter (25.8%) of children were reported by caregivers to have used emergency room or urgent care services for an illness, injury, accident, or poisoning in the year before the interview. Compared with children living in other settings, children living at home with biological parents were less likely to have received a recent well-child checkup and more likely to have had an overnight hospital stay.

Mental health services

Overall, 16.7% of children had received one or more outpatient psychiatric services. Twelve percent (12.0%) had received specialty outpatient mental health services, 7.0% had received help from their family physician for a mental health problem, 10.8% had used school-based mental health services, and 6.4% were using psychotropic medications. When compared with children without behavior problems, children reported to have behavior problems on the Achenbach scales were 4 to 5 times as likely to have received each type of mental health service. Although rates of unmet mental health services needs seen here were lower than those for most U.S. children 3 to 17 years old (Kataoka et al., 2002), rates of unmet mental health needs among these children were still surprisingly high: 65.1% of children who had behavior problems did not receive a single mental health service.

Special education services

Almost a quarter (22.6%) of children were receiving special education services through an Individualized Education Plan (IEP), a higher rate than that reported for all U.S. children 6 to 21 years old. According to teachers, a little more than half of the children had been receiving such services for longer than a year. Nearly two thirds of those with an IEP were classified as speech impaired. Developmental delays, learning disabilities, attention-deficit/hyperactivity disorder, and emotional disturbance were also common IEP classifications. Children in this population with scores on developmental measures indicating needs likely to interfere with school success were more likely to have an active IEP than those children not determined to have such needs. However, 62.8% of children determined to potentially benefit from a referral for special education services did not currently have an active IEP.

What Services Do Caregivers and Families Receive?

Child welfare services

Five to 6 years after the index maltreatment investigation, about a tenth of caregivers reported that they were still receiving services that were either provided by or paid for by the CWS. Among those still receiving CWS services, caseworkers reported that 55.9% received family-based services (e.g., family preservation or reunification), 55.6% received parent support services (e.g., parent training), and 41.4% received family counseling. The families of children living in out-of-home settings were more likely than other families to receive the family-based services.

Services to address basic needs

Slightly less than one third of caregivers (32.7%) reported having received some type of assistance for meeting basic living needs (e.g., transportation; food assistance; financial assistance, excluding Temporary Assistance for Needy Families or Supplemental Security Income; housing). Nearly one third of caregivers reported having received regular childcare assistance; 19.3% reported having received services to directly benefit themselves (e.g., job-related services, participation in organized support groups, legal aid); and 11.9% reported having received home assistance services (e.g., home management training). Families living below the federal poverty level were more likely to receive services to meet basic living needs and services to directly assist the caregiver.

Caregiver mental health and substance abuse services

More than a quarter (26.5%) of in-home caregivers had mental health assessments indicating need, but only 25.8% of the group in need received a mental health service. Most commonly, caregivers who received a mental health service reported using psychotropic medication. Only a handful reported visiting a clinic or doctor for mental health problems, and almost none reported using substance abuse services.

Exhibits for Children Aged 1 to 4 at Baseline

A full discussion of children who were older than age 1 at baseline is beyond the scope of this report. Nevertheless, analyses were conducted and exhibits are presented in Appendix B for children aged 1 to 4 at baseline. The analyses paralleled those of the infant sample. Results were similar, with the following notable exceptions:

- Children aged 1 to 4 years old at baseline had *lower* rates of cognitive disability at Wave 5 than children who were infants at baseline.
- Children who were 1 to 4 years old at baseline had somewhat *higher* rates of emotional and behavioral problems at Wave 5 than children who were infants at baseline.
- Children aged 1 to 4 at baseline were *less* likely to be placed outside the home and be adopted than infants at baseline, and the older group's adoptions also took almost 6 months longer when they happened.
- Caseworkers identified *fewer* mental health and substance abuse problems at baseline among caregivers of the children aged 1 to 4 than among caregivers of infants at baseline, which may be related to the higher placement rate for infants.
- Children aged 1 to 4 years old at baseline were less likely to receive child welfare services, family-based services, and parenting support services than children who were infants at baseline.

Conclusions and Implications for Child Welfare Services

Young children are the most likely to be reported to CWS for abuse or neglect, and their cases are the most likely to be substantiated. The innate vulnerability of infants who are abused or neglected makes them of special interest to caseworkers, policy makers, service providers, and the general public. The CWS may indeed have a special responsibility toward these youngest children entering its system.

Findings in this report are in some ways promising. Many children identified in infancy for abuse and neglect fared quite well 5 to 6 years after maltreatment investigation. Most were in good physical health and demonstrated average social competencies. Although their scores on standardized measures of intelligence, academic achievement, and cognitive skills were often below national norms, on average they fell within the typical range of ability. Most children were living at home with at least one biological parent. Of those in out-of-home care, most were living in a permanent home with adoptive parents, kin, or other caregivers.

Despite these positive outcomes, a substantial subpopulation of children experienced placement disruptions, challenges to their developmental well-being, and ongoing unmet service needs. More than half continued to live in poverty. Even for adoptive parents, about half reported income at less than 200% below the federal poverty level, suggesting the need for continuing supportive services for this group. Of those children who were placed outside the home, most had multiple placements and had spent almost 2 years in placement. These findings point to the challenges faced by families, children, and caseworkers in establishing permanent, stable placements even for these youngest children entering the CWS.

Although a fair proportion of children were developing within the expected ranges of normalcy by the time they were 5 to 6 years old, their scores on measures of intellectual and language functioning tended to be lower than the average for all children. Children showed significantly higher rates of externalizing behavior problems, and 5.9% to 28.9% demonstrated risks for a physical, cognitive, and emotional or behavioral disability. Even though one fifth (22.6%) of children were receiving special education services by the time they were 5 to 6 years old, at least an additional third were likely candidates because of cognitive, language, or behavioral-emotional problems. Sixty-five percent (65.1%) of children noted to have behavior problems did not receive a single mental health service. These levels of unmet social service needs underscore the important role for the CWS in securing cross-agency ties and service collaboration for children identified through its investigations. Linking children to preventive, developmentally oriented early intervention services may be particularly critical for infants entering the CWS.

When these children were infants, many caregivers had substance abuse and mental health problems, some suffered from domestic violence, and many had poor parenting skills. By the time the children were 5 to 6 years old, more than a quarter (25.7%) of in-home caregivers had mental health assessments indicating need, but only about a quarter of them reported having used a mental health service. These results show that a significant proportion of children are still facing a number of family risk factors that can compromise their ability to adapt and successfully integrate into society. Identifying and meeting caregiver service needs may be especially important for preventing future child maltreatment.

This report describes children who were infants when they experienced their first contact with CWS. NSCAW will continue to follow the life course of other children (e.g., children in early childhood, young adulthood) entering the CWS, in order to gather data about services received, well-being, and placement stability. This information will chronicle the life outcomes for children and families that have come into contact with the CWS and will therefore enrich our understanding of the problems these families face and the solutions that are possible.

1. Infants Involved with Child Welfare a Special Responsibility

In recent years, the development of very young children (aged 0 to 6 years) has captured the public imagination. The topic has appeared on the covers of major news magazines, garnered attention from celebrities, and led to fads such as playing Mozart during gestation to boost children's IQs. Despite its faddishness, attention to the first years of life is justified, both because of what we have long known about the importance of early childhood for development and because of new knowledge from neuroscience about its impact on children's well-being. This report focuses on a population of children for whom knowledge about early child development is especially critical—children who, as infants, were involved in investigations of child maltreatment by child welfare services. Though they may not grace the cover of magazines or engage celebrity interest, and are far from any parenting fad, as infants many of these children faced major disruption in their development and major risks to their well-being thereafter. Knowledge about the safety, care, and well-being of these children and the service response to their needs is badly needed. Moreover, we need to follow these children over time, to see how their well-being as infants may be related to their ongoing development. In children aged 5 to 6, we can see what role the challenges that began in infancy may play as they adapt to school and start to make friends. This report concentrates on these children at age 5 to 6 years.

This report uses data from the National Survey of Child and Adolescent Well-Being (NSCAW), a longitudinal study of a national probability sample of children involved with child welfare. NSCAW originated in the Personal Responsibility and Work Opportunity Reconciliation Act of 1996, which directed the Department of Health and Human Services to carry out a national study of children who are at risk for maltreatment or are otherwise involved with the child welfare system (CWS; see NSCAW Research Group, 2002: U.S. Department of Health and Human Services, Administration for Children and Families, 2005b). NSCAW has gathered data on children's safety, permanency of living situations, well-being, and services at baseline (approximately 4 months after the completion of a child welfare investigation or assessment), 1½ years, 3 years, and 5 years from baseline. Baseline data were collected in 1999– 2000, while data from the 5- to 6-year follow-up were collected in 2005 2006.

This report is the first in a series presenting findings from the Wave 5 follow-up. It focuses on the 962 children who were infants (0 to 12 months) when first involved in investigations of abuse and neglect and whose caregivers were available to participate in the Wave 5 follow-up. This represents 85% of the children in this group at baseline (see below). By the time of this follow-up, these children were 5 to 6 years old.

Our research questions are as follows:

- How well are these children doing in terms of development, physical and mental health, and success beginning school?
- To what extent have their living situations remained stable or changed, and are they living in permanent homes?
- What services are children and caregivers receiving and do the services match their needs?

Although a full investigation of older children was beyond the scope of this report, the results of additional analyses of children who were 1 to 4 years old at baseline are presented in a series of exhibits in Appendix B. These analyses parallel the analyses for the infant population for the most part, and exhibits with the same numerals (e.g., Exhibit 1-2, Exhibit B.1-2) generally contain parallel information.

The Nature of the Special Responsibility

Our society has a special responsibility for infants who become involved with the CWS through investigations of child maltreatment. Abuse or neglect during this most vulnerable age can place infants in immediate peril. In 2004, an estimated 671 infants died from child abuse and neglect in the United States (U.S. Department of Health and Human Services, 2006a). Child maltreatment during infancy can have a profound effect on children's physical and cognitive development, even affecting the structure and functioning of their brains (see e.g., Stien & Kendall, 2003). It can also interfere with fundamental components of children's well-being and development, such as those described as the critical focus of early intervention: "(1) self- regulation, (2) the establishment of early relationships and (3) knowledge acquisition and the development of specific skills" (National Research Council and Institute of Medicine, 2000, p. 5).

Previous research, including research using NSCAW, shows that less than one third of investigations overall lead to a substantiation of the abuse or neglect allegation. However, a number of allegations are not substantiated for lack of evidence, even when caseworkers judge children to have suffered harm or be at moderate to high risk (U.S. Department of Health and Human Services, 2008a). Moreover, research has found that even children in unsubstantiated cases have disproportionate exposure to risks, have disproportionate rates of developmental deficits and mental health problems, and, in some cases, experience family violence at home and disruption in care. In many ways, outcomes for children in unsubstantiated cases are little different from those for children in substantiated cases.

Society's responsibility for these children is even larger when child welfare services takes custody of the children. CWS takes custody when a child is placed in foster care and often when placed with kin. CWS then has legal responsibility for ensuring that children are kept in a safe and stable environment, are returned home whenever possible, and receive services needed to address maltreatment, ensure positive development, or both. Although most of the children are long past their involvement with CWS, 5 or 6 years after the index investigation that made them eligible for NSCAW, we nevertheless have a responsibility to understand their development. Child abuse and neglect can have long-term negative effects on child victims' cognitive, emotional, and social development.

Moreover, many children faced multiple risk factors impeding their development and many faced developmental delays and behavioral and emotional difficulties that can have a longterm negative effect on subsequent achievement of critical skills. As we discuss below, follow- up reports at 18 and 36 months showed a high prevalence of continuing difficulties.

Purpose of the Report

Our purpose is to gather information to help us better understand these children's needs, inform policy makers and practitioners, and support service improvements. We provide an overview of these children's status at age 5 to 6 years. Using data from caregivers and from standardized assessments of the children themselves, we present data on their well-being, current safety, the stability and permanency of their current living situation, and the services they and their caregivers receive. Given the limited scope of this report, this analysis raises many more questions than it can address. One of our goals is to stimulate more NSCAW research to explore such matters as case pathways, change over time, patterns of disability and resiliency, systems issues and effects, and impact at multiple levels.

NSCAW is available to all qualified researchers through the National Data Archive on Child Abuse and Neglect (NDACAN) at Cornell University (see www.ndacan.cornell.edu). To date, numerous peer-reviewed journal articles and other publications have appeared using NSCAW data (see Wallace, Nahm, Luba, & Cross, 2006), and additional analyses by dozens of different investigators are in progress.

NSCAW Methods

The methodology of NSCAW provides a number of advantages for this analysis, while also entailing some limitations. We give a brief overview of the methodology here; detailed explanations of methods are presented in several available documents (Christ & Biemer, 2005; NSCAW Research Group, 2002; U.S. Department of Health and Human Services, 2005b).

The NSCAW cohort includes 5,501 children aged birth to 14 years (at the time of sampling), who had contact with the CWS within a 15-month period beginning in October 1999. These children were selected from 92 Primary Sampling Units (PSUs) in 97 counties nationwide. The sample of investigated/assessed cases included both cases that received ongoing services and cases that did not receive services, either because they were not substantiated or because it was determined that services were not required.

This sample design required oversampling of infants (to ensure there would be enough cases going through to permanency planning), sexual abuse cases (to ensure there would be enough cases to have sufficient statistical power to analyze this kind of abuse alone), and cases receiving ongoing services after investigation (to ensure adequate power to understand the process of services). This approach allows for generation of national estimates for the full population of children and families entering the system, with power to consider key subgroups of the child welfare population. Weighted percentages are used to provide the most accurate population estimates possible (Christ & Biemer, 2005).

Exhibit 1-1 gives an overview of how and from whom data are collected in NSCAW. NSCAW provides the widest range of informants of any major study of child welfare. Children, caregivers (permanent, foster, and kin), caseworkers, and teachers all participate. Interviews include use of standardized instruments measuring safety, child development, child well-being, service delivery and other constructs, as well as questionnaire items specially designed for this study. Data were collected from children and caregivers in face-to-face interviews conducted in their homes. To help ensure respondents' privacy and comfort reporting personal information, sensitive data collection in the home was conducted through an audio computer-assisted self- interviewing system, in which caregivers, following voiced instructions given to them through headphones, entered data directly into laptop computers.

Exhibit 1-1. Timeline of NSCAW Data Collection

	Wave 1	Wave 2	Wave 3	Wave 4	Wave 5
Start and end dates	11/15/99– 04/3 0/0 1	10/01/00– 03/31/02	04/0 1/0 1– 09/30/02	08/01/02– 02/28/04	09/05/05– 11/15/07
Months after close of investigation	2–6	12	18	36	59–96
Respondent					
Child	X		X	X	X
Current caregiver	X	X	X	X	X
Investigator/services caseworker	X	X	X	X	X
Teacher	X		X	X	X

Wave 5 (the 5- to 6-year follow-up) was atypical in that it was fielded by age cohort rather than by the time interval since investigation or assessment close. Children in the infant cohort (younger than 13 months old at the time of sampling) were fielded first, when they were 5 to 6 years old, from September 2005 to February 2006. Children 13 to 48 months old at the time of sampling were fielded next, from February to December 2006. Young adults who had turned 18 years old by April 30, 2006, were fielded in July 2006. The remaining children's cases were fielded from March to November 2007.

The data collected touched on a wide range of constructs in four domains: safety, permanency, well-being, and service delivery. Below is a partial list of the constructs measured:

- Investigation outcomes
- Child placement, reunification, and adoption
- Living environment
- Cognitive development
- Social skills and support
- Child physical and mental health
- Child behavior problems
- School functioning
- Parental aggression and neglect
- Parental risk factors
- Child welfare services
- Child mental health services
- Family services

There are some differences in the data collected for each case, depending on whether the main child caregiver was a permanent or nonpermanent caregiver. The designation *nonpermanent* is used for caregivers of children in out-of-home placements: formal kinship care, in which a child lives with relatives; family foster care, where care is provided by an unrelated foster parent; or, rarely, other residential settings (e.g., residential treatment center, group home). The designation *permanent* is given to caregivers of children in in-home situations: living with biological or adoptive parents or informally with relatives. The main questionnaire differences by type of caregivers are the following: (1) only permanent caregivers are queried about alcohol dependence, drug dependence, involvement with the law, discipline and child maltreatment, and domestic violence (females only); (2) only nonpermanent caregivers are queried about services received by foster caregivers; and (3) foster and adoptive parents are queried about permanency planning. Detailed description of the instruments used is provided in the baseline report, available at http://www.acf.hhs.gov/programs/opre/abuse_neglect/nscaw/. (For a brief overview, see Appendix A.)

The 5- to 6-year follow-up for children who were infants at baseline

Baseline data were collected 4-5 months after the close of the index CWS investigation. Data collection at 1½ years, 3 years, and 5 years included the vast majority of the same variables as the baseline set. The mean time between the 5- to 6-year follow-up and the previous 3-year follow-up (when children were between 3 and 4 years old) was 30 months, with a range of 21 to 44 months. Thus, at Wave 5, children were between 5 and 6.5 years old.

We learned from caregivers on attempts at follow-up interviews that 10 children among those who were infants at baseline had died. Thus the eligible child and caregiver sample for the purpose of calculating response rates was 1,186 (1,196 in the original sample minus 10 deceased). The overall weighted response rate was 85.1%; the weighted response rate for children was 84.5%. For Wave 5 analysis, placement of children was classified as in home with biological parents, in home with adoptive parents, in home with kin or other caregiver, or out of home. The "kin or other" in-home caregivers were 89.4% kin, and 10.6% nonrelative caregivers (e.g., family friends).

Analysis in this report

This report uses simple data analytic methods to profile infants involved with CWS at a 5- to 6-year follow-up on a number of different variables related to child well-being, placement and permanency and service delivery. We report means and percentages and associated standard errors. In the vast majority of analyses, we compare groups by the key demographic variables of child sex, child race-ethnicity, and children's living setting at the follow-up. We also compare outcomes by severity of maltreatment, and presence of disability or a chronic health condition, and report these results when they are statistically significant. Most analysis uses straightforward bivariate methods such as contingency table analysis with a Pearson χ^2 test (adapted for use with a complex survey sample) and comparison of means using *t* or *F* tests.

A simple analysis plan like this has limitations of course. The most important concerns comparisons on 5- to 6-year follow-up outcomes that involve certain group variables: child living setting, disability status (physical, cognitive or emotional) and chronic health condition. The interpretation of differences on outcomes by groups represented by these variables is ambiguous. We will not be able to determine whether being a member of a certain group made a certain outcome more likely, or whether children on a path to a certain outcome tend to end up in certain groups. If, for example, children who are adopted are more likely to have a chronic health condition, we do not know whether this is because agencies give priority in arranging adoptions to children with health conditions, or if adoptive parents are more conscientious about getting health care for their children and identifying chronic problems. Future NSCAW research that takes advantage of the longitudinal nature of NSCAW data will yield more interpretable results, but is beyond the modest scope of this report.

Exhibit 1-2. Child Characteristics Infant Population at Wave 5

Child Characteristic	Total[1] % (SE)	In Home: Biological Parent[2] % (SE)	In Home: Adoptive Parent[3] % (SE)	In Home: Kin and Other[4] % (SE)	Out of Home[5] % (SE)
Total	100	61.7 (3.6)	16.7 (1.9)	15.3 (1.8)	6.4 (1.5)
Child's sex					
Male	50.3 (3.2)	55.4 (4.3)	39.0 (4.9)	44.7 (6.3)	43.4 (11.1)
Female	49.8 (3.2)	44.6 (4.3)	61.0 (4.9)	55.3 (6.3)	56.6 (11.1)
Child's age					
4	0.1 (0.1)	0.0 (0.0)	0.0 (0.0)	0.4 (0.0)	0.0 (0.0)
5	67.1 (3.5)	61.9 (4.3)	82.9 (4.0)	74.2 (5.4)	59.6 (12.1)
6	31.6 (3.4)	36.1 (4.2)	17.1 (4.0)	25.4 (5.4)	40.4 (12.1)
7	1.2 (1.5)	2.0 (1.5)	0.0 (0.0)	0.0 (0.0)	0.0 (0.0)
Child's race/ethnicity					
Black	30.1 (3.2)	27.3 (3.8)	34.6 (5.7)	38.5 (5.0)	25.2 (9.6)
White	43.3 (3.6)	48.8 (4.9)	32.7 (6.3)	35.7 (5.7)	35.2 (12.2)
Hispanic	20.8 (2.1)	19.4 (3.1)	18.1 (4.7)	23.3 (5.6)	36.0 (11.8)
Other	5.8 (1.4)	4.5 (1.2)	14.6 (5.4)	2.6 (1.5)	3.5 (2.9)
Grade in school					
Not in school[6]	3.5 (0.9)	4.1 (1.4)	2.2 (0.9)	3.4 (2.2)	0.0 (0.0)
Preschool and other[7]	4.5 (1.0)	4.3 (1.4)	7.0 (1.7)	1.9 (1.6)	6.0 (5.8)
Kindergarten	72.9 (2.6)	71.6 (3.4)	77.2 (4.0)	77.3 (5.1)	76.6 (12.9)
First grade	17.9 (2.2)	18.0 (2.6)	13.6 (3.8)	17.5 (4.9)	17.4 (12.3)
Second grade	1.2 (0.9)	2.0 (1.5)	0.0 (0.0)	0.0 (0.0)	0.0 (0.0)

Note: All analyses are on weighted data; Ns are unweighted. Pearson χ^2 tests for cluster samples were used for initial significance tests. Asterisks denote statistical significance of differences across setting types for each covariate (*$p < .05$).

[1] N (minimum) = 921.

[2] N (minimum) = 494.

[3] N (minimum) = 224.

[4] N (minimum) = 159.

[5] N (minimum) = 44.

[6] A valid Pearson χ^2 test was impossible because of sparse cell sizes.

[7] Includes nursery school, Head Start, and other ungraded placements.

This Population at the Wave 5 Follow-up

Exhibit 1-2 gives an overview of sociodemographic characteristics at the Wave 5 follow-up of those children who were infants at baseline, by type of living arrangement at this follow- up. About half the sample is male, 99% of children are 5 or 6 years old. Less than half (43%) are White, 30% are Black, 21% are Hispanic, and 6% are "Other." About 73% are in kindergarten and 18% are in first grade. Exhibit 1-3 gives a similar overview of the caregivers at the 5- to 6- year follow-up by type of living arrangement for children. The majority of caregivers are females (93%), more than half are 25 to 44 years old, and 13% are less than 25 years old. More than half (55%) are White, 27% Black, 13% Hispanic, and 6% Other. Only one third of caregivers have more than high school education. Almost half live under the federal poverty level. About half of caregivers have fulltime or part time employment. Less than half of caregivers are married but the majority live with other adults in the home (70%). About a quarter have four or more children in the home.

Child Development from Age 0 to 6

The literature on normal child development, as well as previous research on the consequences of child maltreatment, guided the selection of measures used and analyzed in NSCAW. A brief overview of key developmental issues provides a context for understanding the results for children involved in CWS investigations at infancy.

Social-emotional competence

Children who have been maltreated are at risk in terms of their social and emotional competency, which is essential for children to develop a sense of wellbeing and to function well with peers and in school (see, e.g., Bolger & Patterson, 2001; Bolger, Patterson, & Kupersmidt, 1998; Rogosch, Cicchetti, & Aber, 1995). Key achievements during the first few years include a representation of the self as distinct from other individuals, the recognition of different feelings, and attachment with a significant adult. The literature indicates that parents who are warm, discipline their children appropriately (e.g., consistent in practices, provide clear expectations for behavior, offer reasons for actions), and provide opportunities for their children to have peer contact are more likely to have children who are socially and emotionally competent (Denham & Grout, 1992; Ladd & Hart, 1992).

By school age, children are learning how to negotiate conflicts and to respond to aggressive behaviors. Children who are successful in making and sustaining friendships become better adjusted in school, whereas children who are rejected by their peers are less likely to be well adjusted (Ladd, 1990; Kochenderfer & Ladd, 1996). The ability to regulate emotions, cooperate, help others, display empathy, and form friendships have been found to be critical for later school success (Raver & Zigler, 1997; Webster-Stratton & Reid, 2004; Blair, 2002). Learning-related social skills are also considered critical by teachers. These include listening, following directions and routines, cooperating, participating in group activities, communicating, taking responsibility, and acquiring self-help skills that facilitate independence (Kemp & Carter, 2005; McClelland & Morrison, 2003). Children entering school with poor learning-related social skills often have low academic achievement (McClelland, Morrison, & Holmes, 2000). Moreover, low learning-related social skills are the most important predictors of referral to special education and of school failure in first grade (Cooper & Speece, 1988).

Exhibit 1-3. Caregiver and Household Characteristics Infant Population at Wave 5

Characteristic	Total (N = 921) % (SE)	In Home: Biological Parent (N = 494) % (SE)	In Home: Adoptive Parent (N = 224) % (SE)	In Home: Other (N = 159) % (SE)	Out of Home (N = 44) % (SE)
Total	100	61.7 (3.6)	16.7 (1.9)	15.3 (1.8)	6.4 (1.5)
Caregiver's sex*					
Male	7.3 (1.7)	10.4 (2.6)	1.2 (0.7)	4.0 (2.1)	0.4 (0.4)
Female	92.7 (1.7)	89.6 (2.6)	98.8 (0.7)	96.0 (2.1)	99.6 (0.4)
Caregiver's age**					
< 25	12.9 (2.0)	19.7 (2.9)	0.4 (0.4)	2.3 (1.3)	5.9 (5.8)
25 – 34	36.6 (2.6)	54.9 (3.0)	4.8 (1.3)	10.3 (5.1)	5.6 (3.2)
35 – 44	26.4 (2.2)	21.2 (2.3)	40.7 (5.4)	23.5 (4.9)	45.8 (12.6)
45 – 54	16.5 (1.9)	4.0 (1.6)	37.3 (5.1)	38.7 (4.9)	29.2 (11.2)
> 54	7.7 (1.4)	0.2 (0.2)	16.8 (5.4)	25.2 (5.4)	13.5 (5.2)
Caregiver's race/ethnicity					
Black	26.7 (3.1)	23.0 (3.7)	29.0 (5.7)	38.3 (5.8)	29.4 (10.9)
White	54.7 (3.9)	58.0 (4.7)	52.9 (5.9)	43.6 (5.6)	53.0 (13.5)
Hispanic	13.0 (2.1)	13.2 (2.7)	14.5 (5.6)	13.1 (5.2)	6.3 (3.5)
Other	5.6 (1.4)	5.8 (1.7)	3.6 (1.5)	5.0 (2.3)	11.3 (7.7)
Caregiver's education**					
Less than high school	25.9 (2.2)	30.3 (3.2)	14.0 (5.8)	24.1 (6.2)	18.1 (9.7)
High school	45.4 (2.8)	49.1 (4.3)	43.1 (5.8)	40.5 (5.5)	26.9 (8.5)
More than high school	28.7 (2.3)	20.4 (2.8)	42.9 (5.6)	35.4 (5.5)	55.1 (11.4)
% of federal poverty level**					
< 50%	18.8 (2.3)	27.2 (3.1)	2.5 (1.4)	10.6 (3.7)	0.0 (0.0)
50 – <100%	26.8 (2.3)	30.9 (3.5)	11.2 (2.0)	30.9 (5.5)	17.1 (9.6)
100 – 200%	27.7 (2.2)	23.2 (2.8)	37.3 (5.9)	24.5 (5.4)	55.6 (11.9)
> 200%	26.7 (2.6)	18.8 (3.5)	49.0 (5.2)	33.9 (5.2)	27.3 (10.9)
Caregiver's employment status**					
Work full time	33.4 (2.8)	36.3 (3.8)	32.8 (5.0)	27.8 (4.6)	19.8 (6.9)
Work part time	19.3 (2.4)	18.6 (2.5)	14.1 (2.9)	20.5 (5.0)	36.8 (13.7)
Unemployed, looking for work	8.9 (1.2)	12.5 (1.8)	0.9 (0.4)	4.1 (1.6)	5.4 (3.8)
Doesn't work	35.9 (2.9)	29.7 (3.6)	47.8 (5.1)	46.8 (7.0)	37.7 (11.4)
Other	2.7 (0.8)	2.9 (1.0)	4.5 (2.4)	0.8 (0.6)	0.3 (0.3)
Caregiver's marital status**					
Married	43.2 (3.7)	34.0 (4.1)	60.0 (5.7)	54.6 (7.5)	60.7 (10.9)
Separated/divorced/widowed	28.3 (2.9)	25.6 (3.4)	29.6 (5.9)	38.0 (7.2)	28.3 (10.3)
Never married	28.5 (2.6)	40.4 (3.6)	10.4 (2.9)	7.5 (3.2)	11.0 (3.2)
Number of children in home					
1	28.4 (2.6)	26.1 (3.4)	33.0 (7.0)	36.8 (6.0)	8.5 (7.8)
2	26.3 (2.5)	28.6 (3.1)	24.9 (5.9)	24.2 (4.9)	12.5 (5.1)
3	20.5 (2.2)	20.9 (2.9)	14.8 (2.9)	15.5 (4.8)	43.0 (12.3)
4	12.8 (2.0)	15.5 (2.9)	10.6 (2.6)	8.6 (3.1)	2.3 (1.7)
5 or more	12.1 (2.0)	9.0 (2.0)	16.7 (4.8)	14.9 (5.3)	23.7 (10.6)
Number of adults in home*					
1	29.7 (3.1)	34.0 (3.2)	26.5 (5.9)	23.0 (5.0)	12.1(6.1)
2	49.2 (3.0)	47.1 (3.5)	50.6 (6.1)	49.1 (8.3)	66.7 (11.9)
3	11.9 (1.7)	10.5 (1.9)	10.8 (2.8)	18.8 (5.2)	12.4 (8.9)
4 or more	9.2 (2.0)	8.5 (2.0)	12.2 (5.0)	9.1 (5.1)	8.8 (5.7)

Note: All analyses are on weighted data; Ns are unweighted. Pearson χ^2 tests for cluster samples were used to test statistical significance. Asterisks denote statistical significance of differences across setting types for each covariate (*$p < .05$, **$p < .01$).

Exhibit 1-4. Caseworker Report on Maltreatment and Risk at Baseline Infant Population at Wave 5

	N	% (SE)
Most serious maltreatment type	**921**	
Physical abuse		19.2 (2.4)
Sexual abuse		1.7 (0.7)
Failure to provide		34.9 (2.7)
Failure to supervise/abandonment		29.0 (3.0)
Emotional, moral/legal, educational maltreatment		4.8 (1.1)
Other		10.5 (1.8)
CWS outcome	877	
Substantiated		38.7 (3.2)
Indicated		8.5 (2.0)
Unsubstantiated		42.5 (3.0)
High risk		3.8 (1.1)
Medium risk		2.0 (0.6)
Low risk		4.6 (1.5)
Level of harm	878	
None		36.9 (3.5)
Mild		25.9 (2.7)
Moderate		20.0 (2.1)
Severe		17.3 (2.1)
Level of risk	802	
None		21.1 (2.6)
Mild		30.2 (2.9)
Moderate		22.6 (2.7)
Severe		26.1 (2.4)
Risk factors		
Prior reports of child maltreatment	872	40.0 (3.4)
Prior investigation of child maltreatment	365	91.6 (2.7)[1]
Prior incident of substantiated child maltreatment	339	66.6 (4.0)
Prior child welfare service history	841	32.4 (2.6)
Child has major special needs or behavioral problems	866	13.8 (1.8)
Active alcohol abuse by primary caregiver	800	14.4 (1.8)
Active alcohol abuse by secondary caregiver	578	18.5 (2.0)
Active drug abuse by primary caregiver	835	29.7 (2.8)
Active drug abuse by secondary caregiver	568	24.4 (3.8)
Primary caregiver has serious mental health problem	831	23.3 (2.8)
Primary caregiver has recent history of arrests	809	20.2 (2.8)
Primary caregiver has intellectual or cognitive impairments	851	11.1 (2.0)
Primary caregiver has physical impairments	867	3.4 (1.3)
Primary caregiver has poor parenting skills	862	42.6 (2.5)
Parent has unreal expectations of child	842	14.8 (1.7)
History of domestic violence against caregiver	813	37.7 (3.3)
Active domestic violence against caregiver	833	22.3 (2.1)
Primary caregiver uses inappropriate or excessive discipline	854	3.6 (1.1)
Secondary caregiver uses inappropriate or excessive discipline	605	6.1 (1.4)
History of abuse or neglect of primary caregiver	754	32.3 (2.8)

Note: Only cases with 5- to 6-year follow-up data analyzed. Percentages and standard errors are weighted. *Ns* are unweighted.

[1] Calculated on those cases with prior reports.

Behavioral regulation and problems

Behavior problems can include externalizing behaviors, such as aggression and delinquency; internalizing behaviors, such as being withdrawn and experiencing anxiety/depression; and social and thought problems. Research indicates that behavior problems in early childhood tend to continue into later childhood and adolescence (Furstenberg, Brooks-Gunn, & Morgan, 1987; Stevenson, Richman, & Graham, 1985). Children who display aggressive, antisocial behaviors when they enter school have social deficits, such as inappropriate play behaviors, lack of social conversation, use of insults, and difficulty in participating in group activities (Coie & Kupersmidt, 1983; Dodge, 1983; Dodge, Lansford & Burks, 2003). As a consequence, antisocial, aggressive children are likely to be rejected by their peer group (Bolger & Patterson, 2001; Coie, Dodge, & Kupersmidt, 1990; Dishion, 1990; Dodge, Coie, & Brakke, 1982), which can lead such children to become more aggressive.

Intellectual abilities and motivation

From earliest infancy, children are acquiring the cognitive structures that allow information to be assimilated from the environment and that promote the linguistic skills that result in communicative skills. These skills include understanding and speaking in words and sentences, maintaining a conversation, and reasoning with and thinking about language. Maltreatment can seriously disrupt these processes (see, e.g., Stien & Kendall, 2003). Maternal responsiveness to the child and age-appropriate stimulation of cognitive/language development (Bradley et al., 2001a, 2001b; Zaslow et al., 2006) help lead to skills in these areas. Motivation and its related behaviors such as persistence, task-direction, and feelings of efficacy emerge during the preschool years and can influence the child's drive to learn (see Busch-Rossnagel, Knauf-Jensen, & Des-Rosiers, 1995; Gottfried, Fleming, & Gottfried, 1998; see McCall, 1995).

NSCAW Results from Baseline and Previous Follow-ups

We enter this analysis already having some knowledge of these children's earlier experience and development from NSCAW data. Exhibit 1-4 provides data from the caseworker report on maltreatment and risk variables for infants at the baseline interview. Regarding the caseworker's baseline report of the most serious maltreatment that the child had experienced, more than a third of cases (35%) were reported for failure to provide, 29% for failure to supervise, 19% for physical abuse, 5% for emotional-moral/legal-educational maltreatment, 2% for sexual abuse, and 11% for other. It is not entirely clear what "other" represents, but it is possible that it includes cases where mothers of newborns are abusing substances or are exposed to domestic violence. Slightly more than one third of the cases (39%) were substantiated. Another 8% of the cases were indicated, a category used in some jurisdictions that provides a classification for cases in which some evidence exists for maltreatment, but not enough for substantiation. A substantial percentage (42%) were not substantiated. In a small number of cases, the maltreatment reports were not formally investigated because in the jurisdiction of record at least some cases are "assessed," not "investigated," and risk is determined. Only 76 infant cases of maltreatment were handled in this way. Placing these cases alongside the substantiated, indicated, and unsubstantiated cases, 4% were at high risk, 2% were at medium risk, and 5% were at low risk. Thus, approximately half of the cases were either not substantiated or were at low risk.

Caseworkers also indicated the kinds of risks that were present in the home. In the infant group, over 40% of families had prior reports of maltreatment, of which 92% were investigated. Two thirds of those investigated were substantiated. Thus, 339 of the families with infants at baseline had a substantiated case of maltreatment prior to the investigation that brought them into the study, although it is not known whether the prior maltreatment involved the index child or caregiver. Nevertheless this high rate of reports indicates a less than optimal environment for child rearing. Other risks that were present in a substantial percentage of the cases include poor parenting (43%), a history of domestic violence against the primary caregiver (38%), active domestic violence against the primary caregiver (22%), a history of maltreatment of primary caregiver (32%), and active drug abuse by the primary caregiver (30%).

Analyses of the data from previous NSCAW reports (see, U.S. Department of Health and Human Services, 2005a, 2005b) provide an idea of how the youngest children were faring in the first three waves (18 months) following the initial investigation. A caveat is that previous NSCAW documents reported results for children who were between the ages of 0 and 2 at baseline. Therefore, they include not only all of the children for this report (ages 0 to 12 months at baseline), but also a substantial number of children between 1 and 2 years of age.

At baseline (5 months after the initial investigation), the large majority (87%) of the children aged 0 to 2 remained in home. By the 1½ -year follow-up, the proportion in home had increased only slightly, to 89%. These youngest children were at high risk for developmental problems. For example, at both baseline and Wave 3, more than 50% scored as high risk for developmental delays (according to the Bayley Infant Neurodevelopmental Screener). The cognitive and language development of these children also lagged behind that of their peers: At both baseline and Wave 3, average scores on the Battelle Developmental Inventory and Preschool Language Scale-3 hovered around the 25th percentile.

Compared to older children, those between the ages of 0 and 2 at baseline were relatively unlikely to have received any services, in spite of their developmental risks. By the 11/2-year follow-up, only 6% of children who remained in home had received any outpatient mental health service. By the 11/2-year follow-up, only 13% had special education needs identified by a professional, 24% had been tested for a learning or developmental problem, 7% had an Individualized Education Plan or an IFSP, and 5% were currently receiving special services. Among children out of home at the 1½ -year follow-up, the proportions receiving services were substantially higher. For example, 19% had received outpatient mental health services, 61% had been tested for a learning or developmental problem, and 11% were receiving special education services.

Providing services to strengthen families is critical to prevent maltreatment and to maintain children in their homes. Caseworkers reported that by the 1½ -year follow-up, three fourths of the families of out-of-home children aged 0 to 2 years, which represents 11% of families, had received some type of family-based service, including intensive family preservation services (13%) and less intensive family preservation service (23%). In addition, nearly three fourths (7 1%) of families whose children were out of home received some type of parenting support services, whether parent training (66%), family counseling (3 8%), or both. Among the families of children who remained in home (89% of the families), the proportions receiving services were substantially lower than among those who were removed from the home, but still notable: 27% received family-based services, and 29% received parenting support services. In addition, many caregivers of children who remained in home reported having received services that helped them meet basic needs, provided either by CWS or other agencies. The services of this type most commonly received were child care (52%); food, financial help, or transportation (49%); and job-related aid, legal aid, or support groups (32%).

In summary, analyses of previous waves indicate that the youngest children in NSCAW are at high risk of developmental delays, but relatively low proportions of the children have received any services; receipt of family-based and parenting support services is more common. The receipt of services is strongly related to the placement status of the child: services to both children and their families are much more common in cases where the child was removed from the home. In the following analyses, we will assess how the youngest of these children (ages 0– 12 months at baseline) were faring at the 5- to 6-year follow-up and we will track trends in their well-being over time.

Guide to the Report

Chapter 2 reviews data on child well-being in terms of caregiver aggression and neglect, health, disability, behavior problems and a variety of measures related to school readiness. Chapter 3 discusses results related to child placement and permanence of children in their living environments. Chapter 4 discusses the services that children and their caregivers receive. Appendix A explains the measures and specially derived variables used.

Appendix B contains tables that provide preliminary results of the Wave 5 follow-up for a different age group of NSCAW children: young children who were aged 1 to 4 years old when they were involved in an investigation of child maltreatment by child welfare services. The Wave 5 young child follow-up was conducted March to December 2006, or about 6 years after the index investigation; 902 children or their caregiver participated in this 6-year follow-up. The data collection methods were identical to those that were reported for the infant sample, with the exception of a few measures that differed on the basis of appropriateness for the age group studied. The research questions addressed by the young child tables were essentially identical to those of the infant. For the most part, tables in Appendix B parallel the tables presented for the infant sample.

2. Children's Well-Being

Ideally, all 5- and 6-year-olds would be physically healthy and growing, their minds would be developing, they would be enjoying school and new friends, their health would be robust, and they would experience self-esteem and a sense of well-being free from depression, anxiety, and behavioral problems. When they enter school, they would be cognitively, emotionally, and socially ready. But the later well-being of infants involved in child maltreatment investigations is at risk, both from whatever maltreatment they may have suffered and from a host of associated risks to development that have been amply documented in previous reports from the National Survey of Child and Adolescent Well-Being (NSCAW).

In addition to our natural interest in children's well-being, there is a policy interest as well, in that the responsibility of child welfare system (CWS) services to promote child well-being is codified in federal regulations (see U.S. Department of Health and Human Services [DHHS], 2000). The federal rule establishing the Child and Family Services Review (CFSR) process sets child well-being as a CWS goal and evaluates state child welfare agencies in part on their efforts to maintain and improve children's well-being. Federal policy holds that CWS has responsibility for promoting children's well-being as well as their safety and permanency in their living situation.

Previous research on the youngest children entering NSCAW indicates that the wellbeing of many of these children was compromised when they were infants and toddlers. As noted earlier, over half of these children showed early signs of developmental delay at earlier measurement points. Notable proportions lagged in cognitive and language development. One question addressed in this chapter is whether these children have been able to overcome their early challenges.

The report of results in this chapter begins with caregivers' reports of their aggression toward and neglect of their children. Next, there is an analysis of health. Then we examine measures of disability and basic living skills. The next section analyzes child behavior problems. There follows an analysis of cognitive, emotional, and social development as measures of children's readiness to enter school. An analysis of their school functioning as based on teacher reports completes the picture of well-being. When appropriate, children's scores are compared to national norms for similarly aged children.

The report also examines how child characteristics are related to different indicators of well-being. Findings are examined in relation to a child's sex, race, and living situation at the 5- to 6-year follow-up. Finally, the report examines the impact of several factors related to the index maltreatment report at baseline; these include the type of maltreatment, the severity of physical abuse or neglect, or the number of different types of maltreatment experienced. When findings related to maltreatment were significant, they are presented in the exhibits. Where such results are not shown or discussed, there was no impact of the maltreatment variables on children's well-being. Note that the limitation mentioned in Chapter 1 applies here: significant group differences on follow-up outcomes do not necessarily mean that being in those groups *caused* those outcomes. Earlier differences on well-being variables may have predisposed children to be in certain groups, as with different living settings or different disability classifications; more complex analyses of NSCAW well-being outcomes at the 5- to 6-year follow-up is needed.

Key Caregiver Aggression and Neglect Results

- Nearly all parents (99%) reported having used some form of nonviolent discipline, primarily explaining why something was wrong and putting the child in time out or sending the child to his or her room.
- Psychological aggression was reported by 78% of caregivers, mainly shouting, yelling, or screaming at the child, or threatening to spank the child.

- Minor physical assault or corporal punishment was reported by nearly two thirds of caregivers (65%).
- Neglect was reported by 12% of caregivers, mostly that they were so caught up with problems that they were not able to show or tell their child that they loved him/her.
- Severe assault and very severe assault were reported by 4% and 0.2% of caregivers respectively.
- Reports on psychological aggression, minor assault, severe assault, and neglect are somewhat lower than in a previous Gallup survey of the general population of parents self-reporting aggression toward their children. Caregivers may have under-reported unsafe behaviors in NSCAW, especially because of the risk of being re-reported to CWS.

Key Children's Physical Health Results

- The vast majority of caregivers (93.5%) reported that their child was in good, very good, or excellent health.
- A fifth of caregivers reported that their child had a chronic health problem. The majority of these children were reportedly suffering from asthma (13% of the total population).
- Approximately 6% of children were reported to have experienced some type of injury, accident, or poisoning in the previous year.
- Children living at home with adoptive parents were the most likely to be reported to have chronic health conditions (32%), compared with children living in other settings.

Key Children's Behavioral Results

- Seventeen percent of children, according to caregivers' report, are in the clinical range on the externalizing behaviors scale (behaviors such as aggression, hyperactivity, and oppositional behavior).
- For internalizing behavior (behaviors signaling anxiety, depression and fears), caregivers reported that only 6% are in the clinical range.
- Girls exhibited slightly but significantly more externalizing behavior problems than boys, as reported by caregivers.
- The percentage in the clinical range on externalizing behavior, according to teacher report, was 9%.
- Only 4% of children were reported by teachers to exhibit proactive aggression; only 7% exhibited reactive aggression.

Key Children's Cognitive, Emotional, and Social Development Results

- Mean scores on tests of cognitive functioning, language skill, and academic achievement were in the low end of the average range, which was significantly below the normative mean.
- Girls had significantly higher scores than boys on both the total language and the auditory comprehension scales of the PLS, and Letter Word Identification scores of the Woodcock-Johnson.
- Children in adoptive homes displayed higher scores on five measures of cognitive language and academic functioning than children in other home settings.
- Teachers rated a lower percentage of this population as demonstrating excellent assertiveness, self-control, and cooperation than of the general population.
- Teachers rated 40% of children as below grade level in language arts and 35% as below grade level in mathematics.

Caregiver Aggression and Neglect

These children were originally involved with CWS because of a report of abuse, neglect or both against them. An important aspect of their well-being, then, is whether they are experiencing aggression or neglect from their caregivers at the 5- to 6-year follow-up. We could not accurately measure this through data on re-reports from the caseworker interview, however, because only 12% of these children had received CWS services since the last follow-up, and also because a recent analysis suggests that caseworkers were not able to provide accurate data on whether there was a later re-report of abuse and neglect in their cases (Biemer, Chiflikyan, Dowd, & Smith, 2007). There is also reason to suspect the accuracy of the Violence Exposure Scale (Shahinfar, Fox, & Leavitt, 2000), a component of the child interview which had questionable reliability overall in NSCAW (see Biemer, Christ, & Wiesen, 2006), and is particularly problematic with 5- and 6-year-olds.

The caregiver interview, however, did ask caregivers about their aggression toward and neglect of their children, using the Conflict Tactics Scale–Parent-Child Version (CTS-PC; Straus, Hamby, Finkelhor, Moore, & Runyan, 1998), and we report results from the CTS-PC here. Caregivers are asked about what tactics (primarily related to discipline) they used in their conflicts with their children. Included are both nonviolent disciplinary tactics and tactics that are mildly or seriously aggressive, from spanking to hitting, slapping, and injurious actions (see Appendix A). The CTS-PC also asks about neglect. It should be noted that caregivers were repeatedly warned in the informed consent process that abusive or neglectful behaviors would be reported to CWS because of mandated reporting laws, which could strengthen reluctance to disclose aggressive tactics. We conducted a comparison of the proportions of caregivers reporting psychological aggression, assault, and neglect between caregivers in the NSCAW survey and a nationally representative sample of parents of children aged 5 to 6 (Straus, Hamby, Finkelhor, Moore, & Runyan, 1998). This analysis indicated that the NSCAW caregivers reported somewhat lower prevalence than the general population on nearly all CTS-PC aggression and neglect scales. It seems likely, therefore, that caregivers tended to withhold information on abusive and neglectful behaviors. Even as an underestimate, however, these results tell us something about the caregiver environment and the risks that some of the children in this population still face at ages 5 and 6.

We present the proportions of caregivers who used each type of tactic in the past year by selected characteristics in Exhibit 2-1. For all tactics, the proportions of caregivers who reported ever having used a tactic were very similar to the proportions of caregivers who reported having used it in the past year. In the past year, nearly all parents (99%) reported having used some form of nonviolent discipline. The most common techniques were explaining why something was wrong (95%) and putting the child in time out or sending the child to his or her room (94%). The use of psychological aggression was reported by 78% of caregivers, primarily shouting, yelling, or screaming at the child (69%) or threatening to spank the child (59%). The use of minor physical assault or corporal punishment was reported by nearly two thirds of caregivers (65%), primarily spanking on the bottom with a bare hand (5 9%) or slapping on the hand, arm, or leg (34%). Much lower proportions of caregivers reported any type of severe assault (4%) or very severe assault (0.2%). Approximately 12% of caregivers reported some form of neglect in the past year—primarily that they were so caught up with problems that they were not able to show or tell their child that they loved him/her (9%). Inability to access needed health care (4%) and inability to provide needed food (3%) were the next most common forms of neglect mentioned.

There were no significant differences between boys and girls in the types of tactics reported. Considering race/ethnicity, minor assault/corporal punishment was most common among non-Hispanic Whites (75%), severe physical assault was most common among non-Hispanic Blacks (8%), and neglect was least common among non-Hispanic Whites (8%). The caregivers of children who had never been in out-of-home placement were significantly more likely to report minor assault/corporal punishment (71%), severe physical assault (5%), and very severe physical assault (0.4%). The percentage of severe physical assault was very close to the percentage of in-home caregivers who scored on the severe violence scale for children aged 0 to 2 at baseline and the 1½ -year follow-up (see U.S. Department of Health and Human Services, 2005b).

The type of maltreatment for which caregivers were reported at baseline was significantly associated with the types of tactics reported by current caregivers. Note of course that many of the caregivers at this follow-up are different from the caregivers who may have maltreated children at baseline, because of placement and other changes in care. When physical abuse was reported at baseline, no current caregivers committed very severe assault, while a very small but significantly higher percentage (0.3%) of caregivers committed very severe assault during this last follow-up period when physical abuse was not reported at baseline. This may be a function of physically abused children being removed from the home close to baseline and now living with substitute caregivers. When failure to provide was reported at baseline, caregivers were significantly more likely to report minor assault/corporal punishment at this follow-up (72% vs. 59% for caregivers of children who were not reported for failure to provide), but were less likely to report very severe assault (0.1% vs. 0.3%). Finally, when failure to supervise was reported at baseline, caregivers at this follow-up were significantly more likely to report neglect (17% vs. 10%).

Previous results on racial/ethnic differences on discipline, corporal punishment, and aggression against children have varied (see Gershoff, 2002, for a relevant literature review), so it is difficult to compare the current results to them. Differences by race and ethnicity could reflect cultural differences in discipline practices as well as differential exposure by race/ethnicity to risk factors that may predispose caregivers to more aggressive responses to their children.

Children who have ever been in out-of-home placement are less likely to experience any form of assault by caregivers. This appears to be due in part to the fact that most children who have ever been out of home are now with adoptive parents or with other in-home caregivers, who report lower levels of assault than biological parents. Moreover, biological parents whose children have ever been out of home report lower levels of assault than those whose children have never been out of home. This may reflect successful CWS action to decrease assault, or fear of revealing aggression by parents who have already have their child removed at least once.

Child Physical Health

Previous NSCAW research indicates that children involved in the child welfare system, particularly those in foster care, are at increased risk for the development of physical health problems as well as chronic health conditions (e.g., Jee, Barth, Szilagzi, Szilagzi, Aida, & Davis, 2006; Leslie, Gordon, Meneken, Premji, Michelmore, & Ganger, 2005). More specifically, previous studies have found anywhere from 26%–82% of children placed in out-of-home care had at least one chronic health condition (Taussig & Culhane, 2005). Findings concerning children's physical health have led some experts to call for comprehensive health screening procedures to be a routine part of social services plans, particularly for children in out-of-home placements (AAP, Committee of Early Childhood, Adoption, and Dependent Care, 2002).

General health characteristics were obtained from caregiver reports. The majority of caregivers (93.5%) reported that their child was in good, very good, or excellent health (Exhibit 2-2). This is comparable with findings within other age groups and across various follow-up periods within NSCAW. It is less than that reported (98.2%) for children between 5 and 11 years of age across the country, and also less than data on children living in poverty nationwide (95.8%; National Health Interview Survey [NHIS]; Bloom & Dey, 2006).

Nonetheless, slightly more than a quarter of caregivers (26.5%) reported that their child had a health problem that "lasts a long time or comes back again and again." When narrowed to include *only* serious chronic health diagnoses (e.g., asthma, diabetes, eczema), approximately 20% of children were reported to be experiencing such conditions, with the majority of them suffering from asthma (13%), followed by severe allergies, other respiratory conditions, and eczema (Exhibit 2-2). Although the rates of chronic health conditions might appear high, it should be noted that recent NHIS findings indicate that 13% of children nationwide who are between 5 and 11 years of age are reported to have asthma (Bloom & Dey, 2006).

Exhibit 2-1. Caregiver Aggression and Neglect Prevalence by Case Characteristics Infant Population at Wave 5

	N (Min)	Nonviolent Discipline % (SE)	Psychological Aggression % (SE)	Minor Assault/ Corporal Punishment % (SE)	Severe Physical Assault % (SE)	Very Severe Assault % (SE)	Neglect % (SE)
Total	899	99.3 (0.3)	77.5 (2.4)	65.2 (2.8)	3.5 (1.0)	0.2 (0.1)	12.3 (1.7)
Sex							
Male	457	99.7 (0.1)	80.8 (3.2)	69.2 (3.9)	4.4 (1.6)	0.2 (0.1)	11.0 (2.3)
Female	442	98.8 (0.6)	74.2 (3.0)	61.1 (3.6)	2.6 (0.7)	0.2 (0.2)	13.6 (2.3)
Race/ethnicity				*	**		**
Black	355	98.2 (1.0)	73.7 (5.5)	57.3 (5.3)	7.5 (2.1)	0.7 (0.4)	17.3 (3.1)
White	316	99.9 (0.1)	81.0 (3.3)	74.5 (4.2)	1.2 (0.7)	0.0 (0.0)	7.8 (1.6)
Hispanic	165	99.4 (0.4)	75.2 (6.2)	58.6 (7.0)	3.5 (2.8)	0.0 (0.0)	13.1 (3.9)
Other	58	100.0 (0.0)	78.2 (7.4)	59.5 (10.1)	0.0 (0.0)	0.0 (0.0)	19.4 (7.2)
Ever in out-of-home placement				*	*	*	
Yes	404	98.7 (0.8)	76.2 (4.8)	56.6 (4.3)	1.7 (0.7)	0.0 (0.0)	8.9 (2.0)
No	457	99.6 (0.2)	80.1 (3.0)	70.5 (3.8)	4.6 (1.4)	0.4 (0.2)	14.0 (2.5)
Child setting				*	*	*	
In home, biological parent	485	99.7 (0.2)	79.9 (3.0)	68.3 (3.5)	4.7 (1.4)	0.3 (0.2)	14.7 (2.4)
Ever out of home	90	99.8 (0.2)	82.5 (5.3)	53.5 (7.1)a	2.4 (1.7)*a	0.0 (0.0)*a	19.0 (5.8)
Never out of home	368	99.7 (0.2)	81.7 (3.3)	71.0 (3.9)	5.1 (1.6)	0.4 (0.2)	13.9 (2.7)
In home, adoptive parent	220	99.6 (0.4)	79.5 (5.1)	59.0 (5.0)	1.5 (0.8)	0.0 (0.0)	7.6 (2.7)
In home, kin, or other caregiver	158	97.4 (1.8)	68.9 (5.6)	63.2 (6.3)	1.5 (0.8)	0.0 (0.0)	8.3 (2.7)
Physical abuse						*	
Yes	209	99.2 (0.5)	79.6 (4.3)	63.5 (6.3)	2.9 (2.1)	0.0 (0.0)	11.8 (3.6)
No	617	99.3 (0.4)	76.0 (3.4)	65.6 (3.1)	3.8 (1.2)	0.3 (0.2)	12.7 (2.0)
Failure to provide				*		*	
Yes	410	99.7 (0.2)	80.3 (3.1)	72.3 (3.1)	6.2 (2.1)	0.1 (0.1)	11.6 (2.1)
No	417	98.9 (0.6)	74.4 (3.6)	59.3 (4.2)	1.5 (0.5)	0.3 (0.2)	13.1 (2.7)
Failure to supervise							*
Yes	281	99.0 (0.8)	73.9 (4.2)	65.8 (4.2)	3.8 (1.8)	0.5 (0.3)	17.2 (3.7)
No	546	99.5 (0.2)	78.9 (2.5)	64.5 (3.4)	3.5 (1.2)	0.1 (0.1)	9.6 (1.5)

Note: Based on caregiver self-report using the Conflict Tactics Scale–Parent-Child version. All analyses are on weighted data; Ns are unweighted. Pearson $\chi 2$ tests for cluster samples were used to test statistical significance. Statistical significance is noted by asterisks in the column above the statistically significant result (*$p < .05$, **$p < .01$).

a Ever out of home significantly different from never out of home.

Exhibit 2-2. Health of Children Infant Population at Wave 5

	N (Min)	In Good Health[1] % (SE)	Caregiver Reports Serious Chronic Health Problem[2] % (SE)
Total	961	93.5 (1.3)	20.5 (2.4)
Sex			
Male	491	92.2 (2.0)	21.2 (3.2)
Female	470	94.8 (1.3)	19.8 (2.8)
Race/ethnicity			
Black	378	91.7 (2.1)	22.1 (3.5)
White	329	94.5 (2.1)	19.9 (3.4)
Hispanic	329	92.6 (3.0)	18.5 (4.9)
Other	62	98.0 (1.1)	21.7 (6.1)
Child setting			**
In home, biological parents	493	94.3 (1.7)	18.8 (2.7)[a]
In home, adoptive parents	224	94.3 (2.3)	31.7 (5.1)[b]
In home, kin, or other caregiver	159	91.3 (3.4)	13.5 (3.3)[a]
Out of home	44	93.4 (4.2)	21.8 (10.8)

Note: All analyses are on weighted data; *Ns* are unweighted. Pearson χ^2 tests for cluster samples were used for initial significance tests. Statistical significance is noted by asterisks in the column above the statistically significant result (***p* < .0 1). Alphabetic superscripts that are different from one another represent statistically significant differences ($\alpha = .05$).

[1] "Good health" was defined as those children whose caregivers reported that they were in "good, very good, or excellent" health.

[2] "Serious Chronic Health Condition" was defined here as one of a number of caregiver-reported diagnoses, as detailed in Appendix A.

Most children reported to have a chronic health condition were also reported to be in relatively good health, with only 20% of caregivers describing the health of their children with chronic health conditions as "fair" or "poor." When compared with children living in other settings, children living at home with adoptive parents were by far the most likely to be reported to have chronic health conditions, followed by children in out-of-home care and those living at home with biological parents. There were no differences in the reports of chronic health conditions by sex, race/ethnicity or type of abuse at baseline.

Approximately 6% of children were reported to have experienced some type of injury, accident, or poisoning that needed the care of a doctor or nurse during the past 12 months. The injuries themselves were most commonly cuts, scrapes, or puncture wounds or broken bones (Exhibit 2-3). The most common circumstances surrounding these accidents or injuries were outdoor play-related injuries (22.3% of the reported injuries), rough-housing with other kids/peers (18.3%), and animal- or insect-inflicted injuries (14.3%). There were no differences in reports of accidents and injuries by sex, race/ethnicity, type of abuse at baseline, current home setting, or the presence of a chronic health condition.

In summary, the overwhelming majority of children were reported to be in good, very good, or excellent health, though somewhat less than the general population. Only a small percentage had suffered serious accidents or injuries requiring the care of a doctor. About one fifth of these children were reported to have a serious chronic health condition, most commonly asthma, with the rate of asthma the same as in the general population. Children with a history of out-of-home placement also were more likely to have chronic health problems. However, these children who were infants when they became involved with CWS do not seem to have the same level of health problems reported by Taussig and Culhane (2005) for the population of children of all ages in foster care.

Child Disability and Basic Living Skills

We also looked at children's risk for development of a cognitive, emotional/behavioral, or physical disability. It is reasonable to consider risk for cognitive, emotional/behavioral, and physical disabilities as indicators of service needs according to the federal definition of "disability" within the Individuals with Disabilities Education Improvement Act of 2004(or IDEA). This could be especially important, as an IDEA disability classification often serves as the precursor to special education service qualification. Within this report, disability risk was operationalized via standardized measures, as well as caregiver or teacher report. *Risk for a cognitive disability* was determined to include any child with a score at the 5- to 6-year follow-up of 2 standard deviations below the mean on the Preschool Language Scales (Zimmerman, Steiner, & Pond, 1992) or the Kaufman Brief Intelligence Test or K-BIT (Kaufman & Kaufman, 1990). *Risk for an emotional or behavioral problem* was determined to include any child with a score greater than 63 according to either caregiver or teacher report on the Total Problems, Externalizing or Internalizing Scales of the Child Behavior Checklist (Achenbach, 1991). *Risk for physical disability* was determined based upon either the caregiver or teacher report. A child was considered at risk for a physical impairment if the caregiver reported having been told that his or her child had a hearing impairment, visual impairment (including blindness), orthopedic impairment, or multiple disabilities at any point over the course of the study. A child was also considered to be at risk for a physical disability if the teacher reported an Individualized Education Plan (IEP) classification due to visual, hearing, orthopedic, or other physical disability.

Exhibit 2-3. Most Common Chronic Health Conditions and Injuries or Accidents Infant Population at Wave 5

Health Condition	% (SE)	
Chronic health problem (*N* = 961)		
Asthma	13.3	(2.0)
Severe allergies	3.9	(1.1)
Other respiratory condition	2.4	(0.7)
Eczema/other skin disorder	1.1	(0.4)
Repeated ear infections	0.8	(0.4)
Serious injury, accident, or poisoning (*N* = 59)[1]		
Cuts, scrapes, puncture	2.3	(0.8)
Broken bone, dislocated joint	1.0	(0.4)
Other	2.5	(0.7)

Note: All analyses are on weighted data; Ns are unweighted.

[1] Caregivers were asked to report on serious accidents and injuries only since the last interview.

Exhibit 2-4. Child Risk for Cognitive, Emotional/Behavioral, and Physical Disabilities Infant Population at Wave 5

	N (Min)	Risk for Cognitive Disability % (SE)	Risk for Emotional/ Behavioral Problem % (SE)	Risk for Physical Disability % (SE)
Total	921	13.0 (2.1)	28.9 (2.6)	5.9 (1.0)
Sex				
Male	472	15.9 (3.5)	26.3 (3.8)	6.8 (1.4)
Female	449	10.0 (2.3)	31.6 (3.5)	5.0 (1.5)
Race/ethnicity				
Black	367	13.3 (3.0)	32.8 (4.4)	7.0 (1.9)
White	310	11.7 (3.4)	28.7 (4.4)	4.5 (1.5)
Hispanic	179	15.7 (4.8)	26.2 (5.7)	4.1 (1.7)
Other	60	—	19.4 (4.3)	
Child setting				
In home, biological parents	493	12.4 (3.0)	25.8 (3.3)	4.5 (1.2)
In home, adoptive parents	224	5.6 (1.3)	27.0 (5.0)	10.2 (3.0)
In home, kin, or other caregiver	159	21.3 (6.0)	26.6 (6.5)	—
Out of home	44		70.4 (8.5)	
Physical maltreatment at baseline		*		*
Yes	213	6.5 (2.3)	31.8 (6.4)	2.8 (1.3)
No	634	15.6 (2.8)	26.7 (2.4)	6.1 (1.2)

Note: See Appendix A for definitions of risk of cognitive disability, emotional/behavioral problem, and physical disability. All analyses are on weighted data; Ns are unweighted. Pearson χ^2 tests for cluster samples were used to test statistical significance. Statistical significance is noted by asterisks in the column above the statistically significant result (*p < .05). Cells are left empty when sample sizes are too small to allow for meaningful estimates (N < 9).

Using these definitions of risk, 13% of children were determined to be at risk for a cognitive disability, 29% at risk for an emotional/behavioral problem, and 6% at risk for a physical disability (Exhibit 2-4). There were no differences in risk for cognitive, emotional/behavioral, or physical disability risks by child sex, race/ethnicity, or the child's setting at 5- to 6-year follow-up. Children who were assessed as physically maltreated at baseline were *less* likely to have risks for cognitive and physical disabilities than other children, perhaps because other children were involved with CWS for reasons (e.g., neglect, parents' having difficulty caring for them) that were more associated with risks for cognitive and physical disabilities.

A child's ability to meet his or her basic functional needs was measured via the daily-living skills domain of the Vineland Screener (Sparrow, Carter, & Cicchetti, 1993), a shortened version of the Vineland Adaptive Behavior Scale (VABS; Sparrow, Balla, & Cicchetti, 1984). For 3- to 5-year-olds, basic daily-living skills assessed included activities such as dressing, toilet- training competence, telling time, using the telephone, using the stove or microwave, and understanding danger from strangers. For children 6 and older, assessed skills included following instructions, understanding how to compliment friends or family members, asking permission to use other's property, and knowing how to avoid trouble situations. According to the VABS manual, scores greater than 84 represent adequate to high functioning and scores below 70 represent low functional ability (Sparrow, Balla, & Cicchetti, 1984). For children described in this report, the average Vineland standard score was 86.04 (SE = 1.1). This indicates that, on the average, children had at least an adequate ability to meet their typical daily basic living needs. Approximately 23% (SE = 2.2) scored below 70 on the daily-living skills domain of the VABs indicating that they did not have an adequate ability to meet their daily living needs. Being at risk for a cognitive, emotional/behavioral, or physical disability increased the likelihood of having some functional impairment in daily-living skills (Exhibit 2-3). For instance, 44% of those at risk for a cognitive disability, 37% of those at risk for an emotional or behavioral problem, and 49% at risk for a physical disability demonstrated problems meeting daily living needs on the VABs (e.g., scores below 70).

Behavior Problems

Child maltreatment can have enduring negative effects on children's mental health (see, e.g., Cicchetti & Lynch, 1995; Kendall-Tackett, Williams, & Finkelhor, 1993), and previous research has found that maltreated children may have increased behavior problems (Shonk & Cicchetti, 2001). However, the relationship between maltreatment in infancy and the mental health status of children at age 5 and 6 has received little attention. At baseline and previous follow-ups, the children in this analysis were simply too young to measure their mental health in any valid and practical way. At this follow-up, however, reasonably valid and reliable teacher and caregiver checklist measures of child behavior problems are available.

In previous NSCAW analyses, a worrisome proportion of the other children scored in the clinical range when they were in this age range. For example, the baseline report (U.S. Department of Health and Human Services, 2005b) reported that 37% of the 4- to 5-year-olds and 40% of the 6- to 10-year-olds scored in the borderline-clinical-to-clinical range on the Child Behavior Checklist, the caregiver checklist of child behavior problems. Burns and colleagues' study of children's mental health in NSCAW reported similar statistics with a slightly different threshold (Burns, Phillips et al., 2004). Thus large proportions of children who were aged 5 to 6 years at NSCAW baseline had mental health problems, significantly greater than the proportion in the clinical range in the general population (see Kataoka, Zhang, & Wells, 2002). Similarly, 37% of the children who were aged 4Y2 to 6Y2 at the 1Y2-year follow-up scored in the borderline clinical or the clinical range (U.S. Department of Health and Human Services, Administration for Children and Families, 2008b). These findings suggest some urgency in the analysis of the behavior problems of children who were infants at baseline and aged 5 and 6 at the latest follow- up.

Caregiver report

Interviewed caregivers completed the Child Behavior Checklist, a 118- item checklist of behavior problems children might have. Externalizing behavior refers to misbehavior that is manifest in the child's external environment, problems such as aggression, hyperactivity, and oppositional behavior. The percentage of children in the clinical range on the Externalizing Score (17.1%) was over twice as high as the percentage in the general population.

Exhibit 2-5. Caregiver Report of Children's Behavior Problems (Child Behavior Checklist) Infant Population at Wave 5

	N	In Clinical Range for Total Score % (SE)	In Clinical Range for Internalizing Score % (SE)	In Clinical Range for Externalizing Score % (SE)
Total	961	18.5 (1.8)	5.5 (1.0)	17.1 (1.8)
Sex				*
Male	491	18.6 (2.8)	6.4 (1.9)	14.0 (2.4)
Female	470	18.4 (3.0)	4.5 (1.4)	20.3 (3.1)
Race/ethnicity				
Black	378	18.9 (3.3)	7.8 (2.0)	16.9 (3.3)
White	329	19.5 (3.3)	4.0 (1.4)	17.9 (3.1)
Hispanic	187	18.7 (4.9)	6.4 (3.3)	18.7 (5.1)
Other	62	7.3 (3.1)	0.9 (0.5)	4.8 (2.1)
Child setting				
In home, biological parents	493	16.5 (2.5)	4.8 (1.4)	14.0 (2.2)
In home, adoptive parents	224	18.3 (3.8)	3.3 (1.4)	18.2 (4.6)
In home, kin, or other caregiver	159	17.1 (4.7)	8.0 (3.1)	10.3 (3.2)
Out of home	44	14.5 (5.4)	12.8 (8.8)	67.1 (9.6)
Chronic health condition				
Yes	221	20.2 (3.9)	6.4 (1.9)	20.4 (4.3)
No	740	18.1 (2.0)	5.2 (1.2)	16.2 (1.8)
Physical disability				
Yes	35	33.7 (12.3)	13.0 (10.0)	8.7 (5.6)
No	926	18.0 (1.8)	5.2 (1.0)	17.4 (1.9)
Cognitive disability				
Yes	109	20.4 (6.3)	7.2 (3.3)	22.2 (7.1)
No	811	18.2 (1.9)	5.3 (1.1)	16.8 (1.8)
Physical abuse (baseline)				
Yes	225	15.2 (4.0)	4.6 (1.6)	17.8 (5.0)
No	660	18.9 (2.2)	5.3 (1 4)	16.4 (2.1)

Note: Instrument used is the Child Behavior Checklist. All analyses are on weighted data; Ns are unweighted. Pearson χ^2 tests for cluster samples were used to test statistical significance. Statistical significance is noted by asterisks in the column above the statistically significant result (*$p < .05$).

On the other hand, only 5.5% of the population was in the clinical range on the internalizing score, a percentage similar to that in the general population. Thus, caregivers reported that these 5 and 6 year olds were about average on behaviors signaling anxiety, depression, and fears. On the Total Problems score, which combines results from the Externalizing and Internalizing scores, 18.5% of children scored in the clinical range, again substantially higher than the percentage in the general population.

Exhibit 2-6. Teacher Report of Children's Behavior Problems Infant Population at Wave 5

	N (Min)	In Clinical Range for Total Score % (SE)	In Clinical Range for Internalizing Score % (SE)	In Clinical Range for Externalizing Score % (SE)
Total	608	7.9 (1.7)	7.6 (1.9)	8.8 (1.6)
Sex				
Male	311	5.3 (2.2)	9.0 (3.3)	5.3 (1.2)
Female	297	10.5 (2.7)	6.2 (1.8)	12.4 (2.8)
Race/ethnicity				*
Black	244	11.7 (3.8)	7.5 (2.8)	16.2 (3.7)[a]
White	214	6.0 (3.8)	7.7 (3.2)	5.5 (1.8)[b]
Hispanic	108	5.5 (4.2)	8.5 (5.0)	2.6 (0.9)[b]
Other	44	8.6 (5.0)	4.5 (3.2)	14.2 (5.5)
Child setting				
In home, biological parents	318	5.9 (2.0)	6.8 (2.7)	7.5 (2.2)
In home, adoptive parents	134	7.7 (3.5)	4.8 (2.1)	10.7 (3.6)
In home, kin, or other caregiver	114	8.5 (3.4)	6.0 (3.4)	13.6 (4.6)
Out of home	31	22.1 (13.2)	19.0 (13.2)	5.1 (4.4)
Chronic health condition				
Yes	135	8.8 (3.3)	14.6 (6.2)	8.8 (3.1)
No	473	7.6 (2.0)	5.6 (1.6)	8.8 (2.0)
Physical disability				
Yes	25	6.4 (6.4)	2.3 (2.1)	16.3 (8.9)
No	583	7.8 (1.7)	7.8 (2.0)	8.5 (1.6)
Cognitive disability				
Yes	57	19.0 (8.0)	12.8 (7.3)	13.9 (6.5)
No	540	6.3 (1.6)	6.5 (1.9)	8.3 (1.7)
Physical abuse (baseline)				
Yes	151	7.0 (2.9)	12.2 (5.0)	8.5 (2.9)
No	411	7.9 (2.1)	4.8 (1.6)	8.0 (1.7)

Note: Instrument used is the Teacher Report Form (TRF). All analyses are on weighted data; *Ns* are unweighted. Pearson χ^2 tests for cluster samples were used to test statistical significance. Statistical significance is noted by asterisks in the column above the statistically significant result (*$p < .05$). Alphabetic superscripts that are different from one another represent statistically significant differences ($\alpha = .05$).

These children had significantly higher scores than average children, but there were few variables within this population that predicted higher or lower scores, as shown in Exhibit 2-5. One that did was surprising. Girls exhibited significantly more externalizing behavior problems than boys.

Teacher report

Teachers completed the Teacher Report Form (TRF), a measure of behavior problems that parallels the Child Behavior Checklist in content and scoring (Exhibit 2-6). The percentage in the clinical range on externalizing behavior was 8.8%, which is only modestly higher than the percentage in the clinical range in the normative population. For internalizing behavior, 7.6% of this population was in the clinical range, about what would be expected for children in general. For the Total score, the percentage in the clinically significant range (7.9%) was only slightly higher than one would expect in the normative population. Among the variables we tested, only one, race/ethnicity, was significantly related to the percentage of children with TRF scores in the clinical range. A significantly higher percentage of children who were Black or in the "Other" category were in the clinical range on the externalizing scale compared with the White and Hispanic categories.

We examined the Attention subscale of the Teacher Rating Form as an indicator of attention problems in this group (Exhibit 2-7). Although the ratings of attention were in the average range, the mean score (52.1) was somewhat elevated as compared to the normative group (50). Girls' scores were significantly higher than boys', but otherwise there were no significant group differences.

Teachers rated children's aggressive behaviors on Dodge and Coie's (1987) Teacher Checklist of Aggression. (Exhibit 2-7). These children were fairly nonaggressive on average, especially concerning proactive or nonprovoked aggression. Although reactive aggression scores were a little higher, the scores of the group as a whole indicated that teachers rated the children between "seldom" and "sometimes" on average. Black children were rated higher than White children on reactive aggression, but otherwise no group differences were significant.

Exhibit 2-7. Teacher Ratings of Attention and Aggressive Behaviors Infant Population at Wave 5

	TRF Attention Problems		Proactive Aggression		Reactive Aggression	
	N	Mean (SE)	*N*	Mean (SE)	*N*	Mean (SE)
Total	636	52.1 (0.2)***	618	4.2 (0.1)	620	6.7 (0.2)
Sex		***				
Male	328	51.5 (0.2)	315	4.3 (0.2)	317	7.0 (0.4)
Female	308	52.8 (0.3)	303	4.0 (0.2)	303	6.5 (0.3)
Race/ethnicity						*
Black	259	52.5 (0.4)	252	4.4 (0.3)	253	7.5 (0.4)[a]
White	218	52.2 (0.4)	210	3.9 (0.2)	210	6.1 (0.3)[b]
Hispanic	114	51.3 (0.3)	113	4.2 (0.2)	114	6.8 (0.4)
Other	44	52.1 (0.4)	42	4.2 (0.4)	42	7.3 (0.7)
Current setting						
In home, biological parents	330	52.0 (0.3)	319	4.1 (0.1)	319	6.7 (0.3)
In home, adoptive parents	145	52.2 (0.4)	142	4.0 (0.2)	142	6.3 (0.3)
In home, kin, or other caregiver	117	52.6 (0.8)	116	4.4 (0.3)	116	7.4 (0.5)
Out of home	32	52.3 (0.8)	31	4.3 (0.6)	33	7.2 (0.8)

Note: Instruments used are the Teacher Report Form (TRF) and the Teacher Rating Instrument of Proactive and Reactive Aggression. All analyses are on weighted data; *N*s are unweighted. Pearson χ^2 tests for cluster samples were used to test statistical significance. For the total, differences in means were tested against means of the standardization sample, which equals 50 for TRF attention problems. Statistical significance is noted by asterisks in the column above the statistically significant result (*$p < .05$, ***$p < .001$). Alphabetic superscripts that are different from one another represent statistically significant differences ($\alpha = .05$).

School Readiness

Previous research suggest that many children who have been maltreated have deficits in cognitive, language, social, and behavioral skills, with some differences beginning in infancy (Bolger, Patterson, & Kupersmidt, 1998; Culp, Watkins, Lawrence, Letts et al., 1991; Kim & Cicchetti, 2003; Shonk & Cicchetti, 2001). The baseline NSCAW report on children during infancy and preschool indicates that more than half (53%) of all children aged 3 to 24 months whose families were investigated for maltreatment were considered to be at high risk for developmental delay or neurological impairment (U.S. Department of Health and Human Services, 2005b). Among children aged 3 or younger, 30% lagged significantly behind average children in both cognitive and language skills. When followed up 1 1/2 years after investigation, children who were 2 years or younger at baseline continued to have significant risks for developmental delay and neurological impairment, and their functioning on measures of cognition and language development was below average.

Given these children's history of developmental challenges, it is important to examine their functioning as they make the transition to school. The analyses below examine development in terms of global cognitive functioning, language skills, social competence, attention, aggression, peer relationships, and academic performance. We examine children's outcomes in these areas overall and by background factors (i.e., sex, race/ethnicity, chronic health conditions) and case characteristics (i.e., maltreatment type, number of out-of-home placements, current setting, severity of physical abuse, and severity of neglect).

There are limitations in the analysis relating to school adjustment. Some children had entered the school system and have information available from their teachers, while 8% had not yet reached kindergarten, resulting in a lack of critical information on their integration to formal schooling. Because of their limited time in formal schooling—most of these children were only in kindergarten—teachers and caregivers may not yet have identified their educational needs.

Cognitive and Language Development

Overall, the children performed in the average range on the Kaufman Brief Intelligence Test (K-BIT; Exhibit 2-8). However, overall scores were about one half of a standard deviation below the mean for children in general on the composite as well as the vocabulary scale and the nonverbal matrices scales. Black children scored significantly lower than one or more other race/ethnicity groups on each K-BIT score. In addition, K-BIT scores differed by setting, children in adoptive homes having higher scores than children in their homes with kin or other nonparental caregivers.

Scores on the Preschool Language Scale (PLS) were also in the average range (Exhibit 2-8), though they were also significantly lower than those of children in general. The sample size for the PLS is lower because it is not used with 6-year-olds. The total language score and the expressive language score were each about one half of a standard deviation below the mean. Girls had significantly higher scores than boys on both the total language and the auditory comprehension scales. Children in out-of-home care had significantly lower PLS total and auditory comprehension scores than children who were living at home with either their biological or adoptive parents. No other differences in cognitive or language scores were found as a function of background or case characteristics.

Early Academic Achievement

Children completed several subtests of the Woodcock Johnson III Tests of Achievement, although only children who were at least 6 were old enough to take the Calculation test. Although mean scores tended to be in the average range, both the Passage Comprehension test, assessing reading comprehension, and the Applied Problems test, measuring math ability were significantly below the mean for children on average (Exhibit 2-9). The difficulties of the population who were involved with CWS at baseline were especially clear on Calculation. Of the 6-year-olds who were eligible for this test, nearly 27% were given missing standard scores because of their inability to successfully complete test items at the lowest level. For the other subtests, between 1% and 2% did not have standard scores.

Girls had significantly higher Letter Word Identification scores than boys, but boys had significantly higher Calculation scores. Black children had significantly lower scores on Woodcock-Johnson Calculation scores than White and "Other" children and lower on Woodcock-Johnson Applied Problems than White children. Woodcock-Johnson scores also differed by setting. Children who had been adopted had significantly higher scores than children in all other groups on Letter Identification and Comprehension and higher scores than children in two groups on Applied Problems. Children who were in out-of-home setting had significantly lower scores than others on Calculation.

Severity of neglect at baseline was significantly related to Passage Comprehension in an unexpected way. Those experiencing mild or moderate neglect at baseline had lower scores than those experiencing severe or grave neglect. The data indicate that the more serious the neglect, the greater the likelihood of adoption [χ^2 (12) = 49.0, p = .0001], suggesting that the finding of elevated Passage Comprehension scores among those who were adopted explains why those with more severe cases of neglect at baseline had higher scores. The relationship between severity of neglect and Calculation is difficult to interpret because samples for this analysis were small— many children were not proficient enough to be scored on this test. It was difficult to test the effect of severity of physical abuse because of small cell sizes, and it was not significantly related Woodcock Johnson scores.

Teachers rated children's performance in academic subjects using a 5-point scale (far below grade to well above grade). Exhibit 2-10 shows the percentage of children rated as below grade/far below grade for four subject areas: Language Arts (e.g., oral language skills, preliteracy, reading, writing, spelling), mathematics, Social Studies, and Science. Although the majority of the children received ratings in each subject area that indicated academic performance that was at grade-level to far above grade-level performance, a sizable percentage performed below or far below grade level in language arts and mathematics (39% and 35.1%, respectively). While no national norms exist for comparison, if ratings were normally distributed, we would expect about 16% to be below average grade level. There were no differences in language arts or mathematics performance ratings by child or background characteristics. However, science and social studies ratings differed by current setting. The highest percentage of children who received below/far below grade level ratings

Exhibit 2-8. Cognitive and Language Test Scores Infant Population at Wave 5

	K-BIT Composite		K-BIT Vocabulary		K-BIT Matrices		PLS Total		PLS Expressive		PLS Comprehension	
	N	Mean (SE)	*N*	Mean (SE)	*N*	Mean (SE)	*N*	Mean (SE)	*N*	Mean (SE)	*N*	Mean (SE)
Total	914	92.9 (1.0)***	914	92.5(1.1)***	921	94.5(1.0)***	686	92.7(1.4)***	686	91.7(1.6)***	686	94.8(1.4)***
Sex								*				*
Male	469	93.0 (1.4)	469	92.5(1.5)	472	94.8 (1.4)	354	90.0(1.7)	354	89.2(1.9)	354	92.5(1.5)
Female	445	92.7 (1.1)	445	92.6(1.2)	449	94.2 (1.2)	332	95.3(2.0)	332	94.1(2.2)	332	97.1(1.7)
Race/ethnicity		***		***		**						
Black	367	88.1 (1.1)[a]	367	87.3(1.2)[a]	367	91.1(1.2)[a]	286	92.1(1.5)	286	93.4(1.4)	286	92.0(1.7)
White	310	96.5 (1.5)[b]	310	97.6(1.5)[b]	310	96.1(1.5)[b]	219	95.1(2.9)	219	92.6(3.1)	219	98.2(2.4)
Hispanic	172	91.9 (1.6)	172	88.4(2.2)[b]	179	96.6(1.6)[b]	138	88.9(3.4)	138	87.6(4.1)	138	92.1(2.4)
Other	60	93.8 (1.5)[b]	60	95.3(1.6)[b]	60	93.4(2.1)	38	92.6(3.3)	38	90.9(5.0)	38	95.3(2.6)
Current Setting		**		*		*		**				**
In home, biological parents	488	93.6 (1.4)	488	92.9(1.4)	483	95.5(1.4)	354	93.5(2.1)[a]	354	92.2(2.2)	354	95.4(1.9)[a]
In home, adoptive parents	223	94.7 (1.0)[a]	223	95.2(1.2) a	224	95.1(1.0)	184	96.0(1.1)[a]	184	95.2(1.8)	184	97.3(1.2)[a]
In home, kin, or other caregiver	158	89.0 (2.3)[b]	158	89.9(2.8)[b]	159	90.1(1.9)	118	90.0(4.1)	118	87.8(4.5)	118	93.9(3.2)
Out of home	44	90.3 (2.0)	44	88.2(4.4)	44	94.1(2.3)	30	81.1(4.6)[b]	30	82.6(5.0)	30	82.8(4.6)[b]

Note: K-BIT = Kaufman Brief Intelligence Test. PLS = Preschool Language Scale. All analyses are on weighted data; Ns are unweighted. Pearson $\chi2$ tests for cluster samples were used to test statistical significance. For the total, means were tested against means of the standardization sample, which equals 100 for all scales in this exhibit. Statistical significance is noted by asterisks in the column above the statistically significant result (*p < .05, **p < .01, ***p < .001). Means that have different superscripts are significantly different from each other ($\alpha = .05$).

Exhibit 2-9. Early Achievement Test Scores at 5 to 6 Years of Age Infant Population at Wave 5

	WJ Letter Identification		WJ Passage Comprehension		WJ Calculation		WJ Applied Problems	
	N	Mean (SE)	*N*	Mean (SE)	*N*	Mean (SE)	*N*	Mean (SE)
Total	904	100.8 (0.7)	897	97.5 (0.7)*	256	94.4 (1.7)	899	91.6 (0.9)***
Sex		***						
Male	460	98.6 (1.0)	458	97.2 (1.0)	132	95.7 (2.6)	455	91.1 (1.3)
Female	444	103.0 (1.0)	439	97.8 (0.9)	124	93.1 (1.7)	444	92.2 (1.0)
Race/ethnicity								*
Black	358	100.3 (1.1)	358	98.8 (1.1)	85	89.8 (2.3)	360	88.6 (1.2)[a]
White	306	100.8 (1.1)	300	97.0 (1.0)	100	95.8 (2.3)	304	93.9 (1.4)[b]
Hispanic	176	101.3 (1.2)	176	96.7 (1.7)	48	94.5 (3.2)	172	91.9 (1.4)
Other	50	101.2 (1.9)	60	97.8 (1.5)	23	103.9 (5.9)	59	90.0 (2.8)
Chronic conditions						**		
Yes	200	101.8 (2.5)	197	97.7 (2.2)	47	88.3 (2.5)	198	91.1 (1.9)
No	703	100.5 (0.8)	699	97.5 (0.8)	209	95.6 (2.0)	700	91.7 (0.9)
Type of maltreatment								**
Physical abuse	208	103.0 (1.6)	206	98.5 (1.3)	71	97.2 (3.6)	206	92.2 (1.8)[a]
Neglect	513	99.8 (0.9)	511	97.1 (1.1)	137	93.0 (1.8)	513	92.7 (0.8)[a]
Other	111	99.6 (2.1)	109	98.5 (1.8)	48	93.8 (4.1)	109	84.9 (2.7)[b]
Current setting		**				***		**
In home, biological parents	486	100.0 (1.0)[a]	482	96.7 (1.0)[a]	147	95.3 (2.3)[a]	481	92.2 (1.2)
In home, adoptive parents	221	104.6 (1.1)[b]	221	101.8 (1.5)[1,b]	46	101.5 (3.0)[2,a]	221	95.2 (1.1)[3,a]
In home, kin, or other caregiver	155	99.6 (1.9)[a]	152	97.1 (1.2)[a]	47	90.8 (2.6)[b]	155	86.5 (3.4)[b]
Out of home	41	101.0 (2.0)[a]	41	95.1 (21.7)[a]	16	83.8 (2.1)[b]	41	88.9 (3.2)[b]
Severity of neglect				**				
Mild	131	98.0 (1.5)	130	95.5 (1.7)[4,a,b]	45	91.6 (2.6)	130	92.6 (1.4)

Exhibit 2-9. (Continued)

	WJ Letter Identification			WJ Passage Comprehension	WJ Calculation		WJ Applied Problems	
	N	Mean (SE)	*N*	Mean (SE)	*N*	Mean (SE)	*N*	Mean (SE)
Moderate	83	96.8 (2.6)	82	91.6 (2.8)[a,c]	24	91.0 (4.0)	84	90.3 (2.2)
Serious	73	102.0 (2.7)	72	102.2 (2.7)[c.e]	13	89.8 (4.6)	73	90.2 (2.1)
Severe	65	102.1 (2.1)	64	97.8 (1.2)[b,e]	20	87.8 (1.5)	65	91.5 (2.7)
Grave	75	104.2 (2.7)	75	101.2 (1.7)[d]	15	97.4 (7.1)	75	95.0 (3.3)

Note: Instruments used are the Woodcock-Johnson III Tests of Cognitive Abilities (WJ). All analyses are on weighted data; Ns are unweighted. Pearson χ^2 tests for cluster samples were used to test statistical significance. For the total, means were tested against means of the standardization sample, which equals 100 for all scales in this exhibit. Statistical significance is noted by asterisks in the column above the statistically significant result (*$p < .05$, **$p < .01$, ***$p < .001$). Alphabetic superscripts that are different from one another represent statistically significant differences ($\alpha = .05$).

1 Children living with adoptive parents had better scores on the WJ Passage Comprehension than children living with biological parents, with kin, or in out-of-home placements.

2 Children living with biological and adoptive parents had better scores on the WJ Calculation than children living with kin or out of home.

3 Children living with adoptive parents had better scores on the WJ Applied Problems than children living with kin or out of home.

4 Information presented in the next chapter shows that children who suffered more serious neglect were more likely to be adopted. These comparisons show that children with the most serious type of neglect had better scores on the WJ Passage Comprehension than children who suffered less severe types of neglect, suggesting that the finding of elevated Passage Comprehension scores among those who were adopted explains why those with more severe cases of neglect at baseline had higher scores.

for social studies (19.9%) was for those in home with their biological parent. The highest percentage of children who received below/far below grade level ratings for science (44.5%) was for those out of home. No other differences were statistically significant.

Exhibit 2-10. Number and Percentage Below Grade Level in Different Academic Domains (Teacher Report) Infant Population at Wave 5

	Language Arts		Mathematics		Social Studies		Science	
	N	% (SE)	*N*	% (SE)	*N*	% (SE)	*N*	% (SE)
Total	237	39.0 (3.4)	203	35.1 (2.9)	67	16.7 (3.3)	74	20.2 (3.8)
Sex						*		**
Male	135	43.2 (4.3)	109	36.7 (4.4)	40	24.0 (4.6)	47	31.2 (5.9)
Female	102	34.7 (4.3)	94	33.5 (4.1)	27	10.3 (3.7)	27	10.2 (3.4)
Race/ethnicity								
Black	95	38.9 (5.7)	87	36.5 (5.1)	32	19.1 (5.6)	40	26.8 (6.8)
White	71	37.3 (5.0)	60	29.7 (4.8)	16	14.0 (5.5)	15	13.1 (5.6)
Hispanic	52	43.0 (8.4)	40	46.5 (8.4)	13	16.8 (7.3)	14	23.7 (9.1)
Other	18	38.5 (7.6)	15	28.5 (7.4)	6	—	5	—
Current setting						*		**
In home, biological parents	125	38.9 (4.3)	103	33.1 (3.9)	35	19.9 (4.5)[a]	39	23.1 (5.1)[a]
In home, adoptive parents	48	33.6 (5.6)	42	33.0 (6.8)	11	13.8 (5.7)	10	5.8 (2.0)[b]
In home, kin, or other caregiver	39	38.9 (7.6)	37	34.6 (7.9)	11	5.5 (2.4)[b]	13	8.8 (4.0)[b]
Out of home	16	41.0 (16.2)	14	46.6 (17.2)	6	—	9	44.5 (16.8)

Note: All analyses are on weighted data; Ns are unweighted. Pearson χ^2 tests for cluster samples were used to test statistical significance. Statistical significance is noted by asterisks in the column above the statistically significant result (*$p < .05$, **$p < .01$). Cells are left empty when sample sizes are too small to allow for meaningful estimates ($N < 9$).

Social Competence

Teachers and caregivers completed several measures of social competence, rating both social skills in total and specific social skills. Although the mean total social skills score (96.4) was in the average range, it was significantly below the mean of children in general (Exhibit 2-11). A greater percentage of children were rated as having "fewer" social skills than in the general population of children (23.5% vs. 15.9%). Children whose most serious maltreatment at baseline was classified as other were rated lower than children whose maltreatment was classified as physical abuse. There were no other differences by child or background characteristics on either mean scores or percentage having fewer social skills.

Teachers' ratings indicated that there were a significantly greater percentage of children in this population (19.2%) with fewer assertive behavior skills than among all children. Similarly, a significantly greater percentage of children were rated as having "fewer" self-control behaviors (19.1%) and cooperative behaviors (27.3%). There were correspondingly smaller percentages of children involved with CWS who had more of these skills than among all children (Exhibit 2-1 1). While 14.7% of boys were rated as having "more" self-control behaviors, only 3.5% of the girls were so rated (Exhibit 2-12). Social skill scores did not differ by race/ethnicity or case characteristics.

Exhibit 2-11. Social Competence Ratings by Teachers Infant Population at Wave 5

	N	SSRS Total Mean (SE)[1]	SSRS Assertion Ratings		
			Fewer Behaviors % (SE)	Average Behaviors % (SE)	More Behaviors % (SE)[2]
Total	613	96.4 (1.0)***	19.2 (2.6)	68.9 (3.4)	11.9 (2.1)***
Sex					
Male	309	97.8 (1.4)	22.3 (3.8)	66.3 (4.4)	11.4 (0.3)
Female	304	95.1 (1.2)	16.2 (3.0)	71.4(0.4)	12.4 (2.7)
Race/ethnicity					
Black	247	93.2 (1.6)	23.2 (4.6)	70.4 (0.5)	6.4 (1.8)
White	209	99.2 (1.7)	16.8 (4.3)	66.0 (5.3)	17.2 (3.6)
Hispanic	114	96.7 (1.9)	18.4 (5.3)	71.1 (6.9)	10.4 (5.7)
Other	42	95.6 (2.9)	18.1 (5.5)	74.6 (5.8)	7.3 (4.4)
Type of maltreatment		*			
Physical abuse	151	99.7 (1.8)[3,a]	11.4 (3.4)	66.6 (6.4)	22.0 (6.1)
Neglect	342	96.1 (1.4)	19.4 (3.3)	72.0 (3.6)	8.7 (1.8)
Other	120	92.5 (1.9)[b]	30.5 (6.8)	62.2 (6.6)	7.3 (0.3)
Current setting					
In home, biological parents	317	97.5 (1.6)	15.6 (3.1)	71.2 (3.8)	13.2 (2.7)
In home, adoptive parents	141	97.1 (2.1)	16.3 (3.9)	76.6 (5.0)	7.1 (3.8)
In home, kin, or other caregiver	112	93.7 (1.8)	30.8 (8.4)	59.1 (8.0)	10.2 (3.3)
Out of home	32	93.6 (2.4)	16.7 (6.2)	64.0 (18.0)	19.3 (13.9)

Note: Instrument used is the Social Skills Rating System (SSRS). All analyses are on weighted data; *Ns* are unweighted. Pearson χ^2 tests for cluster samples were used to test statistical significance. For the total, the mean was tested against the mean of the standardization sample. Statistical significance is noted by asterisks in the column above the statistically significant result (*$p < .05$). Alphabetic superscripts that are different from one another represent statistically significant differences ($\alpha = .05$).

[1] The mean of the normative sample is 100.

[2] The percentage showing more behaviors in the normative sample is 16.

[3] Children whose main type of maltreatment was physical abuse had better SSRS Total scores than children whose main type of maltreatment was classified as "other" (including sexual abuse, abandonment, and emotional abuse).

Exhibit 2-12. Additional Social Competence Ratings by Teachers Infant Population at Wave 5.

	N	SSRS Self-Control Ratings			SSRS Cooperation Ratings			
		Fewer Behaviors % (SE)	Average Behaviors % (SE)	More Behaviors % (SE)[1]	*N*	Fewer Behaviors % (SE)[2]	Average Behaviors % (SE)	More Behaviors % (SE)
Total group	611	19.1(2.5)	71.8(2.8)	9.1(1.8)	611	27.3(3.2)	63.1(3.5)	9.6(1.8)
Sex		*						
Male	309	15.9(2.7)	69.4(4.5)	14.7(3.7)	309	28.5(3.7)	63.7(4.5)	7.7(2.8)
Female	304	22.3(0.4)	74.1(0.4)	3.5(0.1)	302	26.1(4.4)	62.5(4.7)	11.4(2.7)
Race/ethnicity								
Black	247	26.2(4.3)	65.9(4.8)	7.9(1.8)	246	33.9(5.1)	54.2(5.8)	11.9(3.3)
White	209	15.7(3.7)	72.6(3.9)	11.7(3.4)	208	21.2(4.4)	70.2(0.5)	8.6(2.5)
Hispanic	114	13.5(4.5)	81.3(6.3)	5.2(0.3)	114	28.0(7.8)	62.3(8.1)	9.7(5.0)
Other	42	25.2(8.5)	65 (0.9)	9.8(6.8)	42	34.9(8.3)	61.6(8.3)	3.5(2.3)
Current setting								
In home, biological parents	37	18.9(3.3)	70.3(3.6)	10.8(2.6)	37	25.6(0.4)	62.9(4.6)	11.5 (2.7)
In home, adoptive parents	141	16.3(3.9)	77.4(4.4)	6.3(2.2)	140	29.5(6.5)	60.2(6.2)	10.3(4.1)
In home, kin, or other	112							
caregiver		25.0(7.6)	65.3(8.1)	9.7(4.5)	111	23.6 (6.2)	70.9(6.5)	5.4(2.2)
Out of home	32	16.1(8.1)	83.6(8.1)	0.3(0.3)	32	46.6 (11.5)	52.6(11.5)	0.8(0.8)

Note: Instrument used is the Social Skills Rating System (SSRS). Statistical significance is noted by asterisks in the column above the statistically significant result (*$p < .05$). All analyses are on weighted data; Ns are unweighted. Pearson χ^2 tests for cluster samples were used to test statistical significance.

[1] The percentage showing more behaviors in the normative sample is 16.

[2] The percentage showing fewer behaviors in the normative sample is 16.

Exhibit 2-13. Child Social Competence Ratings by Parents Infant Population at Wave 5

		SSRS Total Behavior Ratings			SSRS Assertion Ratings		
	N	**Fewer Behaviors % (SE)**	**Average Behaviors % (SE)**	**More Behaviors % (SE)**	**Fewer Behaviors % (SE)**	**Average Behaviors % (SE)**	**More Behaviors % (SE)**
Total	959	21.8 (1.9)	67.4(2.8)	10.8(2.0)	21.7(2.4)	64.7(2.5)	13.6(2.1)
Sex		***					
Male	491	19.1 (2.9)	65.2(3.9)	15.7(2.7)	25.0(3.6)	59.3(3.6)	15.7(2.7)
Female	468	24.5 (3.0)	69.7(3.4)	5.8(1.9)	18.3(2.9)	70.2(3.1)	11.4(2.7)
Race/ethnicity		*			*		
Black	378	21.9 (3.4)	68.0(3.8)	10.2(2.6)	19.9(3.6)	66.4(3.7)	13.7(3.2)
White	328	16.9 (3.0)	71.3(4.4)	11.8(3.2)	19.5(4.4)	65.4(4.1)	15.1(3.2)
Hispanic	186	33.0 (5.7)	61.0(4.4)	6.0(2.1)	32.5(5.0)	59.4(5.4)	8.1(3.1)
Other	***62***	***14.8 (4.6)***	***61.0(8.3)***	***24.2(6.4)***	***7.4(2.9)***	***71.1(8.0)***	***21.5(7.7)***
Current setting					*		
In home, biological parents	492	21.5 (3.0)	67.1(4.0)	11.5(2.8)	23.6(3.5)	62.1(3.5)	14.3(3.0)
In home, adoptive parents	224	17.4 (3.1)	66.0(4.7)	16.6(3.8)	9.5(2.2)	69.4(4.5)	21.2(4.3)
In home, kin, or other caregiver	159	26.3 (4.9)	68.2(4.6)	5.4(2.1)	27.6(5.9)	64.1(5.6)	8.4(3.1)
Out of home	43	22.3 (10.0)	76.5(10.2)	1.3(1.3)	15.0(9.0)	77.8(10.3)	7.2(5.9)

Note: Instrument used is the Social Skills Rating System (SSRS). All analyses are on weighted data; Ns are unweighted. Pearson χ^2 tests for cluster samples were used to test statistical significance. Statistical significance is noted by asterisks in the column above the statistically significant result (*$p < .05$, ***$p < .001$).

Exhibit 2-14. Additional Social Competence Ratings by Parents Infant Population at Wave 5

		SSRS Self-Control Ratings			SSRS Cooperation Ratings		
	N	Fewer Behaviors % (SE)	Average Behaviors % (SE)	More Behaviors % (SE)[1]	Fewer Behaviors % (SE)	Average Behaviors % (SE)	More Behaviors % (SE)[1]
Total	959	18.7(2.0)	71.6(2.6)	9.7(1.9)	15.2(1.8)	74.7(2.5)	10.0(1.3)
Sex					**		
Male	491	18.3(2.7)	69.4(3.5)	12.3(2.6)	12.3(2.5)	73.7(3.5)	14.0(2.3)
Female	468	19.1(2.9)	73.8(3.6)	7.0(2.0)	18.3(3.0)	75.8(3.6)	6.0(1.7)
Race/ethnicity							
Black	378	19.6(3.3)	69.0(3.9)	11.4(2.8)	14.8(3.2)	76.0(3.5)	9.2(1.9)
White	328	14.7(3.2)	74.8(4.6)	10.5(3.0)	15.4(2.4)	72.4(3.9)	12.2(2.8)
Hispanic	186	26.1(5.0)	69.0(4.7)	4.8(2.0)	14.7(4.1)	80.6(4.4)	4.6(1.6)
Other	62	16.0(6.0)	73.0(7.0)	11.1(4.2)	16.0(6.6)	66.4(9.3)	17.6(5.5)
Current setting		*					
In home, biological parents	492	19.8(2.5)	70.3(3.6)	9.9(2.8)	15.2(2.6)	72.6(3.5)	12.2(2.1)
In home, adoptive parents	224	21.6(5.0)	62.8(6.0)	15.7(3.6)	10.8(2.6)	81.0(3.4)	8.2(2.2)
In home, kin, or other caregiver	159	11.4(3.1)	82.7(4.0)	5.9(2.5)	23.8(6.4)	71.8(6.7)	4.4(1.9)
Out of home	43	15.4(9.0)	83.2(9.1)	1.4(1.3)	4.8(2.2)	91.2(3.5)	4.1(2.2)

Note: Instrument used is the Social Skills Rating System (SSRS). All analyses are on weighted data; *Ns* are unweighted. Pearson χ^2 tests for cluster samples were used to test statistical significance. Statistical significance is noted by asterisks in the column above the statistically significant result (*$p < .05$).

[1] The percentage showing more behaviors in the normative sample is 16.

Exhibit 2-15. Children's Reports of School-Related Perceptions Infant Population at Wave 5

	Loneliness			School Engagement	
	N (Min)	Mean (SE)	% (SE)	*N* (Min)	Mean (SE)
Total	860	23.6 (0.3)	36.2 (2.3)	218	34.0 (0.7)
Sex					
Male	429	23.4 (0.4)	34.9 (3.1)	108	33.4 (0.9)
Female	431	23.7 (0.4)	37.4 (3.5)	110	34.5 (0.8)
Race/ethnicity					
Black	346	24.6 (0.6)	46.5 (4.4)	77	32.5 (0.8)
White	289	23.1 (0.5)	31.2 (3.6)	84	35.2 (0.9)
Hispanic	169	23.0 (0.2)	28.5 (5.2)	36	33.6 (1.6)
Other	53	23.5 (0.8)	44.1 (9.5)	21	34.0 (1.2)
Chronic health condition					
Yes	187	23.2 (0.7)	33.9 (5.2)	37	34.3 (2.2)
No	672	23.7 (0.3)	36.8 (2.7)	181	33.9 (0.6)
Current setting					*
In home, biological parents	463	23.4 (0.4)	33.3 (3.2)	128	33.9 (0.7)[a]
In home, adoptive parents	203	23.0 (0.6)	33.6 (5.0)	36	35.6 (1.0)[b]
In home, kin, or other caregiver	153	24.5 (0.5)	51.7 (6.8)	39	31.4 (1.0)[b]
Out of home	41	24.4 (1.4)	34.0 (12.0)	14	35.7 (3.5)
Severity of neglect		*	*		
Mild	126	24.1(0.9)[1,a]	36.8 (6.4)[1,a,c]	38	33.2 (0.8)
Moderate	80	23.6 (0.8)[a]	33.3 (5.7)[a,c]	20	34.7 (1.2)
Serious	68	22.1 (0.7)[a]	21.1 (6.8)[c]	12	35.1 (3.1)
Severe	63	24.3 (1.2)	49.4 (7.0)[a,b]	19	36.4 (1.1)
Grave	71	27.7 (1.3)[b]	66.1 (8.4)[b]	12	33.1 (1.1)

Note: Instruments used are the Loneliness and Social Dissatisfaction Scale and the School Engagement Scale. All analyses are on weighted data; Ns are unweighted. Pearson $\chi 2$ tests for cluster samples were used to test statistical significance. For the total, differences in means were tested against means of the standardization sample. Statistical significance is noted by asterisks in the column above the statistically significant result (*$p < .05$). Alphabetic superscripts that are different from one another represent statistically significant differences ($\alpha = .05$).

[1] Children whose neglect was characterized as grave indicated greater loneliness than did children whose neglect was classified as mild, moderate, or serious.

Caregivers also rated children on social skills. Because separate scales were used for preschool and elementary school children, we performed separate analyses and results are not tabled. Caregiver ratings of overall social skills of both preschool children and elementary children were in the average range ($M_{\text{preschool}} = 96.9$; $M_{\text{elementary}} = 93.3$), but significantly lower than for children in general. There were no differences by sex or maltreatment type. However, preschool children of different race/ethnicity groups differed significantly on social skills, Wald F (3) = 3.69, $p < .05$. Pairwise contrasts indicated that Hispanic children were rated lower than White children. Social skills ratings of elementary school children differed by severity of neglect, Wald F (4) = 7.03, $p < .001$. Pairwise contrasts indicated that those children who were reported to be seriously neglected at baseline had *higher* social skills ratings than each other group (i.e., mild neglect, moderate neglect, severe neglect, and grave neglect). In addition, those whose neglect was classified as mild had higher ratings than those whose neglect was classified as severe. The reason for these differences is not clear.

When behavior ratings of preschool and elementary children were combined (Exhibit 2-13), 21.8% had fewer social skills than the general population of children on average. This is significantly higher than among children in general, and there is a corresponding smaller percentage of these children with more social skills. Among boys, 15.7% of the males were rated as having more social skills than the general average, but only 5.8% of the girls were rated as highly. A significantly smaller percentage of the population in this report had caregiver ratings in the "more" category for self-control and cooperativeness than would be expected based on the normative sample (9.7% and 10%, respectively; Exhibit 2-13). Differences in the distribution of these ratings were found for several subgroups.

Racial/ethnic differences were found in ratings of assertiveness. The Hispanic subgroup had the highest percentage assertive behaviors that were classified as "fewer" (32.5%); the group classified as "other" had the lowest percentage of "fewer" assertive behaviors (7.4%; Exhibit 2-13). There were also differences in the distribution of assertive behaviors as a function of setting. The subgroup of children who were in homes with kin or other caregiver had the highest percentage classified with "fewer" assertive behaviors (27.6%), whereas the group in adoptive homes had the lowest percentage classified with "fewer" assertive behaviors (9.5%) and the highest percentage classified with "more" assertive behaviors (21.2%).

Differences in self-control behaviors were also found as a function of setting. However, the subgroup who were in adoptive homes had both the highest percentage rated with "fewer" self-control behaviors (21.6%) and the highest percentage rated with "more" self-control behaviors (15.7%; Exhibit 2-14). Finally, girls had a higher percentage than boys of being rated with "fewer" cooperative behaviors (18.3% v. 12.3%) and a lower percentage of being rated with "more" cooperative behaviors (6% v. 14%; Exhibit 2-14).

School-Related Perceptions

Children were asked about their relationships with peers at school and their degree of engagement in school. They completed the Loneliness and Social Dissatisfaction Scale (Cassidy & Asher, 1992), which assesses feelings of loneliness and dissatisfaction with peer support at school (Exhibit 2-15). Data from the scale developers are reported separately for males and females, which requires comparisons to be sex-specific. Both boys and girls had significantly higher loneliness scores than the average group in Cassidy and Asher's sample (M_{males} = 19.3 and $M_{females}$ = 19.5), indicating that children involved as infants with CWS were more lonely than average children at age 5 to 6. There was a significant difference in loneliness ratings by severity of neglect. Children whose neglect was characterized as grave indicated greater loneliness than children whose neglect was classified as mild, moderate, or serious. In addition, a significant difference was found in the percentage classified as lonely among the children as a function of severity of neglect; there were a somewhat higher percentage of children classified as lonely among those who had experienced severe neglect.

The measure of school engagement addressed both children's participation (e.g., completing assignments, paying attention) and their psychological identification with school (e.g., get along with teachers, enjoy school). The mean of 34 indicates that children were positively engaged on average. Children who had never been out of the home and children who had been adopted had higher scores than children who lived with kin or other in-home arrangements.

Conclusions

The results on children's well-being at the 5- to 6-year follow-up are mixed. Most children who entered CWS as infants were in good health, as healthy generally as children who live below the federal poverty level (Bloom & Tonthat, 2002). On average, at 5 to 6 years they displayed cognitive, language, and academic skills within the normal range. However, these findings must be tempered by several less than positive results.

Using a very stringent definition of risk, we found a substantial percentage of the group at risk for cognitive, emotional, or physical disabilities. In particular, 29% of the children were considered to be at risk for an emotional/behavioral problem, and 23% of the children were compromised in their ability to meet their daily living needs.

Although the children's average cognitive and language scores at 5 to 6 years were in the typical range, their mean scores on measures were significantly below the general population mean. The K-BIT verbal and the PLS language scores are comparable with those reported by other researchers who have shown that their samples of maltreated children differed from nonmaltreated samples at early school age (Eigsti & Cicchetti, 2004; Perry, Doran, & Wells, 1983). A substantial proportion of the children had scores low enough to be in the generally accepted range for services in school systems. Notably, this group of children tended to look no better on these measures than children who were 3 to 5 years old at baseline and 4.5 to 6 years old at the 11/2-year follow-up. The children studied in this report were involved in CWS investigations during infancy; many of their families had received services and more than one fifth were eventually adopted. Although it was expected that they would have had a chance to show better developmental outcomes in these domains than the children whose maltreatment was reported later, this was not found. Given the importance of cognitive and language skills for success in school, it would not be surprising if many children subsequently show learning difficulties.

If we add the 27% of children whose Woodcock-Johnson Calculation raw scores were 0 to the 2.5% whose scores were more than 1.5 standard deviations below the mean, almost one third of children were performing below expectation on this scale. Although we do not know the percentage of children in the normative group with raw scores of 0, the large percentage of NSCAW children who have basic difficulty with arithmetic computation is cause for alarm. Almost one fifth were in the risk range on Applied Problems, but the percentage in the risk range on Letter Word Identification and Passage Comprehension was within normal limits. Correspondingly, teachers rated more than one third of children as below or far below grade level in language arts and mathematics achievement. These data suggest that these children are at heightened risk for academic problems. Since 73% of these children were still in kindergarten, it is too soon to understand the full impact on school achievement.

The children also displayed average scores, as a group, on measures of social competence. However, teacher ratings indicated that more than 27% of children had cooperation ratings in the below average range, and teacher and caregiver ratings showed that only 10% had "more" self-control and cooperative behaviors than children in general. Moreover, children had significantly higher loneliness scores than children in general. This finding agrees with previous reports showing that children with histories of maltreatment had difficulty interacting with peers, were less socially competent, and had been avoided or rejected by peers (Bolger & Patterson, 2001; Bolger, Patterson, & Kupersmidt, 1998; Rogosch, Cicchetti, & Aber, 1995). The importance of such skills for school success is well known and suggests that these children are at risk for difficulties managing at school.

Even more troubling is the finding, consistent with previous research (Shonk & Cicchetti, 2001), that children showed increased externalizing behavior problems compared to the general child population. More than twice the expected percentage of children had an Externalizing score in the clinical range. Although children did not display internalizing problems, such problems are more difficult for observers to detect . The studies where such problems have been identified include older children (Kaufman & Cicchetti, 1989; Toth, Manly, & Cicchetti, 1992).

One of our most surprising findings is of sex differences in an unexpected direction. Girls had significantly lower scores on calculation, higher scores on the teacher-rated attention problems scale, less-developed self-control behaviors as rated by teachers, higher externalizing behavior scores as rated by parents, and overall less-developed social behaviors as rated by parents. Although adolescent girls have been reported to perform less well on quantitative measures, such a difference among very young children has not been documented in research. We are also unaware of other research reporting girls showing more behavior problems. Moreover, this finding differs from results reported about children 3 to 5 years of age in previous NSCAW waves. The reasons for the finding are not clear and require further research. Differences may stem from actual sex differences, differences in teachers' appraisal of girls and boys with CWS involvement, or both.

We did not expect so few differences by child and case characteristics. In particular, we found almost no differences by type of maltreatment. Previous research has reported that physical abuse as compared with neglect was linked to more difficulties with peers (Hildyard & Wolfe, 2002; Wodarski, Kurtz, Gaudin, & Howing, 1990), and children who were neglected have been found to display greater language deficits (Allen & Oliver, 1982; Culp et al., 1991) and poorer motivation for school than were children who were physically abused (Eckenrode, Laird, & Doris, 1993; Wodarski et al., 1990).

On the other hand, we did find that the type of living situation was related to children's cognitive, language, and achievement scores, social competence ratings, academic engagement, and chronic health problems. Children who were adopted had higher scores on two of the Woodcock Johnson tests and more optimal social behaviors. We believe that these children were likely to have had a more stable environment in which to develop, although we cannot rule out the possibility that causality runs in the opposite direction, that children with these advantages were more likely to be adopted. As shown in the description of characteristics of caregivers, adoptive caregivers are older, better educated, and less likely to be living in poverty. On the other hand, it must be acknowledged that differences between children were likely to influence which setting they had entered by the Wave 5 follow-up.

Children in out-of-home care at the 5-to-6-year follow-up had lower scores on a variety of cognitive measures and social skills. Our findings are in line with those who have reported high rates of language and learning problems in children living in foster care (Evans, 2001; Evans, Scott, & Schulz, 2004; Halfon, Mendonca, & Berkowitz, 1995; Sawyer & Dubowitz, 1994).

Although the differences among the neglect groups in terms of social skills were not completely interpretable, we did find that children whose neglect was indicated as "grave" were lonelier. As is known, the capacity to form friendships develops from the earliest relationships between caregivers and children as well as from early experiences with peers. It may be that those children whose neglect was of a more serious nature lacked those early experiences critical for forming friendships. In fact, previous research has shown that children with histories of neglect are unpopular and have fewer peers with whom to play (Bolger et al., 1998; Erickson, Egeland, & Pianta, 1989).

Our findings indicate that a substantial proportion of the children are at risk for school-related problems. Their readiness to learn may be compromised by poorly developed language skills, social skills, and peer relationships. Although few child and case characteristics were associated with their outcomes, there do appear to be some subgroups at heightened academic and behavioral risk. Future NSCAW analyses will provide a greater understanding of the trajectories of risk and resilience among young maltreated children.

3. Child Placement and Permanency

The child welfare system (CWS) aims to ensure children's safety and well-being at home, but, in a minority of cases, CWS makes the judgment that children cannot safely stay at home and places children outside the home. Out-of-home placements include kinship care, in which a child lives with relatives; nonkin foster care, or, rarely, other residential settings (e.g., residential treatment center, group home).

Once children are placed, CWS will try to reunify them with their parents or other caregivers whenever possible. But this process often takes considerable time either for families to make the changes to enable reunification or for the court to determine with certainty that a family will be unable to make those changes. Too often placement has led to long-term stays in foster care that do not provide children with the stable, consistent, permanent family environment that they need to be happy and develop fully (U.S. Department of Health and Human Services, Children's Bureau, 2003a). When reunification is impossible, the biological parents' rights to their children are terminated and children adopted. But it can take considerable time for adoptive parents to be found and a considerable wait for the adoption to be finalized, even after a child is living in the adoptive home. Nevertheless, the goal is to place children in permanent homes in a timely way.

In passing the Adoption and Safe Families Act (ASFA) of 1997, Congress recognized the need for permanency and included guidelines for states to achieve permanency for children in placement (U.S. Department of Health and Human Services, 2003b). Among other provisions ASFA decreased from 18 to 12 months the time in foster care for making permanency decisions, and required termination of parental rights when children are in foster care 15 of the previous 22 months (Pinderhughes, Harden, & Guyer, 2007). AFSA also made it easier for states to pursue concurrent planning, which involves working toward reunification but also planning for an alternative permanent setting at the same time (Child Welfare Information Gateway, 2005). Other state and federal reforms aim to reduce the time to finalization of adoption for children in foster care (e.g., Governor's Office of Regulatory Reform, 2003). Yet only a minority of states met standards for stability, reunification, and adoption in the 2001–2002 Child and Family Services Reviews (CFSRs; U.S. Department of Health and Human Services, Children's Bureau, 2003b). In addition, states needed much improvement on achieving permanency outcomes. Finally, adoption was least likely of all services to be designated as a quality service in the states.

Thus, developing permanent homes for children expeditiously is an important goal of child welfare services. Reunification is preferred, but when this is impossible the aim is for timely adoption. Historically, adoption rates for very young children like this group are higher than for older children (Wulczyn, Hislop & Harden, 2002), in large degree because their age makes them more desirable for many prospective adoptive parents.

In this section, we present data on these children's history of placement since the index investigation when they were infants and on their progress toward permanency. We examine reunification, termination of parental rights and adoption. Time is a key variable here, so we investigate time in placement and time to adoption. As we did in Chapter 2 with respect to child well-being, we also examined the relationship of several factors to permanency and placement outcomes. Two variables we consistently used were child sex and race. We also analyzed the association between a variety of maltreatment characteristics and placement or permanency. These included the type of maltreatment reported at baseline, the severity of physical abuse or neglect, and the number of types of maltreatment experienced. Consistent with the previous chapter, children's disabilities continue to be of special interest. Consequently, we frequently present placement and permanency findings specifically for the subgroups of children at-risk for physical, emotional or cognitive disabilities.

A major caveat needs to be acknowledged: The data presented here stop at age 5 to 6, but the outcomes measured here remain to be determined for some of these children. Some may yet be reunified, experience termination of parental rights, or be adopted. Thus the analysis of reunification, termination of parental rights, and adoption do not possess fully accurate rates, because we have not followed all cases out to final disposition.

Key Children's Placement Results

- More than one third of these 5- and 6-year-olds have been placed out of the home at some point in their lives.
- Of the children who were placed, 24% had two placements during their lifetime, and 27% had three or more placements.
- Of children placed, about half the group was in placement for less than 2 years, 38% were in placement for 2 to 4 years, and 13% were in placement for more than 4 years.
- White children were less likely to be placed outside the home (27% of cases), compared with 43% or higher for every other racial/ethnic group.
- Two thirds of children with a physical disability were placed.

- Nearly half of children who experienced physical abuse leading to hospitalization or permanent physical damage were placed.

Key Reunification Results

- Of the children who were out of home at some point during the 5- to 6-year analysis period, 17% were reunified with their birth parents.

Key Termination of Parental Rights Results

- Parental rights were terminated in over one third of the infants-at-baseline population
- More than half of children with a chronic medical condition experienced termination of parental rights.

Key Adoption Results

- Slightly fewer than one fifth of the children were adopted by age 5 to 6.
- Most of those who were adopted had been placed outside the home (78%).
- The median time between placement and adoption was 729 days, almost 2 years.
- Adoption increased as foster care decreased over time.
- Adoption had an upward trend over time: the percentage of children living in adoptive homes was about 1% at baseline, 13% at the 3-year follow-up, and 17% at the 5- to 6-year follow-up.

Placement

More than one third of these 5- and 6-year-olds have been placed out of the home at some point in their lives (Exhibit 3-1). For most of these children, placement came early. At baseline, when they were infants, within 4–5 months after the index investigation, 30.7% of the infants-atbaseline were in out-of-home care (Exhibit 3-2). This is substantially higher than the 11% reported for the NSCAW population as a whole at baseline (U.S. Department of Health and Human Services, 2005b).

Of the children who were placed, 24% had two placements during their lifetime and 27% had three or more placements. One CFSR goal is to limit children to no more than two placements within a 12-month period (U.S. Department of Health and Human Services, 2001), but analyzing the timing of these placements is beyond the scope of this report, so we do not know the extent to which this goal is met for these children.

We examined whether number of out-of-home placements differed by demographics, severity of maltreatment, and chronic health condition and disabilities. Placement differed significantly by the race/ethnicity variable. White children were placed outside the home in 27% of cases, while the percentage placed was 43% or higher for every other racial/ethnic group. Other research has also documented racial differences in placement in foster care (e.g., U.S. Department of Health and Human Services, 2005a).

Almost two thirds of children with a physical disability were placed, a number of them more than once. This was significantly higher than for children without a physical disability. Not surprisingly, severity of abuse at baseline made a difference in terms of placement. Severity of physical abuse was not statistically significant, mainly because of small cell size. But nearly half of children who experienced physical abuse leading to hospitalization or permanent physical damage were placed, more than twice the percentage of those with lesser physical abuse. Severity of neglect was significantly related to placement too. A much higher percentage of children were placed if neglect was serious, severe, or grave than if it was mild or moderate. Finally, the *number of types* of maltreatment (e.g., physical abuse, neglectful supervision) was significantly related to placement: 49% of children who had experienced more than one type of maltreatment were placed outside the home compared to 32% who had experience only one type of maltreatment.

Exhibit 3-1. Number of Out-of-Home Placements Infant Population at Wave 5

	N	Percentage (SE)			
		0 Placements	1 Placement	2 Placements	3 or More Placements
Total	921	62.6 (2.7)	18.4 (1.8)	8.8 (1.2)	10.2 (2.3)
Sex					
Male	475	64.5 (3.9)	16.7 (2.7)	8.6 (2.1)	10.2 (3.1)
Female	446	60.6 (3.2)	20.2 (2.6)	9.0 (1.9)	10.2 (2.4)
Race/ethnicity		*			
Black	361	53.1 (5.4) [a]	25.8 (3.5)	11.6 (3.1)	9.5 (2.4)
White	317	73.2 (3.2)[1,b]	14.1 (2.2)	6.1 (1.4)	6.5 (1.8)
Hispanic	177	56.8 (6.8)[a]	15.8 (4.5)	9.1 (3.2)	18.2 (6.9)
Other	61	53.3 (8.5)[a]	20.9 (5.6)	10.9 (4.2)	15.0 (7.3)
Chronic health condition					
Yes	214	53.7 (5.0)	19.5 (3.7)	10.7 (2.4)	16.1 (4.3)
No	706	64.9 (2.8)	18.2 (1.9)	8.3 (1.4)	8.6 (2.2)
Severity of neglect		**			
Mild	132	81.9 (5.3)[2,a]	10.7 (4.3)	2.5 (1.6)	4.9 (1.9)
Moderate	83	65.7(6.9)[2, c]	14.3 4.4)	12.3 (5.8)	7.7 (3.6)
Serious	74	39.5 (11.0)[b]	30.9 (10.3)	13.9 (6.2)	15.7 (8.6)
Severe	70	29.1 (8.7)[b]	32.8 (6.9)	13.9 (4.7)	24.3 (7.7)
Grave	81	19.1 (8.7)[b]	22.6 (5.7)	11.0 (4.6)	17.0 (7.0)
Physical disability		*			
Yes	58	34.7 (8.2)	23.5 (7.8)	27.5 (7.7)	14.3 (7.3)
No	863	64.3 (2.7)	18.1 (1.8)	7.7 (1.3)	9.9 (2.3)

Note: All analyses are on weighted data; *Ns* are unweighted. Pearson χ^2 tests for cluster samples were used to test statistical significance. Statistical significance is noted by asterisks in the column above the statistically significant result (*$p < .05$, **$p < .0\ 1$). Alphabetic superscripts that are different from one another (within the same category) represent statistically significant differences ($\alpha = .05$).

[1] White children are significantly less likely to be placed out of home than Black, Hispanic, or "Other" children.

[2] Children with mild neglect were less likely to be placed out of home than children with serious, severe, or grave neglect. Children with moderate neglect were less likely to be placed out of home than children with serious and severe neglect.

We also assessed placement over time. Exhibit 3-2 presents the percentage of children in five different settings at each time point of NSCAW measurement. This provides a general picture of children's living environments over time, though there are two significant caveats. We do not know about possible changes in setting in the significant intervals (18 months to approximately 2 years) *in between* measurement time points, in part because of the lack of CWS data for the majority of families. The figure also does not distinguish between children who were in home because they had always been at home and children who were in home because they were placed and then reunified.

A large majority of children were with their original caregivers at each time point, either because they had never left home or they had returned home. Nonkin foster care was provided for 14.1% at baseline, but that declined steadily over time, dropping sharply to 5% at the 3-year follow-up and 3% at the five year follow-up. Correspondingly, adoption had an upward trend: the percentage of children living in adoptive homes was 1% at baseline, 13% at the 3-year follow-up, and 16.9% at the 5- to 6-year follow-up. Parallel to the foster care drop, the sharpest *increase* in adoption was at the 3-year follow-up. The use of kinship care was fairly consistent, ranging from 14.6% to 19.6%, with no apparent trend over time. Other settings (e.g., residential treatment) were used rarely, which is not surprising, given the age of these children.

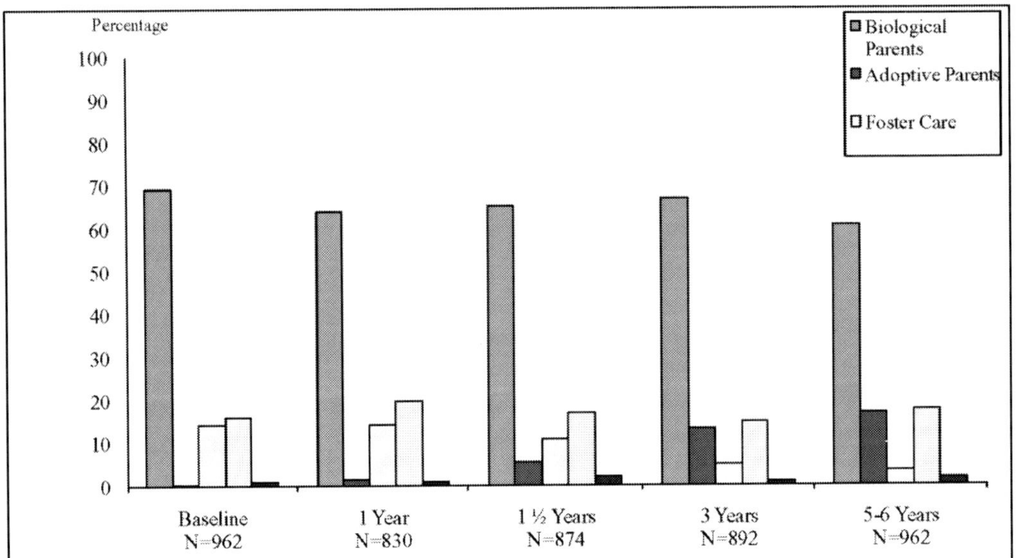

Exhibit 3-2. Distribution of Children by Settings at Each Time Point Infant Population at Wave 5.

Even though the rate of kinship care was fairly consistent, its implications for permanence changed over time. In another analysis (not shown in a table) for the infant-at-baseline population, we considered at each study time point whether kinship care was considered an "out-of-home" or "in-home" placement, the former representing a temporary and the latter a permanent home. At baseline, only 17.4% of kinship placements were considered in home (SE = 4.9). At the 11/2-year follow-up, this increased to 3 5.7% (SE = 6.0), and at the 3-year follow-up, to 52.9% (SE = 8.5). By the 5-year follow-up, 82% of kinship placements were considered permanent (SE = 4.3). Thus there was a trend toward permanence in kinship care just as there was for adoption. Further analysis is needed to determine to what extent this represents the same placement with kin changing from temporary to permanent over time, versus different kinship placements tending at earlier points to be temporary and at later points permanent.

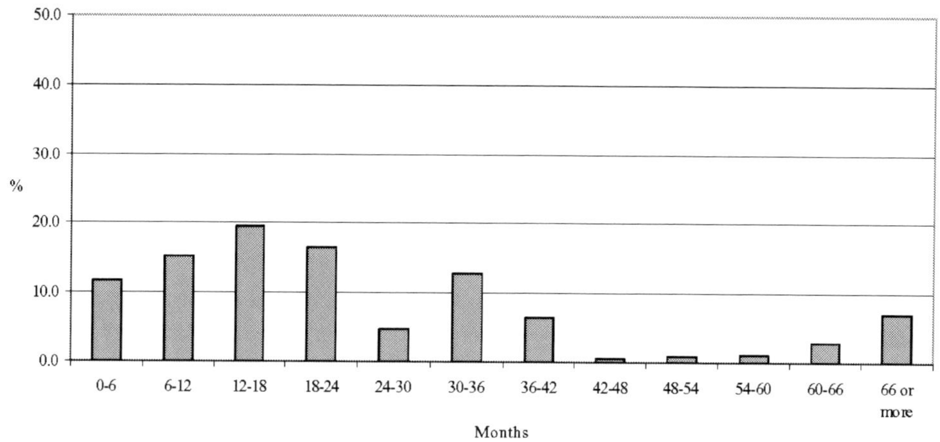

Note: N = 447.

Exhibit 3-3. Time in Placement Infant Population at Wave 5.

Exhibit 3-4. Time in Placement (in Days) Infant Population at Wave 5.

	N	**Mean (SE)**
Total	447	723 (64)
Sex		
Male	224	667 (68)
Female	223	776 (98)
Race/ethnicity		
Black	197	613 (57)
White	130	739 (109)
Hispanic	84	931 (142)
Other	32	573 (55)
Chronic health condition		
Yes	123	892 (126)
No	324	665 (63)
Emotional problems		
Yes	143	838 (108)
No	304	670 (77)

Note: All analyses are on weighted data; *Ns* are unweighted. Pearson χ^2 tests for cluster samples were used to test statistical significance.

Ideally, children should spend as little time in placement as possible, but time in placement is nevertheless substantial in many cases. The report presents the mean amount of time in placement and the time between placement and adoption, but it should be acknowledged that this analysis of time is limited, because it does not take into account the fact that children assessed at this follow-up may yet be reunified or adopted. More sophisticated analysis using event history analysis is needed to assess probability and timeliness of these events more accurately (see e.g., Barth, Courtney, Berrick, & Albert, 1994), but this analysis is beyond the scope of this report and should be addressed in future NSCAW research.

The average time children were in placement was 723 days, which is 1.98 years (this variable is a sum if children had multiple stays in placement). This ranged from 40 days to 2,100 days. See Exhibit 3-3 for the distribution of time in placement in months. A little less than half the group (49.2%) was in placement for less than 2 years. The percentage in placement 2 to 4 years was 38.3%. The percentage in placement more than 4 years is substantially less, but still comprises 12.5% of children in placement. Note that some of these 5- and 6-year-olds had been in placement 66 months or more, almost their entire lives. Time in placement did not vary by sex, race/ethnicity, chronic health condition, or presence of emotional problems (Exhibit 3-4).

Reunification

Of the children reportedly maltreated as infants who were out of home during the 5- to 6-year analysis period, 17% were reunified at some point with their birth parents. No demographic, abuse severity, or child functioning variable was significantly related to the percentage reunified.

This 17% must be interpreted cautiously. As explained above, it is possible that reunification may still be sought and achieved for some of these children after 5 and 6 years, and the rate of reunification can be calculated only when a disposition has been reached for all children in this group. This is particularly true when placement has occurred at different time points for these children (fairly recently for some children).

Nevertheless, the fact that 17% reunified over 5 to 6 years provides us with a rough idea of the role of reunification among cases of infants involved in maltreatment investigation. It suggests that there was only a fairly small probability of reunification once children maltreated as infants were removed from the home. Adoption (43% of those removed from the home) and kinship care (31% of those removed from the home) were much more frequent outcomes once children were removed.

Termination of Parental Rights

When parents severely abuse or neglect a child, abandon the child, or put the safety and well-being of the child at risk because of criminal behavior, substance abuse or dependence, mental illness or other problems, CWS can petition courts for termination of parental rights (TPR). This is generally a necessary step to free children for adoption. Exhibit 3-5 reports the percentage of children in out-of-home placement who experienced TPR and how that varied by characteristics of the child and maltreatment. Because TPR is almost always limited to children who are removed, we limited the analysis to those who had an out-of-home placement. It should be noted that data was missing on termination of parent rights in cases in which there was no caseworker interview. This includes 26% of cases in which adoption was finalized. Thus, given that TPR routinely precedes adoption, data is missing on TPR on finalized adoptions and in other cases in which TPR has taken place but the case was closed and as a consequence there was no active file with CWS, neither a caseworker's interview to confirm TPR.

Parental rights were terminated in over one third of cases that had at least one placement out of home. Over half of children with a chronic medical condition experienced TPR. On the other hand, children with a cognitive disability were less likely than others to experience TPR, though the small cell size meant that the significance of this difference was .0547, just above the , <.05. No other variables examined had a meaningful relationship to TPR.

Adoption

Slightly fewer than one fifth of children were adopted by age 5 to 6 (Exhibit 3-5). Most of those who were adopted had been placed outside the home (78%), but 22% were adopted from the homes they were in at baseline without having been placed during the study period (SE = 4.6). Although several categories in Exhibit 3-5 have percentages adopted that seem high or low; numbers in these groups are small and standard errors relatively large for many categories. There were only two statistically significant predictors of adoption. Children with a chronic health condition were nearly twice as likely to be adopted as those without a chronic health condition. Children with a cognitive disability, on the other hand, were about one third *less* likely to be adopted than children without a cognitive disability.

Typically, termination of parental rights precedes adoption unless there is no caregiver with parental rights. A large majority (85.3%) of children whose parents had their rights terminated were adopted before the 5- to 6-year follow-up, but this left almost 15% of children with TPR not adopted. There were no significant differences on this percentage by demographic variables (sex, race/ethnicity), by severity of abuse, or by current disabilities or chronic health condition.

If children cannot be reunified, it is important for their attachment to a permanent home and for their well-being generally to complete an adoption as soon as possible. The Child and Family Service Review process has a standard that 32% of children should spend no more than 2 years in placement before being adopted.

Nevertheless, adoption can take considerable time. There are more children available for adoption than can be adopted, and it may take considerable time to find adoptive parents. It takes time for parents and children to prepare for adoption through preplacement visits. Even after children move in, considerable time can pass before the adoption works its way through the court system and the adoption is finalized. Moreover, systems issues can lead to delays, as the 2002 Child and Family Service Reviews of the states found (U.S. Department of Health and Human Services, 2003b).

The average time between first placement and adoption was 848 days (more than 2 ½ years; Exhibit 3-6). This is somewhat inflated by outliers, but the median (729) is still substantial. Among this group of children, infants at the time they were involved with CWS, a much higher percentage were adopted within 2 years of placement (49%) than the Child and Family Service Review standard. Race/ethnicity was the only significant predictor of either time in placement or the percentage of children in placement for more than 2 years before adoption. Hispanic children had a significantly longer wait than other groups, though this result was based on only 23 Hispanic adopted children.

Exhibit 3-5. Termination of Parental Rights (TPR) and Adoption Infant Population at Wave 5

	TPR		Adopted[1]	
	N	% (SE)	*N*	% (SE)
Total	780	19.6 (2.4)	962	17.0 (1.9)
Sex		*		*
Male	401	14.6 (2.2)	492	13.7 (2.1)
Female	379	25.3 (3.9)	470	20.4 (2.8)
Race/ethnicity				
Black	322	20.8 (3.6)	378	18.7 (3.1)
White	255	14.0 (2.7)	330	12.5 (2.6)
Hispanic	149	28.3 (6.3)	187	15.7 (3.9)
Other	49	17.9 (6.2)	62	43.7 (10.0)
Chronic health condition		**		**
Yes	182	32.9 (5.6)	221	25.3 (3.8)
No	598	16.0 (2.3)	740	14.9 (2.1)
Physical disability				
Yes	53	25.0 (7.7)	63	30.0 (7.9)
No	727	19.3 (2.4)	899	16.2 (1.8)
Cognitive disability		*		**
Yes	91	9.8 (3.1)	109	7.1 (2.1)
No	657	21.3 (2.6)	811	19.3 (2.3)
Emotional/behavioral problems				
Yes	247	21.4 (4.3)	294	16.6 (3.2)
No	533	18.8 (2.7)	667	17.2 (2.1)
Severity of neglect		***		***
Mild	91	6.0 (2.9)[a]	135	3.9 (1.7)[a]
Moderate	73	16.1 (5.9)	86	11.3 (4.2)[a,b]
Serious	69	19.1 (5.8)[2,b]	77	20.3 (5.5)[3,b,c]
Severe	67	31.0 (7.3)[2,b]	70	31.4 (8.5)[3,c]
Grave	70	31.4 (7.8)[2,b]	83	34.9 (7.1)[3,c]

Note: All analyses are on weighted data; *Ns* are unweighted. Pearson χ^2 tests for cluster samples were used to test statistical significance. Statistical significance is noted by asterisks in the column above the statistically significant result (*$p < .05$, **$p < .01$, ***$p < .001$). Alphabetic superscripts that are different from one another represent statistically significant differences ($\alpha = .05$).

[1] Defined as in an adoptive home at the 5- to 6-year follow-up.

[2] Caregivers of children who suffered serious, severe, or grave neglect were more likely to have their parental rights terminated than caregivers whose children suffered mild neglect.

[3] Children who suffered more severe neglect were more likely to be adopted than children who suffered less severe neglect.

Exhibit 3-6. Time from First Placement to Adoption Finalization (in Days) Infant Population at Wave 5.

	N	Mean (SE)
Total	172	848 (65)
Sex		
Male	80	830 (69)
Female	92	863 (90)
Race/ethnicity		*
Black	73	699 (57)[a]
White	60	835 (59)[a]
Hispanic	23	1,229 (147)[b]
Other	13	638 (126)[a]
Chronic health condition		
Yes	67	944 (111)
No	105	777 (46)
Physical disability		
Yes	19	748 (105)
No	153	861 (168)
Emotional problems		
Yes	50	927 (84)
No	122	817 (84)

Note: Time was counted from the first placement that was not followed by a reunification. Cell sizes for cognitive disability were too small to report means. All analyses are on weighted data; *Ns* are unweighted. Statistical significance is noted by asterisks in the column above the statistically significant result (*$p < .05$). Alphabetic superscripts that are different from one another represent significant differences ($\alpha = .05$).

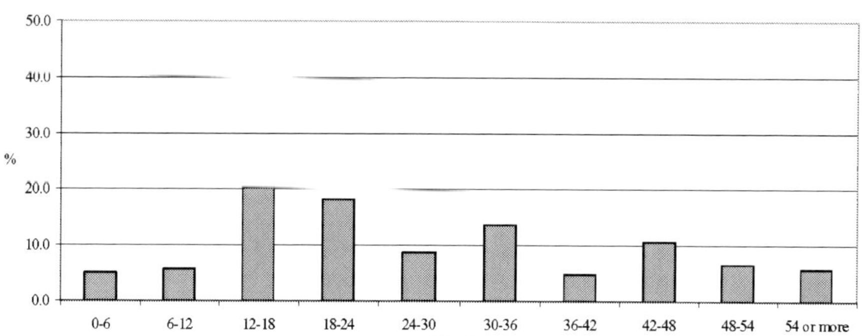

Note: $N = 172$.

Exhibit 3-7. Time from First Placement to Adoption Finalization Infant Population at Wave 5.

Exhibit 3-8. Time from Termination of Parental Rights to Adoption (in Days) Infant Population at Wave 5.

	N	Mean (SE)
Total	155	403 (32)
Sex		
Male	76	429 (38)
Female	79	384 (53)
Race/ethnicity		
Black	58	378 (53)
White	53	415 (40)
Hispanic	33	424 (99)
Other	8	
Chronic health condition		
Yes	54	455 (70)
No	101	373 (29)
Emotional problems		
Yes	49	423 (35)
No	106	394 (44)

Note: All analyses are on weighted data; Ns are unweighted. Pearson χ^2 tests for cluster samples were used to test statistical significance. Cells are left empty when sample sizes are too small to allow for meaningful estimates ($N < 9$). Cell sizes were too small to report means for cognitive and physical disabilities.

Exhibit 3-7 shows the distribution of time between first placement and adoption in months. The range in time span was considerable, from just over one month to about 70 months. A plurality of cases took between 12 and 24 months, but there were meaningful proportions of cases for every interval of duration beyond including 54 months or more.

In many cases, much of the time before adoption took place after parental rights were terminated. The time between TPR and adoption averaged 403 days. This is somewhat skewed by a small number of very high values, but the median (302 days) is still substantial. This time span ranged from 0 days (two cases in which adoption took place on the same day as TPR) to 1,218 days (about 3 years and 4 months). Time from TPR to adoption did not vary by sex, race/ethnicity, chronic health condition, or presence of emotional problems (Exhibit 3-8).

Though this time span appears long, we do not know to what extent this reflects waiting to identify adoptive parents versus waiting for a preadoptive placement to lead officially to adoption. Child welfare agencies frequently place children in preadoptive families, preparing for the possibility of adoption by that family if efforts at reunification fail (Pecora, Whittaker, Maluccio, Barth, & Plotnick, 2000). The effect of waiting for adoption to be official may be less stressful than actually waiting for adoptive parents.

Conclusion

At each time point, a solid majority of these children involved in investigations as infants were in home, and placement and permanency issues did not apply to them. Still, about one third of these children were placed outside the home. Together these data tell a story about them, a story of disruption and difficulty followed by an evolution over a long time period to greater permanency. The disruption was considerable early on: The vast majority of those who were placed entered placement as infants, and a majority of those placed had two or even three or more placements. As other research has shown, Black, Hispanic, and "Other" children were significantly more likely to be placed than White children; this finding, which has been reported previously for all children involved with CWS as a whole, is also true specifically of infants involved with CWS. As other experts have noted (U.S. Department of Health and Human Services, 2003 [a,b]), this disparity points to the need for special preventive measures to be offered to families and to Black, Hispanic, and "Other" communities both to prevent child maltreatment and to be able to use less intrusive and restrictive methods for responding to it. Some of this effort needs to focus specifically on infants.

As has been shown before, progress toward permanency is slow, although there are hopeful signs for these children. On average, children who were placed spent nearly 2 years of their short lives in out-of-home placement. From that point on results were more encouraging. The percentage of children in foster care decreased substantially to a very small percentage by age 5 to 6, paralleled by a substantial increase in the percentage of children adopted. Thus there is evidence of substantially improved permanency by ages 5 and 6. On average, more than a year passed between termination of parental rights and adoption, although for many of these children at least some of this time elapsed while the children were with the caregivers who adopted them.

These results suggest some success for CWS in achieving permanency for these children, who were infants when first involved in the CWS system. However, given the high placement rate, prevention of placement remains an important goal, and given the number of children with 2 or 3 or more placements, stability of placements is still an issue. The time spans before permanency, though longer than ideal, actually exceeded the standards set by the CFSR process.

4. Child and Family Services

Introduction

The preceding chapters have provided evidence that 5- to 6-year-old children reported for maltreatment as infants often experience social and behavioral problems, cognitive deficits, chronic health problems, or physical disabilities. These conditions and their functional impairments are likely indicators of the need for health, mental health, or special education services. Previous research has indicated that children in the child welfare system (CWS), particularly those placed in out-of-home care, do successfully access a diverse array of services, occasionally even more than children in the general population (e.g., Halfon,

Berkowitz, & Klee, 1992; Jonson-Reid, Drake, Kim, Porterfield, & Han, 2004). Given the high levels of need among children in the CWS, however, much of this research also indicates that their unmet need for services remains high (e.g., Burns et al., 2004). Ensuring that these children receive adequate and appropriate services is critical to their future positive development.

Services to strengthen and support children's caregivers and families are also important. Many families of children in the CWS confront a range of problems such as parenting stress, lack of social support, intimate-partner violence, parental substance abuse, or mental health problems, which makes it difficult for them to parent effectively. In this context, providing services to strengthen and support caregivers and families may help support children's development and prevent future child maltreatment.

The purpose of this chapter is to examine what services children, caregivers, and families received, which children and caregivers were more likely to receive different services, and whether service utilization was sufficient to meet needs. Analyses examine the following types of services:

- Children's preventive and urgent health care services,
- Children's outpatient and inpatient mental health services,
- Children's special education services,
- Family CWS services, including family-based and parenting support services,
- Services to address basic needs like shelter and child care, and
- Caregiver mental health and substance abuse services.

Data on service needs and utilization are derived from caseworker, caregiver, and teacher interviews. Which source was used for each service depended upon data availability and which reporter was best positioned to provide information on each type of service. For instance, information on use of CWS services relied on caseworker reports, information regarding special education services relied on teacher reports, and information on use of children's health and mental health services relied on caregiver reports.

For most services, we examined the degree to which need for a particular service matched actual service receipt. We were also interested in which types of caregivers, families, and children were more likely to receive different kinds of services. Consequently, we analyzed findings in relation to a child's sex, race, and placement setting at the 5- to 6-year follow-up. We also examined the impact of other family characteristics on service delivery when they were deemed conceptually relevant. For instance, we examined the impact of the type of child maltreatment on utilization rates of CWS services and the impact of poverty on basic family needs assistance.

It was beyond the scope of this report to examine the impact of caregiver or child welfare services on child outcomes such as placement or well-being. It was also outside the scope of this report to compare the relative influence of various predictors of service utilization rates and patterns. This chapter is primarily intended to provide a descriptive picture of the services received by children who are now 5 to 6 years of age and their families. The chapter is divided into two sections: services to children and services to families or caregivers. Key results for children's services are summarized below.

Key Results for Children's Services

- Most children have received some preventive health service since their last NSCAW interview (30 months on average). Eighty-eight percent have had a well-child checkup in that time period, and nearly all (99%) are reported up to date on immunizations. The proportions of children having received dental care, vision testing, or hearing testing, however, are somewhat lower (70% to 77%).
- Children with chronic health conditions are more likely to receive well-child checkups and to have a consistent health care service location than children without such conditions.
- Children living at home with biological parents are less likely than children living in other settings (e.g., adoptive parents) to have had a recent well-child checkup and are more likely to have used emergency room or urgent care services.
- An estimated 16.7% of children were reported to have received outpatient mental health services since their last interview, most often specialty mental health services.
- Children currently placed out of home were almost twice as likely to use any outpatient mental health service or specialty mental health service as children living in other settings.
- Children whose assessments indicated need for mental health services were more likely to receive them; however, approximately 65% of children in need of mental health services still received none.
- An estimated 22.6% of all children were reported to have an active Individualized Education Plan (IEP) currently. Most of these children were classified as speech impaired, developmentally delayed, or learning disabled.
- Approximately two thirds of children with cognitive disabilities had an IEP, and only one third of children with emotional problems had an IEP. Thus many children potentially in need of special education services were not receiving them.

Children's Preventive and Urgent Health Services

Caregivers reported that most children had received preventive and routine health services since the last interview (Exhibit 4-1).[1] The time since the last interview averages 30 months, with a range from 21 to 44 months. Almost all children (98.5%) were reported to be up to date with their immunizations, and a sizable majority had recently participated in a well-child checkup (88.2%). The high rate of immunizations is particularly notable. At baseline, children aged 0 to 2 years were significantly less likely to be up to date on their immunizations than older children, but almost all of the children who were infants at baseline were up to date with their immunizations by 5 and 6 years of age. The increase is likely because, by the time of the 5- to 6- year follow-up, nearly all of these children had started school, and states require that children be up-to-date on their immunizations to enroll in kindergarten. During the time since the last interview, most children (70% to 77%) also received dental care, vision testing, or hearing testing. Almost all (95.7%) children were reported to have at least one place their child "usually goes when sick or needs advice." This parallels national findings from the NHIS, indicating that approximately 95% of children have a usual place of health care (Bloom & Dey, 2006). Slightly fewer than half (46%) of children had received all of these preventive health care services (dental care, vision and hearing testing, well-child checkup, and immunizations) since the last interview.

The proportion of children receiving these preventive health services did not vary according to the child's sex. Race and the child's current placement setting, however, were associated with access to health services. Black children were significantly more likely than children of other races to receive all of the preventive health services, and were more likely to have recently received a well-child checkup. When compared to children living at home with either adoptive parents or other in-home caregivers and children living out of home, children living at home with their biological parents were the *least* likely to have recently received a well- child checkup or recent vision testing. Previous reports have documented greater health care utilization and medical care costs for children in foster care than among other groups of children receiving medical assistance coverage (e.g., Halfon, Berkowitz, & Klee, 1992).

Consistent with these findings, children living out of home and those adopted were more likely than children living at-home with biological parents or other caregivers to access health care services. It should be noted that only 1% of children in out-of-home placement or living at home with biological parents or some other caregiver had no health insurance, compared to 4% of children living at home with biological parents (not shown). Thus children living at home with biological parents may have slightly greater financial barriers to health service utilization than those in other groups.

As reported earlier, approximately 20% of children had a serious chronic health condition. Access to preventive and routine child health services would be particularly important for this population of children. When compared to children without chronic health conditions, children with chronic health conditions were significantly more likely to have recently received a well-child checkup (95.1%) and to have reported having at least one place they usually go when sick or need health care advice (99.4%).

Caregivers also reported on children's use of urgent care services for illnesses or injuries since the last interview (Exhibit 4-2). Slightly more than one quarter of these children were reported to have used emergency room (ER) or urgent care services for illness or an injury, accident, or poisoning since the last interview. Overnight hospital admissions for illnesses and injuries were much less common (4%). Six percent of caregivers reported contact with a physician or nurse for serious accidents, injuries, or poisonings since the last interview. It should be noted that these may be the same families who reported having used emergency-room care. Nationally, it is estimated that 10% of children aged 5 to 6 are treated for serious accidents, injuries, or poisonings in any given year (National Center for Injury Prevention and Control, n.d.).

Although children's sex, race, and chronic health condition status had no significant association with the likelihood of receiving urgent care health services, the child's current living situation did have a significant association. Children living at home with their biological parents were more likely to have had an overnight hospital admission for an illness or injury and more likely to have received care from a doctor or nurse for serious injuries, accidents, or poisonings than children living out of home or children living in home with either adoptive parents or nonbiological parents.

Exhibit 4-1. Preventive and Routine Child Health Services Infant Population at Wave 5

	N (Min)	All Preventive Services[1] % (SE)	Reported To Have a Usual Health Care Location % (SE)	Dental Care Since Last Interview % (SE)	Vision Testing Since Last Interview % (SE)	Hearing Testing Since Last Interview % (SE)	Well-Child Checkup Since Last Interview % (SE)	Up-to-date Immunizations % (SE)
Total	941	46.4(2.9)	95.7(1.2)	70.2(2.4)	76.9(2.6)	77.0(2.6)	88.2 (1.7)	98.5(0.4)
Sex								
Male	480	43.6(4.1)	95.7(1.8)	70.0(3.8)	73.7(4.2)	75.1(4.0)	86.8 (2.5)	98.7(0.5)
Female	461	49.2(3.4)	95.8(1.6)	70.4(2.6)	80.1(2.9)	78.9(2.9)	89.5 (2.4)	98.3(0.7)
Race/ethnicity		*					*	
Black	368	56.9(5.0)[a]	95.8(1.0)	77.2(3.6)	81.3(4.6)	81.8(4.0)	93.9 (1.7)[3,a]	98.1(0.7)
White	323	42.6(3.5)[2,b]	97.2(1.6)	65.9(3.4)	75.0(3.8)	74.4(3.5)	84.6 (3.1)[b]	98.1(0.8)
Hispanic	184	40.3(5.7)[2,b]	95.0(2.2)	71.0(5.3)	73.3(5.9)	75.3(5.7)	88.8 (3.7)	99.5(0.5)
Other	61	41.0(8.6)	85.4(11.0)	61.2(9.1)	81.2(5.1)	77.1(7.9)	81.5 (6.5)	99.4(0.4)
Child setting					*		**	
In home, biological parents	489	42.3(3.3)	95.0(1.4)	67.8(3.2)	74.2(4.1)[a]	76.5(3.5)	84.0 (2.7)[a]	98.7(0.5)
In home, adoptive parents	219	54.6(6.1)	95.0(4.2)	74.1(5.4)	83.3(3.7)[a]	79.4(4.6)	94.0 (2.3)[5,b]	99.8(0.2)
In home, kin, or other caregiver	154	52.9(5.8)	98.0(1.0)	68.2(5.9)	79.4(5.0)[a]	82.1(4.2)	96.7 (1.5)[5,b]	98.5(0.9)
Out of home	39	50.0(13.7)	97.2(2.7)	82.8(6.0)	96.0(3.3)[4,b]	77.9(11.7)	90.4 (5.7)	96.1(4.0)
Chronic health condition			**				**	
Yes	218	42.7(5.6)	99.4(1.4)	66.0(5.7)	75.2(5.2)	75.1(5.4)	95.1 (2.0)	98.2(1.0)
No	723	47.4(3.3)	94.7(1.3)	71.3(2.8)	77.3(2.6)	77.5(2.7)	86.4 (2.1)	98.6(0.5)

Note: All preventive and routine health care is caregiver-reported since last interview. All analyses are on weighted data; Ns are unweighted. Pearson $\chi 2$ tests for cluster samples were used to test statistical significance. Statistical significance is noted by asterisks in the column above the statistically significant result

(*p < .05, **p < .0 1). Alphabetic superscripts that are different from one another represent significant differences ($\alpha = .05$).

[1] Includes having had up-to-date immunizations and recent dental, vision, hearing, and well-child checkups.

[2] Black children were more likely to receive all preventive services since the last interview than White or Hispanic children.

[3] Black children were more likely to have a well-child check-up since the last interview than White children.

[4] Children out of home were more likely to have their vision tested since the last interview than children living in home with biological parents, children living with adoptive parents, or children living with kin

[5] Children living with adoptive parents and children living with kin or other caregiver were more likely to have a well-child check-up since the last interview than children living with biological parents.

Exhibit 4-2. Child Urgent Medical Care Infant Population at Wave 5

	N (Min)	Emergency Room or Urgent Care for Illness or Injury Since Last Interview % (SE)	Hospital Admission for Illness or Injury Since Last Interview % (SE)	Care from Doctor or Nurse for Serious Injury, Accident, or Poisoning Since Last Interview % (SE)
Total	959	25.8 (2.2)	4.1 (0.9)	5.5 (1.0)
Sex				
Male	489	26.5 (3.4)	3.7 (1.2)	7.7 (1.9)
Female	470	25.1 (3.1)	4.6 (1.3)	3.3 (1.0)
Race/ethnicity				
Black	378	21.8 (3.4)	4.0 (1.3)	5.3 (1.5)
White	328	31.5 (4.2)	4.3 (1.3)	6.7 (1.9)
Hispanic	187	19.6 (5.3)	3.3 (2.1)	2.3 (0.9)
Other	62	26.3 (8.2)	6.7 (4.6)	9.6 (5.1)
Child setting			**	*
In home, biological parents	493	26.9 (3.3)	5.3 (1.4)[1,a]	6.0 (1.6)[a]
In home, adoptive parents	224	21.0 (4.0)	2.1 (0.8)[b]	4.5 (1.1)[a]
In home, kin, or other caregiver	159	24.1 (4.9)	0.6 (0.3)[b]	4.4 (2.0)[a]
Out of home	42	26.4 (12.0)	0.0 (0.0)[1,c]	0.1 (0.1)[2,b]
Chronic health condition				
Yes	221	34.8 (5.0)	7.8 (2.6)	5.3 (1.5)
No	738	23.5 (2.6)	3.2 (0.9)	5.6 (1.2)

Note: All urgent medical care is caregiver-reported since the time of last interview. All analyses are on weighted data; *Ns* are unweighted. Pearson χ^2 tests for cluster samples were used to test statistical significance. Statistical significance is noted by asterisks in the column above the statistically significant result (*$p < .05$, **$p < .0$ 1). Alphabetic superscripts that are different from one another represent significant differences ($\alpha = .05$).

[1] Children out of home did not have any hospital admission for illness or injury since the last interview, in contrast to children living in home with biological parents, children living with adoptive parents, or children living with kin. Children living with biological parents were more likely to have a hospital admission for illness or injuries than children living with adoptive parents, with kin, or out of home.

[2] Children out of home were less likely to need care form a doctor or nurse for a serious injury, accident, or poisoning since the last interview than children living in home with biological parents, children living with adoptive parents, or children living with kin.

Exhibit 4-3. Caregiver Report of Utilization of Child Mental Health Services Infant Population at Wave 5

	N (Min)	Outpatient Mental Health Services[1] % (SE)	Specialty Outpatient Services % (SE)	Family Doctor % (SE)	School-Based Services[2] % (SE)	Current Use of Psychotropic Medication % (SE)
Total	954[3]	16.7 (2.1)	12.0 (1.9)	7.0 (1.3)	10.8 (3.2)	6.4 (1.1)
Sex						
Male	489	19.6 (3.3)	13.7 (2.3)	8.8 (2.0)	14.2 (5.8)	8.2 (1.7)
Female	470	14.1 (2.9)	10.5 (2.7)	5.2 (1.5)	7.3 (3.1)	4.5 (1.3)
Race/ethnicity				**		
Black	376	16.5 (3.8)	10.6 (2.7)	5.5 (1.9)	23.8 (9.2)[4]	7.4 (1.9)
White	329	16.8 (3.0)	11.0 (2.5)	10.6 (2.5)[a]	9.5 (4.8)	5.8 (1.3)
Hispanic	187	19.2 (5.4)	18.3 (5.3)	1.6 (0.7)[b]	1.0 (0.7)	7.0 (2.8)
Other	62	12.2 (4.4)	6.1 (3.4)	7.9 (3.6)	1.4 (1.5)	3.0 (1.6)
Child setting		*	*			**
In home, biological parents	493	10.9 (2.3)[a]	7.5 (2.0)[a]	5.9 (1.8)	10.5 (3.8)	3.1 (1.0)[a]
In home, adoptive parents	224	22.4 (4.1)[5,b]	15.2 (3.7)[a]	10.2 (2.6)	7.5 (4.8)	12.6 (3.3)[6,b]
In home, kin, or other caregiver	158	16.6 (4.8)	11.7 (4.3)[a]	7.4 (2.7)	6.5 (4.2)	10.5 (3.6)
Out of home	43	42.6 (13.4)[5,c]	41.1 (13.2)[7,b]	7.3 (4.2)	1.2 (1.1)	9.3 (4.1)
Child in need of mental health services[8]		***	***	***	*	***
Yes	293	34.9 (4.9)	26.6 (4.9)	15.7 (3.3)	22.7 (7.2)	13.4 (2.6)
No	668	6.8 (1.4)	6.1 (1.1)	3.5 (0.8)	5.5 (3.2)	3.5 (0.9)

Note: Mental health services were reported by caregivers and measured through an adapted version of the Child and Adolescent Services Assessment (CASA; see Appendix A). All analyses are on weighted data; Ns are unweighted. Pearson χ^2 tests for cluster samples were used for initial significance tests. Statistical significance is noted by asterisks in the column above the statistically significant result (*p < .05, **p < .01, ***p < .001). Alphabetic superscripts that are different from one another represent significant differences (α = .05). Cells are left empty when sample sizes are too small to allow for meaningful estimates (N < 9). Caregiver report of mental health service utilization represents services received since last interview.

1 Any outpatient mental health service included use of specialty outpatient (e.g., professional help from a psychologist or social worker, in-home counseling, community-based mental health center), school-based mental health services (e.g., services from a school guidance counselor, social worker, or psychologist), or mental health services performed by a family doctor.

2 Only children 6 years or older were asked about school-based services; consequently, the sample size for these items are smaller (N = 261).

3 The total sample size represents all service categories except school-based services (which included only 261 children).

4 Pearson χ^2 test not conducted because of small expected frequencies.

5 Children living with adoptive parents were more likely to receive outpatient mental health services than children living with biological parents, while children living out of home were more likely to receive outpatient mental health services than children living with biological parents, and adoptive parents.

6 Children living with adoptive parents were more likely to use psychotropic medication than children living with biological parents.

7 Children living out of home were more likely to receive specialty outpatient mental health services than children living with biological parents, adoptive parents, or kin.

8 Children were defined as "in need of mental health services" if either a caregiver or teacher reported an elevated score (> 1.5 standard deviations above the mean) on the caregiver-completed Child Behavior Checklist or teacher-completed Teacher Report Form Total Problems, Internalizing, or Externalizing subscales.

In summary, children aged 5 to 6 years old who entered the CWS in their infancy have relatively good access to preventive health services and access that is comparable to other children in the United States. Children living in home with biological parents had less access to preventive health services and greater use of urgent care services than those living in adoptive homes or in out-of-home placements. For children with a history of maltreatment, active involvement with the CWS may increase access to routine preventive health services and decrease reliance on urgent health care services.

Children's Mental Health Services

Caregivers were asked about whether their child had received help for an emotional, behavioral, learning, or attention problem since the last interview. The questions were framed so that caregivers could respond positively for all service providers or service settings that were applicable. Consequently, children could be reported to have received services from more than one source. Exhibit 4-3 provides reported rates of mental health service use for outpatient mental health services, specialty outpatient mental health services, treatment from a family doctor for a mental health problem, school-based mental health services and use of psychotropic medications. School-based mental health services were analyzed only for children six and older, because few younger children would have access to these services. Outpatient mental health services included any services received from a specialty mental health provider, family doctor, or school professional for an emotional or behavioral problem. Specialty outpatient services referred to services received from a private mental health clinician (i.e., psychiatrist, psychologist, social worker, or psychiatric nurse not working within a community health center), a community mental health center, therapeutic nursery at a mental health or community health center (for 5- year-olds only), or via in-home counseling or crisis services. Caregivers were also asked whether children had received inpatient psychiatric services, which represented all restrictive forms of mental health care, including hospital or emergency room care for mental health problems, residential or group home treatment, emergency shelter, or day treatment. Because only a small number of children were reported to have received inpatient psychiatric services since the time of the last interview (0.8%, SE = .4, unweighted $N = 14$), these services are not included in Exhibit 5-3.[2]

Overall, 16.7% of children were reported to have received outpatient mental health services since their last interview (Exhibit 4-3). A total of 12% received specialty outpatient mental health services. The most commonly utilized specialty outpatient service was "help received from a private mental health professional" (7.5%, not shown). Seven percent of children were reported to have been in contact with their family physician about a mental health problem, and 6.4% were reported to be currently using psychotropic medications. Among 6-year-olds, 10.8% reported having used school-based mental health services.

The most recent national estimates indicate that approximately 2% to 3% of children 3 to 5 years of age and 6% to 9% of children 6 to 17 years of age reported (or were reported) having used mental health services within a 12-month period (Kataoka et al., 2002). Previous analyses have shown that, when compared to all U.S. children, rates of mental health service utilization are higher within a child welfare population. For instance, Burns et al. (2004) found that approximately 7% of 2- to 5–year-olds and 16% of 6- to 10–year-olds at the baseline NSCAW interview had used at least one mental health service over the course of a year. Rates of mental health service utilization remain comparatively high among children who were infants at baseline and followed up at age 5 to 6. Previous research has suggested that CWS may act as a gateway to mental health service access. However, the impact of CWS contact on mental health service access is not as relevant here where, 5 years postbaseline, very few children are still receiving some type of CWS service (16%). Consequently, it is striking to find comparable mental health service utilization rates here to those described within previous NSCAW research using baseline interview data for similarly aged children. Mental health service utilization rates for these 5- to 6-year-olds cannot simply be a function of CWS' current involvement in their lives.

Children's sex was not associated with their utilization of any type of mental health services. With one exception, race was not associated with mental health service utilization patterns. Race was associated only with the receipt of mental health services from a family doctor: White children were significantly more likely than Hispanic children to have consulted with their primary care physician about a mental health problem. The absence of racial differences in most mental health service receipt for these children is contrary to research findings from the general population. Nationally, the research literature demonstrates substantial disparities in children's mental health service utilization by race (e.g., Garland, Lau, Yeh, McCabe, Hough et al., 2005).

The child's current home setting was associated with utilization of most types of mental health services. Children currently placed out of home were anywhere from almost twice as likely to more than five times as likely to use outpatient mental health services or specialty outpatient mental health services as children living at home (Exhibit 4-3). Children living at home with adoptive parents were more than twice as likely as children living at home with their biological parents to use outpatient mental health services and four times as likely to be currently taking a psychotropic medication. Generally, children who have ever lived in out-of-home care or who are currently living outside the home appear more likely to use mental health services. This finding is consistent with similar findings in the literature (e.g., Burns et al., 2004; Hurlburt, Leslie, Landsverk, Barth, Burns, Gibbons, Slymen, & Zhang, 2004). These findings also support previously drawn conclusions that the CWS often acts as a gateway into mental health services for children within the CWS (e.g., Leslie, Hurlburt, James, Landsverk, Slymen, & Zhang, 2005).

As would be expected, children's use of mental health services was significantly higher when caregivers or teachers reported that children had behavior problems (operationalized as having an elevated score on the Child Behavior Checklist or Teacher Report Form—see Appendix A). Children reported to have behavior problems were four to five times more likely to have received each type of mental health service than children not reported to have behavior problems. Nonetheless, rates of unmet need for mental health services were high. For instance, the fact that 35% of children reported to have behavior problems received outpatient mental health services means that 65% did not receive these services. Despite the relatively high level of unmet need for mental health services among these children, one study suggests that the unmet need for all children within the general population is even higher: nearly 80% (Kataoka et al., 2002). So, while rates of unmet mental health needs remain high in this target population, involvement within the CWS does appear to increase children's access to mental health services.

Children's Special Education Services

NSCAW collected data from caregivers on children's need for and receipt of special education services in the time period since the 36-month follow-up interview. For this cohort of children, the time since the 36-month interview represents the period of first school entry (as the children turn 5 to 6 years of age). Consequently, for children who were infants at baseline, the 5- to 6-year follow-up represents the first opportunity to identify school-related special education needs. Caregivers were asked whether they had been told that the child had a learning/developmental problem and, if so, whether the child had an Individualized Education Plan (or IEP) or had received special education services. Nationwide eligibility for special education placement is determined through a comprehensive assessment of the child's abilities, which also forms the basis for the type and level of service a child receives. Children may be diagnosed as having health, cognitive, or emotional challenges that must be addressed within the educational setting.

Approximately 20% of all caregivers reported being told by an education professional since the last interview that their child had a learning problem, special need, or developmental disability (for more specific information see Chapter 3). Of these, 65% were told that these problems would merit special education services. Almost all (95%) caregivers who had been told their children needed special education services reported receiving them.

Exhibit 4-4. Special Education Services Infant Population at Wave 5

	N	Child Has an Active IEP[1] % (SE)
Total	676	22.6 (2.8)
Sex		*
Male	353	28.4 (3.6)
Female	323	17.0 (3.6)
Race/ethnicity		
Black	273	20.5 (4.2)
White	234	23.1 (4.7)
Hispanic	119	25.4 (6.3)
Other	46	18.5 (8.4)
Child setting		
In home, biological parents	336	15.8 (3.2)
In home, adoptive parents	163	27.3 (5.3)
In home, kin, or other caregiver	125	32.5 (8.1)
Out of home	34	18.4 (8.0)
Child in need of special education services[2]		***
Yes	349	37.2 (5.0)
No	331	8.4 (2.2)

Note: All analyses are on weighted data; Ns are unweighted. Pearson χ^2 tests for cluster samples were used to test statistical significance. Statistical significance is noted by asterisks in the column above the statistically significant result (*$p < .05$, ***$p < .001$). IEP = Individualized Education Plan.

[1] Active IEP was determined according to either teacher or caregiver report.

[2] "Need for special education services" was determined by a child's risk of behavior problems, cognitive/learning delays, or functional impairment, as described in Appendix A.

As shown in Exhibit 4-4, according to either caregivers or teachers,[3] 22.6% of all children were reported to currently have an active IEP. This rate is comparable to rates of special education services for all children within NSCAW at both baseline and 18-month follow-up. The rate of 22.6% is much higher than proportions of children reported to be in federally supported special education programs nationally: 5% of all 3- to 5-year-olds and 9% of all 6- to 21-yearolds (U.S. Department of Education, 2005).

Exhibit 4-4 also shows the percentages of children with active IEPs by sex, race, current placement setting, and need. Boys were more likely to have received an IEP than girls. This is consistent with other studies showing greater representation of boys in special education (Hodapp & Fidler, 1999). Contrary to national research which tends to show greater numbers of children of color receiving special education services (e.g., Artiles, Harry, Reschly, & Chinn, 2002; Hosp & Reschly, 2003), there was no association in this population between child race/ethnicity and IEP receipt. Also, IEP receipt was not related to child setting at Wave 5.

As expected, an active IEP was significantly more common when children were determined to have needs that would be likely to interfere with school success (operationalized as having an elevated score on a standardized measure indicating risk for behavior problems, cognitive delays, language delays, or functional impairments).[4] Although need increased the likelihood of receiving special education services, 63% of children determined to need a referral for special education services were not currently reported to have an active IEP. An examination of specific disability types revealed that most children at risk for cognitive disabilities (64%, SE = 9.2) had a current IEP; meanwhile, only 32% (SE = 5.2) of children at risk for behavioral or emotional problems were reported to have an IEP. It should be noted that estimates here of "need" for special education services do not directly correspond to national eligibility requirements for IEP services. In fact, the exact eligibility for IEP services differs from state to state. However, similar to the approach taken here, most states use clinically elevated scores on quantitative measures to determine eligibility for IEP receipt.

For those children reported by teachers to be currently receiving IEP-related special education services, teachers were asked several questions to describe these services in more detail.[5] Teachers were asked to report upon a child's IEP classification, receipt of noninstructional IEP services, educational location, and length of time in special education services. Based upon teacher reports, 78% of students receiving special education services were in a regular class, as opposed to a special school or self-contained classroom (not shown). A little over half had been served by special education for more than 1 year. Most students receiving an IEP were classified as speech impaired (65%) and the most commonly received noninstructional service was speech therapy. Other common IEP classifications included developmental delay, learning disability, ADHD, and emotional disturbance.

Although a higher rate of special education placement has been previously noted for children in the child welfare population (e.g., Jonson-Reid et al., 2004), such findings do not necessarily mean that all the special education needs of children in child welfare are being met. It is important to consider special education needs along with associated service utilization. This report continues to find relatively high rates of unmet special education needs among young children just entering the school system. In particular, in this group of children, those with behavioral and emotional problems that might interfere with academic functioning appear to be more commonly overlooked by the education system than those with cognitive deficits.

Key Results of CWS Services and Services to Meet Basic Family Needs

- As would be expected, the number of families engaged in CWS services appears to be decreasing as increasing time passes since initial CWS maltreatment investigation. An estimated 12% of all caregivers reported that they were still in contact with the CWS. The caseworkers responsible for these families reported that 69% of them had received some type of CWS-delivered service since the time of last interview.
- Approximately 56% of families still involved with CWS received family-based services, most often nonintensive family preservation or reunification services.
- An estimated 56% of those involved with CWS received parenting support services, most frequently parent training.
- When asked about receiving services to meet basic needs, the caregivers of children living at home were most likely to report having received either assistance for their family's basic living needs (e.g., transportation, food, 33%) or regularly needed assistance with child care (30%).
- Services to meet basic needs were more likely received by families living at or below the poverty level. Families of children living at home with biological parents were also more likely to receive these services.
- An estimated 27% of permanent caregivers were determined to be in need of mental health services, and 12% reported having used a mental health service.
- Approximately 26% of permanent caregivers were determined to be in need of substance abuse services, but almost no caregivers reported having used a substance abuse service.
- Biological parents of children living in home were more likely to have mental health and substance abuse needs than other caregivers. They were also more likely to use mental health services.
- While having a mental health need did increase the likelihood that a caregiver received a mental health service, only 26% of those in need of mental health services received one.

Family Child Welfare Services

At the time of the 5- to 6-year follow-up, 12% of all caregivers (unweighted $N = 143$) reported that they were still in contact with CWS and receiving some type of service. Caseworker surveys were attempted for all of these cases; 129 interviews were completed for an 81.8% response rate. Analysis of the receipt of family child welfare services is based solely on data from caseworker interviews. Consequently, it should be noted that results presented here represent the percentage of families reported to be receiving CWS services, not percentages of the entire infant cohort at the 5- to 6-year follow-up. Caseworkers were asked to report upon three different categories of child welfare services: family-based services, parenting support services, and individual parent counseling (Exhibit 5-5). Sixty-nine percent of families still engaged with CWS at the 5- to 6-year follow-up were reported to have received some type of CWS family-based parenting support or parent/guardian counseling service since the time of last interview.

Fifty-six percent of families still involved with CWS were reported by caseworkers to have received family-based services since the last interview period. *Family-based services* are intended to provide support for families who are in crisis or at risk for child maltreatment or child placement into foster homes (Omnibus Reconciliation Act of 1993, Pub. L. 103-66). They also aim to support children's well-being indirectly by increasing the caregiver's ability to provide a good environment for them.

Three different categories of family-based services were recorded. Intensive family preservation or reunification services denote intense, brief services provided in a family's home in the crisis intervention model. The second family-based service category included less intensive forms of family preservation or reunification services to prevent out-of-home placement.

The third category included all other home-based services. These are less intensive than the other two categories and could involve as little as periodic monitoring visits. For this population of children and families still involved with CWS at the 5- to 6-year follow-up, caseworkers most frequently reported the receipt of other home-based services (44%), followed by nonintensive family preservation or reunification services (20%), and finally intensive family preservation or reunification (15%). In other words, when families did receive family-based services, they most commonly received the least intensive type of such service.

Caseworkers reported that 56% of families still involved with CWS had received a parent support service since the last interview. *Parent support services* specifically aim to support caregivers' capacity to parent. Four different categories of parenting support services were recorded: parent training, parent aid, family counseling, and respite services. When parent support services were received, caseworkers reported that families most typically received parent training (34.9%) or the help of a parenting aide (16.3%). Caseworkers finally reported upon the extent to which *family counseling services* may have been recommended to support caregivers and deal with maladaptive behaviors that may put children at risk. Forty-one percent of caregivers still involved with CWS were reported by caseworkers to be receiving individually based family counseling services.

The handful of children who continued to have some CWS contact 5 to 6 years after the index maltreatment investigation lived in a variety of settings (Exhibit 4-5). As might be expected, child setting did impact CWS service receipt. When compared to children living in other settings, children living in out-of-home placements were the most likely to be involved with some type of CWS service. Almost all of these children in out-of-home care (9 8%) were reported to have received a CWS service since the time of last interview. Children living out of home were specifically more likely than children living in home with their caregivers (biological or otherwise) to have received family-based services. Caseworkers were reportedly continuing to work toward family reunification with these children. More interesting, 65% of children living at home with their biological parents were reported to have received some CWS service since last interview. Despite these children remaining in their biological home 5 to 6 years past the index investigation, a sizable portion are still actively involved with CWS to the point that they had received either family-based parenting support or individual counseling services. The receipt of CWS services did not vary based upon caregiver race or a variety of maltreatment variables (e.g., type of maltreatment originally investigated).

As the time since the index investigation passes, we would expect fewer families to be involved with the CWS and fewer families to need CWS services. Results from this analysis confirm this trend. Fewer families at the 5- to 6-year infant follow-up period are receiving family-based CWS services than those noted for all families at previous waves. More specifically, at the 18-month follow-up period, 25% of NSCAW families whose children were living at home and 63% of those living out of home were reported to be receiving family-based services. This trend continued for parent support services and family counseling services. Fewer families of children who were infants at baseline were receiving parent support services and family counseling at the 5- to 6-year follow-up than those reported in previous waves.

Exhibit 4-5 Child Welfare and Other Family Services Infant Population at Wave 5

	N (Min)	Any CWS Service[1] % (SE)	Family-Based Services[2] % (SE)	Parenting Support Services[3] % (SE)	Parents/Guardians Counseled Individually % (SE)
Total	129[4]	68.7 (7.9)	55.9 (9.0)	55.6 (7.3)	41.4 (6.8)
Caregiver race/ethnicity					
Black	36	82.4 (8.6)	75.1 (10.6)	73.7 (10.0)	37.7 (13.3)
White	57	62.5 (11.7)	50.3 (13.6)	48.6 (10.2)	38.3 (9.8)
Hispanic	15	58.0 (18.5)	56.8 (18.5)	44.4 (19.5)	35.7 (16.4)
Other	10	98.3 (1.9)	71.0 (23.1)	92.5 (6.5)	71.0 (23.1)
Child setting		**	**		
In home, biological parent	55	64.6 (1 1.6)[a]	50.8 (13.8)[a]	59.3 (11.2)	48.0 (8.3)
In home, adoptive parent	18	45.1 (15.7)[a]	45.4 (15.9)[a]	29.9 (13.8)	28.3 (12.8)
In home, kin, or other caregiver	22	60.7 (14.9)[a]	45.4 (15.9)[a]	45.5 (16.5)	6.6 (13.1)
Out of home	25	97.7 (1.7)[5,b]	94.3 (3.1)[6,b]	72.0 (15.5)	44.1 (17.5)

Note: All analyses are on weighted data; Ns are unweighted. Pearson χ^2 tests for cluster samples were used for initial significance tests. Statistical significance is noted by asterisks in the column above the statistically significant result (*$p < .05$, **$p < .0$ 1). Alphabetic superscripts that are different from one another represent statistically significant differences ($\alpha = .05$). CWS = child welfare system.

[1] Indicates having received any one of the following types of service: family-based services, parenting support services, or individual counseling.

[2] Indicates having received any home-based service including more or less intensive family preservation or reunification services.

[3] Indicates having received parent training, parent aide services, respite care, or family counseling.

[4] All data based on caseworker interviews (N = 129); this represents 81.8% of all cases reported by caregivers to have received some CWS service since last interview.

[5] Children out of home were more likely to receive CWS services than children living in home with biological parents, children living with adoptive parents, or children living with kin.

[6] Children out of home were more likely to receive family-based services than children living in home with biological parents, children living with adoptive parents, or children living with kin.

Services to Address Basic Needs

Being unable to meet your family's basic living needs (e.g., housing, child care, food) likely exacerbates parenting stress, especially for those living in poverty. This stress may then contribute to child maltreatment. Consequently, addressing these basic family needs has long been a central component of child welfare services. In fact, some argue that families would use fewer child welfare services if their basic needs for housing, income, and medical care were met (Lindsey, 1994). This section of the report describes caregiver reports of services to address basic needs.

Only caregivers of children living *at home* (94% of families) were asked if they had received any of 10 services to address basic needs since the last interview. For ease of presentation, these services were grouped into four categories as follows:

1. Assistance for family's basic living needs
    - Food (e.g., from a soup kitchen or food bank)
    - Financial help (other than Transitional Assistance to Needy Families [TANF] or Social Security Income [SSI])
    - Transportation (from caregiver's home)
    - Emergency shelter/housing
2. Child care receipt on a regular basis
3. Services directly to assist caregiver
    - Job-related services (e.g., job training or help finding a job)
    - Legal aid (not related to child welfare custody or child protective issues)
    - Organized support groups
4. Home assistance
    - Home management training (e.g., budgeting or planning meals)
    - Assistance in the home (e.g., someone coming to caregivers' homes to help with cleaning or minor repairs)

Exhibit 4-6 presents caregiver reports of service receipt across these categories and these are broken down by relevant case characteristics. Thirty-three percent of caregivers reported having received some type of assistance to help meet their family's basic living needs. Among those services in this category, caregivers most frequently reported having received transportation (16%) or food assistance (15%), followed by financial help (10%) and emergency shelter or housing services (3%; not shown). Nearly one third of caregivers reported that they had received some regular help with child care since the last interview. Nineteen percent of caregivers reported having received services intended to directly assist their own basic needs, including received job-related services (10%), organized support groups (8%), and legal aid (5%; not shown). The least frequently utilized service category was "home assistance." Only 12% of caregivers reported having received either home management training (3%) or assistance in the home (10%).

Exhibit 4-6. Services to Address Basic Needs Infant Population at Wave 5

	N (Min)	Assistance for Family's Basic Living Needs[1] % (SE)	Child Care[2] % (SE)	Services to Directly Assist Caregiver[3] % (SE)	Home Assistance[4] % (SE)
Total	971	32.7 (2.8)	30.0% (3.1)	19.3% (2.2)	11.9% (1.7)
Caregiver race/ethnicity			**		
Black	326	29.6 (4.4)	27.0 (4.5)[7,a]	15.6 (2.6)	8.9 (1.9)
White	442	27.2 (3.9)	33.1 (3.7)[7,a]	20.7 (2.8)	11.7 (2.5)
Hispanic	130	39.3 (7.1)	7.0 (3.4)[b]	23.2 (7.9)	17.9 (6.0)
Other	59	32.2 (9.2)	36.2 (10.2)[7,a]	16.0 (7.1)	15.0 (7.2)
Poverty status[5]		***		*	
At/below poverty level	401	47.8 (4.4)	25.6 (3.9)	26.5 (3.8)	12.7 (2.7)
Above poverty level	488	19.6 (2.6)	34.6 (4.3)	15.8 (3.2)	13.4 (2.1)
Child setting[6]		**		**	*
In home, biological parent	493	41.5 (3.9)[8,a]	31.9 (3.7)	25.6 (3.5)[9,a]	13.0 (2.6)
In home, adoptive parent	224	18.4 (4.0)[b]	27.3 (4.8)	15.9 (3.7)	18.2 (4.0)[10,a]
In home, kin, or other caregiver	159	16.4 (4.0)[b]	25.7 (5.6)	8.6 (2.7)[b]	5.8 (2.5)[b]

Note: All analyses are on weighted data; Ns are unweighted. Pearson χ^2 tests for cluster samples were used for initial significance tests. Statistical significance is noted by asterisks in the column above the statistically significant result (*$p < .05$, **$p < .01$, ***$p < .001$). Alphabetic superscripts that are different from one another represent statistically significant differences ($\alpha = .05$).

1 Includes having received any financial assistance, food from a community source, transportation help, or emergency shelter or housing.

2 Indicates having received child care on a regular basis.

3 Indicates that the caregiver has received job-related services, legal aid, or has attended any organized support group.

4 Indicates that having received help with specific home management training or cleaning or help with home repairs.

5 Using the federal poverty status guidelines, this variable is based upon family income for the child's current home setting at Wave 5.

6 Child home setting at Wave 5.

7 White, Black, and "Other" children were more likely to receive child care services than Hispanic children.

8 Families of children living with biological parents were more likely to receive assistance for family's basic living needs than children living with adoptive parents or children living with kin.

9 Families of children living with biological parents were more likely to receive services to directly assist caregivers than families of children living with kin.

10 Families of children living with adoptive parents were more likely to receive home assistance than families of children living with kin.

Some family characteristics did predict receipt of services to meet basic needs. For instance, caregivers living below poverty level at the 5- to 6-year follow-up were more likely to report the receipt of services to assist in meeting their family's basic living needs and services to help themselves. The only significant association between caregiver race and service receipt was for the regular receipt of child care: Hispanic caregivers were least likely to receive child care assistance. The child's living situation was associated with all basic needs services except child care. Children living at home with biological parents were significantly more likely to receive services to meet basic family living needs and services to assist caregivers than children living at home with either adoptive parents or other caregivers. The children of adoptive parents were more likely to receive home management services than those children living at home with "other" caregivers.

When compared to results from previous waves of NSCAW, fewer families within this group had received services to meet basic needs. With regard to services to directly assist caregivers, 34% of families with children 1.5 to 17 years old and living at home at the 18-month follow-up reported having received services, as opposed to the 19% noted here. Similarly, 46% of families had received services to meet basic family needs at 18 months, compared to 33% here. Little to no change occurred, however, in receipt of home assistance (16% at 18 months vs. 12% here).

In summary, the services most commonly received since last interview according to caregivers' reports were those related to (1) assistance for family's basic living needs, and (2) regularly needed assistance with child care. Not surprisingly, caregivers reported to be living at or below the poverty level were more likely than those living above the poverty level to report having received several of these basic need services. Generally, biological parents of children living at home were more likely than adoptive parents or other caregivers caring for children living at home to receive services to assist basic needs. We know that more children living with biological parents were living in poverty at the 5- to 6-year follow-up than children living in other settings. Consequently, this finding likely reflects an income-related inability to provide for a family's basic needs. Families in poverty are more likely to need services to meet their basic needs and more likely to meet eligibility requirements for the receipt of such services.

Caregiver Mental Health and Substance Abuse Services

Previous studies have found that children of parents with psychiatric disorders are two to three times more likely to experience maltreatment than those who do not have a history of mental health problems (Walsh, MacMillan, & Jamieson, 2002). Children whose parents abuse alcohol or other drugs are almost three times more likely to be abused and over four times more likely to be neglected than children of parents who are not substance abusers (Kelleher, Chaffin, Hollenberg, & Fisher, 1994). Increasing the recognition of caregiver behavioral health needs and providing services to alleviate this suffering are likely important components of maltreatment prevention. The following section describes the mental health and substance abuse needs of *permanent* (in-home) caregivers, including adoptive caregivers, along with their behavioral health service utilization since last interview (see footnote 1). Exhibit 5-7 describes reported levels of mental health need, substance abuse need, and mental health service utilization.

Permanent caregivers' needs for mental health and substance abuse services were assessed in five ways: (1) caregivers' responses to questions about the degree to which they perceived themselves as needing help for either a mental health problem or a substance abuse problem; (2) caseworkers' responses to similar questions; (3) caregivers' responses to direct questions about substance abusing behaviors; (4) the sections of the Composite International Diagnostic Interview Short Form (CIDI-SF; WHO, 2003; see Appendix A) on major depression, alcohol dependence, and drug dependence; and (5) the Short Form Health Survey (SF-12; Ware, Kosinski, & Keller, 1996; see Appendix A). According to the caregiver reports, 4% reported that they needed either "a lot" or "some" help with a mental health problem, and only 1% reported that they needed either "a lot" or "some" help with an alcohol or drug problem. These rates of self-reported caregiver mental health and substance abuse needs are comparable to those found for all caregivers at the 18-month follow-up. For those families still in contact with CWS (12% of families), caseworkers were asked about caregiver behavioral health needs. Caseworkers reported that 26% of the caregivers within their caseloads needed mental health services, 12% needed alcohol-related services and 26% needed drug abuse services.

When permanent caregivers were asked directly about substance abusing behaviors, 11.1% of permanent caregivers reported having had used some type of drug "on their own" in the last 12 months. For these questions, "on your own" was described as without a doctor's prescription, in larger amounts than prescribed, or for a longer period than prescribed. Among those reporting to have used a drug on their own, use of analgesics (e.g., codeine, Percodan, morphine and other prescriptions painkillers), was the most common category reported (4.8%), followed by marijuana (4.3%), sedatives (2.2%), and tranquilizers (1.6%). Eight percent of permanent caregivers reported consuming four or more alcoholic drinks in a single day during the past year.

In addition to caregiver and caseworker reports of behavioral health service needs, caregivers' risks for mental health and substance abuse problems were also assessed through two standardized measures. Three sections of the Composite International Diagnostic Interview Short Form (CIDI-SF; WHO, 2003, see Appendix A) were used to assess clinical levels of major depression, alcohol dependence, and drug dependence. Impairing mental health problems were also measured through the Short Form Health Survey (SF-12; Ware, Kosinski, & Keller, 1996, see Appendix A). Caregivers scoring within the clinical range on either of these standardized measures were determined to be at risk for a mental health, alcohol or drug problem and potentially in need of behavioral health services.

When findings from all sources of information on the need for mental health services are combined (Exhibit 4-7), 26.5% of caregivers were determined to be in need of mental health services. To put this in context, a recent national study estimated that the same proportion (26%) of all U.S. adults 18 years and older meet diagnostic criteria for any mental disorder over a 12- month period (Kessler, Chiu, Demler, Merikangas, & Walters, 2005). In this report, there were no significant variations in the need for mental health services by caregiver race/ethnicity, but there were by child setting, with biological parents more likely to need mental health services than adoptive parents. Approximately 2 6.2% of caregivers were determined to be in need of substance abuse services. Need for substance abuse services was significantly lower among Hispanics than among other racial/ethnic groups, and, similar to findings related to mental health services, need was higher among biological parents than among adoptive parents or other in- home caregivers.

Exhibit 4-7. Caregiver Need for Mental Health and Substance Abuse Services and Service Receipt Infant Population at Wave 5

	N	In Need of Mental Health Service[1] % (SE)	In Need of Substance Abuse Service[2] % (SE)	Received Mental Health Service % (SE)
Total	971	26.5 (2.4)	26.2 (2.3)	11.6 (1.6)
			*	
Caregiver race/ethnicity				*
Black	304	23.5 (3.5)	16.6 (2.9)[3,a]	4.7 (2.3)
White	463	27.1 (3.0)	27.6 (3.9)[3,a]	15.6 (2.2)
Hispanic	138	30.3 (6.5)	7.9 (3.4)[b]	7.3 (3.5)
Other	66	23.2 (7.4)	22.4 (9.4)	13.2 (6.1)
Child setting		**		
In home, biological parent	512	24.6 (3.0)[4,a]	25.8 (3.2)[5,a]	13.1 (2.3)
In home, adoptive parent	236	11.9 (3.4)[b]	9.3 (2.7)[b]	9.8 (3.2)
In home, kin, or other caregiver	168	18.3 (5.3)	13.0 (5.1)[b]	9.7 (4.0)
Need for mental health or substance abuse service				
In need of mental health services	216	NA	13.1 (1.7)[6]	29.9 (5.3)
In need of substance abuse services	221	13.1 (1.7)[6]	NA	19.6 (4.9)

Note: All analyses are on weighted data; Ns are unweighted. Pearson χ^2 tests for cluster samples were used to test statistical significance. Statistical significance is noted by asterisks in the column above the statistically significant result (*$p < .05$, **$p < .01$, ***$p < .001$). Alphabetic superscripts that are different from one another represent statistically significant differences ($\alpha = .05$).

[1] Caregivers were determined to be "in need of mental health services" when they met any one of four criteria: (1) caregiver self-reported need for "a lot" or "some" help for a mental health problem, (2) caseworker report of a caregiver's need for a mental health services, (3) self-reported scores within the clinical range on either the Dysthymia and Anhedonia scales of the CIDI-SF, or (4) a score exceeding 1.5 standard deviations below the norm (i.e., a score ≤ 35) on the Mental Health component of the SF-12.

[2] Caregivers were determined to be in need of substance abuse services when they met any one of three criteria: (1) caregiver self-reported need for "a lot" or "some" help for an alcohol or drug problem, (2) caseworker report of caregiver's need for alcohol or drug abuse services, or (3) or scores within the clinical range on either the Alcohol Dependence or Drug Dependence scales of the CIDI-SF.

[3] Caregivers of Black and White children were more likely to need substance abuse services than caregivers of Hispanic children.

[4] Biological caregivers were more likely to need mental health services than adoptive caregivers.

[5] Biological caregivers were more likely to need substance abuse services than adoptive and kin caregivers.

[6] Of the sample of caregivers, 13.1% had both a need for mental health services and a need for substance abuse services.

Despite these indicators of need, few caregivers reported receiving any behavioral health services. The NSCAW survey asked caregivers about services provided through inpatient care, day treatment programs, and clinic/psychiatric services. Approximately 12% of all caregivers reported having received any mental health service since the time of last interview, nearly all of which consisted of the use of medication for a mental health problem (11%). A handful reported having visited a clinic or doctor for a mental health problem. Caregivers who are White are significantly more likely than those who are Black to have received services, and biological parents are more likely to have received services than either adoptive parents or other in-home caregivers. The number of caregivers reported having received substance abuse services is even smaller (unweighted $N = 4$), and almost no caregivers reported having utilized hospital-based or residential psychiatric or substance abuse services. Because so few caregivers reported having received services for substance abuse problems, these data are not in Exhibit 4-7.

While having a mental health service need (using the criteria described above) did make it more likely that a caregiver received a mental health service, the large majority of caregivers determined to be in need of mental health services received none (70%). This finding is comparable to other recent reports of caregivers involved with the CWS (Libby et al., 2006). It should be noted that high levels of unmet mental health needs are not unique to this population. A recent national study found that only 41% of adults with a diagnosable mental disorder reported having received professional help within a 12-month period (Wang, Lane, Olfson, Pincus, Wells, & Kessler, 2005).

There are some limitations to the ways in which NSCAW assesses caregiver substance abuse and mental health needs and service use. For instance, the NSCAW survey does not ask caregivers about therapy received in nonclinical settings or group therapy or participation in self- help groups. Consequently, service utilization rates may be underestimated. Caregivers, particularly those under CWS involvement, may also be biased against reporting either substance abusing behaviors or related service utilization. Despite these limitations, the data still suggest that receipt of services in this population is not adequate for the level of need. By any measure of need, no more than a quarter of those in need of mental health services and almost none of those in need of substance abuse services received them.

Conclusion

The most obvious and promising finding of this chapter is that many children in need of health, mental health, special education, or CWS services did receive them. In fact, being identified as needing a particular service was strongly related to actually receiving such a service. We found that 69% of families still actively involved with CWS were currently receiving some type of CWS-service. Families living below the federal poverty level were more likely to receive services to meet their basic living needs than families with higher incomes. Children with chronic health conditions were more likely to have a consistent pediatric home and to have received a recent well-child checkup than children without chronic health conditions. And finally, children with objectively determined needs for mental health and special education services were far more likely than children without such needs to receive the relevant services.

Involvement with CWS was an important reason some of the children and families in this population received services. The link between CWS and increase rates of service receipt is not unique to children aged 5 to 6 years old who were infants at baseline, but it is consistently supported by previous NSCAW reports and related research (e.g., Leslie, Gordon et al., 2005; Leslie, Hurlburt et al., 2005). The influence of CWS appears to be particularly important with regard to both health and mental health service system access. Having had a history of out-of-home placement (either those now adopted or those currently in out-of-home care) increased the likelihood that a child received both mental health services and well-child checkups. Furthermore, rates of unmet mental health service needs, although still high (65%), were actually found to be lower than published rates of unmet mental health needs for the U.S. child population at large (80%; Kataoka et al., 2002). It should be noted, however, that *current* involvement with CWS is limited as an explanation for increased service use, since only 12% of this population were actively engaged with CWS at the five year follow-up. It is possible that there may be a lasting effect of CWS involvement on engagement with services. Further research should examine this further the influence of CWS involvement on service receipt over time.

When mental health service utilization is examined across children of all ages within the United States, studies most frequently find that mental health services are most commonly provided in schools. For children who were infants at NSCAW baseline, children most typically received more traditional outpatient mental health services. This is not surprising since these children have just started their school experience. On the other hand, 22% of children were reported to already have an active IEP during their early years of school. Further, nearly all caregivers who were told by a professional since the last interview that their child needed special education services reported already receiving them. Once children were identified by the school as needing services, caregivers' reported that most of these children received them. However, many children with needs that might merit a special education referral (e.g., cognitive, developmental, behavioral impairments) were never identified by schools and were not reported by caregivers to have received an IEP.

We know that identifying a child's social, emotional, or behavioral needs is a critical factor in subsequent service utilization. So, while we have highlighted that many children's needs were identified and served, it is critical at the same time to highlight the remaining high levels of *unmet* service needs. For instance, 65% of children with mental health needs did not report having received *any* service since the last interview period. Slightly over half of children with characteristics indicating the need for a special education referral were currently involved in an active IEP.

Levels of unmet service needs are not limited to children. In fact, unmet behavioral health needs among caregivers were even greater than those observed for children. Almost none of caregivers with substance abuse service needs reported having received some kind of substance abuse-related service. Seventy-six percent of caregivers in need of mental health services reported having received none (compared to national estimates of 60% unmet mental health service needs within the U.S. adult population (Kessler, Berglund, Demler, Jin, & Walter, 2005). Although rates of unmet behavioral health care needs are either comparable to or sometimes lower than as those observed for the general U.S. population, they are still remarkably high. Prior research has indicated that the children of parents with psychiatric disorders and the children of parents who abuse substances are more likely to experience maltreatment than the children of parents without such problems (Kelleher, Chaffin, Hollenberg, & Fischer, 1994; Walsh et al., 2002). Given the association between parental mental illness, substance abuse, and child maltreatment, it may be especially critical to meet caregiver behavioral health needs as a means to potentially prevent future child maltreatment and other developmental risks.

There are also obvious windows of missed service opportunity. For instance, although 88% of children had recently received a well-child checkup and 99% reported having at least one usual location of health care, only 16% of those in need of mental health services had received services from their family doctor for a mental health problem. Particularly for young children, primary care offers a promising point of mental health intervention but primarily appears to be a missed opportunity for these children.

This 5- to 6-year follow-up of children identified by CWS for maltreatment as infants indicates that a substantial proportion of children or caregivers have physical health, mental health, or education needs—or a combination of needs. Although many children did receive necessary services, there were substantial remaining unmet needs. Caregivers were even less likely to receive needed services than their children. So, while services are being delivered at a greater rate to those in need, there is still much room for improvement to best facilitate the healthy development of children and families who have been involved in the CWS.

APPENDIX A. TECHNICAL INFORMATION

Scales

Child and Adolescent Services Assessment. Data on the use of mental health services are based on an adapted version of the Child and Adolescent Services Assessment (CASA; Ascher et al., 1996; Burns et al., 1995; Farmer et al., 1994). This instrument gathers information from caregivers and children about an array of child-focused services for emotional or behavioral problems including outpatient and residential care. Outpatient services include: (1) clinic-based specialty mental health services; (2) private practice professionals including psychiatrists, psychologists, social workers, and psychiatric nurses and drug or alcohol clinics; (3) in-home mental health services (e.g., family preservation); and (4) therapeutic nursery/day treatment. Residential services include: (1) hospitalization in a psychiatric hospital or psychiatric unit of a general hospital, (2) hospitalization in a medical inpatient unit for emotional or behavioral problems, and (3) inpatient drug or alcohol detoxification.

Child Behavior Checklist. (Achenbach, 1991). The CBCL was designed to assess children's social competencies and problem behaviors on the basis of "standardized descriptions of behavior rather than diagnostic inferences" (Achenbach, 1991, p. iii). Two versions of the checklist have been developed; one for children aged 1 1/2 to 5 and another for those aged 6 to 18. In this wave of data collection, the version for children aged 6 to 18 was used. The checklist consists of 118 items related to behavior problems. For each item, the child's caregiver indicates how well the behavior describes the child, either now or within the past 6 months, on a 3-point scale: 0, "not true" of the child; 1, "somewhat/sometimes true"; or 2, "very/often true." The caregiver also reports on 20 social competency items such as the amount and quality of the child's participation in sports, hobbies, jobs and chores, and organizations; friendships; and school functioning. For this report, the CBCL *Total Problem* behavior standardized (T) score was used to measure the behavioral well-being of children. In keeping with recommended procedures for classifying the Total T score (Achenbach, 1991; 1992), behavior was classified as Normal (< 60), Borderline (60 to 63), or Clinical (> 63).

Composite International Diagnostic Interview Short Form—Mental Health. The CIDI-SF is a highly standardized interview that screens for mental health and substance use disorders using the criteria established in the Diagnostic and Statistical Manual 3rd Edition, Revised (*DSMIII-R*). The full instrument evaluates the presence of eight disorders: major depression, generalized anxiety, specific phobia, social phobia, agoraphobia, panic attack, alcohol dependence, and drug dependence. For this study, only the sections on major depression, alcohol dependence, and drug dependence were administered. Questions are scripted to ask about the previous 12-month period (Nelson, Kessler, & Mroczek, 2001); the section on depression was administered by in-person interview, while the sections on alcohol and drug dependence were administered by means of audio computer-assisted self-interviewing. The CIDI-SF version used in NSCAW does not indicate comorbidity with other disorders, nor does it differentiate between depression occurring as a primary diagnosis or in the context of other disorders, such as bipolar disorder or schizoaffective disorder.

For alcohol, respondents scored in the dependence range if (1) they indicated that they had consumed four or more drinks in a single day at least once during the past year, and (2) they reported at least three of the seven *DSM-III-R* symptoms of dependence. For drugs, respondents scored in the dependence range if (1) they indicated that they had used any of a variety of substances "on their own" (without a doctor's prescription, in larger amounts than prescribed, or for a longer period than prescribed) during the past year, and (2) they reported at least three of the seven *DSM-III-R* symptoms of dependence.

Kaufman Brief Intelligence Test. (Kaufman & Kaufman, 1990). The Kaufman Brief Intelligence Test is a brief, individually administered screener of verbal and nonverbal intelligence designed for individuals 4 years and older. It includes two subtests: Vocabulary (expressive vocabulary & definitions) and Matrices (ability to perceive relationships and complete analogies). We used the standard score for vocabulary, matrices and total IQ composite. Each is normed to have a mean of 100 and standard deviation of 15.

Loneliness and Social Dissatisfaction Scale. (Cassidy & Asher, 1992). The Loneliness and Social Dissatisfaction Scale assesses children's feelings of loneliness and dissatisfaction with peer support at school using a self-report questionnaire. This is a modification of the version used for older elementary school children. The children rate 16 items such as "Can you find a friend at school when you need one?" on a 3-point scale. We used the total score. Higher scores indicate greater loneliness. Cassidy and Asher (1992) indicated that their administration inadvertently omitted one item; in order to compare means, we prorated our mean by eliminating one item.

Parent-Child Conflict Tactics Scales. (Straus, Hamby, Finkelhor, Moore, & Runyan, 1998). The CTS-PC was developed to measure psychological and physical maltreatment and neglect by parents, as well as nonviolent modes of discipline CTSPC scales include nonviolent discipline (e.g., putting a child in "time out"), psychological aggression (e.g., shouting, yelling, or screaming at a child), physical assault, and neglect. Because items in the physical assault scale range widely in severity, from spanking to burning a child on purpose, the scale may be divided into subscales for minor, severe, and very severe physical assault. In NSCAW, parental report on the CTS-PC measures were obtained from permanent caregivers, including biological parents, adoptive parents, and other in-home caregivers, but excluding foster parents and other out-ofhome caregivers. In this report, we present findings from the nonviolent discipline, psychological aggression, and neglect scales, as well as the physical assault subscales. Measures shown are annual and lifetime prevalence and year chronicity for each scale and each item in each scale. Annual prevalence for each item is the percentage of caregivers who report that they have used the tactic in the past year; lifetime prevalence is the percentage of caregivers who report that they have ever used the tactic. Prevalence for each scale is the percentage of caregivers who report having used any of the tactics in the scale. Among the subset of caregivers who reported having used a tactic at least once in the past year, year chronicity is a measure of how often they used it.

Preschool Language Scale-3. (Zimmerman, Steiner, & Pond, 1992). The PLS-3 measures language development of infants and young children (ages 2 weeks to 6 years, 11 months). The *Auditory Comprehension* subscale measures receptive communication skills, while the *Expressive Communication* subscale measures expressive communication skills with tasks that focus on social communication and vocal development. A *Total Language* score combines these two subscales. PLS-3 scores are standardized with a mean of 100 and standard deviation of 15.

School Engagement. (Safe and Drug Free Schools). This measure assesses children's "connection" to the school experience by means of a self-rating scale. It is designed for children in elementary and middle school. In the current study it was used for all children aged 6 or older. The scale includes 11 items that measure both the behavioral component (participation) and psychological component (identification) of school engagement. Items are measured on a 4-point scale from 1 *never* to 4 *almost always*. We used the total scores. The range in scores is 11 to 44, with higher scores indicating greater connection.

Social Skills Rating System. (SSRS: Gresham & Elliott, 1990). The Social Skills Rating System (SSRS) measures caregiver and teacher perception of the social skills of children between the ages of 3 and 18. Separate versions have been developed for preschool, elementary school, and secondary school. The scores used in this report are based on the caregiver and teacher reports. The SSRS assesses social skills in four domains—cooperation, assertion, responsibility, and self-control—and provides standard scores and competence categories for the total as well as competence categories for the individual domains. The SSRS standardized scores are based on a mean of 100 with a standard deviation of 15. Total scores were categorized as suggested in the SSRS manual (Gresham & Elliott, 1990): Fewer Social Skills (< 85), Average Social Skills (85 to 115), or More Social Skills (> 115). We also included subscale scores and competence categories for the domains of assertion, self-control, and cooperation obtained from both parent and teacher forms.

Short Form Health Survey. The SF-12 is a standardized survey instrument designed to provide an indicator of physical and mental health status. It includes 12 items selected from the Medical Outcomes Study 36-item Short-Form Health Survey (SF-36). The SF-12 is collapsed into two summary scales—a physical health component summary and a mental health component summary. Average scores for the two summary scales have been shown to closely reflect those from the original 36-item form. Furthermore, the SF-12 has demonstrated adequate reliability and validity (see Ware, Kosinski, & Keller, 1996, for more information).

Teacher-Rating Instrument of Proactive and Reactive Aggression. (Dodge & Coie, 1987). The Teacher Rating Instrument of Proactive and Reactive Aggression was designed to measure how children process information regarding aggressive behavior. Reactive aggression includes aggressive behaviors in which children react to provocation, measured by statements such as "Child angry at teasing/threats." Proactive aggression includes aggressive behaviors that are initiated by the child not in response to others actions and includes items such as "Child threatens to get his way." Three statements reflecting each type of aggression are included in the instrument, each of which teachers are asked to rate on a 5-point scale from 1 (*Never)* to 5 (*Very Often)*. The range is 3 to 15 for each type of aggression, with higher scores indicating more aggression.

Teacher's Report Form. (Achenbach System of Empirically Based Assessment 1991). The Teacher's Report Form (TRF) uses the same constructs as the CBCL to evaluate a child's behavior problems. The TRF is different in that it is completed by the child's teacher, rather than a parent, and it includes some items specifically related to behaviors displayed in school. As with the CBCL, two versions of the form have been developed: one for children aged 11/2 to 5 and another for those aged 6 to 18. In this wave of data collection, the version for children aged 6 to 18 was used. Each item on the Problem Section of the TRF contains a statement about a child's behavior. The teacher selects the response that assesses how well each statement describes the child, either currently or within the previous two months. Response choices include: "Not True" (0), "Somewhat or Sometimes True" (1), and "Very True or Often True" (2). For this report, we present Internalizing, Externalizing, and Total Problems T scores as well as the Attention Problems syndrome score, which has a normative mean of 50 and standard deviation of 10.

Vineland Screener. (Sparrow, Carter, & Cicchetti, 1993). We used the daily-living skills domain of the Vineland Screener, a shortened version of the Vineland Adaptive Behavior Scale The scale is administered via a structured interview with the child's caregiver in order to determine the frequency with which the child typically performs a given behavior. For children aged 5 to 6, skills assessed include basic eating and drinking, dressing, toileting, hygiene, housekeeping, time and money concepts, telephone use, and basic safety. Scores were categorized using the classifications suggested in the VABS manual (Sparrow, Balla, & Cicchetti, 1984): Low (< 70), Moderately Low (70 to 84), or Adequate to High (> 84).

Woodcock-Johnson III Tests of Cognitive Abilities. (Woodcock, McGrew, & Mather, 2001). Four subtests were used from the Woodcock Johnson III Tests of Cognitive Abilities. *Letter-Word Identification* is a basic reading skill involving naming letters and reading words aloud from a list. *Calculation* is a test of math achievement measuring the ability to perform arithmetic computation with paper and pencil. *Passage Comprehension* is a measure of reading comprehension in which the individual has to orally supply the missing word removed from each sentence or very brief paragraph. *Applied Problems* is a test of math reasoning requiring the individual to solve oral word-problems. Standardized scores are based on a mean of 100 with a standard deviation of 15.

Derived Variables

Risk for Physical Disability. Risk for physical disability was determined based upon either the caregiver or teacher report. A child was considered at risk for a physical impairment if the caregiver reported having been told that his or her child had a hearing impairment, visual impairment (including blindness), orthopedic impairment, or multiple disabilities at any point over the course of the study. A child was also considered to be at risk for a physical disability if the teacher reported an Individualized Education Plan (IEP) classification due to visual, hearing, orthopedic, or other physical disability.

Risk for Cognitive Disability. Risk for a cognitive disability was determined to include any child with a score at the five year follow-ups of 2 standard deviations below the mean on the Preschool Language Scales (Zimmerman, Steiner, & Pond, 1992) or the Kaufman Brief Intelligence Test or K-BIT (Kaufman & Kaufman, 1990).

Risk for Emotional/Behavioral Problem. Risk for an emotional or behavioral problem was determined to include any child with a score greater than 63 according to either caregiver or teacher report on the Total Problems, Externalizing or Externalizing Scales of the Child Behavior Checklist (Achenbach, 1991)

Serious Chronic Health Condition. Children were characterized as having a serious chronic health condition if the caregiver reported that they had received any of the following diagnoses: AIDS, asthma, anemia, arthritis/joint problems, brain tumor, cerebral palsy, chronic heart condition, diabetes, eczema/other skin disease, epilepsy/fits/convulsions, fetal alcohol syndrome, hernia, high blood pressure, birth defect (e.g., cleft palate), other blood disorder, other respiratory problems, persistent bowel problems, physical deformities, repeated ear infections, severe allergies, sickle cell anemia, or Spina Bifida.

Need for Mental Health Services (Caregivers). Caregivers were determined to be "in need of mental health services" when they met any one of four criteria: (1) caregiver self-reported need for "a lot" or "some" help for a mental health problem, (2) caseworker reported a caregiver's need for mental health services, (3) self-reported scores were within the clinical range on either the Dysthymia and Anhedonia scales of the CIDI-SF, or (4) a score on the Mental Health scale of the SF-12 exceeded 1.5 standard deviations above the norm ($t \geq 65$).

Need for Mental Health Services (Children). Children were defined as "in need of mental health services" if either (1) a caregiver reported an elevated score (>1.5 standard deviations above the mean) on the CBCL; or (2) a teacher reported an elevated score on the Total Problems, Internalizing or Externalizing subscales of the TRF.

Need for Special Education (Children). Children were considered to be in need of a referral for special education services if they met any of the four following criteria: (1) Total Problem, Internalizing or Externalizing t-scores were greater than 65 on either the Child Behavior Checklist or Teacher Report Form, (2) an overall score on the Kaufman Brief Intelligence Test was more than 2 standard deviations below the mean, (3) an overall score on the Preschool Language Scale was more than 2 standard deviations below the mean, or (4) a score on the Vineland Screener was more than 2 standard deviations below the mean.

Need for Substance Abuse Services (Caregivers). Caregivers were determined to be in need of substance abuse services when they met any one of 3 criteria: (1) caregiver self-reported a need for "a lot" or "some" help for an alcohol or drug problem, (2) caseworker reported caregiver had a need for alcohol or drug abuse services, or (3) caregiver scored within the clinical range on either the Alcohol Dependence or Drug Dependence scales of the CIDI-SF.

Specialty Outpatient Mental Health Services. This category refers to services received from a private mental health clinician (i.e., psychiatrist, psychologist, social worker, or psychiatric nurse not working within a community health center), a community mental health center, a therapeutic nursery at a mental health or community health center (for 5-year-olds only), or in-home counseling or crisis services.

Any Outpatient Mental Health Service. This category includes use of specialty outpatient services, school-based mental health services (e.g., services from a school guidance counselor, social worker, or psychologist), and mental health services performed by a family doctor.

Appendix B. Exhibits of Results of 5- to 6-Year Follow-Up for Children Aged 1 to 4 at Baseline

This appendix contains tables that provide preliminary results of the Wave 5 follow-up for a different age group of NSCAW children: young children who were aged 1 to 4 years old when they were involved in an investigation of child maltreatment by child welfare system (CWS) services. The Wave 5 young child follow-up was conducted March–December 2006, or 5 to 6 years after the index investigation. It included the 1,120 children in the child protective services sample component who met the age criteria from 92 child welfare agencies nationwide; 902 children or their caregiver participated at this 6-year follow-up and their data are included in the following exhibits. The data collection methods were identical to those that were reported for the infant sample, with the exception of a few measures that differed on the basis of appropriateness for the age group studied. Complete information about the NSCAW sampling, instrumentation, data collection, weighting and variance estimation, and data availability can be found in other documents (U.S. Department of Health and Human Services, 2005b; U.S. Department of Health and Human Services, 2006b).

Scope of These Exhibits

The research questions addressed by the young child exhibits were essentially identical to those of the infant sample:

- Who are children who have had contact with the CWS during young childhood? What types of maltreatment did they experience? What risks did they face? What environments are these children living in 5 years later.
- How well are these children doing in terms of their physical, psychosocial, cognitive, peer, and academic development? How does this development compare to other children?
- How stable are the children's living situations? Are they now living in permanent homes?
- What services do these children, caregivers and families need? What have they received?

For the most part, these exhibits parallel the exhibits presented in the preceding report on the infant sample, with exhibits with the same number generally including parallel analyses. Exhibit B. 1-1 presents basic information on the difference between the Wave 5 infant and young child tables. The first set (Exhibits 1-1 through 1-4) present information on the background characteristics of the child, caregiver and maltreatment characteristics of the young child population. The second set (Exhibits 2-1 through 2-14) present information on young children's well-being and development. The third set (Exhibits 3-1 through 3-8) concerns the permanency of children's living situation: information on out-of-home placements, termination of parental rights and adoption. The final set (Exhibits 4-1 through 4-7) details the health, mental health, education, child welfare and family support services provided.

As with the infant sample, many of the results in these exhibits are presented by a standard set of covariates: child sex, child race/ethnicity group, child placement setting at Wave 5, and the presence or absence of each of three different types of disability (physical, cognitive and emotional/behavioral). In addition, analyses also broke down results by a range of different maltreatment and maltreatment severity variables, but these were only presented in exhibits when they were statistically significant, to save space. Standard statistical tests (Pearson's χ^2, t, F) adapted for complex samples were performed to identify statistically significant differences by group.

Although children who were between 1 and 4 years old at baseline look similar in many areas to children that were infants at baseline, there were some important differences between the groups. For example, at the time of the index report many of the sociodemographics characteristics of both groups were similar, but the description of the case provided by the caseworker showed more risk factors (e.g., primary caregiver alcohol and drug abuse, mental health problems, arrest history, poor parenting skills) among the infants than the young children. Consistently, infants (38.7%) were more likely to be substantiated than young children (21.8%). In terms of type of index maltreatment, young children were more likely to have been reported for physical abuse (27.8%), while infants were more likely to be reported for failure to provide (34.9%).

By Wave 5, the majority of children who were infants at baseline were 5 and 6 years old, 72.9% were in kindergarten and some were in first grade. Among those who were young children at baseline, the majority were between 7 and 9 years old, in 2nd to 4th grade.

In terms of physical health, children who were infants and young children at the time of the index investigation appear to be in general in good health and similar proportions (about a fifth) have a chronic health problem.

Children who were 1 to 4 years old (3.2%) at baseline had lower rates of cognitive disability at Wave 5 than those who were infants (13.0%). Consistently, those who were young children at baseline had a higher standing relative to their age group on a cognitive functioning test than those who were infants at baseline. Both groups looked similar on social skills, with around a fifth having fewer social skills than expected for their age. Those who were young children at baseline, however, were slightly more likely to have emotional/behavioral problems (36.8% vs. 2 8.9%). According to caregivers' reports, young children (12.5%) were more likely to be in the borderline/clinical range for internalizing problems than those who were infants (5.5%). According to teachers' reports, those who were young children appeared to have more behavioral problems in all areas than those who were infants at baseline (Total: 13.7% vs. 7.9%; Internalizing: 22.0% vs. 7.6%; Externalizing: 13.7% vs. 8.8%, respectively).

A clear area of differences between these groups was placement and adoption. Infants (37.4%) were more likely to be placed out of home than young children (25.0%). As expected, more of those who were infants at baseline experienced termination of parental rights and adoption (19.6% with TPR and 17.0% adopted) than those who were young children (13.1% with TPR and only 6.0% adopted). Those who were older at baseline were not only less likely to be adopted, but also the mean time from first placement to adoption finalization took almost 6 months longer than for those who were infants at baseline (mean number of days: 848 vs. 681).

In terms of preventive services, both groups were likely to receive services and almost all of them were up to date with immunizations, a finding consistent with the majority of them being in the school system which requires immunizations. The use of emergency services was also similar for both groups (about a quarter used the emergency room or urgent care for an injury or illness since the last interview). Both groups had somewhat similar rates of use of outpatient mental health services (less than a fifth for each group), but children who were young children at baseline were more likely to be receiving school-based services than those who were infants (19.8% vs. 10.8%), which is expectable given that they had spent more time in the school system and had more time to be identified as in need. Consistently, those who were young children were more likely to be using psychotropic medication (16.0%) and to have an Individualized Educational Plan (IEP, 37.2%) than those who were infants (psychotropic medication: 6.4%, IEP: 22.6%).

Child welfare and other family services were less likely to be received by those who were young children compared to those who were infants. Thus, among the small percentage that still had contact with CWS at Wave 5 (114 young children and 129 infants), only 7.6% of young children had any CWS service compared to 68.4% of infants. Caregivers of those who were infants at baseline received more family based services (55.9%) and parenting support services (55.6%) than caregivers of those who were young children at baseline (family based services: 5.3%; parenting support services: 5.4%). Importantly, although caseworkers at baseline identified more mental health and substance abuse problems among caregivers of infants than young children, both groups of caregivers had somewhat similar rate of mental health needs at Wave 5 (28.1% among caregivers of those who were young children at baseline, and 26.5% among those who were infants). Nevertheless only a small percentage at each group had received mental health services at Wave 5 (15.4% among caregivers of those who were young children at baseline, and 11.6% among those who were infants).

Exhibit B.1-1. Comparison of Wave 5 Infant and Young Child Samples

	Infant Sample	Young Child Sample
N	962	921
Child age range at baseline (in years)	0 to 1 year	1 to 4 years
Period of data collection	09/2005 to 02/2006	03/2006 to 12/2006
Mean time to follow-up	5.5 years	5.9 years
Child age range at follow-up (in years)	4 to 7 years	6 to 10 years

Exhibit B.1-2. Child Characteristics Young Child Population at Wave 5

Child Characteristic	Total % (SE) (N_{min} = 895)	In Home: Biological Parent (N_{min} = 600)	In Home: Adoptive Parent (N_{min} = 105)	In Home: Kin and Other (N_{min} = 144)	Out of Home (N_{min} = 46)
Total	100	75.11 (2.7)	5.3 (1.2)	15.8 (2.1)	3.8 (1.1)
Child's sex					
Male	51.4 (3.3)	53.9 (3.8)	58.5 (9.5)	35.3 (7.7)	60.0 (13.2)
Female	48.6(3.3)	46.1 (3.8)	41.5 (9.5)	64.7 (7.7)	40.0 (13.2)
Child's age*					
6	12.9 (2.0)	13.7 (2.4)	19.3 (5.8)	7.3 (2.6)	9.9 (4.0)
7	34.2 (2.6)	31.5 (3.2)	57.2 (7.9)	38.9 (7.1)	36.2 (13.2)
8	31.1 (3.0)	31.8 (3.2)	17.6 (6.6)	29.3 (7.6)	44.7 (15.2)
9	21.6 (2.8)	22.7 (3.2)	5.8 (2.4)	24.5 (8.2)	9.2 (4.5)
10	0.2 (0.2)	0.3 (0.2)	0.0 (0.0)	0.0 (0.0)	0.0 (0.0)
Child's race/ethnicity					
Black Non-Hispanic	29.6 (3.4)	27.8 (4.1)	37.5 (8.5)	37.2 (7.3)	21.4 (9.1)
White Non-Hispanic	45.1 (4.5)	47.5 (5.4)	42.0 (7.5)	32.9 (6.7)	52.5 (14.1)
Hispanic	18.5 (2.9)	18.5 (3.5)	16.2 (8.4)	20.4 (8.7)	14.0 (8.7)
Other	6.8 (1.8)	6.2 (2.1)	4.3 (2.2)	9.5 (4.8)	12.2 (10.9)
Urban at baseline*					
Yes	71.7 (6.3)	68.1 (6.9)	93.5 (3.3)	78.4 (7.8)	84.0 (9.3)
Grade in school					
Not in school	0.0 (0.0)	0.1 (0.1)	0.0 (0.0)	0.0 (0.0)	0.0 (0.0)
Preschool/other ungraded setting	0.4 (0.4)	0.0 (0.0)	6.8 (6.6)	0.0(0.0)	0.0 (0.0)
Kindergarten	6.3 (1.3)	5.3 (1.0)	11.0 (5.7)	10.3 (4.9)	3.9 (2.3)
First grade	28.6 (2.9)	28.7 (3.2)	50.3 (10.9)	21.6 (5.4)	26.3 (12.7)
Second grade	28.0 (2.6)	27.6 (3.2)	18.8 (5.8)	36.0 (7.4)	15.7 (5.0)
Third grade	31.4 (3.4)	34.0 (4.1)	11.0 (4.3)	20.8 (6.7)	51.1 (14.6)
Fourth grade	5.2 (1.8)	4.3 (1.8)	2.1 (1.4)	11.4 (7.7)	3.0 (2.7)

Note: All analyses are on weighted data; Ns are unweighted. Pearson χ^2 tests for cluster samples were used for initial significance tests. Asterisks denote statistical significance of differences across setting types for each covariate (*$p < .05$).

Exhibit B.1-3. Caregiver and Household Characteristics Young Child Population at Wave 5

Caregiver Characteristic	Total % (N_{min} = 853)	In Home: Biological Parent (N_{min} = 577)	In Home: Adoptive Parent (N_{min} = 100)	In Home: Other (N_{min} = 134)	Out of Home (N_{min} = 42)
Caregiver's sex*					
Male	14.1 (2.9)	17.5 (3.6)	3.3 (2.0)	4.3 (2.0)	1.3(1.1)
Female	86.0 (2.9)	82.6 (3.6)	96.7 (2.0)	95.7 (2.0)	98.7(1.1)
Caregiver's age***					
< 25	5.5 (1.6)	7.3 (2.2)	0.2 (0.2)	0.1 (0.1)	0.0(0.0)
25–34	51.9 (3.9)	65.9 (4.1)	12.9 (4.4)	9.5 (3.4)	3.2(2.0)
35–44	21.2 (2.8)	21.9 (3.2)	26.1 (7.5)	14.3 (5.2)	30.1(13.4)
45–54	16.0 (2.4)	4.6 (1.3)	37.7 (8.5)	56.3 (7.0)	45.3(15.1)
> 54	5.4 (1.0)	0.4 (0.3)	23.2 (9.1)	19.8 (5.4)	21.3(9.0)
Caregiver's race/ethnicity					
Black	23.6 (3.8)	22.1 (4.0)	19.9 (7.5)	30.8 (8.0)	30.9(13.4)
White	51.4 (4.2)	54.7 (4.9)	59.4 (9.9)	30.5 (5.7)	60.1(13.8)
Hispanic	16.8 (2.8)	16.5 (3.2)	13.8 (7.9)	22.0 (8.9)	4.6(2.7)
Other	8.2 (2.1)	6.7 (2.1)	6.9 (3.4)	16.8 (6.6)	4.4(2.7)
Caregiver's education**					
Less than high school	20.6 (2.6)	21.9 (3.2)	2.7 (1.8)	22.5 (7.2)	12.5(7.9)
High school	50.0 (3.1)	50.6 (4.2)	42.2 (8.3)	47.8 (8.4)	57.8(13.8)
More than high school	29.3(3.6)	27.4 (4.6)	55.1 (8.5)	29.7 (7.7)	29.7(11.8)
% of federal poverty level***					
< 50%	13.5 (2.2)	17.0 (2.8)	0.2 (0.2)	3.0 (1.4)	0.7(0.8)
50–< 100%	26.6 (2.5)	29.6 (3.3)	5.3 (3.1)	20.0 (5.9)	22.2(13.6)
100–200%	28.8 (3.0)	28.1 (3.1)	34.1 (11.4)	28.1 (5.7)	37.3 (17.8)
> 200%	31.1 (3.0)	25.3 (3.2)	60.4 (10.7)	48.8 (8.2)	39.7 (15.7)
Caregiver's employment status*					
Work full time	42.4 (3.4)	43.7 (4.0)	47.3 (8.4)	37.0 (8.8)	32.2 (14.5)
Work part time	17.0 (2.5)	19.0 (3.0)	10.9 (4.2)	11.9 (5.6)	6.2 (2.4)
Unemployed, looking for work	8.5 (1.5)	9.9 (1.9)	1.1 (0.7)	5.3 (3.5)	3.6 (2.3)
Doesn't work	31.1 (3.3)	26.3 (3.2)	40.4 (8.2)	45.0 (9.4)	55.4 (14.5)
Other	1.0 (0.4)	1.1 (0.4)	0.4 (0.4)	0.8 (0.5)	2.6 (2.2)
Caregiver's marital status***					
Married	43.9 (3.1)	36.5 (3.9)	77.5 (7.9)	66.2 (6.9)	50.9 (14.6)
Separated/divorced/widowed	26.5 (2.7)	26.4 (3.3)	19.2 (7.6)	24.7 (6.6)	45.6 (15.0)
Never married	29.7 (3.9)	37.1 (4.8)	3.4 (1.5)	9.1 (4.0)	3.6 (2.0)
Number of children in home***					
1	17.2 (2.6)	17.5 (3.0)	28.4 (9.2)	10.5 (3.5)	24.1 (9.7)
2	36.9 (3.1)	40.4 (3.3)	19.0 (5.2)	33.7 (9.7)	5.4 (2.7)
3	25.2 (3.0)	25.1 (3.2)	8.4 (3.5)	32.8 (9.0)	19.9 (9.2)
4	12.0 (2.5)	11.5 (2.3)	26.9 (8.7)	10.9 (5.0)	5.5 (3.0)
5 or more	8.7 (1.3)	5.5 (0.9)	17.4 (6.6)	12.2 (5.5)	45.1 (13.5)
Number of adults in home*					
1	32.5 (3.0)	37.7 (3.9)	19.5 (7.2)	15.2 (4.0)	20.1 (7.1)
2	46.9 (3.5)	45.9 (4.2)	62.1 (7.6)	46.8 (9.3)	46.2 (15.1)
3	14.0 (2.3)	11.0 (2.4)	15.2 (6.6)	23.1 (8.7)	33.3 (17.7)
4 or more	6.6 (2.1)	5.4 (2.1)	3.3 (1.4)	14.8 (7.1)	0.3 (0.4)

Note: All analyses are on weighted data; Ns are unweighted. Pearson χ^2 tests for cluster samples were used to test statistical significance. Asterisks denote statistical significance of differences across setting types for each covariate (*$p < .05$, **$p < .01$, ***$p < .001$).

Exhibit B.1-4. Caseworker Report on Maltreatment and Risk at Baseline Young Child Population at Wave 5

	N	% (SE)
Most serious maltreatment type	**827**	
Physical abuse		27.8 (3.3)
Sexual abuse		6.1 (1.3)
Failure to provide		20.0 (2.6)
Failure to supervise/abandonment		37.7 (3.5)
Emotional, moral/legal, educational maltreatment		4.3 (2.1)
Other		4.1 (1.5)
CWS outcome	835	
Substantiated		21.8 (2.6)
Indicated		9.3 (2.2)
Unsubstantiated		52.7 (4.8)
High risk		3.1 (1.8)
Medium risk		3.2 (1.4)
Low risk		9.9 (3.2)
Level of harm	838	
None		44.3 (4.2)
Mild		28.2 (3.4)
Moderate		19.2 (2.1)
Severe		8.4 (1.6)
Level of risk	733	
None		31.8 (4.2)
Mild		32.0 (3.7)
Moderate		24.6 (2.8)
Severe		11.6 (1.9)
Risk factors		
Prior reports of child maltreatment	828	38.2 (3.3)
Prior investigation of child maltreatment	366	94.5 (1.7)
Prior incident of substantiated child maltreatment	314	50.9 (5.5)
Prior child welfare service history	791	26.4 (3.6)
Child has major special needs or behavioral problems	825	9.5 (1.2)
Active alcohol abuse by primary caregiver	787	8.2 (1.6)
Active alcohol abuse by secondary caregiver	583	11.1 (2.0)
Active drug abuse by primary caregiver	785	9.2 (1.7)
Active drug abuse by secondary caregiver	571	7.0 (1.1)
Primary caregiver has serious mental health problem	794	14.2 (2.0)
Primary caregiver has recent history of arrests	768	13.4 (2.7)
Primary caregiver has intellectual or cognitive impairments	813	5.4 (1.2)
Primary caregiver has physical impairments	821	2.5 (0.8)
Primary caregiver has poor parenting skills	817	31.8 (3.4)
Parent has unreal expectations of child	806	17.5 (3.0)
History of domestic violence against caregiver	775	29.3 (3.1)
Active domestic violence against caregiver	807	15.2 (2.2)
Primary caregiver uses inappropriate or excessive discipline	821	7.3 (2.2)
Secondary caregiver uses inappropriate or excessive discipline	598	6.9 (1.5)
History of abuse or neglect of primary caregiver	698	22.2 (3.5)

Note: Only cases with 5- to 6-year follow-up data analyzed. Percentages and standard errors are based on an analysis of weighted data. Ns are unweighted.

Exhibit B.2-1. Caregiver Aggression and Neglect Prevalence by Case Characteristics Young Child Population at Wave 5

Case Characteristic	*N* (Min)	Nonviolent Discipline % (SE)	Psychological Aggression % (SE)	Minor Assault/ Corporal Punishment % (SE)	Severe Physical Assault % (SE)	Very Severe Assault % (SE)	Neglect % (SE)
Total	837	98.0 (0.8)	84.5 (2.3)	64.1 (3.5)	5.4 (1.6)	0.7 (0.3)	19.7 (2.6)
Sex							
Male	445	98.7 (0.8)	87.1 (3.1)	65.3 (5.2)	3.4 (1.1)	1.0 (0.4)	16.2 (2.9)
Female	392	97.4 (1.4)	81.7 (4.0)	62.7 (4.9)	7.5 (3.0)	0.6 (0.4)	23.4 (4.3)
Race/ethnicity					*		
Black	277	98.7 (1.3)	84.5 (5.4)	69.9 (5.7)	9.4 (3.4)	1.1 (0.8)	21.2 (5.2)
White	368	97.9 (1.5)	85.1 (2.4)	66.6 (3.7)	3.3 (1.5)	0.5 (0.3)	22.0 (3.4)
Hispanic	136	97.2 (1.7)	83.4 (7.6)	51.5 (9.7)	3.3 (1.8)	0.5 (0.4)	12.1 (3.6)
Other	54	98.7 (1.3)	81.6 (8.9)	53.2 (13.6)	8.4 (5.8)	1.4 (1.4)	20.5 (10.8)
Ever in out-of-home placement							*
Yes	278	97.8 (1.7)	85.6 (3.8)	60.8 (7.0)	4.9 (2.3)	0.9 (0.7)	11.7 (3.4)
No	525	98.0 (1.0)	84.2 (2.6)	64.5 (3.8)	5.7 (1.8)	0.7 (0.4)	22.3 (2.9)
Child setting In home, biological parent							*
Ever out of home	108	98.8 (1.2)	85.4 (2.4)	67.6 (10.4)	2.8 (1.5)	2.5 (1.9)	13.8 (4.7)
Never out of home	456	97.8 (1.1)	83.9 (3.0)	64.0 (3.9)	4.9 (1.5)	0.7 (0.4)	22.7[a](2.8)
In home, adoptive parent	102	93.2 (6.6)	78.3 (8.7)	58.2 (8.9)	2.1 (1.6)	0.1 (0.1)	5.9[b](3.2)
In home, kin, or other caregiver	142	99.7 (0.2)	87.5 (4.0)	62.4 (8.7)	10.7 (7.9)	0.5 (0.5)	15.7 (7.7)
Physical abuse at baseline			*				
Yes	233	99.1 (0.7)	90.1 (3.3)	72.0 (7.0)	4.5 (2.0)	0.8 (0.6)	21.0 (5.6)
No	557	97.3 (1.3)	81.1 (2.9)	58.6 (3.8)	5.9 (2.1)	0.5 (0.2)	19.1 (3.1)
Failure to provide at baseline				**			
Yes	276	96.2 (2.4)	72.8 (7.1)	46.3 (6.6)	2.5 (1.0)	1.0 (0.8)	11.6 (3.0)
No	514	97.6 (0.7)	89.0 (2.7)	69.9 (4.1)	6.5 (2.3)	0.5 (0.3)	12.0 (3.8)
Failure to supervise at baseline							
Yes	395	98.4 (1.4)	85.8 (4.0)	64.1 (5.7)	4.4 (1.5)	0.5 (0.3)	17.5 (3.3)
No	395	98.0 (1.0)	83.1 (2.5)	62.7 4.9)	6.2 (2.8)	0.7 (0.5)	22.0 (3.9)

Note: Based on caregiver self-report using Conflict Tactics Scale–Parent-Child version. All analyses are on weighted data; *Ns* are unweighted. Pearson χ^2 tests for cluster samples were used to test statistical significance. Statistical significance is noted by asterisks in the column above the statistically significant result (*$p < .05$, **$p < .01$). The percentages with different superscripts are significantly different from each other ($\alpha = .05$).

Exhibit B.2-2. Health of Children Young Child Population at Wave 5

Child Characteristic	*N* (Min)	In Good Health[1] % (SE)	Caregiver Reports Serious Chronic Health Problem[2] % (SE)
Total	896	96.9 (.85)	23.1 (2.7)
Sex			
Male	476	97.8 (1.2)	22.9 (4.3)
Female	422	96.3 (1.4)	23.3 (3.0)
Race/ethnicity			
Black	301	96.6 (1.5)	19.3 (3.9)
White	387	96.7 (1.1)	31.5 (3.8)
Hispanic	149	96.4 (3.0)	16.0 (5.2)
Other	59	100.0 (0.0)	5.3 (2.6)
Child setting			
In home, biological parents	601	96.6 (1.0)	15.9 (2.4)
In home, adoptive parents	105	92.0 (6.6)	30.0 (9.5)
In home, kin, or other caregiver	144	100.0 (0.3)	20.1 (6.6)
Out of home	48	97.8 (1.6)	11.0 (5.3)

Note: All analyses are on weighted data; Ns are unweighted. Pearson χ^2 tests for cluster samples were used for initial significance tests.

[1] "Good health" was defined as those children whose caregivers reported that there were in "good, very good, or excellent" health.

[2] "Serious chronic health condition" was defined here as one of a number of caregiver-reported diagnoses, as detailed in Appendix A.

Exhibit B.2-3. Most Common Chronic Health Conditions and Injuries or Accidents Young Child Population at Wave 5

Health Condition	% (SE)
Chronic health problem	
Asthma	9.8(1.7)
Severe allergies	3.8(1.0)
Other respiratory condition	1.2(0.5)
Eczema/other skin disorder	1.9(0.7)
Repeated ear infections	1.2(0.5)
Serious injury, accident, or poisoning[1]	
Cuts, scrapes, puncture	3.1(0.9)
Broken bone, dislocated joint	0.3(0.1)
Other	3.6(1.3)

Note: N = 897. All analyses are on weighted data; *N*s are unweighted.

[1] Caregivers were asked to report upon serious accidents and injuries only since the last interview.

Exhibit B.2-4. Child Risk for Cognitive, Emotional/Behavioral, and Physical Disabilities Young Child Population at Wave 5

Child Characteristic	*N* (Min)	Risk for Cognitive Disability % (SE)	Risk for Emotional/ Behavioral Problem % (SE)	Risk for Physical Disability % (SE)
Total	865	3.2 (0.9)	36.8 (3.6)	4.9 (1.4)
Sex				
Male	456	1.3 (0.5)	37.8 (5.0)	3.7 (1.2)
Female	411	5.1 (1.9)	35.7 (3.8)	6.2 (2.7)
Race/ethnicity				
Black	288	5.8 (2.6)	32.0 (5.8)	2.1 (1.3)
White	379	2.6 (1.2)	41.2 (4.6)	5.2 (1.2)
Hispanic	139	1.6 (0.9)	34.1 (9.7)	9.2 (7.0)
Other	59	0.1 (0.1)	34.7 (15.1)	4.0 (5.2)
Child setting				
In home, biological parents	587	2.8 (1.0)	36.3 (4.6)	3.9 (1.8)
In home, adoptive parents	98	2.3 (1.4)	51.6 (8.1)	11.3 (6.7)
In home, kin, or other caregiver	136	5.7 (3.7)	34.8 (7.4)	8.6 (3.6)
Out of home	46	1.1 (0.8)	32.2 (12.4)	1.6 (1.5)
Physical maltreatment at baseline				
Yes	246	3.0 (1.8)	44.2 (6.5)	5.2 (2.0)
No	591	3.4 (1.2)	33.3 (3.8)	5.2 (2.2)
Clinically significant Vineland score			*	
Yes	20	48.1 (15.8)	18.5 (4.7)	30.5 (13.5)
No	81	51.9 (15.8)	81.5 (4.7)	69.5 (13.5)

Note: See Appendix A for definitions of risk of cognitive disability, emotional/behavioral problem, and physical disability. All analyses are on weighted data; *Ns* are unweighted. Pearson χ^2 tests for cluster samples were used to test statistical significance. Statistical significance is noted by asterisks in the column above the statistically significant result (*$p < .05$).

Exhibit B.2-5. Caregiver Report of Children's Behavior Problems Young Child Population at Wave 5

Child Characteristic	*N*	In Clinical Range		
		Total Score % (SE)	Internalizing Score % (SE)	Externalizing Score % (SE)
Total	897	20.3 (2.7)	12.5 (2.0)	15.4 (1.9)
Sex				
Male	476	22.7 (3.6)	15.4 (3.6)	14.2 (2.4)
Female	421	17.8 (2.8)	9.4 (1.8)	16.7 (2.6)
Race/ethnicity		*		
Black	301	15.5 (3.4)	8.1 (2.4)	15.2 (3.5)
White	387	27.5 (4.2)	15.6 (3.3)	19.9 (3.3)
Hispanic	148	14.3 (4.7)	13.4 (7.5)	8.4 (3.5)
Other	59	12.2 (5.9)	9.3 (5.9)	6.8 (3.5)
Child setting				
In home, biological parents	600	17.7 (2.9)	11.8 (2.7)	12.9 (2.0)
In home, adoptive parents	105	35.1 (9.9)	21.3 (8.6)	35.0 (9.9)
In home, kin, or other caregiver	144	26.7 (5.6)	15.5 (5.0)	17.7 (4.8)
Out of home	48	25.9 (10.8)	1.9 (1.5)	29.2 (12.0)
Chronic health condition		***		*
Yes	177	44.0 (6.4)	22.4 (5.9)	28.1 (6.5)
No	719	15.6 (2.3)	10.5 (2.5)	12.9 (1.8)
Physical disability				
Yes	62	34.6 (13.9)	23.1 (11.5)	27.8 (12.2)
No	835	19.5 (2.8)	11.8 (2.2)	14.7 (1.8)
Cognitive disability				
Yes	38	38.5 (15.6)	16.3 (14.2)	30.9 (14.2)
No	826	19.7 (2.8)	12.5 (2.1)	14.8 (2.0)
Failure to provide at baseline			**	*
Yes	293	15.6 (4.7)	6.6 (1.6)	8.8 (2.3)
No	546	23.0 (3.5)	15.5 (3.3)	18.7 (2.6)

Note: Instrument used is the Child Behavior Checklist. All analyses are on weighted data; *N*s are unweighted. Pearson $\chi 2$ tests for cluster samples were used to test statistical significance. Statistical significance is noted by asterisks in the column above the statistically significant result (*$p < .05$, **$p < .01$, ***$p < .001$).

Exhibit B.2-6. Teacher Report of Children's Behavior Problems Young Child Population at Wave 5

Child Characteristic	*N* (Min)	In Clinical Range		
		Total Score % (SE)	Internalizing Score % (SE)	Externalizing Score % (SE)
Total	558	13.7 (2.8)	22.0 (3.4)	13.7 (2.9)
Sex				
Male	289	11.4 (3.5)	23.7 (4.9)	11.5 (3.4)
Female	269	16.2 (4.2)	20.0 (4.7)	16.0 (4.1)
Race/ethnicity		*		
Black	172	21.2 (6.6)	20.4 (7.4)	24.5 (6.9)
White	259	9.0 (2.3)	22.2 (4.8)	7.9 (2.0)
Hispanic	88	20.3 (10.6)	29.0 (11.4)	6.8 (4.2)
Other	38	0.7 (0.6)	2.3 (1.3)	31.6 (19.3)
Child setting				
In home, biological parents	386	14.1 (3.3)	24.5 (4.6)	13.9 (3.7)
In home, adoptive parents	59	19.4 (11.9)	11.2 (5.3)	23.5 (11.7)
In home, kin, or other caregiver	86	11.9 (4.9)	16.0 (8.1)	11.4 (5.0)
Out of home	27	6.3 (3.6)	6.0 (3.7)	6.9 (3.2)
Chronic health condition			*	
Yes	115	11.2 (4.3)	40.1 (8.8)	10.1 (2.9)
No	442	14.5 (3.4)	18.4 (3.4)	14.7 (3.5)
Physical disability				
Yes	33	34.5 (20.6)	41.6 (22.6)	6.6 (4.0)
No	525	12.3 (2.4)	20.8 (3.6)	14.2 (3.1)
Cognitive disability				
Yes	20	15.0 (9.5)	20.3 (11.8)	7.8 (5.4)
No	525	13.8 (2.9)	22.2 (3.5)	13.8 (3.0)
Neglectful supervision at baseline*				
Yes	258	15.6 (5.4)	27.8 (4.7)	18.0 (5.5)
No	264	12.9 (3.1)	15.7 (3.6)	10.5 (2.7)

Note: Instrument used is the Teacher Report Form (TRF). All analyses are on weighted data; *Ns* are unweighted. Pearson χ^2 tests for cluster samples were used to test statistical significance. Statistical significance is noted by asterisks in the column above the statistically significant result (*$p < .05$).

Exhibit B.2-7. Teacher Ratings of Attention and Aggressive Behaviors Young Child Population at Wave 5

Child Characteristic	TRF Attention Problems		Proactive Aggression		Reactive Aggression	
	N	Mean (SE)	*N*	Mean (SE)	*N*	Mean (SE)
Total	598	52.4 (0.2)***	553	4.5 (0.2)	553	6.9(0.3)
Sex		*				*
Male	309	51.6 (0.3)	283	4.6 (0.3)	283	7.5(0.4)
Female	289	52.9 (0.4)	270	4.4 (0.2)	270	6.2(0.3)
Race/ethnicity				*		*
Black	188	51.8 (0.4)	176	5.3 (0.4)[a]	176	7.8(0.6)[a]
White	274	52.2 (0.3)	254	4.4 (0.2)[b]	254	7.0(0.4)[a,c]
Hispanic	94	52.5 (1.1)	87	4.0 (0.4)[b]	87	5.8(0.5)[b,d]
Other	41	53.2 (0.8)	35	3.8 (0.3)[b]	35	5.4(0.7)[c,d]
Chronic health conditions						
Yes	130	53.1 (0.6)	122	5.1 (0.5)	122	7.6(0.5)
No	467	52.0 (0.3)	430	4.4 (0.2)	430	6.8(0.3)
Setting						
In home, biological parents	410	52.3 (0.3)	377	4.5 (0.2)	377	7.0(0.3)
In home, adoptive parents	65	51.4 (0.4)	58	4.1 (0.3)	58	6.4(0.8)
In home, kin, or other caregiver	93	52.4 (0.6)	90	4.7 (0.4)	90	6.6(0.7)
Out of home	30	51.3 (0.4)	28	4.8 (0.8)	28	7.1(1.5)
Severity of abuse						
Dangerous acts	37	51.1 (0.5)	35	4.9 (0.8)	35	6.6(1.0)
Marks	45	52.1 (0.7)	38	4.6 (0.6)	38	6.7(0.8)
Hospital < 24 hours	16	52.1 (1.0)	16	4.3 (0.6)	16	6.4(0.4)
Hospital >24 hours	10	51.4 (0.7)	9	4.5 (0.8)	9	6.6(0.9)
Severity of neglect		**		***		*
Mild	125[1,2]	52.2 (0.4)[a]	116[3]	4.4 (0.3)[a]	116	6.6(0.5)[a]
Moderate	79	53.4 (0.6)[a]	69	5.7 (0.4)[b]	69	8.6(0.5)[b]
Serious	54	52.3 (0.4)[a]	53	4.2 (0.4)[a,c]	53	6.2(0.6)[a]
Severe	38	51.6 (0.7)[a]	37	3.9 (0.3)[a,c]	37	7.0(0.9)
Grave	17	58.9 (1.8)[b]	15	3.4 (0.4)[c]	15	8.1(0.3)[b]

Note: Instruments used are the Teacher Report Form (TRF) and the Teacher-Rating Instrument of Proactive and Reactive Aggression. All analyses are on weighted data; *N*s are unweighted. Pearson χ^2 tests for cluster samples were used to test statistical significance. For the total, differences in means were tested against means of the standardization sample. Statistical significance is noted by asterisks in the column above the statistically significant result (*$p < .05$, **$p < .01$, ***$p < .005$). Alphabetic superscripts that are different from one another represent significant differences (α = .05).

[1] The linear trend was significant ($p < .005$).

[2] The quadratic trend was significant ($p < .00$ 1).

[3] The linear trend was significant ($p < .00$ 1).

Exhibit B.2-8 Cognitive Test Scores Young Child Population at Wave 5

Child Characteristic	K-BIT Composite		K-BIT Vocabulary		K-BIT Matrices	
	N	Mean (SE)	*N*	Mean (SE)	*N*	Mean (SE)
Total	867	96.3 (0.8)***	867	93.6 (0.9)***	870	99.6 (1.1)
Sex						
Male	456	97.3 (1.1)	456	94.6 (1.2)	456	100.6 (1.8)
Female	411	95.2 (1.3)	411	92.6 (1.4)	414	98.6 (1.2)
Race/ethnicity		**		***		
Black	288	92.0 (1.8)[a]	288	88.0 (2.4)[a]	288	97.2 (1.9)
White	379	99.1 (1.2)[b]	379	98.5 (1.4)[b]	379	99.9 (1.1)
Hispanic	139	96.2 (3.1)	139	90.1 (2.0)c	142	102.8 (3.7)
Other	59	97.2 (1.6)[b]	59	95.0 (2.0)[b,c]	59	100.0 (2.4)
Chronic health condition						*
Yes	167	93.6 (2.3)	167	93.1 (2.4)	167	95.0 (2.2)
No	697	96.9 (0.8)	697	93.7 (1.0)	700	100.6 (1.2)
Current setting						**
In home, biological parents	587	97.7 (0.9)[a]	587	94.8 (1.0)[a]	589	101.0 (1.3)[a]
In home, adoptive parents	98	93.7 (1.7)[b]	98	94.1 (2.0)	98	94.3 (1.9)[b]
In home, kin, or other caregiver	136	90.9 (2.7)[b]	136	88.6 (2.7)[b]	137	94.6 (2.6)
Out of home	46	94.3 (1.8)	46	91.5 (2.4)	46	98.4 (1.7)
Severity of abuse						*
Dangerous acts	45	101.9 (5.0)	45	95.5 (3.3)	46	107.7 (6.4)[1]
Marks	69	96.1 (3.2)	69	95.4 (4.0)	69	97.7 (3.2)
Hospital < 24 hours	27	92.5 (3.9)	27	92.9 (5.8)	27	93.7 (2.2)[a]
Hospital >24 hours	13	96.3 (5.2)	13	87.7 (4.8)	13	106.1 (5.2)[b]
Severity of neglect		*				*
Mild	171	97.1 (1.4)[a]	171	93.3 (1.7)[a]	171	101.6 (1.4)[a]
Moderate	122	89.6 (1.7)[b]	122	87.8 (1.9)[b]	122	93.5 (1.8)[b]
Serious	76	94.2 (1.9)	76	91.1 (2.2)	76	98.3 (1.6)
Severe	53	95.6 (1.6)[a]	53	93.5 (1.8)[a]	54	98.5 (1.6)[a]
Grave	27	94.7 (2.3)	27	91.7 (2.7)	27	99.3 (1.7)[a]

Note: All analyses are on weighted data; Ns are unweighted. Pearson χ^2 tests for cluster samples were used to test statistical significance. For the total, differences in means were tested against means of the standardization sample. Statistical significance is noted by asterisks in the column above the statistically significant result (*p < .05, **p < .01, ***p < .00 1). Means that have different superscripts are significantly different from each other (α = .05). K-BIT = Kaufman Brief Intelligence Test.

[1] Quadratic trend was significant (p < .05).

Exhibit B.2-9. Early Achievement Test Scores at 6 to 10 Years of Age Young Child Population at Wave 5

Child Characteristic	WJ Letter Identification		WJ Passage Comprehension		WJ Calculation		WJ Applied Problems	
	N	Mean (SE)	*N*	Mean (SE)	*N*	Mean (SE)	*N*	Mean (SE)
Total	862	100.4 (0.9)	852	92.7 (0.8)***	844	99.3 (1.0)	856	99.4 (1.0)
Sex								
Male	453	99.9 (1.3)	449	91.9 (1.3)	446	99.2 (1.5)	450	99.8 (1.5)
Female	409	100.9 (1.3)	403	93.6 (1.1)	398	99.4 (1.2)	406	98.9 (1.5)
Race/ethnicity								
Black	284	98.5 (2.1)	282	90.8 (1.9)	281	98.8 (1.9)	282	95.8 (1.9)
White	379	100.8 (1.6)	375	93.6 (1.2)	367	99.7 (1.2)	377	101.1 (1.7)
Hispanic	138	101.5 (2.5)	135	93.4 (2.4)	136	99.4 (2.3)	137	100.7 (3.5)
Other	59	104.3 (2.9)	58	94.1 (2.5)	58	99.0 (2.6)	58	99.8 (1.8)
Chronic health condition								
Yes	166	95.8 (3.2)	164	90.3 (2.4)	156	98.5 (1.9)	165	95.4 (3.0)
No	693	101.4 (0.9)	685	93.4 (0.9)	685	99.5 (1.1)	688	100.2 (1.1)
Current setting						*		
In home, biological parents	581	101.4 (1.0)	576	93.3 (0.9)	574	99.8 (1.2)[a]	578	100.6 (1.2)[a]
In home, adoptive parents	98	101.1 (1.0)	96	93.8 (2.2)	95	95.4 (2.1)	96	96.6 (2.0)
In home, kin, or other caregiver	137	96.2 (3.5)	136	90.7 (2.4)	133	99.2 (1.7)	137	95.2 (3.1)
Out of home	46	97.7 (4.2)	44	87.6 (4.5)	42	94.2 (2.2)[b]	45	96.4 (1.4)[b]
Severity of abuse		**		*				*
Dangerous acts	44	111.3 (3.4)[a,1]	44	101.0 (2.7)[a,1]	45	106.8 (2.8)	441	109.1 (4.9)[a]
Marks	69	97.2 (3.9)[b]	67	91.6 (3.1)[b]	67	97.4 (2.6)	68	97.7 (4.9)
Hospital < 24 hours	27	96.4 (2.5)[b]	27	89.9 (2.3)[b]	26	96.7 (4.9)	27	91.6 (3.3)[b]
Hospital >24 hours	13	105.5 (9.7)	12	101.1 (7.8)	12	104.8 (6.9)	12	107.1 (8.3)
Severity of neglect								
Mild	169	99.6 (2.2)	167	91.7 (1.6)	166	99.7 (1.9)	169	99.7 (1.8)[a]
Moderate	121	96.6 (1.9)	119	91.0 (1.4)	120	96.3 (2.5)	121	95.5 (2.2)
Serious	75	103.3 (5.1)	74	93.6 (2.0)	74	95.8 (3.0)	74	98.4 (1.6)
Severe	54	96.8 (2.0)	54	89.5 (1.6)	53	99.1 (6.4)	54	93.7 (2.1)[b]
Grave	27	99.4 (2.8)	26	93.2 (3.5)	25	95.1 (2.9)	26	98.8 (2.0)

Note: Instruments used are the Woodcock Johnson III Tests of Achievement (WJ). All analyses are on weighted data; Ns are unweighted. Pearson χ^2 tests for cluster samples were used to test statistical significance. For the Total line, means were tested against means of the standardization sample. Statistical significance is noted by asterisks in the column above the statistically significant result (*p < .05, **p < .0 1). Alphabetic superscripts that are different from one another represent statistically significant differences ($\alpha = .05$).

[1] The quadratic trend was significant ($p < .01$).

Exhibit B.2-10. Number and Percentage Below Grade Level in Different Academic Domains (Teacher Report) Young Child Population at Wave 5

Child Characteristic	Language Arts		Mathematics		Social Studies			Science
	N	% (SE)	*N*	% (SE)	*N*	% (SE)	*N*	% (SE)
Total	520	36.1(4.0)	517	37.2(4.1)	375	19.9(4.0)	377	19.4(4.0)
Sex								*
Male	273	38.3(5.5)	272	38.0(6.5)	195	27.5(6.8)	196	25.0(6.8)
Female	247	33.4(5.5)	245	36.2(5.8)	180	11.2(3.5)	181	12.6(3.7)
Race/ethnicity								
Black	161	38.5(7.7)	159	40.8(8.8)	123	22.6(7.7)	121	20.2(8.4)
White	243	37.0(4.9)	241	41.9(5.7)	164	25.8(6.6)	163	26.6(7.0)
Hispanic	80	27.5(7.5)	80	22.3(7.7)	58	13.3(6.3)	61	13.2(6.1)
Other	35	47.0(19.5)	36	35.6(20.2)	29	0.5(0.4)	31	2.1(1.8)
Chronic health conditions								
Yes	110	48.8(7.9)	107	43.2(8.7)	67	19.9(9.7)	65	20.3(10.2)
No	410	33.0(4.2)	410	35.9(4.5)	308	19.9(4.5)	312	19.3(4.6)
Current setting								
In home, biological parents	352	34.2(4.8)	348	39.6(4.9)	254	20.1(5.0)	255	20.8(5.1)
In home, adoptive parents	56	49.2(14.2)	56	22.8(8.0)	40	46.3(17.4)	43	17.4(8.0)
In home, kin, or other caregiver	87	39.8(9.0)	87	28.3(9.8)	65	7.3(3.4)	64	7.3(3.4)
Out of home	25	43.8(14.3)	26	43.6(14.2)	16	44.7(17.4)	15	42.5(17.8)

Note: All analyses are on weighted data; Ns are unweighted. Pearson χ^2 tests for cluster samples were used to test statistical significance. For the total, differences in means were tested against means of the standardization sample. Statistical significance is noted by asterisks in the column above the statistically significant result (*$p < .05$).

Exhibit B.2-11. Social Competence Ratings by Teacher Young Child Population at Wave 5

Child Characteristic	*N*	SSRS Total Mean (SE)	SSRS Assertion Ratings		
			Fewer Behaviors % (SE)	Average Behaviors % (SE)	More Behaviors % (SE)
Total	553	94.6 (1.3)***	19.5(3.1)	71.7(3.7)	8.8 (2.9)*
Sex					
Male	283	94.5 (2.2)	21.8(4.7)	70.0(5.5)	8.2 (4.1)
Female	270	94.7 (1.3)	17.0(5.0)	73.5(6.1)	9.5 (4.6)
Race/ethnicity		*			
Black	176	97.0 (3.2)	13.1(3.5)	71.7(7.2)	15.2 (7.6)
White	254	93.8 (1.2)[a]	18.1(3.4)	73.8(5.2)	8.1 (4.7)
Hispanic	87	91.4 (4.2)[a]	33.9(12.0)	64.1(12.3)	2.0 (0.7)
Other	35	101.9 (2.2)[b]	6.2(3.3)	85.4(8.8)	8.4 (8.0)
Chronic health condition					
Yes	122	92.6 (1.7)	17.6(4.6)	76.3(5.3)	6.2 (14.1)
No	430	95.0 (1.6)	20.3(3.9)	70.0(4.6)	9.6 (3.6)
Current setting					
In home, biological parents	377	94.7 (1.7)	22.0(4.3)	68.4(4.9)	9.6 (3.7)

Exhibit B.2-11. (Continued)

Child Characteristic	*N*	SSRS Total Mean (SE)	SSRS Assertion Ratings		
			Fewer Behaviors % (SE)	Average Behaviors % (SE)	More Behaviors % (SE)
In home, adoptive parents	58	97.7 (6.5)	14.0(5.6)	70.0(12.5)	16.0 (12.0)
In home, kin, or other caregiver	90	92.9 (2.2)	12.8(3.9)	82.8(4.7)	4.4 (3.0)
Out of home	28	95.3 (3.1)	5.6(3.3)	91.4(4.2)	3.1 (2.8)
Severity of neglect		***			
Mild	116	94.9 (1.5)a [1,2]	17.9(4.9)	76.7(5.7)	5.3 (2.5)
Moderate	69	88.5 (2.3)[c]	20.1(4.9)	71.2(6.3)	8.6 (5.6)
Serious	53	93.4 (2.9)a, [c]	30.4(13.4)	65.9(13.7)	3.7 (2.4)
Severe	37	99.2 (2.4)[a]	7.1(4.4)	89.2(5.7)	3.7 (3.4)
Grave	15	80.7 (2.7)[b]	86.7(11.8)	13.3(11.8)	0.0

Note: Instrument used is the Social Skills Rating System (SSRS). All analyses are on weighted data; *N*s are unweighted. Pearson χ^2 tests for cluster samples were used to test statistical significance. For the total, differences in means were tested against means of the standardization sample. Statistical significance is noted by asterisks in the column above the statistically significant result (*$p < .05$, ***$p < .001$). Means that have different alphabetic superscripts are significantly different from each other ($\alpha = .05$).

[1] Linear trend is significant ($p < .05$).

[2] Quadratic trend is significant ($p < .05$).

Exhibit B.2-12. Additional Social Competence Ratings by Teachers Young Child Population at Wave 5

Child Characteristic	*N*	SSRS Self-Control Ratings			SSRS Cooperation Ratings		
		Fewer % (SE)	Average % (SE)	More % (SE)	Fewer % (SE)	Average % (SE)	More % (SE)
Total	553	21.8 (3.3)	68.4 (3.8)	9.9(2.7)	30.8(3.3)	58.4(3.8)	10.8(2.8)
Sex							
Male	283	18.2 (3.9)	69.2 (5.4)	12.6(4.5)	32.1(5.0)	59.5(5.5)	8.4(4.4)
Female	270	25.8 (5.6)	67.5 (5.7)	6.7(2.6	29.2(4.7)	57.3(5.5)	13.4(3.4)
Race/ethnicity							
Black	176	23.0 (5.7)	63.4 (8.1)	13.5(7.7)	33.4(7.7)	51.5(8.6)	15.1(7.7)
White	254	17.9 (4.4)	76.8 (4.6)	5.2(2.4)	29.6(4.1)	63.0(4.5)	7.3(3.0)
Hispanic	87	31.4 (12.1)	49.7 (12.9)	37.1(6.7)	35.4(11.8)	55.6(11.5)	9.0(3.3)
Other	35	8.8 (4.8)	90.4 (5.0)	0.8(0.6)	13.2(5.4)	59.9(17.6)	26.9(13.6)
Chronic health condition							
Yes	122	20.4 (6.4)	71.2 (6.8)	6.7(3.3)	33.8(6.5)	61.6(6.7)	4.6(2.9)
No	430	22.0 (3.7)	67.1 (4.5)	10.8(3.3)	30.5(3.8)	57.0(4.3)	12.6(3.4)
Current setting							
In home, biological parents	377	18.6 (3.4)	70.6 (4.5)	10.9(3.3)	31.5(4.1)	56.0(4.6)	12.4(3.7)
In home, adoptive parents	58	24.4 (12.7)	43.3 (12.4)	32.4(14.7)	30.0(12.7)	55.5(14.4)	14.6(12.0)
In home, kin, or other caregiver	90	32.3 (10.8)	62.6 (10.6)	1.1(0.6)	30.2(8.1)	65.2(8.3)	4.6(2.1)
Out of home	28	23.7 (12.5)	76.3 (12.5)	0.0	20.1(12.6)	79.9(12.6)	0.0

Note: Instrument used is the Social Skills Rating System (SSRS). All analyses are on weighted data; *N*s are unweighted. Pearson χ^2 tests for cluster samples were used to test statistical significance.

Exhibit B.2-13. Child Social Competence Ratings by Parents Young Child Population at Wave 5

Child Characteristic	*N*	SSRS Total Mean (SE)	SSRS Assertion Ratings		
			Fewer Behaviors % (SE)	Average Behaviors % (SE)	More Behaviors % (SE)
Total	898	93.2(1.0)***	12.1 (2.2)	59.0(3.5)	28.9(3.2)***
Sex			*		
Male	476	94.0(1.6)	5.5 (2.8)	43.9(4.4)	50.6(4.0)
Female	422	92.3(1.4)	19.0 (3.8)	74.9(4.2)	6.0(3.2)
Race/ethnicity					
Black	301	92.4(1.5)	10.3 (2.8)	63.8(4.8)	25.9(4.7)
White	387	92.6(1.5)	10.6 (3.0)	60.6(4.4)	28.8(5.1)
Hispanic	149	94.4(3.9)	22.7 (8.4)	45.9(10.7)	31.3(10.1)
Other	59	96.5(1.8)	1.7 (1.1)	67.3(11.5)	31.0(11.2)
Chronic health conditions		**	**		
Yes	177	86.9(2.3)	16.5 (5.4)	71.6(5.9)	11.9(3.5)
No	720	94.5(1.1)	11.3 (2.5)	56.9(3.8)	31.8(3.7)
Current setting					
In home, biological parents	601	94.1(1.1)[a]	10.6 (2.4)	57.9(4.0)	31.5(3.9)
In home, adoptive parents	105	84.4(3.9)[b]	28.3 (8.9)	57.9(8.0)	13.8(4.8)
In home, kin, or other caregiver	144	92.3(2.6)	15.4 (6.9)	64.6(7.2)	20.0(6.0)
Out of home	48	90.6(3.5)	4.6 (2.1)	58.7(15.3)	36.6(16.1)
Severity of neglect		*			
Mild	175	92.4(1.9)[1]	10.4 (3.6)	57.4(6.6)	32.3(6.2)
Moderate	127	91.0(2.0)[a]	10.6 (5.0)	72.8(6.1)	16.7(5.2)
Serious	80	89.2(3.9)[a]	17.7 (10.2)	68.6(10.7)	13.7(5.0)
Severe	57	98.4(3.1)	5.5 (2.5)	48.8(10.2)	45.6(10.8)
Grave	28	98.0(2.0)[b]	4.7 (2.8)	89.9(6.1)	5.4(4.2)

Note: Instrument used is the Social Skills Rating System (SSRS). All analyses are on weighted data; *N*s are unweighted. Pearson χ^2 tests for cluster samples were used to test statistical significance. For the total, differences in means were tested against means of the standardization sample. Statistical significance is noted by asterisks in the column above the statistically significant result (*$p < .05$, **$p < .005$, ***$p < .001$).

[1] The linear trend was significant ($p < .05$)

Exhibit B.2-14. Additional Social Competence Ratings by Parents Young Child Population at Wave 5

Child Characteristic	SSRS Self-Control Ratings				SSRS Cooperation Ratings			
	N	Fewer Behaviors % (SE)	Average Behaviors % (SE)	More Behaviors % (SE)	*N*	Fewer Behaviors % (SE)	Average Behaviors % (SE)	More Behaviors % (SE)
Total	898	24.2(2.6)	68.2(2.8)	7.6(1.8)	898	17.0(2.1)	66.4(2.8)	16.7(2.2)
Sex								
Male	476	20.2(3.4)	71.4(3.9)	8.4(2.9)	476	18.8 (3.2)	63.0(3.8)	18.2(3.4)
Female	422	28.6(3.6)	64.7(4.0)	6.8(1.9)	422	15.0 (2.5)	70.0(4.4)	15.1(3.4)
Race/ethnicity								
Black	301	24.6(4.7)	69.4(4.9)	6.0(2.0)	301	16.2(3.0)	67.4(6.3)	16.4(4.8)
White	387	23.7(3.5)	71.0(3.9)	5.3(1.8)	387	17.0(2.9)	68.9(4.1)	14.1(3.4)
Hispanic	149	22.9(7.4)	60.0(9.3)	17.1(7.9)	149	17.4(7.4)	60.3(9.1)	22.4(9.0)
Other	59	32.1(15.2)	64.0(14.5)	3.9(2.9)	59	20.2(11.2)	63.1(12.3)	16.7(7.8)
Type of maltreatment								
Physical abuse	247	23.0(5.2)	69.1(6.1)	7.9(4.0)	247	16.6(3.9)	63.3(6.0)	20.0(5.6)
Neglect	504	26.6(3.5)	64.9(3.6)	8.4(2.3)	504	18.1(2.8)	67.4(3.4)	14.5(2.8)
Other	147	18.6(5.4)	77.5(5.6)	3.9(1.9)	147	13.7(4.3)	70.0(6.3)	16.3(6.7)
Chronic health conditions								
Yes	177	31.7(5.8)	63.2(6.0)	5.1(2.3)	177	26.8(6.0)	60.4(6.7)	12.8(4.5)
No	720	22.9(3.1)	68.9(3.4)	8.2(2.1)	720	15.1(2.4)	67.2(3.2)	17.6(2.5)
Setting								
In home, biological parents	601	24.4(3.2)	67.4(3.3)	8.3(2.3)	601	15.5(2.4)	67.0(3.2)	17.4(2.7)
In home, adoptive parents	105	34.3(10.1)	63.1(10.1)	2.6(1.5)	105	36.1(10.1)	56.2(10.2)	7.7(3.0)
In home, kin, or other caregiver	144	18.9(6.6)	73.9(6.3)	7.2(2.9)	144	17.6(6.4)	67.7(8.7)	14.7(5.9)
Out of home	48	29.6(12.1)	67.7(12.3)	2.7(2.2)	48	17.3(9.4)	60.9(14.4)	21.8(11.7)

Note: Instrument used is the Social Skills Rating System (SSRS). All analyses are on weighted data; *N*s are unweighted. Pearson χ^2 tests for cluster samples were used to test statistical significance. For the total, differences in means were tested against means of the standardization sample.

Exhibit B.2-15. Children's Reports of School-Related Perceptions Young Child Population at Wave 5

	Loneliness (5–7 yrs)		Loneliness (8+ yrs)		Loneliness		School Engagement	
	N	Mean (SE)	*N*	Mean (SE)	*N*	% (SE)	*N*	Mean (SE)
Total	477	22.6(0.6)	368	34.2 (1.3)	845	28.1 (3.6)	846	34.5(0.3)
Sex								
Male	251	23.1(0.6)	190	33.7 (1.8)	441	39.4 (4.7)	443	34.3(0.4)
Female	226	22.1(0.9)	178	34.8 (1.7)	404	26.7 (5.7)	403	34.7(0.4)
Race/ethnicity								
Black	171	21.5(1.0)	109	34.9 (2.8)	280	27.1 (4.2)	281	33.4(0.8)
White	201	23.5(0.8)	166	33.7 (1.8)	367	29.1 (5.6)	367	34.4(0.5)
Hispanic	78	22.5(0.9)	60	34.8 (3.4)	138	32.6 (9.3)	138	35.9(0.8)
Other	26	22.4(0.9)	32	34.6 (3.0)	58	15.9 (8.0)	58	35.6(1.2)
Chronic health conditions								
Yes	104	22.4(1.3)	57	36.3 (2.8)	161	34.4 (6.6)	161	33.0(1.1)
No	372	22.7(0.6)	309	34.0 (1.5)	681	27.2 (3.9)	682	34.8(0.3)
Current setting								
In home, biological parents	313	23.2(0.5)[1]	260	34.4 (1.6)	573	30.5 (3.9)	574	34.6(0.4)
In home, adoptive parents	66	23.5(1.4)	28	34.9 (3.4)	94	29.8 (9.8)	94	33.7(0.5)
In home, kin, or other caregiver	74	19.9(1.9)	63	32.9 (2.0)	137	17.5 (6.9)	136	34.1(1.4)
Out of home	24	21.6(0.8)	17	36.8 (5.0)	41	23.4 (9.6)	42	34.7(1.8)
Severity of neglect								
Mild	98	22.9(0.9)	68	34.9 (2.5)	166	34.5 (6.2)	166	34.6(0.7)
Moderate	63	24.3(2.0)	57	34.0 (3.2)	120	33.3 (10.3)	121	33.8(0.7)
Serious	51	24.6(1.4)	22	30.1 (2.6)	73	32.2 (9.3)	73	34.2(0.8)
Severe	32	22.5(1.2)	21	31.6 (3.8)	53	20.2 (8.3)	54	35.0(1.0)
Grave	17	24.6(0.3)	8	30.9 (3.4)	25	80.8 (11.5)	25	35.0(0.6)

Note: Instruments used are the Loneliness and Social Dissatisfaction Scale and the School Engagement Scale. All analyses are on weighted data; *N*s are unweighted. Pearson χ^2 tests for cluster samples were used to test statistical significance. For the total, differences in means were tested against means of the standardization sample.

[1] Significant linear trend ($p < .05$), although F test on comparison of means was not significant.

Exhibit B.3-1 Number of Out-of-Home Placements Young Child Population at Wave 5

Child Characteristic	*N*	Percentage (SE)			
		0 Placements	1 Placement	2 Placements	3 or More Placements
Total	864	75.0 (2.6)	10.9 (1.9)	7.8 (1.7)	6.3 (1.4)
Sex					
Male	459	75.6 (3.8)	8.2 (2.3)	11.0 (3.2)	5.1 (1.5)
Female	405	74.3 (3.7)	13.7 (3.3)	4.5 (1.4)	7.5 (2.5)
Race/ethnicity					
Black/non-Hispanic	288	74.6 (5.4)	7.9 (2.3)	12.6 (4.6)	4.8 (1.8)
White/non-Hispanic	375	76.9 (4.0)	10.9 (2.8)	6.3 (2.2)	5.9 (1.8)
Hispanic	140	74.4 (7.2)	12.1 (6.6)	3.1 (1.8)	10.4 (5.8)
Other	59	64.0 (11.5)	21.7 (10.2)	10.2 (6.6)	4.1 (3.0)
Chronic health condition*					
Yes	172	78.1 (5.2)	7.7 (2.4)	11.4 (4.2)	2.7 (0.9)
No	689	75.4 (3.1)	11.5 (2.3)	6.0 (1.8)	7.1 (1.7)
Physical disability					
Yes	49	68.9 (14.1)	11.2 (9.0)	15.0 (10.7)	4.9 (2.7)
No	811	75.4 (2.9)	10.8 (2.2)	7.5 (1.8)	6.4 (1.5)
Cognitive disability					
Yes	38	61.9 (15.0)	10.7 (6.3)	10.4 (9.3)	17.1 (11.2)
No	795	76.0 (2.7)	11.0 (2.0)	7.3 (1.8)	5.6 (1.4)
Emotional problems					
Yes	330	73.8 (3.9)	10.1 (2.1)	8.6 (3.3)	7.5 (2.0)
No	532	76.0 (4.0)	11.1 (3.0)	7.3 (2.0)	5.6 (1.9)

Note: All analyses are on weighted data; *N*s are unweighted. Pearson $\chi 2$ tests for cluster samples were used to test statistical significance (*$p < .05$).

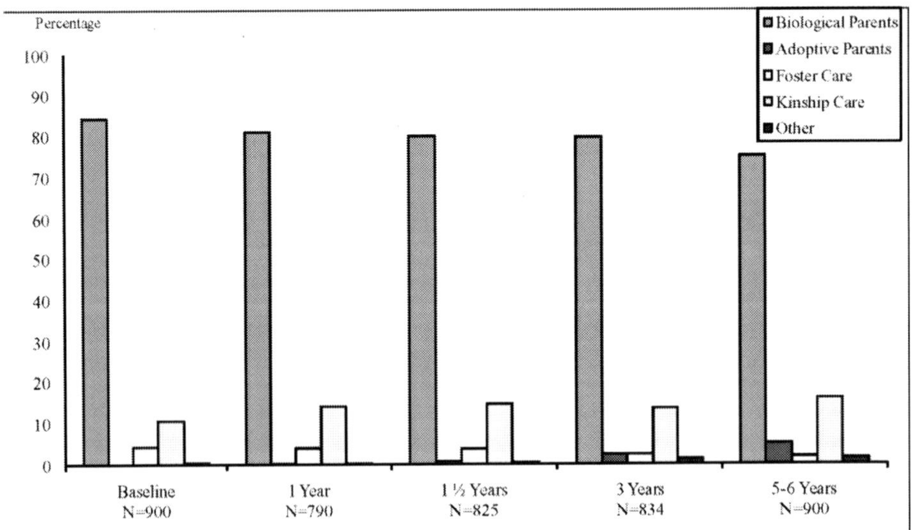

Exhibit B.3-2. Distribution of Children by Settings at Each Time Point Young Child Population at Wave 5.

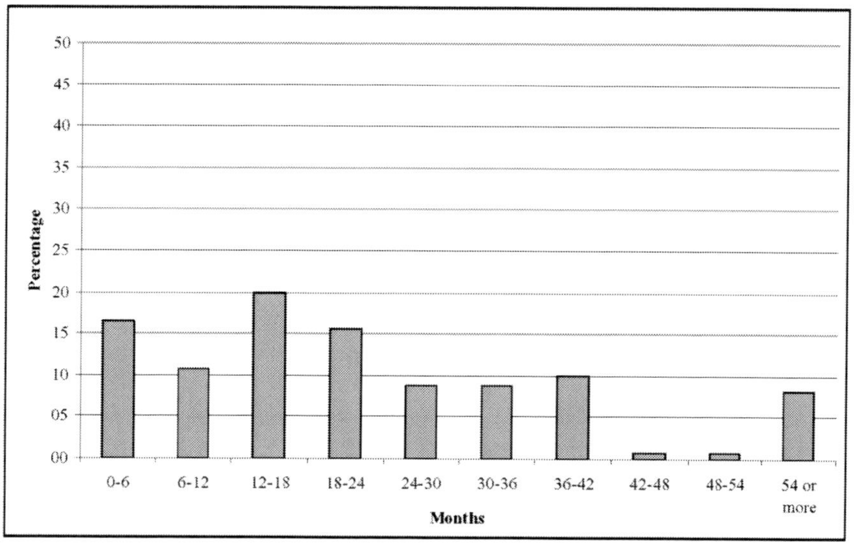

Note: $N = 318$.

Exhibit B.3-3. Time in Placement Young Child Population at Wave 5.

Exhibit B.3-4. Time in Placement (in Days) Young Child Population at Wave 5

Child Characteristic	*N*	Mean (SE)
Total	**324**	**675 (061)**
Sex		*
Male	171	670 (097)
Female	153	681 (075)
Race/ethnicity		
Black	125	641 (134)
White	119	608 (065)
Hispanic	55	888 (161)
Other	25	658 (116)
Chronic health condition		
Yes	68	614 (081)
No	253	706 (074)
Physical disability		
Yes	31	680 (162)
No	293	675 (063)
Cognitive disability		
Yes	15	491 (141)
No	293	681 (064)
Emotional problems		
Yes	136	696 (127)
No	186	673 (064)
Physical maltreatment		**

Exhibit B.3-4. (Continued)

Child Characteristic	*N*	Mean (SE)
Yes	84	430 (070)
No	218	769 (072)
Severity of neglect		*
Mild	40	497 (1 13)[a]
Moderate	53	940 (1 10)[b]
Serious	59	658 (108)
Severe	29	499 (124)[a]
Grave	18	940 (186)[b]

Note: Only children who have had at least one out-of-home placement are included in these analyses. All analyses are on weighted data; *N*s are unweighted. Pearson χ^2 tests for cluster samples were used to test statistical significance. Statistical significance is noted by asterisks in the column above the statistically significant result (*$p < .05$, **$p < .0$ 1). Alphabetic superscripts that are different from one another represent significant differences ($\alpha = .05$), except that the p for the difference between severe and grave neglect equals .056.

Exhibit B.3-5. Termination of Parental Rights and Adoption Young Child Population at Wave 5

Child Characteristic	*N* (Min)	TPR % (SE)	Adopted % (SE)
Total	651	13.1 (2.4)	6.0 (1.2)
Sex			
Male	348	10.9 (2.3)	7.0 (2.1)
Female	303	15.8 (4.0)	5.0 (1.2)
Race/ethnicity			
Black	207	7.7 (2.9)	8.8 (2.5)
White	292	18.2 (3.9)	5.3 (1.5)
Hispanic	103	11.3 (4.1)	4.6 (2.7)
Other	47	8.5 (4.4)	3.3 (1.3)
Chronic health condition			
Yes	127	8.5 (3.0)	9.8 (3.5)
No	522	14.0 (2.8)	5.3 (1.2)
Physical disability			
Yes	44	18.8 (8.6)	17.5 (8.2)
No	607	12.8 (2.6)	5.3 (1.2)
Cognitive disability		*	
Yes	30	2.0 (1.6)	3.4 (2.3)
No	602	13.5 (2.5)	5.5 (1.2)
Emotional/behavioral problems		*	
Yes	255	7.2 (2.7)	8.0 (2.1)
No	393	16.9 (3.4)	4.9 (1.2)
No. of types of maltreatment			*
One	404	15.2 (3.2)	3.2 (0.9)
Two or more	206	9.3 (2.7)	13.0 (3.6)

Note: All analyses are on weighted data; *N*s are unweighted. Pearson χ^2 tests for cluster samples were used to test statistical significance. Statistical significance is noted by asterisks in the column above the statistically significant result (*$p < .05$, **$p < .0$ 1). TPR = termination of parental rights.

Exhibit B.3-6. Time from First Placement to Adoption Finalization (in Days) Young Child Population at Wave 5

Child Characteristic	*N*	Mean (SE)
Total	88	681 (061)
Sex		
Male	46	758 (060)
Female	42	597 (101)
Race/ethnicity		
Black	28	758 (100)
White	34	631 (096)
Hispanic	17	678 (124)
Other	9	689 (219)
Chronic health condition		
Yes	12	797 (091)
No	75	676 (064)
Emotional problems		
Yes	27	644 (110)
No	60	698 (071)

Note: Time was counted from the first placement that was not followed by a reunification. All analyses are on weighted data; *N*s are unweighted. Pearson χ^2 tests for cluster samples were used to test statistical significance. Cell sizes were too small to test cognitive and physical disabilities.

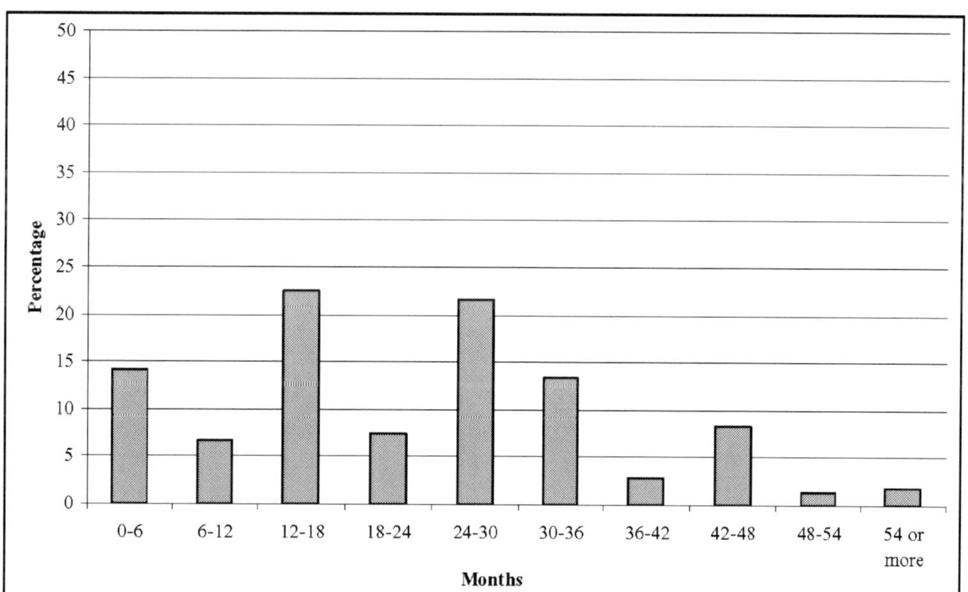

Note: *N* = 88.

Exhibit B.3-7. Time from First Placement to Adoption Finalization Young Child Population at Wave 5.

Exhibit B.3-8. Time from Termination of Parental Rights to Adoption (in Days) Young Child Population at Wave 5

Child Characteristic	*N*	Mean (SE)
Total	64	648 (50)
Sex		***
Male	30	872 (65)
Female	34	371 (73)
Race/ethnicity[a]		***
Black	21	844 (114)[b]
White	23	298 (040)[a]
Hispanic	14	749 (169)[b]
Other	8	—
Chronic health condition		
Yes	17	583 (173)
No	47	676 (120)
Emotional problems		
Yes	30	720 (127)
No	34	544 (139)

Note: All analyses are on weighted data; Ns are unweighted. Pearson χ^2 tests for cluster samples were used to test statistical significance. Statistical significance is noted by asterisks in the column above the statistically significant result (*$p < .05$, **$p < .01$, ***$p < .001$). Alphabetic superscripts that are different from one another represent statistically significant differences ($\alpha = .05$).

Exhibit B.4-1. Preventive and Routine Child Health Services Young Child Population at Wave 5

Child Characteristic	*N* (Min)	All Preventive Services[1] % (SE)	Reported To Have a Pediatric Home % (SE)	Dental Care Since Last Interview % (SE)	Vision Testing Since Last Interview % (SE)	Hearing Testing Since Last Interview % (SE)	Well-Child Checkup Since Last Interview % (SE)	Up-to-Date Immunizations % (SE)
Total	889	46.4 (3.9)	95.9 (1.2)	74.9 (4.1)	79.8 (3.0)	78.5 (3.0)	77.3 (2.7)	99.7 (0.3)
Sex								
Male	453	46.7 (4.8)	97.7 (0.8)	73.9 (4.8)	76.2 (4.6)	75.8 (4.7)	78.4 (4.4)	99.5 (0.4)
Female	397	46.0 (4.7)	94.1 (2.4)	75.9 (4.9)	83.7 (3.6)	81.4 (3.3)	76.3 (3.3)	99.9 (0.1)
Race/ethnicity								
Black	139	50.3 (5.4)	92.0 (3.4)	75.6 (5.6)	80.3 (5.2)	83.5 (4.7)	75.2 (5.5)	99.1 (0.6)
White	187	44.6 (6.1)	97.4 (1.2)	75.3 (6.9)	80.5 (3.9)	75.8 (4.5)	74.7 (4.1)	100.0 (0.0)
Hispanic	77	45.2 (9.7)	97.3 (1.3)	70.9 (10.1)	81.6 (6.2)	83.3 (6.0)	87.6 (5.2)	99.9 (0.1)
Other	28	47.9 (14.2)	100.0 (0.0)	78.5 (10.7)	69.1 (13.1)	61.0 (14.1)	82.1 (10.9)	100.0 (0.0)
Child setting		*		*			*	
In home, biological parents	597	43.8 (4.7)[a]	96.3 (1.1)	71.0 (4.9)[a]	80.4 (3.3)	75.7 (3.7)[a]	75.5 (3.4)[a]	99.7 (0.2)
In home, adoptive parents	105	70.1 (6.3)[b]	99.6 (0.4)	94.6 (3.0)[b]	88.0 (5.7)	85.8 (6.5)	93.2 (2.8)[b]	100.0 (0.0)
In home, kin, or other caregiver	143	50.5 (7.3)[a]	92.3 (5.4)	83.8 (5.5)	75.5 (7.8)	86.0 (4.0)[b]	80.5 (5.7)	99.5 (0.5)
Out of home	44	47.2 (15.3)	99.2 (0.6)	88.7 (7.7)	73.1 (17.6)	92.8 (4.8)[b]	78.2 (11.0)	99.9 (0.1)
Chronic health condition		*						
Yes	175	59.3 (6.3)	98.8 (0.8)	82.7 (5.0)	84.8 (5.7)	80.4 (5.8)	80.1 (5.8)	99.9 (0.1)
No	714	44.2 (4.4)	95.3 (1.5)	73.0 (4.5)	79.6 (3.2)	77.8 (2.5)	76.8 (3.1)	99.7 (0.2)

Note: All preventive and routine health care is caregiver-reported since last interview. All analyses are on weighted data; *N*s are unweighted. Pearson χ^2 tests for cluster samples were used to test statistical significance. Statistical significance is noted by asterisks in the column above the statistically significant result (*$p < .05$, **$p < .01$). Alphabetic superscripts that are different from one another represent significant differences $\alpha = .05$).

[1] Includes having had up-to-date immunizations and recent dental, vision, hearing, and well-child checkups.

Exhibit B.4-2. Child Urgent Medical Care Young Child Population at Wave 5

Child Characteristic	*N* (Min)	Emergency Room or Urgent Care for Illness or Injury Since Last Interview % (SE)	Hospital Admission for Illness or Injury Since Last Interview % (SE)	Care from Doctor or Nurse for Serious Injury, Accident, or Poisoning Since Last Interview % (SE)
Total	892	23.3 (2.5)	5.5 (1.8)	7.1 (1.5)
Sex				
Male	474	23.1 (3.8)	2.9 (1.2)	7.5 (2.2)
Female	418	23.7 (3.2)	7.8 (3.2)	6.2 (2.0)
Race/ethnicity		*		
Black	299	23.9 (4.9)[a]	6.9 (3.3)	7.1 (3.9)
White	387	28.1 (4.4)[a]	4.4 (1.5)	9.1 (2.1)
Hispanic	149	10.2 (3.3)[b]	7.1 (6.8)	3.2 (2.7)
Other	59	24.7 (15.2)	0.2 (0.2)	2.0 (1.4)
Child setting				
In home, biological parents	600	25.6 (3.4)	5.2 (2.1)	6.9 (1.7)
In home, adoptive parents	104	18.5 (5.4)	3.0 (1.6)	5.9 (2.9)
In home, kin, or other caregiver	144	17.5 (4.7)	7.7 (5.5)	8.7 (4.9)
Out of home	44	11.1 (8.0)	1.6 (1.1)	1.0 (0.7)
Chronic health condition		*		
Yes	168	38.2 (6.1)	4.3 (2.0)	10.8 (4.4)
No	680	20.9 (3.1)	5.7 (2.1)	6.3 (1.7)

Note: All urgent medical care is caregiver-reported since the time of last interview. All analyses are on weighted data; *N*s are unweighted. Pearson χ^2 tests for cluster samples were used to test statistical significance. Statistical significance is noted by asterisks in the column above the statistically significant result (*$p < .05$, **$p < .01$). Alphabetic superscripts that are different from one another represent significant differences ($\alpha = .05$).

Exhibit B.4-3. Caregiver Report of Utilization of Child Mental Health Services Young Child Population at Wave 5

Child Characteristic	N (Min)	Outpatient Mental Health Services[1] % (SE)	Specialty Outpatient Services % (SE)	Family Doctor % (SE)	School-Based Services[2] % (SE)	Current Use of Psychotropic Medication % (SE)
Total	895	29.7 (3.0)	16.4 (2.6)	11.1 (1.8)	19.8 (2.7)	16.0 (2.3)
Sex						*
Male	475	34.0 (4.4)	18.0 (3.6)	13.3 (2.3)	22.8 (4.0)	21.2 (3.5)
Female	420	25.0 (3.4)	14.7 (3.0)	8.8 (2.2)	16.6 (3.3)	10.6 (2.6)
Race/ethnicity		**			**	
Black	300	26.5 (5.5)	12.7 (4.2)	7.0 (2.0)	18.5 (5.3)	4.9 (4.5)
White	38	38.0 (3.8)[a]	21.4 (4.2)	15.4 (3.2)	26.0 (3.5)[a]	18.0 (3.8)
Hispanic	149	18.6 (5.3)[b]	13.6 (4.6)	8.2 (3.7)	7.8 (2.7)[b]	18.0 (5.4)
Other	59	16.9 (6.8)[b]	8.0 (5.6)	9.5 (5.8)	15.3 (6.7)	3.6 (1.8)
Child setting		*	*	*		*
In home, biological parents	600	25.6 (3.4)[a]	11.8 (2.8)[a]	8.3 (1.6)[a]	19.0 (3.2)	13.5 (2.3)[a]
In home, adoptive parents	105	49.6 (10.1)[b]	26.5 (8.8)	32.8 (10.3)[b]	19.2 (5.4)	45.6 (8.4)[b]
In home, kin, or other caregiver	144	32.5 (6.7)[a]	27.5 (6.6)[b]	13.8 (4.7)	20.1 (6.9)	15.7 (6.2)[b]
Out of home	45	71.5 (12.8)[b]	49.4 (14.6)[b]	29.3 (9.7)[b]	38.5 (12.6)	27.2 (12.1)
Child in need of mental health services[3]		***	***	***	***	***
Yes	350	52.2 (5.8)	32.1 (5.5)	22.3 (4.3)	38.6 (5.9)	29.3 (3.9)
No	545	16.5 (2.8)	7.2 (1.8)	4.5 (1.1)	8.7 (2.0)	8.3 (2.3)

Note: Mental health services were reported by caregivers and measured through an adapted version of the Child and Adolescent Services Assessment. All analyses are on weighted data; *N*s are unweighted. Pearson χ^2 tests for cluster samples were used for initial significance tests. Statistical significance is noted by asterisks in the column above the statistically significant result (*$p < .05$, **$p < .01$, ***$p < .001$). Alphabetic superscripts that are different from one another represent significant differences (á = .05). Caregiver report of mental health service utilization represents services received since last interview.

[1] Any outpatient mental health service included use of specialty outpatient (e.g., professional help from a psychologist or social worker, in-home counseling, community-based mental health center), school-based mental health services (e.g., services from a school guidance counselor, social worker, or psychologist), or mental health services performed by a family doctor.

[2] Only children 6 years or older were asked about school-based services; consequently, the sample size for these items are smaller ($N = 261$).

[3] Children were defined as "in need of mental health services" if either a caregiver or teacher reported an elevated score (> 1.5 standard deviations above the mean) on the caregiver-completed Child Behavior Checklist or teacher-completed Teacher Report Form Total Problems, Internalizing, or Externalizing subscales.

Exhibit B.4-4. Special Education Services Young Child Population at Wave 5

Child Characteristic	*N* (Min)	Child Has an Active IEP[1] % (SE)
Total	645	25.7 (2.8)
Sex		**
Male	340	33.8 (4.9)
Female	305	16.6 (3.3)
Race/ethnicity		
Black	197	36.0 (8.1)
White	299	25.9 (3.9)
Hispanic	104	16.5 (5.8)
Other	44	17.1 (8.2)
Child setting		
In home, biological parents	435	22.8 (3.8)
In home, adoptive parents	75	49.3 (11.5)
In home, kin, or other caregiver	102	32.0 (8.2)
Out of home	33	24.4 (13.4)
Child in need of special education services[2]		***
Yes	333	37.2 (4.7)
No	312	14.0 (3.0)

Note: All analyses are on weighted data; *N*s are unweighted. Pearson χ^2 tests for cluster samples were used to test statistical significance. Statistical significance is noted by asterisks in the column above the statistically significant result (*$p < .05$, **$p < .01$, ***$p < .001$).

[1] Active Individualized Education Plan (IEP) was determined according to either teacher or caregiver report.

[2] "Need for special education services" was determined by a child's risk of behavior problems, cognitive/learning delays, or functional impairment, as described in Appendix A.

Exhibit B.4-5. Child Welfare and Other Family Services Young Child Population at Wave 5

Child Characteristic	*N* (Min)	Any CWS Service[1] % (SE)	Family-Based Services[2] % (SE)	Parenting Support Services[3] % (SE)	Parents/Guardians Counseled Individually % (SE)
Total	138[4]	65.5 (7.3)	44.3 (6.9)	47.0 (9.1)	36.7 (6.6)
Caregiver race/ethnicity			**	*	
Black	42	31.1 (11.9)	16.1 (6.9)[a]	15.5 (7.0)[a]	26.9 (12.2)
White	65	76.5 (8.5)	56.7 (7.8)[b]	67.9 (9.8)[b]	37.3 (7.7)
Hispanic	22	53.0 (20.1)	9.7 (4.5)	11.8 (5.8)	43.0 (21.3)
Other	9	80.8 (12.4)	74.3 (11.6)	37.5 (26.2)	40.2 (22.8)
Child setting					
In home, biological parent	72	60.1 (9.6)	33.5 (9.3)	39.3 (10.6)	34.0 (10.1)
In home, adoptive parent	19	36.6 (14.1)	36.0 (13.9)	30.4 (12.8)	12.7 (7.9)
In home, kin, or other caregiver	14	83.1 (12.1)	52.4 (19.0)	68.5 (16.7)	66.4 (17.2)
Out of home	32	84.3 (6.8)	72.8 (12.6)	64.7 (14.4)	37.7 (19.6)

Note: All analyses are on weighted data; Ns are unweighted. Pearson $\chi2$ tests for cluster samples were used to test statistical significance. Statistical significance is noted by asterisks in the column above the statistically significant result (*$p < .05$, **$p < .01$, ***$p < .001$). Alphabetic superscripts that are different from one another represent statistically significant differences ($\alpha = .05$).

[1] Indicates having received any one of the following types of service: family-based services, parenting support services, or individual counseling.

[2] Indicates having received any home-based service including more or less intensive family preservation or reunification services.

[3] Indicates having received parent training, parent aide services, respite care, or family counseling.

[4] All data based upon caseworker interviews ($N = 150$); this represents 76.0% of all cases reported by caregivers to have received some child welfare system service since last interview.

Exhibit B.4-6. Services to Address Basic Needs Young Child Population at Wave 5

Child Characteristic	*N* (Min)	Assistance for Family's Basic Living Needs[1] % (SE)	Child Care[2] % (SE)	Services to Directly Assist Caregiver[3] % (SE)	Home Assistance[4] % (SE)
Total	844	25.4 (2.9)	22.7 (3.0)	15.5 (1.8)	9.2 (1.8)
Caregiver race/ethnicity					
Black	233	23.2 (6.2)	20.6 (4.9)	14.5 (3.6)	6.8 (2.5)
White	447	27.4 (3.6)	20.2 (3.4)	18.4 (3.6)	8.7 (2.3)
Hispanic	26	16.5 (5.1)	25.5 (7.9)	11.9 (4.3)	13.7 (7.9)
Other	14	21.1 (9.9)	47.4 (14.3)	21.1 (8.7)	9.4 (5.8)
Poverty status[5]		**			**
At/below poverty level	357	38.3 (5.4)	19.0 (3.9)	17.4 (3.8)	4.3 (1.3)
Above poverty level	454	18.6 (2.6)	26.7 (4.8)	16.1 (2.7)	13.2 (3.0)
Child setting			*	*	*
In home, biological parent	600	27.5 (3.3)	25.7 (3.8)	16.9 (2.4)[b]	8.7 (2.1)[b]
In home, adoptive parent	105	15.4 (7.0)	12.8 (4.4)	29.8 (7.7)[a]	30.6 (9.5)[a]
In home, kin, or other caregiver	143	18.6 (5.6)	11.6 (4.8)	7.7 (2.9)[b]	4.3 (2.6)[b]

Note: All analyses are on weighted data; *N*s are unweighted. Pearson $\chi 2$ tests for cluster samples were used for initial significance tests. Statistical significance is noted by asterisks in the column above the statistically significant result (*$p < .05$, **$p < .01$, ***$p < .001$). Alphabetic superscripts that are different from one another represent significant differences ($\alpha = .05$).

[1] Includes having received any financial assistance, food from a community source, transportation help, or emergency shelter or housing.

[2] Indicates having received child care assistance on a regular basis.

[3] Indicates that the caregiver has received job-related services, legal aid, or has attended any organized support group.

[4] Indicates having received help with specific home management training or cleaning or help with home repairs.

[5] Using the federal poverty status guidelines, this variable is based upon family income for the child's current home setting at Wave 5.

Exhibit B.4-7. Caregiver Need for Mental Health and Substance Abuse Services and Service Receipt Young Child Population at Wave 5

Child Characteristic	*N* (Min)	In Need of Mental Health Service[1] % (SE)	In Need of Substance Abuse Service[2] % (SE)	Received Mental Health Service % (SE)
Total	846	28.1 (3.0)	20.8 (2.4)	15.4 (2.8)
Caregiver race/ethnicity			*	**
Black	225	25.7 (5.4)	14.3 (4.3)[a]	9.7 (5.4)
White	447	29.4 (4.1)	27.4 (3.5)[b]	23.6 (4.6)[a]
Hispanic	124	17.4 (5.2)	9.4 (3.9)[a]	2.3 (1.2)[b]
Other	50	48.8 (12.7)	21.8 (7.8)	8.7 (4.4)[b]
Child setting				**
In home biological parent	600	29.5 (3.5)	21.6 (2.8)	17.6 (3.6)[a]
In home adoptive parent	105	23.6 (8.9)	15.5 (7.0)	20.2 (8.8)
In home, kin, or other caregiver	143	23.7 (8.6)	13.0 (4.2)	3.4 (1.3)[b]
Need for mental health or substance abuse service				
In need of mental health services	233	NA	31.7 (4.3)	36.3 (6.4)
In need of substance abuse services	191	42.4 (6.8)	NA	24.4 (6.7)

Note: All analyses are on weighted data; *Ns* are unweighted. Pearson χ^2 tests for cluster samples were used to test statistical significance. Statistical significance is noted by asterisks in the column above the statistically significant result (*$p < .05$, **$p < .01$, ***$p < .001$). Alphabetic superscripts that are different from one another represent significant differences ($\alpha = .05$). NA = not applicable.

[1] Caregiver was determined to be "in need of mental health services" when she or he met any one of four criteria: (1) caregiver self-reported need for "a lot" or "some" help for a mental health problem, (2) caseworker report of a caregiver's need for a mental health services, (3) self-reported scores within the clinical range on either the Dysthymia and Anhedonia scales of the CIDI-SF, or (4) a score exceeding 1.5 standard deviations above the norm ($t \leq$) on the Mental Health component of the SF-1 2. [b]A caregiver was determined to be in need of substance abuse services when he or she met any one of three criteria: (1) caregiver self-reported need for "a lot" or "some" help for an alcohol or drug problem, (2) caseworker report of caregiver's need for alcohol or drug abuse services, or (3) or scores within the clinical range on either the Alcohol Dependence or Drug Dependence scales of the CIDI-SF.

[2] A caregiver was determined to be in need of substance abuse services when they met any one of three criteria: (1) caregiver self-reported need for "a lot" or "some" help for an alcohol or drug problem, (2) caseworker report of caregiver's need for alcohol or drug abuse services, or (3) or scores within the clinical range on either the Alcohol Dependence or Drug Dependence scales of the CIDI-SF. [b]Black < White ($p < .05$); [c]White > Hispanic ($p < .05$); [d] White > Hispanic ($p < .05$).

REFERENCES

[1] AAP Committee on Early Childhood, A. & Dependent Care (2002). Health care of young children in foster care. *Pediatrics, 109*(3), 536–541.

[2] Achenbach, T. M. (1991). *Manual for the Child Behavior Checklist/4–18 and 1991 Profile*. Burlington, VT, University of Vermont, Department of Psychiatry.

[3] Achenbach, T. M. (1992). *Manual for the Child Behavior Checklist/2–3 and 1992 Profile*. Burlington, VT, University of Vermont, Department of Psychiatry.

[4] Allen, R. E. & Oliver, J. M. (1982). The effects of child maltreatment on language development. *Child Abuse & Neglect, 6(3)*, 299–305.

[5] Artiles, A. J., Harry, B., Reschly, D. J. & Chinn, P. C. (2002). Over-identification of students of color in special education: A Critical overview. *Multicultural Perspectives, 4,* 3-10.

[6] Ascher, B. H., Farmer, E. M. Z. & Burns, B. J. (1996). The Child and Adolescent Services Assessment (CASA): Description and psychometrics. *Journal of Emotional and Behavioral Disorders, 4(1)*, 12–20.

[7] Barth, R. P., Courtney, M., Berrick, J. D. & Albert, V. (1994). From child abuse to permanency planning: Child welfare services pathways and placements. New York: Aldine de Gruyter.

[8] Biemer, P. P., Chiflikyan, R., Dowd, K. & Smith, K. (2007). *What child welfare agency administrative records tell us about the accuracy of survey reports of abuse or neglect.* Paper presented at the proceedings of the International Statistics Institute, Lisbon, Portugal.

[9] Biemer, P., Christ, S. L. & Wiesen, C. (2006). *Reliability Assessment of the National Survey on Child and Adolescent Well-Being*. Odlum Institute, University of North Carolina. Chapel Hill, NC: UNC.

[10] Blair, C. (2002). School readiness. Integrating cognition and emotion in a neurobiological conceptualization of children's functioning at school entry. *American Psychologist, 57(2)*, 111–127.

[11] Bloom, B. & Dey, A. N. (2006). Summary health statistics for U.S. children: National Health Interview Survey, 2004. *Vital Health Statistics 10(227)*, 1-85.

[12] Bloom, B. & Tonthat, L. (2002). Summary health statistics for U.S. children: National Health Interview Survey, 1997. *Vital Health Statistics, 10(203)*, 1-53.

[13] Bolger, K. E. & Patterson, C. J. (2001). Developmental pathways from child maltreatment to peer rejection. *Child Development, 72(2)*, 549-568.

[14] Bolger, K. E., Patterson, C. J. & Kupersmidt, J. B. (1998). Peer relationships and self-esteem among children who have been maltreated. *Child Development, 69*, 1171–1197.

[15] Bradley, R. H., Corwyn, R. F., McAdoo, H. P. & Coll, C. G. (2001a). The home environments of children in the United States part I: variations by age, ethnicity, and poverty status. *Child Development, 72(6)*, 1844–1867.

[16] Bradley, R. H., Corwyn, R. F. & Burchinal, M. (2001b). The home environments of children in the United States Part II: Relations with behavioral development through age thirteen. *Child Development, 72,* 1868–1886.

[17] Burns, B. J., Phillips, S. D., Wagner, H. R., Barth, R. P., Kolko, D. J., Campbell, Y., et al. (2004). Mental health need and access to mental health services by youths involved

with child welfare: a national survey. *Journal of the American Academy of Child Adolescent Psychiatry, 43(8)*, 960–970.

[18] Burns, B. J., Costello, E. J., Angold, A., Tweed, D., Stangl, D., Farmer, E. M. Z., et al. (1995). DataWatch: Children's mental health service use across service sectors. *Health Affairs, 14(3)*, 147–159.

[19] Busch-Rossnagel, N., Knauf-Jensen, D. & DesRosiers, F. (1995). Mothers and others: The role of the socializing environment in the development of mastery motivation. In R. MacTurk & G. Morgan (Eds.), *Mastery Motivation: Origins, Conceptualizations, and Applications:Advances in Applied Developmental Psychology, 12*,117–146. Norwood, NJ: Ablex Publishing Corporation.

[20] Cassidy, J. & Asher, S. R. (1992). Loneliness and peer relationships in young children. *Child Development, 63*, 350–365.

[21] Child Welfare Information Gateway (2005). Concurrent planning: What the evidence shows. Issue Brief. Retrieved January 3, 2007, from http://www.childwelfare.gov/pubs/issue_briefs/concurrent_evidence/concurrent_evidence .pdf

[22] Christ, S. & Biemer, P. (2005). *National Survey of Child and Adolescent Well-Being (NSCA W) Statistical Users' Manual.* Washington, DC: Administration for Children and Families.

[23] Cicchetti, D. & Lynch, M. (1995). Failures in the expectable environment and their impact on individual development: The case of child maltreatment. In D. Cicchetti & D. J. Cohen (Eds.), *Developmental psychopathology: Risk, disorder, and adaptation, 2*, 32–71. New York: Wiley.

[24] Coie, J. D. & Kupersmidt, J. B. (1983). A Behavioral Analysis of Emerging Social Status in Boy's Groups. *Child Development, 54*, 1400–1416.

[25] Coie, J. D., Dodge, K. A. & Kupersmidt, J. B. (1990). Peer group behavior and social status. In S. R. Asher & J. D. Coie (Eds.), *Peer Rejection in Childhood* (pp. 17–59). Cambridge: Cambridge University Press.

[26] Cooper, D. H. & Speece, D. L. (1988). A novel methodology for the study of children at risk for school failure. *The Journal of Special Education, 22(2)*, 186–198.

[27] Culp, R. E., Watkins, R. V., Lawrence, H., Letts, D., Kelly, D. J. & Rice, M. L. (1991). Maltreated children's language and speech development: Abused, neglected, and abused and neglected. *First Language, 11(33)*, 377–389.

[28] Denham, S. A. & Grout, L. (1992). Mothers' emotional expressiveness and coping: Relations with preschoolers' social-emotional competence. *Genetic, Social, and General Psychology Monographs, 118*, 3–101.

[29] Dishion, T. J. (1990). The family ecology of boys' peer relations in middle childhood. *Child Development, 61*:874–892.

[30] Dodge, K. A. (1983). Behavioral antecedents of peer social status. *Child Development, 54(6)*, 1386–1399.

[31] Dodge, K. A. & Coie, J. D. (1987). Social-information-processing factors in reactive and proactive aggression in children's peer groups. *Journal of Personality and Social Psychology, 53(6)*, 1146–1158.

[32] Dodge, K. A., Coie, J. D. & Brakke, N. P. (1982). Behavior patterns of socially rejected and neglected preadolescents: The roles of social approach and aggression. *Journal of Abnormal Child Psychology, 10*, 389–410.

[33] Dodge, K. A., Lansford, J. E., Burks, V. S., Bates, J. E., Petit, G. S., Fontaine, R. & Price, J. M. (2003). Peer rejection and social information-processing factors in the development of aggressive behavior problems in children. *Child Development , 74,* 374–3 93.

[34] Eckenrode, J., Laird, M. & Doris, J. (1993). Academic performance and disciplinary problems among abused and neglected children. *Development Psychology, 29,* 5 3–62.

[35] Eigsti, I. M. & Cicchetti, D. (2004). The impact of child maltreatment on expressive syntax at 60 months. *Developmental Science, 7,* 88–102.

[36] Erickson, M. F., Egeland, B. & Pianta, R. (1989). The effects of maltreatment on the development of young children. In D. Cicchetti & V. Carlson (Eds.), *Child maltreatment: Theory and research on the causes and consequences of child abuse and neglect* (pp. 647–684). New York: Cambridge University Press.

[37] Evans, L. D. (2001). Interactional models of learning disabilities: Evidence from students entering foster care. *Psychology in the Schools, 38,* 381–390.

[38] Evans, L. D., Scott, S. S. & Schulz, E. G. (2004). The need for educational assessment of children entering foster care. *Child Welfare, 83,* 565–580.

[39] Farmer, E. M. Z., Angold, A., Burns, B. J. & Costello, E. J. (1994). Reliability of self-reported service use: test-retest consistency of children's responses to the Child and Adolescent Services Assessment (CASA): description and psychometrics. *Child Family Studies, 3,* 307–325.

[40] Furstenberg, F. F., Brooks-Gunn, J. & Morgan, P. (1987). Adolescent mothers and their children in later life. *Family Planning Perspectives, 19(4)*, 142–151.

[41] Gershoff, E.T. (2002). Corporal punishment by parents and associated child behaviors and experiences: A meta-analytic and theoretical review. *Psychological bulletin, 128,* 539– 579.

[42] Gottfried, A. E., Fleming, J. S. & Gottfried, A. W. (1998). Role of cognitively stimulating home environment in children's academic intrinsic motivation: A longitudinal study *Child Development, 69(5)*, 1448–1460.

[43] Governor's Office of Regulatory Reform (May 21, 2003). Governor Pataki, Chief Judge Kaye, Mayor Bloomberg announce joint effort to streamline New York's adoption system: Includes the adoption of 5,000 children by year's end. Press release. Albany, NY: Governor's Office of Regulatory Reform.

[44] Gresham, F. M. & Elliott, S. N. (1990). *Social Skills Rating Scale.* Circle Pines, MN: American Guidance Service.

[45] Halfon, N., Mendonca, A. & Berkowitz, G. (1995). Health status of children in foster care. The experience of the Center for the Vulnerable Child. *Archives of Pediatrics & Adolescent Medicine, 149(4)*, 386–392.

[46] Halfon, N., Berkowitz, G. & Klee, L. (1992). Children in foster care in California: An examination of Medicaid reimbursed health services utilization. *Pediatrics, 89*(6 Pt 2), 1230–1237.

[47] Hildyard, K. L. & Wolfe, D. A. (2002). Child neglect: Developmental issues and outcomes. *Child Abuse and Neglect, 26,* 679–695.

[48] Hodapp, R. M. & Fidler, D. J. (1999). Special education and genetics: Connections for the 21st century. *Journal of Special Education, 33(3)*, 130–137.

[49] Hosp, J. L. & Reschly, D. J. (2003). Referral rates for intervention or assessment: A meta-analysis of racial differences. *Journal of Special Education, 37(2)*, 67–80.

[50] Hurlburt, M. S., Leslie, L. K., Landsverk, J., Barth, R. P., Burns, B. J., Gibbons, R. D., Slymen, D. J. & Zhang, J. (2004). Contextual predictors of mental health service use among children open to child welfare. *Archives of General Psychiatry, 61(12)*, 1217–1224.

[51] Jee, S. H., Barth, R. P., Szilagyi, M. A., Szilagyi, P. G., Aida, M. & Davis, M. M. (2006). Factors associated with chronic conditions among children in foster care. *Journal of Health Care for the Poor & Underserved, 17(2)*, 328–341.

[52] Jonson-Reid, M., Drake, B., Kim, J., Porterfield, S. & Han, L. (2004). A prospective analysis of the relationship between reported child maltreatment and special education eligibility among poor children. *Child Maltreatment, 9(4)*, 3 82–394.

[53] Kataoka, S. H., Zhang, L. & Wells, K. B. (2002). Unmet need for mental health care among U.S. children: Variation by ethnicity and insurance status. *American Journal of Psychiatry, 159(9)*, 1548–1555.

[54] Kaufman, J. & Cicchetti, D. (1989). Effects of maltreatment on school-age children's socioemotional development: Assessments in a day-care setting. *Developmental Psychology, 25*, 516–524.

[55] Kaufman, A. & Kaufman, N. (1990). Kaufman Brief Intelligence Test (K-BIT): American Guidance Service, Inc.

[56] Kelleher, K., Chaffin, M., Hollenberg, J. & Fischer, E. (1994). Alcohol and drug abuse disorders among physically abusive and neglectful parents in a community-based sample. *American Journal of Public Health, 84*, 1586–1590.

[57] Kemp, C. & Carter, M. (2005). Identifying skills for promoting successful inclusion in kindergarten. *Journal of Intellectual & Developmental Disability, 30(1)*, 31–44.

[58] Kendall-Tackett, K. A., Williams, L. M. & Finkelhor, D. (1993). Impact of sexual abuse on children: A review and synthesis of recent empirical studies. *Psychological Bulletin, 113(1)*, 164–180.

[59] Kessler, R. C., Berglund, P., Demler, O., Jin, R., Merikangas, K. R. & Walters, E. E. (2005). Lifetime prevalence and age-of-onset distributions of *DSM-IV* disorders in the National Comorbidity Survey Replication. *Archives of General Psychiatry, 62(6)*, 593–602.

[60] Kessler, R. C., Chiu, W. T., Demler, O., Merikangas, K. R. & Walters, E. E. (2005). Prevalence, severity, and comorbidity of 12-month *DSM-IV* disorders in the National Comorbidity Survey Replication. *Archives of General Psychiatry, 62(6)*, 617–627.

[61] Kim, J. & Cicchetti, D. (2003). Social self-efficacy and behavior problems in maltreated children. *Journal of clinical child and adolescent psychology, 32*, 106–117.

[62] Kochenderfer, B. J. & Ladd, G. W. (1996). Peer victimization: Manifestations and relations to school adjustment in kindergarten. *Journal of School Psychology, 34(3)*, 267–283.

[63] Ladd, G. W. (1990). Having Friends, Keeping Friends, Making Friends, and Being Liked by Peers in the Classroom: Predictors of Children's Early School Adjustment? *Child Development, 61(4)*, 1081–1100.

[64] Ladd, G. W. & Hart, C. H. (1992). Creating informal play opportunities: Are parents' and preschoolers' initiations related to children's competence with peers? *Developmental Psychology, 28*, 1179–1187.

[65] Leslie, L. K., Gordon, J. N., Meneken, L., Premji, K., Michelmore, K. L. & Ganger, W. (2005). The physical, developmental, and mental health needs of young children in

child welfare by initial placement type. *Developmental and Behavioral Pediatrics, 26(3)*, 177–185.

[66] Leslie, L. K., Hurlburt, M. S., James, S., Landverk, J., Slymen, D. J. & Zhang, J. (2005). Relationship between entry into child welfare and mental health service use. *Psychiatric Services, 56(8)*, 981–987.

[67] Libby, A. M., Orton, H. D., Barth, R. P., Webb, M. B., Burns, B. J., Wood, P., et al. (2006). Alcohol, drug, and mental health specialty treatment services and race/ethnicity: a national study of children and families involved with child welfare. *American Journal of Public Health, 96(4)*, 628–631.

[68] Lindsey, D. (1994). *The welfare of children*. New York: Oxford University Press.

[69] McCall, R. B. (1995). On definitions and measures of mastery motivation. In R. H. MacTurk & G. A. Morgan (Eds.), *Mastery motivation: Origins, conceptualization, and applications* (pp. 273–292). Norwood, NJ: Ablex Publishing Co.

[70] McClelland, M. M. & Morrison, F. J. (2003). The emergence of learning-related social skills in preschool children. *Early Childhood Research Quarterly, 18(2)*, 206–224.

[71] McClelland, M. M., Morrison, F. J. & Holmes, D. L. (2000). Children at risk for early academic problems: The role of learning-related social skills. *Early Childhood Research Quarterly, 15(3)*, 307–329.

[72] National Center for Injury Prevention and Control (n.d.). *WISQARS Nonfatal Injury Report.* Retrieved January 25, 2007 from http://webappa.cdc.gov/sasweb/ncipc/nfirates2001.html

[73] National Research Council & Institute of Medicine. (2000). Early childhood intervention: Views from the field. Report of a Workshop. Committee on Integrating the Science of Early Childhood Development. Shonkoff, J. P., Phillips, D.A., Keilty, B. (Eds.). Board on Children, Youth, and Families, *Commission on Behavioral and Social Sciences and Education*. Washington, DC: National Academy Press.

[74] Nelson, C.B., Kessler, R.C. & Mroczek, D. (2001). Scoring the World Health Organization's Composite International Diagnostic Interview Short-Form (CIDI-SF; v1 .0 NOV98).

[75] NSCAW Research Group (2002). Methodological lessons from the National Survey of Child and Adolescent Well-Being: The first three years of the USA's first national probability study of children and families investigated for abuse and neglect. *Child and Youth Services Review, 24*(6/7), 513–541.

[76] Pecora, P. J., Whittaker, J. K., Maluccio, A. N., Barth, R. P. & Plotnick, R. D. (2000). *The child welfare challenge* (2nd ed.). New York: Aldine de Gruyter.

[77] Perry, M. A., Doran, L. D. & Wells, E. A. (1983). Developmental and behavioral characteristics of the physically abused child. *Journal of Clinical Child Psychology, 12*, 320–324.

[78] Pinderhughes, E. E., Harden, B. J. & Guyer, A. E. (2007). Children in foster care. In J. L. Aber, S. J. Bishop-Josef, S. M. Jones, K. T. McLearn & D. A. Phillips (Eds.), *Child development and social policy: Knowledge for action* (pp. 201–216). Washington, DC: American Psychological Association.

[79] Raver, C. C. & Zigler, E. E. (1997). Social competence: An untapped dimension in evaluating Head Start's success. *Early Childhood Research Quarterly, 12,* 363–3 85.

[80] Rogosch, F. A., Cicchetti, D. & Aber, J. L. (1995). The role of child maltreatment in early deviations in cognitive and affective processing abilities and later peer relationship problems. *Development and Psychopathology, 7,* 591–609.

[81] Sawyer, R. J. & Dubowitz, H. (1994). School performance of children in kinship care. *Child Abuse & Neglect, 18,* 587–597.

[82] Shahinfar, A., Fox, N. & Leavitt, L. (2000). Preschool children's exposure to violence: Relation of behavior problems to parent and child reports. *American Journal of Orthopsychiatry, 70(1)*, 115–125.

[83] Shonk, S. M. & Cicchetti, D. (2001). Maltreatment, competency deficits, and risk for academic and behavioral maladjustment *Developmental Psychology, 3 7(1)*, 3–17.

[84] Sparrow, S. S., Balla, D. A. & Cicchetti, D. V. (1984). *Vineland Adaptive Behavior Scales: Interview Edition, Survey Form Manual*. Circle Pines, MN: American Guidance Service.

[85] Sparrow, S. S., Carter, A. S. & Cicchetti, D. V. (1993). *Vineland Screener: Overview, reliability, validity, administration, and scoring*. New Haven, CT: Yale University Child Study Center.

[86] Stien, P.T. & Kendall, J.C. (2003). Psychological trauma and the developing brain: Neurologically based interventions for troubled children. Binghamton, NY: Haworth.

[87] Stevenson, J., Richman, N. & Graham, P. (1985). Behaviour problems and language abilities at three years and behavioural deviance at eight years *Journal of Child Psychology and Psychiatry and Allied Disciplines, 26,* 215–230.

[88] Straus, M. A. (1996). Spanking and the making of a violent society. *Pediatrics, 98*(4 suppl.), 837–842.

[89] Straus, M. A., Hamby, S. L., Finkelhor, D., Moore, D. W. & Runyan, D. (1998). Identification of child maltreatment with the parent-child conflict tactics scales: Development and psychometric data for a national sample of American parents. *Child Abuse & Neglect, 22(4)*, 249–270.

[90] Taussig, H. N. & Culhane, S. E. (2005). *Foster care as an intervention for abused and neglected children*. Kingston, NJ: Civic Research Institute.

[91] Toth, S. L., Manly, J. T. & Cicchetti, D. (1992). Child maltreatment and vulnerability to depression. *Development and Psychopathology, 4,* 97–112.

[92] U.S. Department of Education (2005). 25th Annual (2003) Report to Congress on the Implementation of the Individuals with Disabilities Act (Vol. 1): U.S. Department of Education.

[93] U.S. Department of Health and Human Services (2000). *HHS issues final child welfare regulations to improve services and outcomes for children*. Retrieved November 30, 2006, from http://www.acf.hhs.gov/news/press/2000/cwelfare.htm

[94] U.S. Department of Health and Human Services, Administration for Children and Families (2001). *Background paper: Child and Family Services reviews national standards*. Retrieved December 28, 2006, from http://www.acf.hhs.gov/programs/cb/cwmonitoring/legislation/background.htm

[95] U.S. Department of Health and Human Services, Administration for Children and Families (2005a). *The adoption and foster care analysis and reporting system (FACARS) report: Preliminary FY 2003 estimates as of April, 2005*. Washington, DC: Children's Bureau.

[96] U.S. Department of Health and Human Services, Administration for Children and Families (2005b). *National Survey of Child and Adolescent Well-Being (NSCA W): CPS sample component, Wave 1 data analysis report.* Washington, DC: Author.

[97] U.S. Department of Health and Human Services, Administration on Children, Youth and Families. (2006a). *Child maltreatment 2004.* Washington, DC: U.S. Government Printing Office.

[98] U.S. Department of Health and Human Services, Administration for Children and Families (2006b). *National Survey of Child and Adolescent Well-Being: Combined Waves 1–5 Data File Users Manual, Restricted Release Version.* Washington, DC: Administration for Children and Families.

[99] U.S. Department of Health and Human Services, Administration for Children and Families. (2008a). *How do caseworker judgments predict substantiation of child maltreatment?* Research Brief. Washington, DC: Author.

[100] U.S. Department of Health and Human Services, Administration for Children and Families. (2008b). The well-being of children 18 months following a child maltreatment investigation: An 18-month follow-up report from the National Survey of Child and Adolescent Well-Being. Washington, DC: Author.

[101] U.S. Department of Health and Human Services, Children's Bureau (2003a). *Child welfare outcomes 2003: Annual report.* Washington, DC: Children's Bureau.

[102] U.S. Department of Health and Human Services, Children's Bureau, & Administration for Children and Families (2003b). Results of the 2001 & 2002 child and family service reviews. Retrieved January 3, 2007, from http://www.acf.hhs.gov/programs/cb/cwmonitoring/results/results/results.ppt

[103] Wallace, I., Nahm, E., Luba, A. & Cross, T.P. (2006). *List of NSCA W-related publications.* Research Triangle Park, NC: RTI International.

[104] Walsh, C., MacMillan, H. & Jamieson, E. (2002). The relationship between parental psychiatric disorder and child physical and sexual abuse: Findings from the Ontario Health Supplement. *Child Abuse & Neglect, 26(1)*, 1–22.

[105] Wang, P. S., Lane, M., Olfson, M., Pincus, H. A., Wells, K. B. & Kessler, R. C. (2005). Twelve-month use of mental health services in the United States: Results from the National Comorbidity Survey Replication. *Archives of General Psychiatry, 62(6)*, 629–640.

[106] Ware, J., Jr., Kosinski, M. & Keller, S. D. (1996). A 12-item short-form health survey: Construction of scales and preliminary tests of reliability and validity. *Medical Care, 34(3)*, 220–233.

[107] Webster-Stratton, C. & Reid, J. (2004). Strengthening social and emotional competence in young children—The foundation for early school readiness and success. *Infants and Young Children, 17,* 96–113.

[108] World Health Organization. (2002). *World Report on Violence and Health.* Geneva: Author.

[109] Wodarski, J. S., Kurtz, P. D., Gaudin, J. M. & Howing, P. T. (1990). Maltreatment and the school-age child: Major academic, socioemotional, and adaptive outcomes. *Social Work, 35,* 506–513.

[110] Woodcock, R. W., McGrew, K. S. & Mather, N. (2001). *Examiner's manual. Woodcock- Johnson III Tests of Cognitive Abilities.* Itasca, IL: Riverside Publishing.

[111] Wulczyn, F., Hislop, K. B. & Harden, B. J. (2002). The placement of infants in foster care. *Infant Mental Health Journal, 23,* 454–475.

[112] Zaslow, M. J., Gallagher, M., Hair, E. C., Egeland, B., Weinfield, N. S., Ogawa, J. R., et al. (2006). Longitudinal prediction of child outcomes from differing measures of parenting in a low income sample. *Developmental Psychology, 42(1)*, 27–37.

[113] Zimmerman, I. L., Steiner, V. G. & Pond, R. E. (1992). *PLS-3: Preschool Language Scale-3.* San Antonio, TX: The Psychological Corporation.

End Notes

[1] Unless noted otherwise, caregivers were asked to report on their or their child's service utilization since last contact with NSCAW (or last interview). Service utilization reports do not represent lifetime utilization; they only represent utilization during the specific time period. For 92% of the children, this represented the time between Wave 4 and Wave 5 data collection periods (a recall period of 12 to 24 months). Eight percent of the children at Wave 5 did not have service utilization data from Wave 4. So, this small portion reported on service utilization over the course of more than 2 years. It should be noted that longer reporting periods may increase the opportunity for caregiver recall bias.

[2] For derived categories of service utilization (e.g., "outpatient service use"), an individual was considered to have utilized services in that category if they positively endorsed at least one service question item among those included in the overarching category (even when data was missing in other questions). If an individual validly answered "no" to one or more service questions in an overarching category but had missing responses for one or more other questions in the category, the person was coded as having missing data for the category (rather than concluding that services were not utilized).

[3] Teacher data were collected for 82.9% of the infant follow-up cases at this wave. Where teacher report data were missing, the caregiver report was used to positively identify IEP receipt. If teacher data were missing and the caregiver report was negative, a case was coded as missing (rather than assume no IEP existed).

[4] Children were considered to be in need of a referral for special education services if they met any of the four following criteria: (1) Total Problem, Internalizing or Externalizing t-scores greater than 65 on either the Child Behavior Checklist or Teacher Report Form, (2) an overall score on the Kaufman Brief Intelligence Test more than two standard deviations below the mean, (3) an overall score on the Preschool Language Scale more than two standard deviations below the mean, or (4) a score of more than two standard deviations below the mean on the Vineland Adaptive Behavior Scale Screener. See Appendix A for a detailed description of these measures.

[5] During the 5- to 6-year infant follow-up, caseworker surveys were attempted for all children whose caregivers reported having received any CWS service since the last interview (12%; unweighted $N = 143$). A total of 143 caseworker interviews were attempted and 129 interviews were completed for an unweighted response rate of 8 1.8%.

In: Child Welfare System: Transitions
Editors: Aubrey D. Wilson and Sally G. Ryan
ISBN: 978-1-61324-713-6

Chapter 2

CHILDREN INVOLVED WITH CHILD WELFARE: A TRANSITION TO ADOLESCENCE

United States Department of Health and Human Services

EXECUTIVE SUMMARY

The National Survey of Child and Adolescent Well-Being (NSCAW) is a longitudinal study of a national probability sample of children involved with the child welfare system (CWS). NSCAW originated in the Personal Responsibility and Work Opportunity Reconciliation Act of 1996, which directed the U.S. Department of Health and Human Services to carry out a national study of children at risk for maltreatment or otherwise involved with the CWS. The sample, which represents the population of children and families who entered child protective services within a 15-month period (October 1999 through December 2000), included 5,501 children (aged zero to 14 years at the time of sampling) from 92 child welfare agencies nationwide. NSCAW gathered data on children's safety, permanency of living situation, well-being, and services at five points in time. Baseline data were collected approximately 4 months after the completion of the index CWS maltreatment investigation; follow-up data were collected 1 year (Wave 2), 1½ years (Wave 3), 3 years (Wave 4), and 6 to 7 years later (Wave 5).

Purpose of the Report

This report is the third in a series presenting findings from the NSCAW Wave 5 follow-up. It provides information about 1,484 adolescents who were reported for maltreatment to the CWS when they were between 3 and 11 years old (baseline). Some children's cases were closed after investigation; others had a case opened to CWS services. Although the majority remained at home after investigation, a small proportion were removed from their homes. Now, 6 to 7 years after the child protective services investigation, these adolescents are 11 to 17 years old. This report summarizes the safety, well-being, and service needs of both these adolescents and their caregivers at Wave 5. The report is organized into six main sections:

Safety, Adolescent Well-Being, Services Received by Adolescents, Adolescents' Caregivers, Services Received by Adolescents' Caregivers, and Child Welfare System Services.

Adolescent Characteristics

Key characteristics found for this sample are as follows:

- *Adolescents' age, sex, and race/ethnicity.* The largest age group (making up 39.0%) of adolescents comprised 15- to 17-year-olds, with 3 1.0% being 11 to 12 years old and 29.9% being 13 to 14 years old. Approximately half were male (51.0%). A plurality were White (48.1%), 26.9% were Black, 19.1% were Hispanic, and 6.0% described their race/ethnicity as "other."
- *Living situation.* At Wave 5 most adolescents were living at home with their biological parents (77.2%). Almost a sixth (16.1%) were living with a kin primary caregiver; 3.1%, with adoptive parents; 2.0%, in foster care; and 1.7%, in a group home or other type of residential treatment center.
- *Primary type of abuse.* At the time of the index report of child maltreatment, caseworkers reported that 25.9% of cases were reported for physical abuse; 25.0%, for failure to supervise; 22.8%, for failure to provide; 11.4%, for sexual abuse; 7.2%, for emotional abuse; 5.5%, for moral/legal, educational maltreatment or other maltreatment; and 2.1%, for abandonment. More than a quarter (2 8.5%) of these cases were substantiated.[1]
- *Prior child welfare system involvement.* Caseworkers reported that 53.5% of families had been previously reported for child maltreatment. Among those with a prior report, the majority were investigated (94.9%), and 55.6% were substantiated.
- *Caseworker risk assessment at investigation.* At baseline, caseworkers had been asked about their perceptions of caregivers' risk factors. Caseworkers reported that 29.9% of caregivers had poor parenting skills, 27.3% had a history of suffering domestic violence, 23.7% had a childhood history of abuse or neglect themselves, and 20.3% identified the child as having major special needs or behavioral problems.
- *Out-of-home placement history.* Only a quarter (22.6%) of these adolescents had *ever* lived out of home at some point during the study. Across Waves 1 through 5, most adolescents remained at home with their biological parents.

Safety

Key findings about adolescents' safety were as follows:

- *Caregiver aggression and neglect.* Caregivers and adolescents completed the Conflict Tactics Scale–Parent-Child Version to assess caregivers' aggression and neglect. More than three quarters (81.7%) of caregivers reported using psychologically aggressive disciplinary tactics in the year preceding the Wave 5 interview. A full 40.1% used corporal punishment or other minor hitting. Much lower proportions of caregivers reported any type of severe assault (7.0%) or very severe assault (2.3%). Almost a third (32.9%) of caregivers reported the occurrence of some form of neglect in the year before the interview. Reporting on their own experiences (using the Conflict Tactics Scale), 5 7.6% of adolescents indicated that psychological aggression was used by their caregivers. The receipt of minor physical assault or corporal punishment was reported by 30.0% of adolescents. Low percentages of adolescents reported receipt of any type of severe physical assault (9.6%) or very severe physical assault (5.8%).

- *Witnessing and experiencing violence.* On the Violence Exposure Scale— Revised, 20.8% of adolescents reported seeing an adult at their home yelling at another person, while 2 8.2% reported an adult yelling at them. Almost one out of every five adolescents (18.1%) reported seeing an adult spanking a child; only 4.1% reported that an adult has recently spanked them. A small number of adolescents (5.7%) reported seeing an adult stealing at their home. The witnessing of other violent incidents was reported by a very low percentage of adolescents.

Adolescent Well-Being

Key findings about adolescents' well-being were as follows:

- *Physical health.* The majority of adolescents (94.6%) were reported by caregivers to be in good, very good, or excellent health; 10.6% of caregivers reported that adolescents had a serious chronic health condition (e.g., asthma, diabetes, eczema).
- *Mental health.* On the Children's Depression Inventory, 5.0% of adolescents had a score in the clinical range. On the Posttraumatic Stress scale of the Trauma Symptom Checklist for Children, 5.9% of adolescents had a score in the clinical range.
- *Adolescent behavior.* Scores on the Child Behavior Checklist (CBCL) developed by Achenbach and colleagues were used as indicators of adolescents' mental health, behavioral functioning, and emotional functioning. According to caregivers' report on the CBCL, 26.9% of adolescents scored in the borderline or clinical range of scores on the Externalizing behaviors scale; 15.4%, on Internalizing behaviors scale; and 23.2%, on the Total Problems Scale. According to adolescents' Youth Self-Report, 21.0% of adolescents scored in the borderline or clinical range of scores on the Externalizing behaviors scale; 6.9%, on Internalizing behaviors scales; and 14.3%, on the Total Problems scale.
- *Substance use.* A third of adolescents (33.5%) reported that they used alcohol at some time during their life, 28.7% reported use of cigarettes, 17.9% reported use of marijuana or hashish, 6.5% reported use of chewing tobacco or snuff, 6.4% reported illicit use of prescription medication, 2.6% had reported use of hard drugs (cocaine, crack, or heroin), and 2.3% reported that they had used inhalants. Adolescents also reported on their use of substances in the 30 days preceding the assessment: 14.6% had smoked cigarettes, 13.1% had used alcohol, 8.0% had used marijuana, 3.3% had illicitly used prescription medication, 2.6% had used chewing tobacco or snuff, and less than 1% had used hard drugs or inhalants.

- *Sexual behavior.* Between a quarter and a third (28.4%) of adolescents had at some time had sex. Younger adolescents were less likely to have had sex than older adolescents.
- *Illegal activity.* Using the Self-Report Delinquency Scale, adolescents reported any illegal activity. The most common type of illegal activity was a status offense (25.6%), followed by public disorder (22.7%), minor theft (15.3%) and simple assault (15.3%). Fewer than 10% had damaged property, sold drugs, or committed either a serious property crime or felony assault.
- *Involvement with the law.* Nearly 8.1% of adolescents reported that they had been arrested or picked up by the police at least once in the 6 months prior to interview. According to caregivers, 10.6% of adolescents had a court appearance in the previous 12 months, 5.7% were placed on probation, and less than 1% spent time in a detention center or correctional facility.
- *Cognitive development.* Results of the Kaufman Brief Intelligence Test showed that adolescents performed within the normative range on the Matrices subscale. Overall scores were approximately one half of a standard deviation below the normative mean on the Composite and Vocabulary scales.
- *Academic achievement.* Results of the Woodcock-Johnson III Tests of Cognitive Abilities showed that adolescents performed at least half of a standard deviation below the normative mean on Letter-Word Identification, Calculation, Passage Comprehension, and Applied Problems.
- *Social competence.* Caregiver responses to the Social Skills Rating System suggested that most of these youths were functioning within the average range; however, a greater percentage of adolescents were rated as having "fewer" social skills than the general population.

Adolescent Services

Key findings about adolescents' access to and use of services were as follows:

- *Insurance status.* A majority of adolescents (64.4%) were insured through Medicaid or some other state-funded insurance, 26.2% had private insurance, less than 1% had CHAMPUS, and 8.6% were uninsured.
- *Preventive health services.* More than three quarters of caregivers (75.7%) reported that adolescents had received a wellness check-up in the 12 months prior to the interview. Almost all adolescents were reported as up-to-date in immunizations (99.2%), and most (92.3%) had a usual source of care. More than half of adolescents had recently participated in vision testing (71.9%) and hearing testing (59.9%), and 72.2% had received dental care in the 12 months prior to the interview. More than a third (34.3%) had received all of these preventive health care services.
- *Urgent health services.* Slightly more than a quarter (27.0%) of adolescents were reported as having used the emergency room or urgent-care services for an illness or an injury in the 12 months preceding the interview. Overnight hospital admissions

for illnesses and injuries were less common (5.1%). About 11.6% of adolescents had contact with a physician or nurse for serious accidents, injuries, or poisonings.

- *Special education services.* More than a quarter (25.9%) of all adolescents were reported by their teacher or caregivers to currently have an active Individualized Education Plan (IEP).
- *Mental health services.* Almost a third (30.1%) of adolescents had received any mental health service since previous interview. Almost a fifth (18.9%) received specialty outpatient services, 8.6% received nonspecialty mental health services from a family doctor, and 17.9% received school-based mental health services. Inpatient mental health services were received by 6.3%, while 16.5% were currently using psychotropic medication.

- *Need for independent-living skills training.* Most adolescents reported that they knew how to shop for and prepare meals (92.9%), use public transportation (79.5%), and interview for a job (65.6%). About half knew how to obtain family planning (51.7%) and how to obtain medical and dental care (46.0%). Only 29.5% knew how to apply for college, and only 14.6% had taken drivers education.

Adolescents' Caregivers

Key characteristics of the adolescents' caregivers were as follows:

- *Caregiver's physical health.* According to their own self-reports, the majority of caregivers (73.4%) were in *good*, *very good*, or *excellent* health. The mean score on the Physical Health Component of the 12-Item Short Form Health Survey (SF- 12) was 45.6, one half of a standard deviation below the national norm.
- *Caregiver's mental health.* The mean score on the Mental Health Component of the SF-12 was 49.4, well within the national norm. Depression in permanent caregivers was assessed with the Composite International Diagnostic Interview Short Form (CIDI-SF). 20.9% of caregivers had a score in the clinical range for major depression in the previous 12 months.
- *Domestic violence.* Female permanent caregivers reported on their experiences of severe and less severe physical intimate partner violence (IPV), using the Conflict Tactics Scale. Among them, 8.9% had been victims of IPV during the 12 months preceding the interview: 8.3% had suffered acts of less severe violence; 4.8% had suffered severe physical violence.
- *Caregivers' involvement with the law.* A few permanent caregivers (3.3%) reported that they had been arrested in the year before the interview. Very few (1.2%) reported that they had been convicted in the previous 12 months, and only 0.9% reported having been placed on probation.
- *Services to address basic needs.* Permanent caregivers were asked about services received to address their family's basic living needs. The most commonly reported service was food from a community source (19.2%), followed by financial help (10.7%), excluding Temporary Assistance for Needy Families (TANF) and

Supplemental Security Income (S SI), and help with transportation (10.1%). When permanent caregivers were also asked about their receipt of federal or state-supported services, 10.5% reported that they had received TANF, or welfare, and 14.0% had received benefits from the Special Supplemental Nutrition Program for Women, Infants, and Children (WIC). Receipt of food stamps was reported by 3 8.8% of caregivers. More than a quarter of caregivers (28.5%) reported having received SSI, and 9.5% reported having received housing support.

- *Caregivers' mental health services.* Permanent caregivers were asked to report on mental health services received through inpatient care, day treatment programs, and outpatient clinic or psychiatric services. Few (5.5%) caregivers reported receipt of mental health services since the previous interview.

Child Welfare System Services

Key findings about adolescents' and their families' receipt of child welfare service were as follows:

- *Adolescents with an open child welfare system case.* At Wave 5, 13.6% of all adolescents' caregivers reported that they were still in contact with the CWS and receiving some kind of service. Most of the adolescents were living at home with biological parents (51.3%), 16.7% were in foster care, 15.0% were in kin care, 10.7% were in group homes or residential programs, and 6.4% were with adoptive parents.
- *Child welfare systems services received.* Caseworkers for adolescents with open CWS cases were asked to report on whether an adolescent and his or her family received several different child welfare services. Commonly received services were help with identifying or gaining access to other services (43.2%), family counseling (39.8%), individual parent counseling (38.1%), parent training (35.8%), services to prevent out-of-home placement (32.5%), other nonintensive home-based services (26.9%), and family preservation or reunification services (17.5%).

INTRODUCTION

The transition to adolescence is a critical developmental juncture that facilitates future independence. A successful transition hinges on adolescents' educational achievements, acquisition of skills and abilities, and physical and mental health (Fuligni & Hardway, 2004). Adolescence is also marked by the potential onset of unique developmental risks, including delinquency, substance use, sexual experimentation, or school-related problems (Centers for Disease Control and Prevention, 2008). Although a majority of adolescents will pass through this developmental period without undue stress (Eccles, 1999), for those with a history of CWS reports alleging child maltreatment this period can be difficult. The National Survey of America's Families, examining children who had been involved with CWS, found that among adolescents, 32% had been suspended or expelled from school in the previous year, and 39% had low levels of engagement in school (Kortenkamp & Ehrle, 2002). A second study at the time of adolescents' contact with the CWS reported that 65.7% of adolescents 11 to14 years old had clinically significant emotional or behavioral problems (Burns et al., 2004), 3 8.3% had used alcohol, 17.3% had used marijuana, and 10% reportedly had been arrested in the previous 6 months (Administration for Children and Families, 2005). This report describes the transition to adolescence for youth who were involved with the CWS as children. It provides a broad description of adolescents' feelings, cognitive development, and academic achievement; relationship with caregivers and peers; physical and mental health; and their need and use of services. It also provides a description of their caregivers' well-being and service needs.

This report uses data from NSCAW, a longitudinal study of a national probability sample of children involved with child welfare. NSCAW originated in the Personal Responsibility and Work Opportunity Reconciliation Act of 1996, which directed the U.S. Department of Health and Human Services to conduct a national study of children at risk for maltreatment or otherwise involved with the CWS (NSCAW Research Group, 2002). NSCAW gathered data on children's safety, permanency of living situation, well-being, and services at five points in time. A detailed description of the instruments used in NSCAW is provided in the baseline report, available at http://www.acf.hhs.gov/programs/opre/abuse_neglect/nscaw/. The Technical Appendix to this report provides a brief overview of instruments and main derived variables.

Methods

NSCAW involved 5,501 children aged birth to 14 years (at the time of sampling), who had contact with the CWS within a 15-month period beginning in October 1999. These children were selected from 92 primary sampling units in 97 counties nationwide. The sample of investigated or assessed cases included both cases that received ongoing services and cases that did not receive services because either allegations were not substantiated, or it was determined that services were not required. Data was collected at five points in time (waves) between 1999 and 2007.

This sample design required oversampling of infants (to ensure there would be a sufficient number of cases arriving at the stage of permanency planning), sexual abuse cases (to ensure that there would be enough cases to have sufficient statistical power to analyze this kind of abuse specifically), and cases receiving ongoing services after investigation (to ensure adequate power to understand the process of service provision). This approach allowed for generation of national estimates for the full population of children and families entering the system, with power to consider key subgroups of the child welfare population. Weighted percentages were used to provide the most accurate population estimates possible (Christ & Biemer, 2005).

Exhibit 1 gives an overview of when and from whom data was collected in NSCAW. NSCAW provides the widest range of informants of any major study of child welfare: Data were collected from the children, adolescents, or young adults (Wave 5 only) reported for maltreatment; current caregivers (primarily biological parents, foster parents, or kin); caseworkers; and teachers. Questionnaires used standardized instruments measuring safety, child development, child well-being, service delivery, and other constructs, as well as items specially designed for this study. For children, young adults, and caregivers, data were collected in face- to-face interviews conducted in their homes. To help ensure their privacy and comfort in reporting personal information, sensitive data (e.g., substance use, sexual behavior, delinquency, victimization) were collected by means of audio computer-assisted self-interviewing, with which respondents enter data directly into laptop computers after receiving verbal instructions through headphones attached to the laptop.

Data for Waves 1 to 4 were collected for the entire sample according to the time interval since the investigation of maltreatment was closed (2 to 6 months, 12 months, 18 months, and 36 months after the investigation). In contrast, data for Wave 5 were collected by age cohort. Data collection for Wave 5 began in September 2005 and ended in December 2007 (see Exhibit 1). Exhibit 2 describes overall NSCAW weighted response rates by wave.

NSCAW is available to all qualified researchers through the National Data Archive on Child Abuse and Neglect (NDACAN) at Cornell University (see www.ndacan.cornell.edu). The data analyzed in this report have been released through NDACAN in NSCAW data version 5.4.1. Additional detailed explanations of NSCAW methods are presented in several available documents (Administration for Children and Families, 2005; Christ & Biemer, 2005; NSCAW Research Group, 2002).

Purpose of the Report

The purpose of this report is to describe the safety, well-being, and service needs of a nationally representative sample of adolescents who had been reported for maltreatment to the CWS when they were between 3 and 11 years old (baseline). The sample for this report is 1,484 adolescents 11 to 17 years of age at the time of the Wave 5 interview. Throughout the report, this sample is referred to as *adolescents.*

Baseline data were collected one to 10 months after the close of the index CWS investigation (with a median time of 4 months). Baseline data included interviews with caregivers (permanent and nonpermanent), caseworkers, children, and teachers. Data collection at Wave 3 (1½ years later), Wave 4 (3 years later), and Wave 5 included the same variables as the baseline set. Data collection at Wave 2 included only caseworker and caregiver interviews.

Wave 5 interviews for the adolescents described in this report were conducted between March and December 2007. Adolescent Wave 5 data were collected 6 to 8 years after baseline. The mean time between Wave 5 and Wave 4 (when adolescents were between 6 and 14 years old) was 49 months, with a range of 40 to 63 months.

In some cases, nationally representative data from other studies are available for many of the variables that are collected in NSCAW. Where these data are available, they are provided as a means for examining NSCAW findings in the context of similar information for the general population of adolescents.

Adolescent Characteristics at Wave 5

Exhibit 3 gives an overview of some key characteristics of adolescents at Wave 5. Approximately half of the sample was male (5 1.0%). The majority of adolescents were 15 to 17 years old (3 9.0%), 31.0% were 11 to 12 years old, and 29.9% were 13 to 14 years old.

The majority were White (48.1%), 26.9 % were Black, 19.1 % were Hispanic, and 6.0% described their race/ethnicity as "other." Most children were in 7th or 8th grade (30.3%) or 9th or 10th grade (28.2%), 25.1% were in 5th or 6th grade, 1.5% were in 4th grade or lower, and 2.6% were not in school. More than half (64.4%) reported Medicaid as their primary health insurance. More than a quarter (27.0%) reported private insurance, and 8.6% reported no health insurance. Adolescents living in home with biological parents were less likely to have Medicaid and more likely to have private insurance than adolescents with other living arrangements (Medicaid was had among 60.0% of adolescents in home with biological parents, compared with 88.4% among those in home with adoptive parents, 75.3% among those living with kin, 79.1% among those in foster care, and 99.0% among those in group homes or residential programs).

At Wave 5 most adolescents were living at home with their biological parents (77.2%), while 16.1% were living with a kin primary caregiver. Kin caregivers included grandparents, aunts or uncles, siblings, or other relatives; the *kin caregiver* designation does not necessarily imply formal, CWS-recognized kinship care. At Wave 5, 3.1% of adolescents were living at home with adoptive parents, 2.0% were living in foster care, and 1.7% were living in a group home or other type of residential treatment center. For NSCAW, *residential treatment center* was defined as a self-contained treatment facility for youth with emotional problems; *group home* was defined as a smaller residential treatment center. Because of the small number of adolescents living in a residential treatment center and group homes, results were combined in the analysis.

Caregiver Characteristics at Wave 5

Exhibit 4 provides an overview of the adolescents' caregivers at Wave 5. The majority of caregivers were female (90.9%). The largest group's members were 35 to 44 years old (44.4%). More than half (52.2%) were White; 24.6%, Black; 17.3%, Hispanic; and 5.9% "other." About a third of caregivers (34.2%) reported having more than a high school education, and 42.3% reportedly lived beneath the federal poverty level. Most caregivers had full-time or part-time employment (64.0%). Only 36.9% of caregivers were married, but the majority lived with other adults in the home (63.1%). More than a fifth (22.6%) had four or more children living in the home.

Exhibit 4 also describes these characteristics by type of caregiver (biological parent, adoptive parent, kin caregiver, or foster caregiver). There were differences with regard to age, poverty level, employment status, and marital status. These differences are detailed within exhibit footnotes. For example, biological parents were more likely to report living in poverty at Wave 5 than adoptive or foster parents; kin caregivers were more likely to live in poverty at Wave 5 than adoptive parents. Biological parents were also less likely to be married than foster, kin, and adoptive caregivers.

Caseworker Reports of Adolescents' Maltreatment at Baseline

Exhibit 5 provides information on adolescents' maltreatment history as reported by caseworkers at the NSCAW baseline interview. In terms of the most serious type of maltreatment reported, 25.9% of cases were for physical abuse, 25.0% were for failure to supervise the child, 22.8% were for failure to provide for the child, 11.4% were for sexual abuse, 7.2% were for emotional abuse, 5.5% were for moral/legal or educational maltreatment or other maltreatment, and 2.1% were for abandonment. More than a quarter (28.5%) of these cases were substantiated. Another 7.2% of the cases were *indicated*, a classification used in some jurisdictions in cases for which some evidence exists for maltreatment but not enough for substantiation. More than half (52.7%) of cases were not substantiated. Less than 1% of cases were classified as *high risk*, 2.8% were classified as *medium risk*, and 8.0% were classified as *low risk*.

At the baseline risk assessment, caseworkers also indicated the level of harm that they believed to have occurred and the kinds of risks that were present in the adolescents' homes. For 45.0% of cases, the caseworker assessed that no harm had occurred; the level of harm was judged to be mild for 29.6% of cases, moderate for 19.5%, and severe for 5.9%. The most common risk factor (53.5% of families) was having prior CWS reports of maltreatment. Among those with a prior report, the majority were investigated (94.9%), and 55.6% were substantiated. Notably, these prior reports are at the family level and do not reference the incident reported at NSCAW baseline; therefore they may be unrelated to the index child in NSCAW. Other risks that were present in a substantial percentage of the cases included poor parenting skills (29.9%), a history of domestic violence against the primary caregiver (27.3%), a history of abuse or neglect of the primary caregiver (23.7%), and the child's having major special needs or behavioral problems (20.3%).

Adolescents' Out-of-Home Placement History

In order to comprehensively convey adolescents' living situations since the time of the index report, this subsection describes adolescent placement history across Waves 1 to 5. *Placement history* refers to the adolescent's living situation (in-home with biological parents versus out of home) from Waves 1 to 5. *Out of home* indicates that an adolescent was not living in a home with a biological parent at the time of the interview. *Out-of-home placement* may mean being in foster care, being in kinship care, or living in a group home or other residential treatment facility. As Exhibit 6 shows, less than a quarter (22.6%) of adolescents had *ever* lived out of home at some point during the study period. In other words, over the course of the study period, most adolescents remained at home with their biological parents. The large majority of adolescents never experienced a placement; however, 13.3% experienced one out-of-home placement during the study period, 6.1% experienced 2 to 3 out-of-home placements, and 3.2% experienced 4 or more out-of-home placements. Adolescents living with biological parents at Wave 5 were more likely than all other adolescents to have never been placed out of home (88.9%, compared with 12.0% among adopted, 5 1.8% among those with kin, and 0% among those in foster care and group homes). Adolescents living with kin were significantly less likely to have been placed or to have several placements than adolescents in foster care and group or residential care.

Guide to the Report

This report describes a nationally representative sample of adolescents who were reported for maltreatment to the CWS when they were between 3 and 11 years old (baseline). It summarizes the safety, well-being, and service needs of both the adolescents and their caregivers at Wave 5. The report is organized into six sections, which include the following constructs:

- safety (caregiver aggression and neglect, exposure to violence);
- adolescent well-being (physical and mental health, substance use, sexual behavior, illegal activity, cognitive development, academic achievement, and social competence);
- services received by adolescents (insurance coverage, health and mental health services, and special education services);
- adolescents' caregivers (caregivers' physical and mental health, experiences with IPV, and involvement with the law);
- services received by adolescent caregivers (services to meet basic family needs and mental health services); and
- CWS services (characteristics of adolescents with an open CWS case; CWS services received at Wave 5).

Safety

This section describes the safety of adolescents' living environments at Wave 5 in two ways: (1) by summarizing caregiver- and adolescent-reported caregivers' aggression and neglect, and (2) by describing adolescents' experiences of maltreatment and exposure to violence.

Caregivers' Aggression and Neglect

Caregivers reported their aggression toward and neglect of their children, using the Conflict Tactics Scale–Parent-Child Version (CTS-PC; Straus, Hamby, Finkelhor, Moore, & Runyan, 1998). Caregivers were asked what tactics (primarily related to discipline) they used in their conflicts with their children. Included were both nonviolent disciplinary tactics and tactics that are mildly or seriously aggressive, from spanking to hitting, slapping, and injurious actions (see Technical Appendix). The CTS-PC also asked caregivers about neglect and sexual abuse.[2]

The percentage of caregivers who used each tactic in the previous year is presented by selected characteristics in Exhibit 7. In the previous year, nearly all caregivers (95.2%) reported having used some form of nonviolent discipline (e.g., explaining why something was wrong). The use of psychological aggression was reported by 81.7% of caregivers (e.g., shouting, yelling, or screaming at the adolescent). The use of minor physical assault or corporal punishment was reported by 40.1% of caregivers (shaking; hitting on the bottom with a hard object; spanking on bottom with a bare hand; slapping on the hand, arm, or leg; pinching). Lower percentages of caregivers reported any kind of severe assault (7.0%; hitting with fist or kicking hard, hitting on another part of the body with a hard object, throwing or knocking the child down, slapping on the face, head, or ears). Very severe assault was reported by 2.3% of caregivers (grabbing around the neck and choking, beating up by hitting repeatedly as hard as possible, burning or scalding on purpose, threatening with a knife or gun). Approximately 32.9% of caregivers reported some form of neglect in the previous year (e.g., that they were so "caught up" in their own problems that they were not able to show or tell their child that they loved him or her, that they were unable to provide needed food).

Caregiver-reported discipline tactics differed significantly by an adolescent's gender and age. Caregivers of male adolescents were significantly more likely to report using severe physical assault (10.2%) than caregivers of female adolescents (3.7%). Caregivers were less likely to use nonviolent discipline with adolescents 15 to 17 years old than with younger adolescents. Similarly, caregivers of older adolescents were less likely to report using minor assaults than caregivers of younger adolescents. Caregivers of adolescents 11 to 12 years old (92.3%) were more likely to report using psychological aggression than caregivers of 13- to 14- year-olds (80.1) or 15- to 17-year-olds (73.9%). Caregivers of adolescents 11 to 12 years old were also more likely to report severe physical assault (10.4% for 11- to 12-year-olds, as opposed to 3.4% for 15- to 17-year-olds). In terms of placement, biological parents were slightly less likely to use nonviolent discipline techniques than adoptive parents (95.6%, as opposed to 100.0%). No significant differences were found by race/ethnicity.

Adolescents also reported by A-CASI on the tactics used by their main caregiver in the previous year to resolve conflicts (Exhibit 8). A majority of adolescents (82.6%) reported that their caregiver used some form of nonviolent discipline. Receipt of psychological aggression was reported by 57.6% of adolescents, a rate significantly lower than the use rate reported by caregivers (81.7%). The receipt of minor physical assault or corporal punishment was reported by 30.0% of adolescents, a rate also significantly lower than that reported by caregivers (40.1%). Although lower percentages of adolescents reported receipt of any type of severe physical assault (9.6%) or very severe physical assault (5.8%), the report of severe physical assault by adolescents was significantly higher than the report by caregivers (7.0%).

Caregiver disciplinary tactics from an adolescent's self-report differed by gender and race/ethnicity. Female adolescents were significantly more likely to report receipt of minor assault or corporal punishment (35.3%) than male adolescents (24.7%). Severe physical assault was more common among Black adolescents (19.8%), than among White adolescents (7.3%), Hispanic adolescents (1.9%), and adolescents of "other" race/ethnicity (5.2%). Very severe physical assault was also more common among Black adolescents (10.3%), than among Hispanic adolescents (2.3%) and adolescents of "other" race/ethnicity (2.5%). White adolescents (7.3%) were more likely to report receipt of severe physical assault than Hispanic adolescents (1.9%). No significance differences were found by adolescents' age or placement at Wave 5.

Witnessing and Experiencing Violence

To help explain adolescents' experiences of maltreatment and exposure to violence, the Violence Exposure Scale–Revised (VEX-R; Fox & Leavitt, 1995) was used for adolescents' reports of witnessing and experiencing violence from someone living in the household. The VEX-R is a cartoon-based scale of exposure to violence; it requires respondents to report how often they have either witnessed or been victims of violent acts at home. Exhibit 9 shows reported exposure to violence in the previous 30 to 90 days. Two dimensions of violence were reported: witnessing of violence (the adolescent saw an adult shove another person, saw an adult slap another person, saw an adult beat up another person, saw an adult point a gun at another person, saw an adult stab or shoot another person), and being a victim of violence (an adult threw something at the adolescent, shoved the adolescent, slapped the adolescent, or beat up the adolescent). The most common type of incident reported by adolescents was yelling: About a fifth (20.8%) of adolescents reported seeing or hearing an adult in their home yell at other persons, while 2 8.2% reported that an adult had yelled at them. Almost one out of every five adolescents (18.1%) reported seeing an adult spank a child; only 4.1% reported that an adult had recently spanked them. Some adolescents (5.7%) reported seeing an adult stealing in their home. All other types of violent incidents were reported by very low percentages of adolescents.

Adolescent Well-Being

This section of the report describes the current well-being of adolescents at Wave 5. Included are descriptions of their physical and mental health, substance use, sexual behavior, illegal activity, cognitive development, academic achievement, and social competence.

Physical Health

According to caregivers' report, the majority of adolescents (94.6%) were in good health (reported to be in *good*, *very good*, or *excellent* health; Exhibit 10). This percentage is lower than the percentage of adolescents (aged 12 to 17 years) nationally who reported being in good health (9 8.0%) in the National Health Interview Survey (NHIS; Adams, Barnes, & Vickerie, 2008). As seen in Exhibit 10, the overall physical health of female adolescents was worse than that of male adolescents (91.6% of females were in good health, compared with 97.4% of male adolescents). No significant differences in health status were found by age, race/ethnicity, or placement at Wave 5. Only 10.6% of caregivers reported that adolescents had a serious chronic health condition (e.g., asthma, diabetes, eczema), a finding similar to estimates from the NHIS of chronic health conditions among children 12 to 17 years old (Bloom & Cohen, 2007). White adolescents (13.4%) were more likely to be reported as having chronic health conditions than Hispanic adolescents (4.7%). No significant differences in chronic health conditions were found by sex, age, or placement at Wave 5.

Mental Health

Depression in adolescents was assessed with the Children's Depression Inventory (CDI; Kovacs, 1992). Following the CDI manual scoring, 5.0% of adolescents had a score in the clinical range for depression, according to their reported feelings for the previous 2 weeks (Exhibit 11). Female adolescents (9.1%) were more likely to have a score in the clinical range than male adolescents (1.0%). No significant differences in depression were found by age, race/ethnicity, or placement at Wave 5. Estimates of depression are similar to national estimates drawn from the general adolescent population, estimates that range from 4.3% among 12- 13- year-olds to 11.5% among 16- to 17-year-olds (Office of Applied Studies, 2008).

Trauma was measured with a clinical scale (Posttraumatic Stress) from the Trauma Symptom Checklist for Children (Briere, 1996). The Posttraumatic Stress scale evaluates posttraumatic symptomatology in children and adolescents, including the effects of child abuse (sexual, physical, and psychological) and neglect, other interpersonal violence, witnessing trauma to others, major accidents, and disasters (Briere, 1996). The percentage of adolescents who had a score in the clinical range on the Posttraumatic Stress scale was 5.9%; no significant differences were found by sex, age, race/ethnicity, or placement at Wave 5.

Adolescents' Behavior

Scores on the behavioral checklists developed by Achenbach and colleagues were used as indicators of adolescents' mental health and behavioral and emotional functioning. Externalizing, Internalizing, and Total Problem behaviors are reported here for the Child Behavior Checklist (Achenbach, 1991), Parent Report (caregivers), and the Youth Self-Report (adolescents; Achenbach & Rescorla, 2001). Based on caregivers' reports (Exhibit 12), the percentage of adolescents in the borderline or clinical range of scores was 26.9% for externalizing behaviors, 15.4% for internalizing behaviors, and 23.2% on the Total Problems scale. These percentages are higher than those found in the normative sample for each of these scales (8%; Achenbach & Rescorla, 2001). Male adolescents (19.5%) were significantly more likely to have an internalizing score in the clinical range than female adolescents (11.2%). White adolescents (27.8%) were significantly more likely to have a Total Problems score in the clinical range than Hispanic adolescents (11.1%). Adolescents living in group home or residential facilities were significantly more likely (87.3%) to have an internalizing score in the clinical range than adolescents living with biological parents (13.9%), with adoptive parents (24.9%), with kin (9.9%), or in foster care (43.9%). No significant differences in CBCL scores were found by age.

Based on adolescents' self-report (Exhibit 13), the proportion with scores in the borderline or clinical range was 21.0% for externalizing behaviors, 6.9% for internalizing behaviors, and 14.3% on the Total Problems scale. The percentage of clinically significant internalizing problems here are consistent with rates found in the Youth Self-Report normative sample. Female adolescents (27.4%) were significantly more likely to have an externalizing score in the clinical range than male adolescents (14.8%). Adolescents living with biological parents (7.7%) were significantly more likely to have an internalizing score in the clinical range than adolescents living with kin (2.2%). No significant differences in Youth Self-Report scores were found by age or race/ethnicity.

Substance Use

Alcohol and drug dependence were measured by self-report on items from the Monitoring the Future (Johnston, O'Malley, Bachman, & Schulenberg, 2007) and Youth Risk Behavior (Centers for Disease Control and Prevention, 1999) surveys. Adolescents were asked about lifetime substance use, as well as use, in the previous 30 days, of several different substances, including alcohol and tobacco. A third of adolescents (33.5%) reported that they had used alcohol at some time during their lives, 28.7% reported use of cigarettes, 17.9% reported use of marijuana or hashish, 6.5% reported use of chewing tobacco or snuff, 6.4% reported illicit use of prescription medication, 2.6% reported use of hard drugs (cocaine, crack, or heroin), and 2.3% reported use of inhalants. Adolescents also reported on their use of substances in the 30 days preceding interview: 14.6% had smoked cigarettes, 13.1% had used alcohol, 8.0% had used marijuana, 3.3% had illicitly used prescription medication, 2.6% had used chewing tobacco or snuff, and less than 1% had used hard drugs or inhalants in the 30-day period.

In comparison, national statistics for adolescents between the ages of 12 and 17 are slightly higher for use of alcohol: 15.9% had binged or engaged in heavy alcohol use in the 30 days before being interviewed, as opposed to the 13.1% in NSCAW who had engaged in any use of alcohol in the preceding 30 days. Use of cigarettes in the general population was lower: 9.8% used cigarettes in the 30 days preceding interview, as opposed to the 14.6% in this study. For other estimates, consumption in the general population of adolescents resembles that for this sample: 6.7% used marijuana, 3.3% used prescription medication illicitly, 1.2% used inhalants, and less than 1% used cocaine, heroin, or hallucinogens (Office of Applied Studies, 2008).

Sexual Behavior

Sexual behavior was measured by self-report. Less than a third (28.4% of these adolescents) had ever had sex (Exhibit 15). Adolescents between the ages of 11 and 12 (2.7%) were significantly less likely to have had sex than adolescents 13 to 14 years old (22.2%) or 15 to 17 years old (53.2%). Similarly, adolescents 13 to 14 years old were significantly less likely to have had sex than adolescents 15 to 17 years old. Black adolescents (37.6%) were significantly more likely to have had sex than White (22.7%) and "other" (15.8%) adolescents. Male and female adolescents did not differ significantly from each other in terms of having had sex. In addition, no significant differences in having had sex were found by placement at Wave 5.

The percentage of adolescents that had had sex was slightly higher in NSCAW than that reported nationally for males and females in the 2007 Youth Risk Behavior Surveillance System (YRBSS), although comparisons are limited by the fact that the YRBSS reports estimates by grade rather than age. In the general population of freshman, 32.8% had had sex, as opposed to 39.9% of 15-year-olds in this study. In the general population of sophomores, 43.8% had had sex, as opposed to the 54.9% of 16-year-olds in this study, while, in the general population of juniors, 55.5% had had sex, as opposed to the 67.5% of 17-year-olds in this study. Notably, in the general population of seniors, 64.6% had had sex, which almost matches the percentage of 17-year-olds who had had sex in this study (Centers for Disease Control and Prevention, 2008).

Illegal Activity

Adolescents reported any illegal activity they had engaged in, using the Self-Report Delinquency Scale developed for the National Youth Survey (Elliott, Huizinga, & Ageton, 1985). Each type of delinquent act is reported in Exhibit 16. The most common delinquent act was "skipping" school (16.5%), followed by being "loud, rowdy, or unruly in a public place so that people complained about it or [the adolescent] got in trouble" (16.0%), hitting someone "with the intention of hurting him or her" (13.5%), running away (7.8%), and being involved in a gang fight (7.2%). The most common type of illegal activity (Exhibit 17) was a status offense (25.6%), followed by public disorder (22.7%), minor theft (15.3%), and simple assault (15.3%). Fewer than 10% had damaged property, sold drugs, or committed either serious property crime or felony assault.

Illegal activity varied by sex, age, and race/ethnicity. Male adolescents (20.4%) were significantly more likely than female adolescents (10.0%) to have engaged in minor theft. Adolescents aged 11 to 12 years were less likely than older adolescents to have committed a status offense, to have damaged property, to have committed a felony assault, or to have sold drugs. Adolescents aged 13 to 14 years were less likely than adolescents 15 to 17 to have committed a status offense. Illegal activity also differed by race/ethnicity. White adolescents were less likely than Black to have committed a status offense or engaged in public disorder. White adolescents and adolescents of "other" race/ethnicity were less likely to have committed serious property crime than Hispanic or Black adolescents. Black adolescents were more likely than White adolescents and Hispanic adolescents to have committed simple assault. There were no significant differences in illegal activity by placement at Wave 5.

National-level data on self-reported illegal activity is available for adolescents through the National Longitudinal Survey of Youth (NLSY97; McCurley, 2006). About 6% of male adolescents in the general population sold drugs in the previous 12 months, a rate similar to that of male adolescents in this study (7.1%). Vandalism or damaging property in the general population of male adolescents was 18%, which was higher than among male adolescents in this study (8.0%), while minor theft (14%), major theft or serious property crime (5%), and running away (5%) in the general population of males were lower than among male adolescents in this study (minor theft at 20.4%, major theft at 11.4%, and running away at 7.3%). Comparison of the same type of illegal activities between female adolescents in the general population and females in this study showed that similarly small percentages ran away, sold drugs, or committed theft.

Adolescent Involvement with the Law

Adolescents also reported whether they had been arrested or picked up by the police for something other than a minor traffic offense, with 8.1% reporting that they had been arrested or picked up by the police at least once in the 6 months prior to interview (Exhibit 18). The percentage arrested was much higher for male adolescents (11.8%) than for female adolescents (4.3%). No significant differences in arrest were found by age, race/ethnicity, or placement at Wave 5.

Caregivers also reported on adolescents' involvement with the law (Exhibit 19). Caregivers reported on court appearances for misbehaving (i.e. delinquency, running away, truancy, or other offenses, excluding probation review hearings), probation, and time spent in correctional facilities. Among all adolescents, 10.6% had a court appearance in the previous 12 months, 5.7% were placed on probation, and less than 1% spent time in a detention center or correctional facility. Male adolescents were more likely than female adolescents to have had a court appearance, to be placed on probation, and to have spent time in a detention center or correctional facility. Older adolescents were more likely than younger adolescents to have had a court appearance and to have been placed on probation. No significant differences were found by race/ethnicity or placement at Wave 5.

Cognitive Development

Cognitive development was measured with the Kaufman Brief Intelligence Test (K-BIT; Kaufman & Kaufman, 2004). It includes two subtests: Vocabulary (expressive vocabulary and knowledge of word definitions) and Matrices (a nonverbal assessment of the ability to perceive relationships and to complete analogies). A third scale provides a total score (Composite). Overall, adolescents performed in conformance with the normative average of 100 on the Matrices subscale (mean score: 96.1; Exhibit 20); however, overall scores for adolescents were about one half of one standard deviation below the mean on the Composite and on the Vocabulary scale (mean scores of 91.5 and 88.5, respectively). Adolescents 11 to 12 years old scored significantly higher than older adolescents on the K-BIT Composite and Matrices. White adolescents scored significantly higher than Black adolescents on the K-BIT Composite and scored higher than all other adolescents on vocabulary. In addition, K-BIT scores differed by setting. For K-BIT Composite and Matrices, Adolescents in group homes or residential programs had significantly lower mean scores than adolescents in foster care. No significant differences were found by sex.

Exhibit 21 provides the percentage of adolescents with low (defined as a score between –1 and –1.99 standard deviations) and very low scores (defined as scores –2 standard deviations or more below the mean) on the K-BIT scales. This information provides an estimate of risk for cognitive disabilities and a potential indicator of service need according to the definition of *disability* in the federal Individuals with Disabilities Education Improvement Act of 2004. The percentage of adolescents who scored between –1.0 and –1.99 standard deviations was 21.5% for the Composite scale, 23.1% for Vocabulary, and 19.1% for Matrices. The proportion who scored –2 standard deviations or more below the mean was 8.7% for the Composite scale, 13.0% for Vocabulary, and 5.9% for Matrices. Adolescents 11 to 12 years old were significantly less likely than older adolescents to have scores lower than –2 standard deviations, as opposed to the higher than —1 standard deviation for the Composite and Matrices scales. White adolescents were significantly less likely than Black adolescents to have scores between –1 and –1.99 standard deviations, as opposed to the score higher than –1 standard deviation, for the Vocabulary scale.

In the K-BIT normative sample, which is meant to represent the general population, 13.5% of adolescents had a score between –1 and –1.99 standard deviations, while 2.3% had a score of –2 standard deviations. More adolescents in this study had scores of –2 standard deviations, varying across the three K-BIT subscales between 13.0% and 5.9%. More adolescents in this study than in the general population also had scores between –1 and –1.99 standard deviations, varying across subscales between 23.1% and 19.1%.

Academic Achievement

The Woodcock-Johnson III Tests of Cognitive Abilities (Woodcock, McGrew, & Mather, 2001) were used to assess academic achievement (see Technical Appendix). Four subtests were used from the Woodcock-Johnson: the *Letter-Word Identification* subtest measures a basic reading skill involving naming letters and reading words aloud from a list. *Calculation* is a math achievement subtest measuring the ability to perform arithmetic computation with paper and pencil. *Passage Comprehension* is a subtest of reading comprehension in which the individual has to orally supply the missing word removed from each sentence or very brief paragraph. *Applied Problems* is a subtest of math reasoning requiring the individual to solve oral word-problems. On average, adolescents scored at least half a standard deviation below the normative mean of 100 in all categories. The mean score for Letter-Word Identification was 93.4, for Passage Comprehension it was 85.7 for Calculation it was 88.3, and for Applied Problems it was 88.9 (Exhibit 22). Adolescents 11 to 12 years old scored significantly higher than older adolescents on all subscales of the Woodcock-Johnson. White adolescents scored significantly higher than Black adolescents on the Woodcock-Johnson Letter- Word Identification and higher than Black adolescents and adolescents of "other" race/ethnicity in Passage Comprehension. In addition, Woodcock-Johnson scores differed by setting, adolescents in group homes or residential programs had significantly lower mean scores than all other adolescents in Passage Comprehension, Calculation, and Applied Problems. No significant differences were found by sex.

The percentage who scored between –1.0 and –1.99 standard deviations was 19.1% for Letter-Word Identification, 26.1% for Passage Comprehension, 24.3% for Calculation, and 21.8% for Applied Problems (Exhibit 23). The percentage who scored –2 standard deviations or more below the mean was 10.0% for Letter-Word Identification, 11.7% for Passage Comprehension, 12.7% for Calculation, and 8.1% for Applied Problems. Younger adolescents were significantly less likely than older adolescents to have scores –2 standard deviations or between –1 to –1.99 standard deviations, as opposed to scores higher than –1 standard deviation on all subscales of the Woodcock-Johnson. Black adolescents were significantly more likely than White and Hispanic adolescents to have scores between –1 to –1.99, as opposed to scores higher than –1 standard deviation for Word-Letter identification, Calculation, and Applied Problems; nevertheless, Black adolescents were significantly less likely than White adolescents to have scores –2 standard deviations, as opposed to scores–1 to –1.99 standard deviations for Word- Letter Identification, Calculation, and Applied Problems. Hispanic adolescents were also less likely than White and Black adolescents to have a score –2 standard deviations, as opposed to scores higher than –1 standard deviation for Calculation. Adolescents living with adoptive parents and those living in foster care were less likely than adolescents living with biological parents or in kin care to have scores between –1 and –1.99 standard deviations, as opposed to scores higher than –1 standard deviation, for the letter identification scale.

As with the K-BIT, for the Woodcock-Johnson III Tests of Cognitive Abilities (Woodcock et al., 2001), in the general population 13.5% of adolescents had a score between –1 and –1.99 standard deviations, while 2.3% had a score of –2 standard deviations. Higher percentages of adolescents in this study had scores –2 standard deviations, varying among the four Woodcock-Johnson subscales between 12.7% and 8.1%. More adolescents in this study than in the general population also had scores between –1 and –1.99 standard deviations, varying among subscales from 26.1% to 19.1%.

Social Competence

Adolescents' social competence was measured with the Social Skills Rating System (SSRS; Gresham & Elliott, 1990), which was administered to caregivers. The mean total social skills score (96.5) was in the average range (SSSR mean for the normative population is 100, standard deviation is 15; Exhibit 24). Nevertheless, a greater percentage of adolescents were rated as having "fewer" social skills than those in the general population of adolescents (20.6%, as opposed to 15.9%). Adolescents living in foster care and group homes or residential programs had significantly lower mean social skills scores than adolescents living at home with biological parents, adoptive parents, or kin caregivers. Adolescents in foster and group or residential care were also more likely to be rated as having fewer social skills than adolescents living with biological parents, with adoptive parents, with kin, or in foster care. There were no other differences by adolescents' sex, age, and race/ethnicity on either mean scores or percentage having fewer social skills.

School-Related Perceptions

Adolescents were asked about their relationships with peers at school and their degree of engagement in school. They completed the Loneliness and Social Dissatisfaction Scale (Asher & Wheeler, 1985), which assesses feelings of loneliness and dissatisfaction with peer support at school (Exhibit 25a). Three quarters of adolescents reported that *most of the time* or *always* it was easy for them to make friends at school. They also frequently reported that they "got along with" other adolescents at school, could find a friend when they needed one, and were well liked by the kids at school. Consistent with this information, more than 80% of adolescents reported that they *never* or *hardly ever* lacked friends, had no one to talk to at school, felt alone at school, or felt left out. Less than 5% reported that they *most of the time* or *always* did not have a single friend at school, were lonely at school, felt left out, and had nobody to talk at school. The mean loneliness score (Exhibit 25b) was 27.3. For this scale, higher scores indicate more loneliness. Significant differences in loneliness mean scores emerged by race/ethnicity and placement at Wave 5. Black adolescents had lower mean loneliness scores than White adolescents, Hispanic adolescents, and adolescents of "other" race/ethnicity. In addition, adolescents in kin care had lower mean loneliness scores than adolescents living in foster care. No significant differences were found by gender or age.

Adolescents also completed the School Engagement scale used in the Safe and Drug Free Schools survey (Sylvia, Thorne, & Tashjian, 1997). This measure assesses adolescents' "connection" to school. The scale includes 11 items that measure both the behavioral component (e.g., completing assignments, paying attention) and psychological component (e.g., getting along with teachers, enjoying school) of school engagement (Exhibit 26). More than half of adolescents (54.8%) reported that they enjoyed being in school *often* or *almost always* and found their classes interesting (55.6%). Only 6.2% *almost always* hated being in school. Most adolescents reported that *often* or *almost always* they tried to do their best work in school (86.5%), listened carefully or paid attention in school (76.0%), and finished their homework (73.1%). Adolescents also reported that *often* or *almost always* they "got along with" teachers (75.3%) and other students (79.9%). About a fifth reported that they *often* or *almost always* failed to complete their assignments (21.5%) and found the school work too hard to understand (22.7%), while 11.0% were sent to the office or had to stay after school due to misbehavior.

Parental Monitoring

Parental monitoring was assessed with a 5-item scale that reflects the adolescent's perception of parents' rules (Dishion, Patterson, Stoolmiller, & Skinner, 1991). Most adolescents reported that they *never* or *almost never* left home without telling their caregivers or leaving a note (71.4%; Exhibit 27). Most adolescents also reported that *pretty often* or *very often* their caregivers knew where they were when they were away from home (8 8.4%) and with whom (84.0%). More than three quarters of adolescents (81.6%) reported that *pretty often* or *very often* their caregiver would tell them what time to be home and they would tell their caregivers when they expected to return (66.7%).

ADOLESCENT SERVICES

This section of the report describes services received by adolescents across a variety of domains: physical health (preventive and urgent care), special education, mental health, and need for independent-living skills training. Because insurance coverage is often an important factor in predicting service receipt, the section begins with a summary of adolescent insurance status at Wave 5.

Insurance Status

Caregivers of adolescents were asked the adolescent's current insurance status, with reference to the following categories: (1) Medicaid or another state-funded program (e.g., State Children's Health Insurance Program), (2) private insurance (including health maintenance organizations, preferred provider organizations, independent practice associations, fee for service, Blue Cross Blue Shield, or employer plan), (3) Civilian Health and Medical Program of the Uniformed Services (CHAMPUS; military insurance), or (4) no insurance of any kind (uninsured). Medicaid or state-funded insurance was the most commonly held type of health insurance among adolescents (64.4%). About a quarter (26.2%) had private insurance, and less than 1% had CHAMPUS. The 2008 NHIS showed a very different distribution of insurance status in the general population of adolescents: 64.2% of adolescents had private insurance, 23.0% had Medicaid, and 1.9% had other types of insurance (Adams et al., 2008). Among adolescents in this study, 8.6% were uninsured, a rate that is lower than the national rate for 12- to 17-year-olds (12.6%), according to the Annual Social and Economic Supplement to the Current Population Survey of the U.S. Census Bureau (DeNavas-Walt, Proctor, Smith, & U.S. Census Bureau, 2008) and lower than the 10.9% reported by the 2007 NHIS (Adams et al., 2008).

Exhibit 28 shows variations in insurance status by gender, age, race, and placement at Wave 5. Adolescents living with their biological parents were significantly less likely to have Medicaid or state funded insurance (60.0%) than adolescents living with kin (75.3%) and adolescents living in foster care (79.1%). No significant differences in insurance status were found by gender, age, or race/ethnicity.

Preventive Health Services

About three quarters (75.7%) of caregivers reported that their adolescent had received a wellness checkup in the 12 months prior to interview (Exhibit 29). Almost all adolescents were reported as up-to-date in immunizations (99.2%). Most (92.3%) of adolescents were reported to have a usual source of care, a rate approximating that of the general population of adolescents 12 to 17 nationally (93.1%; Bloom & Cohen, 2007). More than half of adolescents had recently participated in vision testing (71.9%) and hearing testing (59.9%). Almost three quarters (72.2%) of adolescents had received dental care in the 12 months prior to interview, a rate lower than that of the general population of adolescents 12 to 17 nationally (82.9%; Bloom & Cohen, 2007). About one third of adolescents (34.3%) had received all of these preventive health care services (dental care, vision and hearing testing, and checkup) in the 12 months before the interview.

The percentage of adolescents receiving preventive health services varied significantly according to age, race/ethnicity, placement at Wave 5, and insurance status. Adolescents aged 11 to 12 years (81.3%) were significantly more likely to have received vision testing than adolescents 15 to 17 years old (64.8%), while adolescents aged 15 to 17 years old (48.4%) were significantly less likely to have received hearing testing than adolescents 11 to 12 years old (69.0%) or 13 to 14 years old (65.3%). White adolescents (53.4%) were significantly less likely to have received hearing testing than Black (66.8%) and Hispanic adolescents (68.5%), while Black adolescents (89.9%) were significantly more likely to have received a wellness checkup than White (70.3%) and Hispanic adolescents (71.4%). Across many of these preventive services, adolescents in group homes and in foster care were significantly more likely to have received services than adolescents in all other living arrangements. More than 90% of adolescents in group homes and in foster care had received any of the preventive services, as opposed to the 61.7% to 91.3% of adolescents living with biological parents. As might have been expected, adolescents without insurance (10.7%) were significantly less likely to have received all preventive services in the 12 months prior to interview than adolescents with Medicaid (36.6%) and adolescents with private insurance (37.7%). Similarly, adolescents without insurance (43.8%) were significantly less likely to have received dental care in the 12 months prior to interview than adolescents with Medicaid

(76.6%) and adolescents with private insurance (73.1%). No significant differences in use of preventive health services were found by gender.

Urgent Health Care Services for Illnesses, Accidents, or Injuries

Caregivers reported on adolescents' use of urgent-care services for illnesses or injuries in the 12 months prior to interview (Exhibit 30). Slightly more than a quarter (27.0%) of adolescents reportedly used the emergency room (ER) or urgent-care services for an illness or an injury in the previous 12 months. Overnight hospital admissions for illnesses and injuries were less common (5.1%), although higher than among the general population of adolescents 12 to 17 years old (2.5%; Adams et al., 2008). About 11.6% of adolescents had contact with a physician or nurse for serious accidents, injuries, or poisonings. This rate is lower than the 26% prevalence of injuries among adolescents in the United States, according to the 200 1/2002 Health Behaviour in School Age Children study. This World Health Organization collaborative, national study used the same question as NSCAW about contact with a physician or nurse for serious accidents, injuries, or poisonings (Pickett et al., 2005).

Adolescent use of urgent-care services for illnesses or injuries varied significantly according to age, race/ethnicity, and insurance status. Younger adolescents were less likely than older adolescents to have used ER and urgent care services and to have had hospital admissions and care from a doctor or nurse for serious injuries. Hispanic adolescents (3.0%) were less likely than Black (13.4%) and White (13.1%) adolescents to have had care from a doctor or nurse for a serious injury, accident, or poisoning. Adolescents who had Medicaid (7.5%) were more likely than those who had private insurance (0.8%) to have an overnight hospital admission for an illness or injury. No significant differences in use of urgent health services, overnight hospital admission, or care from a doctor or nurse for an injury, accident, or poisoning were found by gender or by placement at Wave 5.

Special Education Services

Schoolteachers were asked whether the adolescents had an Individualized Educational Plan (IEP), a legal document developed when a student receives special education services. In addition to teachers, caregivers were asked whether the adolescent had an IEP or was receiving special education services. The presence of an IEP was determined by teacher's report when available; when a teacher's report was unavailable, determination was based on the caregiver's report.[3]

As shown in Exhibit 31, 25.9% of NSCAW adolescents were reported to currently have an active IEP, a rate that is higher than comparable national estimates. Nationally, the percentage of adolescents aged 12 to 17 years and receiving special education services in 2007 was 7.8% (Adams et al., 2008). The U.S. Department of Education, on the basis of data collected from 2000 to 2001, reported that 12.8% of students of public schools had an IEP. Male adolescents were more likely to have received an IEP than female adolescents (3 3.2%, compared with 18.2%). This distribution is consistent with other studies showing greater representation of boys in special education (Hodapp & Fidler, 1999). Contrary to national research, which tends to show greater numbers of children of color receiving special education services (e.g., Artiles, Harry, Reschly, & Chinn, 2002; Hosp & Reschly, 2003), there was no association in this population between adolescents' race/ethnicity and IEP receipt. IEP receipt was related to placement at Wave 5. Adolescents living in residential treatment or group homes (85%) were more likely to have an IEP than adolescents living with biological parents (26.2%), adoptive parents (3 9.4%), kin caregivers (15.8%), or foster caregivers (26.3%).

Nationwide, eligibility for special education placement is determined through a comprehensive assessment of the adolescent's abilities, which also forms the basis for the type and level of service he or she receives. Adolescents may be diagnosed as having health, cognitive, or emotional challenges that must be addressed in the educational setting. To estimate the level of special education needs in this population, "need" was operationalized as an adolescent's having an elevated score on a standardized measure indicating risk for behavioral problems, cognitive delays, or limited academic achievement.[4] With this procedure, 56.4% of these adolescents were estimated as having elevated risk: 7.3% had a risk of cognitive problems, 35.4% had a risk of behavioral problems, and 13.7% had both types of risk. There were no significant differences in need by gender, race/ethnicity, or placement at Wave 5.

As expected, an active IEP was significantly more common when adolescents were determined to have these cognitive or behavioral needs that might interfere with school success. Adolescents with both cognitive and behavioral needs were more likely to have an active IEP than adolescents with only one type of need. Although need increased an adolescent's likelihood of receiving special education services, 58.2% of adolescents determined to be in need of a referral for special education services due to cognitive problems were not currently reported to have an active IEP. Among adolescents with behavioral needs, 78.8% did not have an active IEP. Adolescents with both types of problems (behavioral and cognitive) were more likely than those with one type of problem to have an active IEP (69.6%). Estimates here of "need" for special education services do not directly correspond to national eligibility requirements for IEP services. In fact, the exact eligibility for IEP services differs from state to state. Nonetheless, adopting criteria similar to the approach taken here, most states use clinically elevated scores on quantitative measures to determine eligibility for IEP receipt.

Mental Health Services

Caregivers were asked whether their adolescent had received help for an emotional, behavioral, learning, or attentional problem since the previous interview (the mean time between Wave 5 and Wave 4 was 49 months, with a range of 40 to 63 months). Mental health service use questions were framed so that caregivers of adolescents could respond positively for all service providers or service settings that were applicable; consequently, caregivers could report receipt of services from more than one source. All questions included the following phrasing: "Since (date of last interview) has your child received any (name of service) for emotional, behavioral, learning, attentional, or substance abuse problems?"

Almost a third (30.1%) of adolescents received some kind of mental health services (whether specialty outpatient services, inpatient mental health services, family doctor, or school- based services for emotional or behavioral problems; Exhibit 32). When the analysis of services was restricted to specialty outpatient services, the percentage that received services was 18.9%, while 8.6% received nonspecialty mental health services from a family doctor, and 17.9% received school-based services mental health services. Inpatient mental health services were received by 6.3%, whereas estimates of the use of inpatient mental health services in the general population of 12- to 17-year-olds are 2.5%, according to the 2007 National Survey on Drug Use and Health (Office of Applied Studies, 2008). Moreover, in the current study 16.5% of 12- to 17- year-olds were currently using psychotropic medication, a percentage substantially higher than the percentage for the general population of adolescents 12 to 17 years old who were prescribed a psychotropic medication in the 12 months prior to assessment (6.0%; Simpson, Cohen, Pastor, & Reuben, 2008).

Mental health service use differed significantly by gender, age, and race/ethnicity. Male adolescents were more likely than female adolescents to have received specialty outpatient services (23.6%, compared with 14.0%) and to be using psychotropic medication (23.7%, compared with 8.9%). Adolescents 15 to 17 years old (12.2%) were more likely than adolescents 11 to 12 years old (0.6%) or 13 to 14 years old (4.5%) to have received inpatient mental health services. White adolescents were more likely than Hispanic adolescents to have received specialty outpatient mental health services (24.1%, compared with 8.1%) and more likely than Black and Hispanic adolescents to be using psychotropic medication (22.7% of White adolescents, compared with 12.3% of Black and 6.1% of Hispanic adolescents).

Mental health service use differed also by placement at Wave 5 and insurance status. Adolescents in foster (86.6%) and group home or residential facilities care (95.1%) at Wave 5 were more likely than adolescents living in other settings to have received any mental health services (less than 40% for any other group). Specifically, adolescents in foster and group care were more likely than adolescents in other placements to have received specialty outpatient services and to be using psychotropic medication. Adolescents living with adoptive parents (33.9%) were more likely than adolescents living with biological parents (14.9%) to have received specialty outpatient mental health services. In terms of insurance status, adolescents who had Medicaid (3 6.5%) were more likely than those who had private insurance (18.9%) to have received mental health services and more likely than those with private insurance and those who were uninsured to have received specialty mental health outpatient services, inpatient mental health services, and family doctor services, as well as to be using psychotropic medication. The only significant difference between adolescents with private insurance and uninsured adolescents was on current use of psychotropic medication: Adolescents who had private insurance (7.7%) were more likely to use psychotropic medications than uninsured adolescents (0.6%).

Mental health services were significantly more common among those adolescents determined to be "in need" of mental health services. Adolescents' needs for mental health services were assessed with the following instruments: the CDI (Kovacs, 1992), the Trauma Symptom Checklist for Children (Briere, 1996), the CBCL (Achenbach, 1991), the Youth Self- Report (Achenbach & Rescorla, 2001), and the Teacher's Report Form (Achenbach & Rescorla, 2001). Scores in the clinical range on any of these standardized measures identified the adolescent as at risk for a mental health problem and potentially in need of behavioral health services. When findings from all sources of information on the need for mental health services were combined, 49.4% of adolescents were determined to be in need of mental health services. Estimates of mental health problems in the general population of 16- to 17-year-olds are less than half the rates found here, which vary between 15.2%, according to the National

Health Interview Survey, and 20.8%, according to the National Survey of American Families (Kataoka, Zhang, & Wells, 2002).

Among those determined to be in need of mental health services, 44.6% received any mental health service, 2 8.9% received any specialty outpatient mental health service, and 11.9% received any inpatient mental health service. Levels of needed mental health service use here were higher than levels estimated from the general population of 12- to 17-year-olds living in the United States. The National Health Interview Survey estimated that 23.0% of U.S. adolescents in need of mental health services received them in the 12 months before interview (Kataoka et al., 2002). Although this estimate is almost half that found in NSCAW, it should be noted that caregivers here were asked about services since the most recent previous interview. This reporting period, "since last interview," varied between one and 2 years.

Need for Independent-Living, Education, and Job-Related Skills Training

For the past 20 years, federal funds have been provided to states to help adolescents receiving CWS services develop independent-living skills and to support their making the transition to independent living. Adolescents 14 and older were queried about their independent-living, education, and job- related skills as indicators of their need for independent-living services. Notably, independent- living services are usually intended for youth in out-of-home placements. Because the majority of adolescents in this report were living at home with their biological parents, these services may not be particularly applicable to the majority of them; no significant differences were found, however, by placement type.

In response to these questions about independent living, the great majority of adolescents reported that they knew how to shop for and prepare meals (92.9%), use public transportation (79.5%), and interview for a job (65.6%). About half knew how to obtain family planning (51.7%) and how to obtain medical and dental care (46.0%). Nevertheless, only 29.5% knew how to apply for college, and only 14.6% had taken drivers education (Exhibit 33).

Female adolescents were more likely than males to know how to obtain family planning (61.5%, compared with 42.9%) and how to get medical or dental care (55.6% compared to 3 7.4%). As expected, adolescents 14 (1.3%) and 15 (7.6%) were less likely to have taken drivers education than those 16 (22.6%) and 17 (3 1.8%). Adolescents 14 (28.3%) were less likely to know how to obtain family planning than those 15, 16, and 17 (over 50%). No significant differences were found by race/ethnicity or by placement at Wave 5.

ADOLESCENTS' CAREGIVERS

This section of the report describes some key aspects of caregiver well-being (physical and mental health, IPV, and involvement with the law), as well as caregivers' receipt of services for themselves or their family.

Caregivers' Physical Health

Adolescents' caregivers were asked to rate their own physical health from *poor* to *excellent.* According to their own self-reports, the majority (73.4%) of caregivers were in good health (*good*, *very good*, or *excellent;* Exhibit 34). This percentage is lower than that for comparably aged adults in the NHIS (Center on the Developing Child at Harvard University, 2007). In the NHIS 94.1% of adults aged1 8 to 44 and 84.8% of adults aged 45 to 64 reported being in good, very good, or excellent health. Self-report of caregiver's health varied by type of caregiver, but not by race/ethnicity. Foster caregivers (9 6.9%) and group home or residential program caregivers (100%) were significantly more likely to describe themselves as being in good health than biological parents (74.4%) and kin caregivers (64.0%).

Another measure of overall health, the 12-Item Short Form Health Survey (SF-12; see Technical Appendix), suggests that caregivers' physical health was comparable to that of the U.S. adult population. The mean score on the Physical Health Component of the SF-12 was 45.6. Although this score is within the national norm (national norm of 50, standard deviation of 10), it is one half of a standard deviation below the mean. Consistent with the previous findings, report of caregivers' health on the Physical Health Component of the SF-12 varied by type of caregiver, but not by the caregiver's race/ethnicity. Foster caregivers and group home or residential program caregivers described themselves as significantly healthier than biological parents, adoptive parents, and kin caregivers described themselves. Biological parents described themselves as significantly healthier than kin caregivers described themselves.

Caregivers' Mental Health

Caregivers' mental health was assessed via the Mental Health Component of the SF-12. The mean score on the Mental Health Component of the SF-12 was 49.4 (Exhibit 35). This score falls well within the national norm (national norm of 50, standard deviation of 10), indicating caregivers' mental health was comparable to that of the U.S. adult population. Report of caregivers' mental health on the SF-12 varied by type of caregiver but not by caregiver race/ethnicity. Biological parents described themselves as in significantly worse mental health than adoptive parents, foster caregivers, or group home caregivers described themselves.

Depression in permanent caregivers (biological parents, adoptive parents, and kin caregivers) was assessed with the CIDI-SF, a screening scale of the World Health Organization (Kessler, Andrews, Mroczek, Ustun, & Wittchen, 1998; see Technical Appendix). Slightly more than a fifth (20.9%) of caregivers had a score in the clinical range for major depression in the 12 months prior to interview (Exhibit 36). There were no significant differences based upon race/ethnicity or type of caregiver. This rate of depression is higher than that found through the National Comorbidity Survey Replication (NCS-R; Wang, Lane, Olfson, Pincus, Wells, & Kessler, 2005), which used the CIDI to assess depression among U.S. adults aged 18 years or older. The NCS-R found a 6.7% prevalence of major depressive disorder in the year prior to interview and 9.5% prevalence of any mood disorder in the 12 months preceding the interview (Kessler, Chiu, Demler, & Walters, 2005).

Domestic Violence

Female permanent caregivers reported on their experiences of severe and less severe physical IPV, using the Conflict Tactics Scale (Straus, 1979; Exhibit 37; see Technical Appendix). 8.9% of female caregivers were victims of IPV during the 12 months prior to interview: 8.3% suffered acts of less severe violence (had something thrown at them; were pushed, grabbed or shoved; were slapped), and 4.8% had suffered severe physical violence (had been kicked, bitten, or hit with a fist; hit or subject to attempted hitting with something; beaten up; choked; threatened with knife or gun; had a knife or gun used against them). Nationally, the annual prevalence of IPV reported for females of all ages is lower (1.3%; Tjaden & Thoennes, 2000). Almost a quarter (24.0%) of female caregivers had been victims of physical IPV at some point in their lives. This finding is only slightly higher than the national 22.1% lifetime prevalence for IPV among adult females (Tjaden & Thoennes, 2000).

Involvement with the Law

Permanent caregivers were asked about whether they had been arrested, convicted, or put on probation in the past 12 months (Exhibit 38); 3.3% of permanent caregivers reported that they had been arrested in the past year. The rate differed by race/ethnicity and type of caregiver. Hispanic caregivers were significantly less likely to have been arrested in the previous 12 months than Black and White caregivers. Biological parents were significantly more likely to have been arrested in the previous 12 months than adoptive parents. Beyond arrest, 1.2% of caregivers reported that they had been convicted in the past 12 months, and 0.9% reported having been placed on probation. There were no significant differences by race/ethnicity or type of caregiver for reports of conviction or probation.

Caregivers' Receipt of Services to Address Basic Needs

Permanent caregivers were asked about a number of different services that they might have received to address their family's basic living needs (e.g., housing, child care, food). The most commonly reported service was food from a community source (19.2%), followed by financial help (10.7%), excluding Temporary Assistance for Needy Families (TANF) and Supplemental Security Income (SSI), and help with transportation (10.1%; Exhibit 39). Other services included attendance at any organized support group (8.6%), regular help with child care (7.8%), in-home cleaning or repair help (5.2%), job-related services (4.9%), legal aid (4.6%), home management training (1.9%), and emergency shelter or housing (0.8%).

All caregivers, both permanent and nonpermanent, were asked about having received several federal or state-supported services to assist in meeting basic family needs in the 12 months prior to interview. For some of these services (e.g., TANF, welfare, or WIC benefits), one criterion for eligibility is being a poor parent raising children; other services are associated with poverty (such as food stamps) or having a disability (such as SSI benefits). More than a third of adolescents' caregivers were living in poverty at Wave 5 and were thus likely eligible for some of these federal or state supported services.

Well over half of caregivers (60.9%) had received some type of federal service in the past year (Exhibit 40): 10.5% had received TANF, or welfare, and 14.0% had received WIC benefits. Receipt of food stamps was reported by 38.8% of caregivers. More than a quarter (2 8.5%) of caregivers reported having received SSI, and 9.5% reported having received housing support. This receipt of federal or state-supported services was higher than that reported in national data from 2006 (Administration for Children and Families, 2008). The percentages of caregivers receiving TANF, food stamps, and SSI were higher than the national rates of 1.5% for TANF, 8.9% for food stamps, and 2.2% for SSI among all U.S. adults 18 to 64 years of age (Administration for Children and Families, 2008).

Receipt of federal or state-supported services differed by race/ethnicity. White caregivers were significantly less likely to receive WIC than Black and Hispanic caregivers. White caregivers were significantly less likely to receive food stamps than Black caregivers. Black caregivers were significantly more likely to receive housing support than White and Hispanic caregivers. Receipt of federal or state-supported services also differed by type of caregiver. Biological parents and kin caregivers were more likely to receive any federal service than adoptive parents and foster caregivers. Specifically, biological parents were more likely to receive TANF, food stamps and housing support than adoptive parents and foster caregivers. They were also more likely to receive food stamps and housing support than group home caregivers. Kin caregivers were more likely to receive housing support than all other caregiver types. Kin caregivers were also more likely to receive TANF and food stamps than adoptive parents and foster caregivers.

Caregivers' Need for and Receipt of Mental Health Services

Permanent caregivers were asked to report on receipt of mental health services provided through inpatient care, day treatment programs, and outpatient clinics or psychiatric services. Few (5.5%) caregivers reported the receipt of mental health services since the previous interview (Exhibit 41), a rate lower than national estimates of past-year mental health specialty service use among U.S. adults in NCS-R (8.8%; Wang et al., 2005). The NCS-R includes treatment by a psychiatrist (4.5%) or a *nonpsychiatrist mental health specialist* (6.3%; defined as a psychologist or other nonpsychiatrist mental health professional in any setting, social worker, or counselor in a mental health specialty setting, or use of a mental health hotline).

There were significant differences in receipt of mental health services by type of caregiver and insurance status. Biological parents were significantly more likely to have received a mental health service than adoptive parents and kin caregivers. Caregivers with Medicaid were significantly more likely to have used a mental health service than caregivers with private insurance. Receipt of permanent caregiver's mental health services did not vary by caregiver's race/ethnicity.

Caregivers' need for mental health services was examined to determine whether mental health service receipt adequately addressed service needs. Permanent caregivers were determined to be "in need of mental health services" when they met any one of four criteria: (1) the caregiver self-reported the need for "a lot" or "some" help for a mental health problem, (2) a caseworker reported a caregiver's need for a mental health services, (3) self-reported scores were within the clinical range on the major depression scale of the CIDI-SF, or (4) a score exceeded 1.5 standard deviations below the norm (i.e., a score <35) on the Mental Health Component of the SF-12. By this definition, 26.6% of permanent caregivers were determined to be in need of mental health services. Of these, 9.5% had received some mental health service since the previous interview. The NCS-R found that 41.1% of those with a diagnosable mental disorder received professional help in the past year (Olfson, Marcus, Tedeschi, & Wan, 2006; Wang et al., 2005), a proportion much larger than reported here for permanent caregivers.

CHILD WELFARE SYSTEM SERVICES

This final section of the report describes characteristics of adolescents with an open CWS case at Wave 5. At the Wave 5 follow-up, 13.6% (unweighted n = 242) of all adolescent caregivers reported that they were still in contact with the CWS and receiving some type of service. Caseworker surveys were attempted for all of these cases; 214 interviews were completed for an 88.9% response rate. This section of the report summarizes caseworkers' report of the CWS services received by these adolescents and their families.

Characteristics of Adolescents with an Open Child Welfare Case at Wave 5

Exhibit 42 describes the demographic characteristics of adolescents with an open CWS case at Wave 5. Almost half (46.6%) of these adolescents were male; 53.4% were female. Most adolescents were 11 to 12 years old (38.1%); 29.7% were 13 to 14 years old; and 32.2% were 15 to 17 years old. The majority were White (5 1.0%), 26.8% were Hispanic, 18.2% were Black, and 4.0% were of "other" race/ethnicity. Most of the adolescents were living at home with biological parents (51.3%), with 16.7% living in foster care, 15.0% in kin care, 10.7% in group homes or residential programs, and 6.4% with adoptive parents.

Caseworker Report of Services Received by Adolescents with an Open Child Welfare Case

Caseworkers of adolescents with an open CWS case were asked to report on whether an adolescent and his or her family received several different child welfare services. CWS service receipt was based solely on caseworker report; consequently, it should be noted that these results represent the percentage of adolescents with an open CWS case reported to be receiving CWS services, not percentages of the entire adolescent cohort at Wave 5.

Exhibit 43 displays the percentages of cases receiving a variety of caseworker-reported services. The most commonly received CWS service was help with identifying or gaining access to other services (received by 43.2% of all adolescents with an open CWS case). Other commonly received services included family counseling (39.8%), individual parent counseling (3 8.1%), parent training (35.8%), services to prevent out-of-home placement (32.5%), other nonintensive home-based services (26.9%), and family preservation or reunification services (17.5%).

Exhibit 1. Time Line of Data Collection

	Wave				
	1	2	3	4	5[a]
Start and end dates	11/15/99–	10/01/00–	04/0 1/0 1–	08/01/02–	09/05/05–
	04/30/01	03/31/02	09/30/02	02/28/04	12/23/07
Months after close of investigation	2–6	12	18	36	57–98 [b]
Respondent					
Child	X		X	X	X
Current caregiver	X	X	X	X	X
Investigator/services caseworker	X	X	X	X	X
Teacher	X		X	X	X
Young adult					X

[a] Interviews were conducted with children, current caregivers, services caseworkers, and teachers at Wave 5 for children younger than 18 years at the time of the Wave 5 interview. For those aged 18 or older at Wave 5, only a young adult interview was conducted.

[b] This interval refers to the time period for the infant, young child, adolescent, and young adult cohorts at Wave 5. Adolescents at Wave 5 were interviewed 74 to 98 months after the close of the child welfare system investigation.

Exhibit 2. Overall Weighted Response Rates by Wave

	Wave				
	1	2	3	4	5
Overall Weighted Response Rate	64.2%	86.7%	86.6%	85.3%	77.6

Exhibit 3. Characteristics of the Adolescent Population at Wave 5

		Total *N* = 1,484		In home biological parents *n* = 1,019		In home adoptive parents *n* = 100		Kin care *n* = 268		Foster care *n* = 59		Group or residential Care *n* = 35	
	N	%	*SE*	%	*SE*	%	*SE*	%	*SE*	%	*SE*	%	*SE*
Total	1,484	100.0	0.0	77.2	1.8	3.1	0.9	16.1	1.9	2.0	0.6	1.7	0.5
Gender	1,484												
Male	730	51.0	3.0	51.2	3.2	58.5	15.1	46.2	6.0	69.0	13.3	54.3	15.6
Female	754	49.0	3.0	48.8	3.2	41.5	15.1	53.8	6.0	31.0	13.3	45.7	15.6
Age (years) [a]	1,484												
11–12	435	31.0	2.6	32.5	3.2	33.9	15.1	28.2	5.2	19.3	12.7	1.0	0.7
13–14	426	29.9	2.9	31.1	3.5	41.0	14.5	25.3	5.1	11.0	4.4	22.4	15.6
15–17	623	39.0	2.5	36.4	3.1	25.1	9.0	46.5	5.1	69.7	12.8	76.6	15.6
Race/ethnicity	1,483												
Black	448	26.9	3.1	24.8	3.4	15.9	6.5	38.4	6.9	25.6	12.6	35.1	16.4

Exhibit 3. (Continued)

		Total $N = 1{,}484$		In home biological parents $n = 1{,}019$		In home adoptive parents $n = 100$		Kin care $n = 268$		Foster care $n = 59$		Group or residential Care $n = 35$	
	N	%	*SE*	%	*SE*	%	*SE*	%	*SE*	%	*SE*	%	*SE*
White	681	48.1	3.9	47.6	3.9	78.1	7.8	44.7	7.4	35.8	12.1	61.6	16.3
Hispanic	269	19.1	2.7	21.5	3.0	3.7	2.1	10.5	4.7	30.7	16.2	1.4	0.9
Other	85	6.0	1.2	6.1	1.3	2.3	1.7	6.4	2.9	7.9	6.7	2.0	1.7
Grade in school	1,436												
Not in school	50	2.6	0.7	2.3	0.7	0.0	0.0	4.3	2.6	0.4	0.4	—	—
4th or under	21	1.5	0.5	1.6	0.7	0.7	0.7	1.4	0.7	1.4	1.4	—	—
5th–6th	314	25.1	2.4	25.1	2.8	30.7	15.2	24.7	5.5	21.1	14.0	—	—
7th–8th	453	30.3	2.6	32.6	3.0	25.2	8.5	22.1	4.4	5.2	2.9	—	—
9th–10th	425	28.2	2.2	27.3	2.6	39.1	14.5	27.4	5.7	58.4	14.9	—	—
11th–12th	173	12.4	1.8	11.1	2.1	4.4	2.6	20.1	5.8	13.6	7.9	—	—
Insurance status [b]	1,466												
Medicaid	1,013	64.4	2.6	60.0	3.4	88.4	4.6	75.3	4.7	79.1	17.1	99.0	0.8
Private	343	27.0	2.5	31.5	3.0	11.6	4.6	14.6	3.8	0.0	0.0	1.0	0.8
Uninsured	110	8.6	1.5	8.5	1.7	0.0	0.0	10.1	3.9	20.9	17.1	0.0	0.0

Note: All analyses were on weighted data; *N*s are unweighted. Reported Ns vary slightly across analyses because of missing data in some variable categories. Pearson χ^2 tests for cluster samples were used for significance tests. School grade was not available for the majority of adolescents in group care.

[a] Adolescents in home with biological parents, adoptive parents, or kin were significantly more likely to be 11 to 12 years old, while adolescents in group home were more likely to be 15 to 17 years old ($p < .01$).

[b] Adolescents in home with biological parents were significantly more likely to have private insurance than those in home with adoptive parents, kin, or foster parents or those in group homes, who were more likely to have Medicaid ($p < .05$). Adolescents in home with biological parents were also significantly more likely to be uninsured than adolescents living with adoptive parents or in group homes ($p < .05$).

Exhibit 4. Characteristics of Caregivers for the Adolescent Population at Wave 5

Caregiver Characteristic		Total		Biological parents $n = 1{,}011$		Adoptive parents $n = 100$		Kin caregivers $n = 266$		Foster caregivers $n = 55$	
	N	%	*SE*	%	*SE*	%	*SE*	%	*SE*	%	*SE*
Total	1,484	100.0	0.0	77.2	1.8	3.1	0.9	16.1	1.9	2.0	0.6
Gender	1,435										
Male	161	9.1	1.7	9.8	2.0	3.6	2.6	7.2	2.6	5.7	3.1
Female	1,274	90.9	1.7	90.2	2.0	96.5	2.6	92.8	2.6	94.3	3.1
Age (years) [a]	1,435										
<25	9	0.2	0.2	—	—	—	—	—	—	—	—
25–34	370	28.4	2.0	29.8	2.4	3.4	2.5	26.4	6.2	22.4	14.1
35–44	591	44.4	2.3	52.1	2.7	29.2	15.5	13.6	3.8	18.6	9.3
45–54	298	18.9	2.0	16.5	1.9	45.7	14.4	22.5	7.4	42.0	16.2
>54	167	8.1	1.1	1.5	0.9	21.7	7.8	36.1	6.0	17.1	8.9
Race/ethnicity	1,435										
Black	404	24.6	3.4	23.2	3.4	12.3	5.3	31.1	6.9	41.2	16.3
White	741	52.2	3.8	51.1	3.9	79.9	7.1	54.7	6.2	34.7	12.6
Hispanic	210	17.3	3.2	19.5	3.6	5.6	3.2	8.5	4.6	23.1	14.4
Other	82	5.9	1.4	6.3	1.5	2.2	1.2	5.7	2.9	1.0	0.9
Education	1,434										
Less than high school	308	22.8	2.2	21.9	2.2	7.8	5.5	32.1	5.5	9.1	7.3
High school	686	42.9	2.1	45.5	2.4	51.3	14.4	31.5	5.3	22.6	8.9
More than high school	436	34.2	2.3	32.5	2.5	40.9	14.3	36.4	6.8	68.3	11.8
Percentage of federal poverty level [b]	1,392										
<50	199	18.2	2.5	20.7	2.9	0.2	0.2	11.9	4.7	2.4	2.0
50–99	352	24.1	2.3	24.0	2.5	4.3	2.9	31.8	6.3	1.6	1.7
100–200	468	32.5	2.6	32.1	3.6	51.6	14.6	32.0	5.3	19.5	8.1
>200	373	25.3	2.3	23.3	2.9	44.0	14.7	24.4	4.4	76.5	9.5
Employment status [c]	1,435										
Work, full time	598	49.0	2.4	51.8	2.6	40.2	14.8	34.3	5.2	71.0	11.3
Work, part time	217	15.0	2.2	14.6	2.7	24.5	15.1	16.4	5.3	4.4	2.5
Unemployed, looking for work	123	7.8	1.3	9.4	1.5	4.0	2.8	1.9	0.9	0.0	0.0
Does not work	455	25.4	2.3	21.1	2.7	27.1	9.3	45.7	5.5	22.4	10.0
Other	42	2.8	0.8	3.0	1.0	4.4	3.5	1.7	0.9	2.2	1.4
Marital status [d]	1,433										
Married	554	36.9	2.6	32.0	2.9	68.7	10.4	52.5	7.0	52.0	16.1
Separated	171	11.5	1.4	13.6	1.7	0.8	0.6	4.4	1.6	0.3	0.3
Divorced	3,42	28.4	2.9	32.5	3.6	13.1	6.4	12.7	4.5	20.4	13.8
Widowed	58	3.2	0.8	1.4	0.6	4.2	2.7	9.1	3.0	24.6	17.9
Never married	308	20.1	2.7	20.5	3.3	13.2	5.7	21.3	6.4	2.7	1.8

Exhibit 4. (Continued)

Caregiver Characteristic	Total			Biological parents n = 1,011		Adoptive parents n = 100		Kin caregivers n = 266		Foster caregivers n = 55	
	N	%	*SE*	%	*SE*	%	*SE*	%	*SE*	%	*SE*
Number of children in home	1,481										
1	405	28.6	2.0	27.2	2.0	36.0	15.3	27.5	5.3	17.5	7.9
2	379	25.0	2.3	25.9	2.4	13.6	5.3	26.4	6.6	15.5	7.6
3	328	23.9	1.8	25.6	2.2	13.0	5.7	18.6	4.7	39.0	14.0
4	203	13.1	1.6	12.6	1.8	9.8	5.6	16.0	4.5	22.4	16.6
5 or more	166	9.5	1.6	8.6	1.9	27.7	14.9	11.6	4.0	5.5	2.6
Number of adults in home	1,481										
1	533	36.9	2.7	37.4	3.1	25.6	9.3	31.5	6.5	31.3	13.6
2	686	44.2	2.3	45.3	2.6	41.5	14.5	46.6	6.1	14.8	5.7
3	184	13.1	1.8	12.3	1.8	8.5	4.0	15.2	5.0	41.6	15.1
4 or more	78	5.9	1.1	5.0	1.3	24.5	15.2	6.7	3.7	12.4	7.9

Note: All analyses were on weighted data; *N*s are unweighted. Reported Ns vary slightly across analyses because of missing data in some variable categories. Pearson χ^2 tests for cluster samples were used for significance tests. Information was available for only biological parents, adoptive parents, kin caregivers, and foster caregivers.

[a] Biological parents were significantly more likely to be aged 25 to 34 or 35 to 44 years than adoptive parents and kin, who were more likely to be older than 44 ($p < .05$).

[b] Biological parents were significantly more likely to subsist below the federal poverty level than adoptive and foster parents ($p < .05$). Kin were significantly more likely to subsist below the federal poverty level than adoptive parents ($p < .05$).

[c] Foster caregivers were significantly more likely to work full time than biological parents, while biological parents were significantly more likely to work full time than kin caregivers ($p < .05$).

[d] Biological parents were significantly less likely to be married than adoptive, kin, or foster caregivers ($p < .05$).

Exhibit 5. Baseline Child Maltreatment and Risk as Reported by Caseworkers for the Adolescent Population at Wave 5

	N	%	*SE*
Most serious maltreatment type	1,366		
Physical abuse	322	25.9	2.3
Sexual abuse	222	11.4	2.2
Failure to provide	262	22.8	2.3
Failure to supervise	355	25.0	2.6
Emotional abuse	90	7.2	1.6
Moral/legal, educational, or other maltreatment	84	5.5	1.0
Abandonment	31	2.1	0.8
Child welfare system outcome	1,380		
Substantiated	595	28.5	2.8
Indicated	197	7.2	1.5

Exhibit 5. (Continued)

	N	%	*SE*
Unsubstantiated	450	52.7	2.7
High risk	34	0.9	0.3
Medium risk	41	2.8	1.8
Low risk	63	8.0	1.8
Level of harm	1,372		
None	360	45.0	2.4
Mild	397	29.6	2.9
Moderate	414	19.5	2.6
Severe	201	5.9	1.1
Level of risk	1,240		
None	237	32.1	2.9
Mild	360	36.9	2.4
Moderate	410	23.6	2.2
Severe	233	7.5	1.2
Risk factors			
Prior reports of child maltreatment	1,362	53.5	2.6
Prior investigation of child maltreatment	763	94.9	2.1
Prior incident of substantiated child maltreatment	707	55.6	4.6
Prior child welfare service history	1,305	31.2	2.8
Child had major special needs or behavioral problems	1,357	20.3	2.6
Active alcohol abuse by primary caregiver	1,299	8.1	1.3
Active alcohol abuse by secondary caregiver	907	9.9	1.8
Active drug abuse by primary caregiver	1,286	8.1	1.4
Active drug abuse by secondary caregiver	895	9.7	1.8
Primary caregiver had serious mental health problem	1,315	16.2	2.2
Primary caregiver had recent history of arrests	1,275	12.4	1.9
Primary caregiver had intellectual or cognitive impairments	1,339	8.1	1.6
Primary caregiver had physical impairments	1,350	6.6	1.1
Primary caregiver had poor parenting skills	1,356	29.9	2.4
Parent had unreal expectations of child	1,327	15.0	1.7
History of domestic violence against caregiver	1,293	27.3	2.7
Active domestic violence against caregiver	1,326	14.3	2.1
Primary caregiver used inappropriate or excessive discipline	1,341	6.9	1.1
Secondary caregiver used inappropriate or excessive discipline	963	12.0	1.8
History of abuse or neglect of primary caregiver	1,121	23.7	2.6

Note: All analyses were on weighted data; *N*s are unweighted. Reported Ns vary slightly across analyses because of missing data in some variable categories.

Exhibit 6. Placement History for the Adolescent Population at Wave 5

		Total		In home biological parents $n = 1{,}019$		In home adoptive parents $n = 100$		Kin care $n = 268$		Foster care $n = 59$		Group or residential care $n = 35$	
	N	%	*SE*	%	*SE*	%	*SE*	%	*SE*	%	*SE*	%	*SE*
Total	1,481	100.0	0.0	77.2	1.8	3.1	0.9	16.1	1.9	2.0	0.6	1.7	0.5
Out-of-home placement history [a]	1,403												
Ever placed out of home	571	22.6	2.1	11.1	1.6	88.0	5.2	48.2	7.8	100.0	0.0	100.0	0.0
Number of out-of-home placements [b]	1,400												
0	829	77.4	2.1	88.9	1.6	12.0	5.2	51.8	7.8	0.0	0.0	0.0	0.0
1	294	13.3	1.8	7.5	1.5	25.6	9.0	37.5	7.5	2.0	1.3	41.8	15.9
2–3	155	6.1	1.2	2.9	0.8	37.1	14.7	9.5	4.1	46.0	15.5	20.6	13.3
4 or more	122	3.2	0.9	0.7	0.2	25.3	16.2	1.2	0.6	52.0	15.3	37.6	15.6

Note: All analyses were on weighted data; *N*s are unweighted. Reported *N*s vary slightly across analyses because of missing data in some variable categories. Pearson χ^2 tests for cluster samples were used for significance tests.

[a] Adolescents in home with biological parents were significantly less likely to have been placed out of home than all other adolescents ($p < .001$). Similarly, adolescents living with kin were significantly less likely to have been placed out of home than adolescents adopted, in foster care, or in group care ($p < .001$).

[b] Adolescents in home with biological parents were more likely to have zero out-of-home placements than all other adolescents ($p < .05$). Adolescents in kin care were less likely to have two or more placements than adolescents adopted, in foster care, or in group care ($p < .05$).

Exhibit 7. Caregivers' Self-Reported Aggression toward and Neglect of Adolescents in the Previous Year, by Characteristics of the Adolescent Population at Wave 5

		Nonviolent discipline		Psychological aggression		Minor assault or corporal punishment		Severe physical assault		Very severe assault		Neglect		Sexual abuse	
	N	%	*SE*	%	*SE*	%	*SE*	%	*SE*	%	*SE*	%	*SE*	%	*SE*
Total	1,346	95.2	1.4	81.7	2.3	40.1	3.3	7.0	1.3	2.3	0.9	32.9	2.3	1.5	0.6
Gender	1,346							*							
Male	652	96.5	1.5	81.7	2.8	40.7	4.5	10.2	2.3	3.6	1.6	33.0	2.5	0.7	0.3
Female	694	93.8	2.2	81.8	3.1	39.5	4.1	3.7	1.0	1.0	0.6	32.9	3.9	2.3	1.2
Age (years)	1,346	**		**		***		*							
11–12	412	97.3	2.2	92.3[a]	2.2	53.8	5.2	10.4[b]	3.3	3.8	2.4	32.9	5.0	0.3	0.2
13–14	390	99.4	0.4	80.1	3.9	43.0	5.5	7.8	2.3	0.5	0.3	39.9	3.7	1.5	0.6
15–17	544	89.9[c]	2.9	73.9	3.8	26.0[d]	4.2	3.4	1.2	2.6	1.1	27.3	3.8	2.5	1.5
Race/ethnicity	1,345														
Black	406	94.3	3.1	90.2	2.3	48.5	4.6	10.0	3.2	2.8	1.2	34.6	4.8	2.0	1.0
White	621	95.0	1.8	81.7	3.6	34.8	4.4	5.3	1.7	2.3	1.6	29.5	3.6	1.8	1.2

Exhibit 7. (Continued)

		Nonviolent discipline		Psychological aggression		Minor assault or corporal punishment		Severe physical assault		Very severe assault		Neglect		Sexual abuse	
	N	%	*SE*	%	*SE*	%	*SE*	%	*SE*	%	*SE*	%	*SE*	%	*SE*
Hispanic	243	96.5	2.2	76.4	5.8	45.9	8.2	7.4	3.3	2.6	1.8	37.1	5.1	0.3	0.2
Other	75	96.4	2.9	61.3	11.0	27.8	10.2	5.9	3.7	0.0	0.0	39.0	10.0	0.1	0.2
Placement at Wave 5	1,346	*													
In home biological parents	1,003	95.6 [e]	1.4	80.8	2.8	41.6	3.4	7.1	1.4	2.5	1.0	34.4	2.6	1.7	0.8
In home adoptive parents	100	100.0	0.0	95.6	2.9	46.8	14.9	4.1	2.7	0.2	0.2	19.9	7.5	0.4	0.4
Kin care	243	92.0	4.7	83.6	4.4	31.1	6.6	6.8	4.6	1.8	1.2	27.6	5.8	0.4	0.2

Note: The instrument used was the Conflict Tactics Scale Parent-Child Version (Straus et al., 1998). All analyses were on weighted data; *N*s are unweighted. Reported Ns vary slightly across analyses because of missing data in some variable categories. Pearson χ^2 tests for cluster samples were used for significance tests. Asterisks indicate statistical significance (*$p < .05$, **$p < .01$, ***$p < .001$). Asterisks in a column apply to the subsequent results for the covariate. Foster and group or residential caregivers were not asked about aggression and neglect.

[a] The 11- to 12-year-olds were significantly more likely to receive psychological aggression than 13- to 14-year-olds ($p < .05$) or 15- to 17-year-olds ($p < .001$).

[b] The 11- to 12-year-olds were significantly more likely to receive severe physical assault than 15- to 17-year-olds ($p < .05$).

[c] The 15- to 17-year-olds were significantly less likely to receive nonviolent discipline than 11- to 12-year-olds ($p < .05$) or 13- to 14-year-olds ($p < .001$).

[d] The 15- to 17-year-olds were significantly less likely to receive minor assault or corporal punishment than 11- to 12-year-olds ($p < .00 1$) or 13- to 14-year-olds ($p < .01$).

[e] Adolescents living in home with biological parents were significantly less likely to receive nonviolent discipline than adolescents living with adoptive parents ($p < .05$).

Exhibit 8. Adolescent-Reported Aggression and Neglect from a Caregiver in the Previous Year, by Characteristics of the Adolescent Population at Wave 5

	N	Nonviolent Discipline		Psychological Aggression		Minor Assault or Corporal Punishment		Severe Physical Assault		Very Severe Assault	
		%	*SE*	%	*SE*	%	*SE*	%	*SE*	%	*SE*
Total	1,332	82.6	2.6	57.6	3.0	30.0	2.7	9.6	1.7	5.8	1.0
Gender	1,332					*					
Male	634	81.1	2.9	52.5	3.4	24.7	3.0	9.2	1.7	7.3	1.6
Female	698	84.2	3.4	62.8	4.4	35.3	3.9	9.9	2.3	4.2	1.2
Age (years)	1,332										
11–12	391	81.4	3.9	52.0	5.1	36.3	4.3	7.9	2.0	5.9	1.8
13–14	385	77.9	5.4	64.6	4.7	32.8	6.1	12.5	3.3	4.9	1.5
15–17	556	87.0	2.7	56.7	4.7	23.2	4.0	8.7	2.5	6.3	1.9
Race/ethnicity	1,331							**		*	
Black	405	85.0	4.0	61.9	4.6	39.5	5.8	19.8 [a]	4.1	10.3 [b]	2.6

Exhibit 8. (Continued)

	N	Nonviolent Discipline		Psychological Aggression		Minor Assault or Corporal Punishment		Severe Physical Assault		Very Severe Assault	
		%	*SE*	%	*SE*	%	*SE*	%	*SE*	%	*SE*
White	616	82.7	2.5	57.6	3.7	27.6	2.9	7.3 [c]	1.8	4.9	1.4
Hispanic	235	76.2	6.5	50.9	8.1	25.4	6.0	1.9	0.9	2.3	1.2
Other	75	91.0	4.1	59.2	12.0	20.5	6.7	5.2	2.2	2.5	1.5
Placement at Wave 5	1,331										
In home biological parents	924	82.8	2.9	58.0	3.3	29.9	2.9	9.6	1.7	5.4	1.1
In home adoptive parents	86	72.7	17.3	65.3	12.3	20.8	7.8	12.1	5.8	6.4	4.4
Kin care	244	81.9	4.7	60.6	5.4	34.2	5.8	7.6	2.2	7.6	2.4
Foster care	49	87.0	8.0	49.7	16.5	5.0	2.5	3.7	2.2	3.3	2.2
Group home or residential program	28	99.1	0.9	64.9	17.1	40.3	20.1	38.6	20.7	6.4	3.7

Note: Instrument used was the Conflict Tactics Scale Parent-Child (Straus et al., 1998). All analyses were on weighted data; Ns are unweighted. Reported Ns vary slightly across analyses because of missing data in some variable categories. Pearson χ^2 tests for cluster samples were used for significance tests. Asterisks indicate statistical significance (*$p < .05$, ** $p < .01$). Asterisks in a column apply to the subsequent results for the covariate.

[a] Black adolescents were significantly more likely to report having received severe physical assault than White ($p < .01$), "Other" ($p < .01$), or Hispanic ($p <$ 001).

[b] Black adolescents were significantly more likely to report having received very severe assault than Hispanic ($p < .01$) and "Other" ($p < .05$).

[c] White adolescents were significantly more likely to report having received severe physical assault than Hispanic ($p < .05$).

Exhibit 9. Adolescents' Reports of Recent Domestic Violence at Wave 5

			Yes
Type of Incident	*N*	%	*SE*
Violence witnessing items			
Adolescent saw adult yell at other	1,177	20.8	2.6
Adolescent saw adult throw something at other	1,298	2.9	0.7
Adolescent saw adult shove other	1,291	3.4	0.8
Adolescent saw adult slap other	1,292	3.9	1.1
Adolescent saw adult beat up other	1,307	1.2	0.5
Adolescent saw adult steal at home	1,299	5.7	1.4
Adolescent saw adult point knife or gun at other	1,312	1.2	0.6
Adolescent saw adult stab other	1,325	0.2	0.2
Adolescent saw adult shoot other	1,326	0.2	0.2
Adolescent saw person arrested at home	1,311	2.1	0.9
Adolescent saw person deal drugs at home	1,304	0.9	0.4
Adolescent saw child being spanked	1,276	18.1	1.9
Violence victimization items			
Adult yelled at the adolescent	1,218	28.2	2.6

Exhibit 9. (Continued)

			Yes
Type of Incident	*N*	%	*SE*
Adult threw something at the adolescent	1,299	2.9	0.8
Adult shoved the adolescent "really hard"	1,302	2.9	0.8
Adult slapped the adolescent "really hard"	1,292	2.5	0.7
Adult beat up the adolescent	1,287	1.4	0.5
Adult pointed a gun or knife at the adolescent	1,320	0.3	0.2
Adult spanked the adolescent	1,266	4.1	1.0

Note: Instrument used was the Violence Exposure Scale–Revised (Fox & Leavitt, 1995). All analyses were on weighted data; *N*s are unweighted. Reported Ns vary slightly across analyses because of missing data in some variable categories.

Exhibit 10. Adolescents' Caregiver-Reported Physical Health and Chronic Conditions, by Characteristics of the Adolescent Population at Wave 5

		Good Health		Chronic Health Condition at Wave 5	
	N	%	*SE*	%	*SE*
Total	1,467	94.6	1.1	10.6	1.5
Gender	1,467	**			
Male	722	97.4	0.9	8.8	1.8
Female	745	91.6	1.9	12.6	2.1
Age (years)	1,467				
11–12	432	95.9	1.5	15.2	2.9
13–14	422	96.3	1.1	7.7	1.7
15–17	613	92.2	2.3	9.2	2.2
Race/ethnicity	1,466			*	
Black	447	95.1	2.1	8.1	1.7
White	674	94.8	1.7	13.4 [a]	2.4
Hispanic	262	94.8	2.6	4.7	2.1
Other	83	89.6	7.0	18.8	7.8
Placement at Wave 5	1,465				
In home biological parents	1,010	94.1	1.3	10.5	1.7
In home adoptive parents	100	99.3	0.5	9.7	4.6
Kin care	266	94.9	2.7	11.7	3.3
Foster care	57	98.8	1.3	12.6	8.6
Group home or residential program	32	98.0	1.3	6.9	4.3

Note: All analyses were on weighted data; *N*s are unweighted. Reported *N*s vary slightly across analyses because of missing data in some variable categories. Pearson χ^2 tests for cluster samples were used for significance tests. Asterisks indicate statistical significance (*$p < .05$, **$p < .01$,). Asterisks in a column apply to the subsequent results for the covariate.

[a] White adolescents had a significantly greater number of chronic health conditions than Hispanic ($p < .05$).

Exhibit 11. Adolescents' Self-Reported Depression and Trauma, by Characteristics of the Adolescent Population at Wave 5

	N	Depression			Trauma	
		%	*SE*	*N*	%	*SE*
Total	1,394	5.0	1.1	1,397	5.9	1.0
Gender	1,394	***		1,397		
Male	674	1.0	0.4	675	6.5	1.7
Female	720	9.1	2.2	722	5.4	1.5
Age (years)	1,394			1,397		
11–12	414	3.8	1.5	417	5.8	1.6
13–14	408	5.2	2.5	409	9.1	2.7
15–17	572	5.7	1.7	571	3.6	1.3
Race/ethnicity	1,393			1,396		
Black	424	7.9	2.4	425	5.9	1.8
White	642	4.3	1.4	644	7.1	1.6
Hispanic	248	2.3	1.4	248	4.1	2.2
Other	79	5.1	3.6	79	2.4	1.6
Placement at Wave 5	1,392			1,395		
In home biological parents	961	4.8	1.4	963	5.9	1.2
In home adoptive parents	93	3.9	2.1	93	4.6	2.5
Kin care	251	4.1	1.9	252	6.9	2.3
Foster care	56	10.2	7.5	56	0.1	0.1
Group home or residential program	31	18.3	12.2	31	10.1	9.9

Note: Instruments used were the Children's Depression Inventory (Kovacs, 1992) and the Posttraumatic Stress subscale from the Trauma Symptom Checklist for Children (Briere, 1996). All analyses were on weighted data; *N*s are unweighted. Reported *N*s vary slightly across analyses because of missing data in some variable categories. Pearson χ^2 tests for cluster samples were used for significance tests. Asterisks indicate statistical significance (***$p < .001$). Asterisks in the column apply to the subsequent results for the covariate.

Exhibit 12. Adolescents' Caregiver-Reported Behavioral Problems, by Characteristics of the Adolescent Population at Wave 5

	N	Total score in clinical range		Internalizing score in clinical range		Externalizing score in clinical range	
		%	*SE*	%	*SE*	%	*SE*
Total	1,468	23.2	2.3	15.4	1.8	26.9	2.5
Gender	1,468			**			
Male	723	25.5	3.3	19.5	2.8	25.5	3.4
Female	745	20.8	2.7	11.2	1.8	28.4	3.2
Age (years)	1,468						
11–12	432	23.4	3.5	17.7	2.8	29.9	4.1
13–14	422	20.0	4.2	10.6	2.8	21.4	4.2
15–17	614	25.6	4.1	17.2	3.0	28.9	4.1
Race/ethnicity	1,467	*					
Black	447	22.0	4.0	13.8	3.4	31.5	5.0
White	675	27.8 [a]	2.7	18.0	2.2	27.0	2.9

Exhibit 12. (Continued)

	N	Total score in clinical range		Internalizing score in clinical range		Externalizing score in clinical range	
		%	*SE*	%	*SE*	%	*SE*
Hispanic	263	11.1	3.8	11.6	3.7	20.7	5.7
Other	82	29.5	11.0	13.8	5.2	25.2	10.9
Placement at Wave 5	1,466			*			
In home biological parents	1,010	21.6	2.5	13.9	2.0	25.5	2.6
In home adoptive parents	100	29.8	10.4	24.4	9.2	30.0	10.3
Kin care	267	21.8	4.6	9.9	2.3	25.3	5.4
Foster care	57	28.8	10.6	43.9	15.2	33.9	11.7
Group home or residential program	32	97.0	1.6	87.3[b]	6.5	94.4	2.9

Note: Instrument used was the Child Behavior Checklist (Achenbach, 1991; Achenbach & Rescorla, 2001). All analyses were on weighted data; *N*s are unweighted. Reported *N*s vary slightly across analyses because of missing data in some variable categories. Pearson χ^2 tests for cluster samples were used for significance tests. Asterisks indicate statistical significance (*$p < .05$, **$p < .01$). Asterisks in a column apply to the subsequent results for the covariate.

[a] White adolescents were significantly more likely to have a clinically elevated Total Problems score than Hispanic adolescents ($p < .01$).

[b] Adolescents in group homes were significantly more likely to have a clinically elevated Internalizing scale score than adolescents in home with biological parents ($p < .0\ 1$), adolescents in home with adoptive parents ($p < .0\ 1$), adolescents living with kin ($p < .01$), or adolescents in foster care ($p < .05$).

Exhibit 13. Adolescents' Self-Reported Behavioral Problems, by Characteristics of the Adolescent Population at Wave 5

	N	Total score in clinical range		Internalizing score in clinical range		Externalizing score in clinical range	
		%	*SE*	%	*SE*	%	*SE*
Total	1,403	14.3	2.0	6.9	1.1	21.0	3.1
Gender	1,403					*	
Male	679	12.0	2.7	7.6	1.8	14.8	3.9
Female	724	16.7	2.4	6.3	1.6	27.4	4.1
Age (years)	1,403						
11–12	418	11.0	2.3	6.1	1.8	16.3	4.0
13–14	410	20.2	4.9	6.7	2.1	22.3	5.4
15–17	575	12.4	2.6	7.8	2.3	23.9	4.4
Race/ethnicity	1,402						
Black	425	14.0	2.9	6.6	2.0	27.1	5.4
White	646	15.6	2.7	6.3	1.7	20.4	3.7
Hispanic	251	11.8	6.3	8.6	3.5	14.6	6.8
Other	80	12.7	7.0	8.4	6.5	18.6	7.7
Placement at Wave 5	1,401			*			
In home biological parents	967	14.9	2.5	7.7[a]	1.4	20.3	3.1

Exhibit 13. (Continued)

	N	Total score in clinical range		Internalizing score in clinical range		Externalizing score in clinical range	
		%	*SE*	%	*SE*	%	*SE*
In home adoptive parents	95	11.4	5.6	4.9	2.9	9.4	4.6
Kin care	252	9.3	3.9	2.2	1.0	24.5	6.6
Foster care	56	20.5	10.3	23.7	17.7	20.6	10.3
Group home or residential program	31	38.7	18.7	1.7	1.4	52.1	16.8

Note: Instrument used was the Youth Self-Report (Achenbach, 1991; Achenbach & Rescorla, 2001). All analyses were on weighted data; *N*s are unweighted. Reported *N*s vary slightly across analyses because of missing data in some variable categories. Pearson χ^2 tests for cluster samples were used for significance tests. Asterisks indicate statistical significance (*$p < .05$). An asterisk in a column applies to the subsequent results for the covariate.

[a] Adolescents living with biological parents were significantly more likely to have a clinically elevated Internalizing scale score than adolescents living with kin ($p < .05$).

Exhibit 14. Adolescents' Substance Use as Self-Reported at Wave 5

Substance		Ever used		Used in past 30 days	
	N	%	*SE*	%	*SE*
Alcohol	1,341	33.5	2.2	13.1	1.7
Cigarettes	1,344	28.7	2.8	14.6	2.0
Chewing tobacco or snuff	1,344	6.5	1.2	2.6	0.9
Marijuana or hashish	1,347	17.9	2.3	8.0	1.4
Inhalants	1,347	2.3	0.8	0.8	0.3
Cocaine, crack, or heroin	1,349	2.6	1.0	0.8	0.3
Nonprescribed medications	1,347	6.4	1.5	3.3	1.0

Note: Items used were from Monitoring the Future (Johnston et al., 2007) and Youth Risk Behavior (Centers for Disease Control and Prevention, 1999). All analyses were on weighted data; *N*s are unweighted. Reported Ns vary slightly across analyses because of missing data in some variable categories.

Exhibit 15. Adolescents' Sexual Experience, by Characteristics of the Adolescent Population at Wave 5

		Ever had sex	
	N	%	SE
Total	1,338	28.4	2.1
Gender	1,338		
Male	644	30.7	3.7
Female	694	26.1	3.4
Age (years)	1,338		
11–12	395	*** 2.7 [a]	1.0
13–14	383	22.2 [b]	5.8

Exhibit 15. (Continued)

	N	%	SE
15–17	560	53.2	3.8
Race/ethnicity	1,337		
Black	412	* 37.6 [c]	4.3
White	618	22.7	2.9
Hispanic	231	33.9	6.4
Other	76	15.8	5.5
Placement at Wave 5	1,336		
In home biological parents	932	27.3	2.4
In home adoptive parents	82	7.9	5.0
Kin care	244	32.4	6.6
Foster care	49	41.0	16.8
Group home/residential program	29	73.1	13.0

Note: All analyses were on weighted data; *N*s are unweighted. Reported *N*s vary slightly across analyses because of missing data in some variable categories. Pearson χ^2 tests for cluster samples were used for significance tests. Asterisks indicate statistical significance (*$p < .05$, ***$p < .001$). Asterisks in a column apply to the subsequent results for the covariate.

[a] The 11- to 12-year-olds were significantly less likely to have ever had sex than the 13- to 14-year-olds ($p < .001$) or 15- to 17-year-olds ($p < .001$).

[b] The 13- to 14-year-olds were significantly less likely to have ever had sex than the 15- to 17-year-olds ($p < .00$ 1).

[c] Black adolescents were significantly more likely to have had sex than White adolescents ($p < .01$) or adolescents of "Other" racial identity ($p < .05$).

Exhibit 16. Delinquent Acts Committed by Adolescents in the Previous 6 Months, as Self-Reported at Wave 5

Delinquent act	*N*	%	*SE*
Status offense			
Ran away	1,345	7.8	1.3
Skipped school	1,350	16.5	1.6
Lied about age for movie admittance	1,348	6.6	1.2
Public disorder			
Hitchhiked	1,346	1.1	0.5
Was loud, rowdy, or unruly in public	1,348	16.0	2.5
Was drunk in a public place	1,352	3.8	1.5
Begged for money or things	1,352	2.6	0.7
Carried a hidden weapon	1,350	6.6	1.5
Paid for having sex	1,343	1.7	0.8
Damaged property			
Damaged property	1,346	7.5	1.5
Minor theft			
Stole things worth less than $5	1,345	5.8	1.3
Went joyriding	1,343	2.9	1.0

Exhibit 16. (Continued)

Delinquent act	*N*	%	*SE*
Stole things worth more than $5 but less than $50	1,348	3.1	0.9
Avoided paying for things such as movies, bus rides, or subway rides	1,344	7.0	1.5
Took something from a store without paying for it	1,346	5.5	1.0
Pickpocketed (snatched wallet or purse)	1,346	2.4	1.0
Serious property crime			
Stole vehicle or attempted to steal vehicle	1,344	0.7	0.3
Stole items worth more than $50 but less than $100	1,344	1.2	0.5
Bought or sold stolen goods	1,344	2.5	0.9
Entered or tried to enter a building to steal	1,344	3.6	1.0
Stole items worth more than $100	1,345	1.6	0.6
Took items from a car	1,347	4.8	1.3
Set fire to a house, building, car, or other property	1,346	0.6	0.4
Used false checks	1,343	0.8	0.3
Used credit cards without permission	1,345	0.6	0.2
Deliberately sold an item above its value	1,343	3.9	1.1
Simple assault			
Threw objects, such as rocks or bottles, at another person	1,343	3.5	0.9
Hit someone with the intention of hurting him or her	1,344	13.5	2.2
Felony assault			
Attacked someone with the intention to hurt, harm, or kill	1,345	1.0	0.3
Used threats or weapon to take money or things from another person	1,343	0.4	0.2
Had or tried to have sexual relations with someone against his or her will	1,343	0.4	0.2
Physically hurt or threatened another to have sex against his or her will	1,342	0.5	0.3
Was involved in a gang fight	1,344	7.2	1.6
Sold drugs			
Sold marijuana or hashish	1,339	5.0	1.5
Sold hard drugs	1,338	0.8	0.5

Note: Instrument used was the Self-Report Delinquency Scale (Elliott et al., 1985). All analyses were on weighted data; *N*s are unweighted. Reported Ns vary slightly across analyses because of missing data in some variable categories.

Exhibit 17. Types of Self-Reported Delinquent Acts Committed by Adolescents in the Previous 6 Months, by Characteristics of the Adolescent Population at Wave 5

	N	Status offense		Public disorder		Damaged property		Minor theft		Serious property crime		Simple assault		Felony assault		Sold drugs	
		%	*SE*	%	*SE*	%	*SE*	%	*SE*	%	*SE*	%	*SE*	%	*SE*	%	*SE*
Total	1,354	25.6	2.1	22.7	2.8	7.5	1.5	15.3	2.0	9.6	1.7	15.3	2.2	8.1	1.6	5.1	1.5
Gender	1,354							**									
Male	648	23.5	3.4	24.6	4.2	8.0	1.9	20.4	3.1	11.4	2.5	17.9	3.1	11.1	2.8	7.1	2.7
Female	706	27.7	3.5	20.7	3.0	7.0	2.1	10.0	2.1	7.7	2.0	12.5	2.6	5.1	1.4	3.0	1.3
Age (years)	1,354	***				***								**		**	
11–12	400	10.4 [a]	3.1	15.1	3.4	1.4[b]	0.5	11.5	3.8	6.1	2.9	14.7	3.7	2.3[c]	0.7	0.2[d]	0.1
13–14	391	25.1 [e]	4.0	23.6	6.3	9.5	3.7	17.1	2.9	14.2	3.0	15.1	4.2	14.1	4.7	7.2	4.3
15–17	563	37.7	4.1	27.9	4.0	10.7	2.7	16.8	3.0	8.9	2.4	15.8	3.7	8.2	2.3	7.2	2.3
Race/ethnicity	1,353	*		*						**		**					
Black	414	31.2	4.4	32.1[f]	4.8	11.1	3.5	15.6	2.7	12.5 [g]	2.7	27.4[h]	4.6	8.9	2.7	4.6	2.1
White	624	20.7 [i]	2.5	18.5	2.5	6.5	1.9	13.4	2.9	5.3	1.7	10.6	2.4	4.9	1.6	4.1	1.6
Hispanic	39	33.6	6.7	18.1	7.1	4.6	3.0	21.1	4.7	18.9[j]	4.9	7.8	3.7	17.0	7.4	9.9	6.8
Other	76	16.2	5.3	28.0	11.7	8.1	3.8	11.7	4.7	3.5	2.2	21.4	11.6	4.7	2.5	0.4	0.3
Placement at Wave 5	1,352																
In home biological parents	939	25.2	2.7	22.9	2.9	6.4	1.7	14.5	2.1	8.9	2.0	12.5	2.2	9.0	2.0	5.8	1.9
In home adoptive parents	86	16.4	7.1	14.9	7.9	4.8	4.1	13.5	7.6	1.6	1.0	7.2	4.6	4.7	4.0	0.0	0.0
Kin care	248	24.3	5.7	22.7	5.6	6.0	2.6	12.5	5.5	8.5	4.0	23.8	7.1	3.1	1.4	1.3	0.9
Foster care	49	45.7	16.3	15.3	8.6	43.0	17.2	43.1	17.0	35.9	17.3	55.1	15.4	26.7	18.4	2.4	1.9
Group home or residential program	30	57.8	17.2	41.0	19.7	54.6	18.3	63.5	14.4	45.4	19.3	33.0	21.0	2.1	1.7	29.4	22.0

Note: Instrument used was the Self-Report Delinquency Scale (Elliott et al., 1985). All analyses were on weighted data; Ns are unweighted. Reported *N*s vary slightly across analyses because of missing data in some variable categories. Pearson χ^2 tests for cluster samples were used for significance tests. Asterisks indicate statistical significance (*$p < .05$, **$p < .01$, ***$p < .001$). Asterisks in a column apply to the subsequent results for the covariate.

[a] The 11- to 12-year-olds were significantly less likely to commit a status offense than the 13- to 14-year-olds ($p < .01$) or 15- to 17-year-olds ($p < .001$).

[b] The 11- to 12-year-olds were significantly less likely to have damaged property than the 13- to 14-year-olds ($p < .05$) or 15- to 17-year-olds ($p < .01$).

[c] The 11- to 12-year-olds were significantly less likely to have committed felony assault than the 13- to 14-year-olds and 15- to 17-year-olds ($p < .05$).

[d] The 11- to 12-year-olds were significantly less likely to have sold drugs than the 15- to 17-year- olds ($p < .01$).

[e] The 13- to 14-year-olds were significantly less likely to commit a status offense than the 15- to 17-year-olds ($p < .05$).

[f] Black adolescents were significantly more likely to have committed public disorder than White ($p < .0 1$).

[g] Black adolescents were significantly more likely to have committed a serious property crime than White ($p < .05$) or Other ($p < .05$).

[h] Black adolescents were significantly more likely to have committed simple assault than White ($p < .01$) or Hispanic ($p < .0 1$).

[i] Black adolescents were significantly more likely to have committed a status offense than White ($p < .05$).

[j] Hispanic adolescents were significantly more likely to have committed a serious property crime than White ($p < .05$) or Other ($p < .05$).

Exhibit 18. Adolescents' Self-Reported Arrests in the Previous 6 Months, by Characteristics of the Adolescent Population at Wave 5

	N	Arrested or picked up by police	
		%	*SE*
Total	1,338	8.1	1.7
Gender	1,338	*	
Male	639	11.8	3.0
Female	699	4.3	1.6
Age (years)	1,338		
11–12	392	3.4	1.8
13–14	386	9.9	4.4
15–17	560	10.5	3.0
Race/ethnicity	1,337		
Black	404	11.3	3.6
White	620	4.3	1.4
Hispanic	237	15.8	6.8
Other	76	2.5	1.8
Placement at Wave 5	1,336		
In home biological parents	930	7.6	2.1
In home adoptive parents	85	4.5	4.1
Kin care	244	9.3	4.6
Foster care	48	1.7	1.7
Group home or residential program	29	43.3	19.8

Note: Instrument used was the Self-Report Delinquency Scale (Elliott et al., 1985). All analyses were on weighted data; *N*s are unweighted. Reported *N*s vary slightly across analyses because of missing data in some variable categories. Pearson χ^2 tests for cluster samples were used for significance tests. Asterisks indicate statistical significance (*$p < .05$). The asterisk in the column applies to the subsequent results for the covariate.

Exhibit 19. Adolescents' Caregiver-Reported Involvement with the Law in the Previous 12 Months, by Characteristics of the Adolescent Population at Wave 5

		Had a court appearance for behavioral problem		Was Placed on probation for behavioral offense		Spent time in detention center or correctional facility	
	N	%	*SE*	%	*SE*	%	*SE*
Total	1,460	10.6	1.5	5.7	1.4	0.8	0.3
Gender	1,460	*		*		*	
Male	718	14.5	2.7	8.5	2.4	1.4	0.5
Female	742	6.5	1.6	2.8	1.1	0.1	0.1
Age (years)	1,460	***		**			
11–12	431	2.1 [a]	0.7	1.1 [b]	0.6	0.5	0.3
13–14	420	9.5	2.8	4.8	2.2	0.3	0.2
15–17	609	18.4	3.6	10.2	3.2	1.4	0.6
Race/ethnicity	1,459						
Black	444	12.9	3.3	7.3	2.9	1.1	0.7
White	670	9.4	2.1	3.8	1.5	0.8	0.4

Exhibit 19. (Continued)

		Had a court appearance for behavioral problem		Was Placed on probation for behavioral offense		Spent time in detention center or correctional facility	
	N	%	*SE*	%	*SE*	%	*SE*
Hispanic	262	8.5	3.4	5.8	3.2	0.5	0.5
Other	83	17.0	9.4	13.7	9.6	0.0	0.0
Placement at Wave 5	1,458						
In home biological parents	1,009	10.7	1.9	5.8	1.6	0.8	0.3
In home adoptive parents	99	4.0	2.7	1.2	1.0	2.8	2.5
Kin care	265	8.1	3.3	3.3	2.7	0.1	0.1
Foster care	55	29.4	16.3	24.2	17.0	0.0	0.0
Group home or residential program	30	21.4	11.3	8.7	7.1	0.0	0.0

Note: All analyses were on weighted data; Ns are unweighted. Reported Ns vary slightly across analyses because of missing data in some variable categories. Pearson χ^2 tests for cluster samples were used for significance tests. Asterisks indicate statistical significance (*$p < .05$, **$p < .01$, ***$p < .001$). Asterisks in a column apply to the subsequent results for the covariate.

[a] The 11- to 12-year-olds were significantly less likely to have a court appearance than the 13- to 14-year-olds ($p < .05$) or 15- to 17-year-olds ($p < .001$).

[b] The 11- to 12-year-olds were significantly less likely to be placed on probation than the 15- to 17-year-olds ($p < .01$).

Exhibit 20. Adolescents' Cognitive Test Scores, by Characteristics of the Adolescent Population at Wave 5

	N	K-BIT composite		K-BIT vocabulary		K-BIT matrices	
		Mean	*SE*	Mean	*SE*	Mean	*SE*
Total	1,410	91.5	0.9	88.5	0.8	96.1	1.0
Gender	1,410						
Male	684	92.5	1.2	89.2	1.1	97.0	1.4
Female	726	90.6	1.1	87.7	1.2	95.1	1.1
Age (years)	1,410	***				***	
11–12	419	95.5[a]	1.4	90.5	1.4	101.2[a]	1.4
13–14	410	89.6	1.4	87.7	1.4	93.4	1.6
15–17	581	90.0	1.2	87.6	1.3	94.2	1.2
Race/ethnicity	1,409	**		***			
Black	427	88.8	1.1	85.6	1.1	94.2	1.4
White	648	93.9[b]	1.3	92.0[c]	1.2	96.8	1.4
Hispanic	253	90.3	2.2	84.5	2.1	97.7	2.4
Other	81	88.7	3.2	85.2	3.4	93.9	2.9
Placement at Wave 5	1,408	*					*
In home biological parents	970	91.6	1.0	88.3	0.9	96.5	1.1
In home adoptive parents	95	93.1	4.7	92.0	2.6	95.5	6.0

Exhibit 20. (Continued)

	N	K-BIT composite		K-BIT vocabulary		K-BIT matrices	
		Mean	*SE*	Mean	*SE*	Mean	*SE*
Kin care	253	91.7	1.7	89.7	2.1	95.1	1.5
Foster care	57	92.4	2.0	89.2	2.1	97.3	1.9
Group home or residential program	33	82.1 [d]	5.1	79.8	5.8	87.7[e]	3.7

Note: Instrument used was the Kaufman Brief Intelligence Test (K-BIT; Kaufman & Kaufman, 2004). All analyses were on weighted data; Ns are unweighted. T tests for cluster samples were used to test statistical significance. Asterisks indicate statistical significance (*$p < .05$, **$p < .01$, ***$p <$ .00 1). Asterisks in a column apply to the subsequent results for the covariate.

[a] The 11- to 12-year-olds had a significantly higher mean score than the 13- to 14-year-olds ($p <$ .00 1) or 15- to 17- year-olds ($p < .001$).

[b] White adolescents had a significantly higher mean score than Black ($p < .01$).

[c] White adolescents had a significantly higher mean score than Black ($p < .001$), Hispanic ($p < .01$), and Other ($p < .05$).

[d] Adolescents living in group homes or residential programs had a significantly lower mean score than adolescents living in foster care ($p < .05$).

[e] Adolescents living in group homes or residential programs had a significantly lower mean score than those living in home with biological parents ($p < .05$) or with foster caregivers ($p < .05$).

Exhibit 21. Adolescents' Low Cognitive Test Scores, by Characteristics of the Adolescent Population at Wave 5

	N	K-BIT Composite				K-BIT Vocabulary				K-BIT Matrices			
		-1 to -1.99 *SD*		-2 *SD* or less		-1 to -1.99 *SD*		-2 *SD* or less		-1 to -1.99 *SD*		-2 *SD* or less	
		%	*SE*	%	*SE*	%	*SE*	%	*SE*	%	*SE*	%	*SE*
Total	1,410	21.5	2.0	8.7	1.8	23.1	2.2	13.0	1.8	19.1	2.2	5.9	1.3
Gender	1,410												
Male	684	22.0	3.1	7.0	1.6	23.5	3.1	12.1	2.7	18.5	3.0	6.3	1.6
Female	726	21.0	2.4	10.5	3.2	13.9	3.1	13.9	3.1	19.8	2.9	5.5	1.7
Age (years)	1,410			*								*	
11–12	419	19.1	4.3	3.5[a]	1.2	23.9	3.2	12.0	3.5	13.3	3.8	1.7[b]	0.8
13–14	410	25.7	4.0	11.3	3.1	22.9	3.6	13.1	3.3	23.6	4.4	9.6	3.0
15–17	581	20.3	3.5	10.9	2.6	22.6	3.5	13.7	2.6	20.3	3.5	6.4	1.6
Race/ethnicity	1,409					**							
Black	427	25.1	4.3	8.6	2.1	32.8[c]	5.3	14.1	2.9	19.8	3.6	6.3	1.5
White	648	20.1	2.6	6.4	2.1	16.7	2.4	10.0	2.5	18.7	2.7	6.6	2.1
Hispanic	253	18.6	5.6	14.0	6.2	24.3	6.0	20.3	6.0	16.2	6.3	3.2	1.8
Other	81	26.0	11.2	11.7	7.1	28.0	11.0	9.3	6.8	29.1	11.1	7.7	3.8
Placement at Wave 5	1,408												
In home biological parents	970	22.0	2.1	8.8	1.9	22.7	2.5	14.0	2.2	18.5	2.3	6.3	1.5

Exhibit 21. (Continued)

	N	K-BIT Composite				K-BIT Vocabulary				K-BIT Matrices			
		-1 to -1.99 *SD*		-2 *SD* or less		-1 to -1.99 *SD*		-2 *SD* or less		-1 to -1.99 *SD*		-2 *SD* or less	
		%	*SE*	%	*SE*	%	*SE*	%	*SE*	%	*SE*	%	*SE*
In home adoptive parents	95	36.1	14.7	5.4	3.5	10.9	4.5	8.5	4.6	33.4	15.3	9.4	4.6
Kin care	253	15.4	4.7	8.4	4.1	28.2	7.7	7.5	3.8	18.3	5.3	4.0	1.6
Foster care	57	15.1	7.9	3.8	2.2	16.7	8.4	4.4	2.8	11.6	7.4	2.3	1.3
Group home or residential program	33	39.3	16.0	17.9	14.1	21.9	10.5	36.4	17.6	36.8	17.1	5.5	4.3

Note: Instrument used was the Kaufman Brief Intelligence Test (K-BIT; Kaufman & Kaufman, 2004). All analyses were on weighted data; Ns are unweighted. Reported Ns vary slightly across analyses because of missing data in some variable categories. Pearson χ^2 tests for cluster samples were used for significance tests. Asterisks indicate statistical significance (*$p < .05$, ** $p < .01$). Asterisks in a column apply to the subsequent results for the covariate.

[a] When K-BIT Composite scores 2 SD below the mean were compared with those in the normative range, 11- to 12-year-olds were found to be significantly less likely than 13- to 14-year-olds or 15- to 17-year-olds to have scores 2 or more SD below the mean ($p < .05$).

[b] When K-BIT Matrices scores 2 SD below the mean were compared with those in the normative range, 11- to 12-year-olds were found to be significantly less likely than 13- to 14-year-olds or 15- to 17-year-olds to have scores 2 or more SD below the mean ($p < .0 1$).

[c] When K-BIT Vocabulary scores one to 1.99 SD below the mean were compared with those in the normative range, Black adolescents were found to be significantly more likely than White to have scores one to 1.99 SD below the mean ($p < .0 1$).

Exhibit 22. Adolescents' School Achievement Test Scores, by Characteristics of the Adolescent Population at Wave 5

	N	Woodcock-Johnson letter identification		Woodcock-Johnson passage comprehension		Woodcock-Johnson calculation		Woodcock-Johnson applied problems	
		Mean	*SE*	Mean	*SE*	Mean	*SE*	Mean	*SE*
Total	1,412	93.4	1.1	85.7	1.0	88.3	1.4	88.9	0.8
Gender	1,412								
Male	684	92.6	1.5	84.7	1.4	87.5	1.7	88.7	1.2
Female	728	94.2	1.3	86.7	1.2	89.0	1.9	89.2	1.1
Age (years)	1,412	***		*		***		***	
11–12	419	97.5[a]	1.7	88.3[b]	1.3	95.4[c]	1.6	94.3[d]	1.1
13–14	409	93.4	1.9	85.1	1.7	86.8	3.3	87.9	1.5
15–17	584	90.1	1.7	84.1	1.4	83.7	1.4	85.6	1.2
Race/ethnicity	1,411	*		*					
Black	428	90.8	1.3	83.5	1.2	87.2	1.7	87.8	0.8
White	648	95.2[e]	1.7	87.7[f]	1.5	87.8	2.2	90.4	1.4

Exhibit 22. (Continued)

	N	Woodcock-Johnson letter identification		Woodcock-Johnson passage comprehension		Woodcock-Johnson calculation		Woodcock-Johnson applied problems	
		Mean	*SE*	Mean	*SE*	Mean	*SE*	Mean	*SE*
Hispanic	254	93.7	1.8	84.8	1.9	92.0	2.0	87.7	1.9
Other	81	89.3	4.0	81.5	3.2	85.5	3.5	86.5	2.6
Placement at Wave 5	1,410			*		*		*	
In home biological parents	971	93.1	1.3	85.8	1.2	88.4	1.7	89.3	0.9
In home adoptive parents	95	101.4	5.4	86.8	3.3	96.0	6.5	93.8	5.1
Kin care	254	94.0	2.3	86.8	1.6	88.2	2.6	88.1	1.9
Foster care	57	92.1	3.2	88.3	3.0	84.2	4.1	85.2	3.5
Group home or residential program	33	88.6	6.3	65.4 [g]	10.2	72.6 [h]	6.8	77.1 [h]	4.4

Note: Instrument used was the Woodcock-Johnson III Tests of Cognitive Abilities (Woodcock et al., 2001). All analyses were on weighted data; *N*s are unweighted. T tests for cluster samples were used to test statistical significance. Asterisks indicate statistical significance (*$p < .05$, **$p < .01$, ***$p < .001$). Asterisks in a column apply to the subsequent results for the covariate.

[a] The 11- to 12-year-olds had a significantly higher mean score than the 15- to 17-year-olds ($p < .001$).

[b] The 11- to 12-year-olds had a significantly higher mean score than the 15- to 17-year-olds ($p < .05$).

[c] The 11- to 12-year-olds had a significantly higher mean score than the 13- to 14-year-olds ($p < .01$) and 15- to 17-year-olds ($p < .001$).

[d] The 11- to 12-year-olds had a significantly higher mean score than the 13- to 14-year-olds and 15- to 17-year-olds ($p < .00 1$).

e White adolescents had a significantly higher mean score than Black adolescents ($p < .05$)

[f] White adolescents had a significantly higher mean score than Black adolescents and adolescents of other race/ethnicity ($p < .05$)

[g] Adolescents living in group homes or residential programs had a significantly lower mean score than adolescents in home with biological parents, those with adoptive parents, and those in foster or kin care ($p < .05$).

[h] Adolescents living in group homes or residential programs had a significantly lower mean score than adolescents in home with biological parents, those with adoptive parents, and those in kin care ($p < .05$).

Exhibit 23. Adolescents' Low School Achievement Test Scores, by Characteristics of the Adolescent Population at Wave 5

		Woodcock-Johnson letter identification				Woodcock-Johnson passage comprehension				Woodcock-Johnson calculation				Woodcock-Johnson applied problems			
	N	-1 to -1.99 *SD*		-2 *SD* or less		-1 to -1.99 *SD*		-2 *SD* or less		-1 to -1.99 *SD*		-2 *SD* or less		-1 to -1.99 *SD*		-2 *SD* or less	
		%	*SE*	%	*SE*	%	*SE*	%	*SE*	%	*SE*	%	*SE*	%	*SE*	%	*SE*
Total	1,412	19.1	2.0	10.0	1.7	26.1	2.4	11.7	1.5	24.3	2.2	12.7	2.0	21.8	2.1	8.1	1.2
Gender	1,412																
Male	684	19.2	3.3	11.0	2.0	26.0	3.2	12.2	1.9	24.7	3.4	13.4	2.5	20.7	2.9	8.5	1.8
Female	728	19.0	2.8	8.9	2.3	26.1	3.3	11.2	2.2	23.9	3.1	12.1	2.4	22.8	2.9	7.7	1.8
Age (years)	1,412					**				***		***		**		**	
11–12	419	21.6	4.6	4.5	1.5	25.4	4.6	8.2	2.2	12.4	2.9	6.5[a]	2.1	14.5	3.8	3.3[b]	1.2
13–14	409	20.0	5.4	10.3	3.4	17.9[c]	2.8	13.7	3.4	19.1	3.1	14.7	3.8	16.8	3.5	10.0	3.2
15–17	584	16.4	2.9	14.1	3.3	32.8	3.8	12.8	2.5	37.7[d]	4.2	16.2	2.6	31.3[e]	3.8	10.4	2.5
Race/ethnicity	1,411	* *		* *						* *		*		*		*	
Black	428	28.2[f]	3.5	7.2[g]	1.4	34.8	5.8	10.6	2.2	34.2[h]	5.4	11.7[i]	2.8	35.0[j]	4.7	3.8[k]	1.2
White	648	14.8	2.8	12.7	2.6	19.4	3.0	11.6	2.1	19.9	2.4	16.4	3.0	16.0	2.0	9.5	2.0
Hispanic	254	15.5	4.1	5.4	2.4	29.6	5.9	12.3	3.3	16.0	4.0	6.2[l]	2.4	15.3	4.2	10.2	3.2
Other	81	23.9	11.1	14.5	7.4	29.6	11.3	14.6	7.4	42.0	12.0	8.3	4.2	29.0	10.9	9.5	4.3
Placement at Wave 5	1,410	*															
In home biological parents	971	19.4[m]	2.1	10.1	1.9	26.5	2.8	11.6	1.8	22.4	2.9	13.3	2.5	21.2	2.3	6.6	1.4
In home adoptive parents	95	5.7	3.1	8.8	4.7	14.1	5.3	11.6	5.4	17.7	7.6	10.6	4.9	14.6	6.7	11.1	4.9
Kin care	254	21.4[n]	5.7	8.6	3.2	28.1	6.3	8.3	3.9	35.7	7.0	7.6	3.5	24.3	5.5	11.9	4.4
Foster care	57	3.3	1.6	13.9	7.8	18.5	9.1	14.4	7.8	24.3	10.4	11.7	5.8	29.6	12.0	8.1	4.2
Group home or residential program	33	26.6	15.9	17.7	14.1	16.4	9.3	42.8	17.4	15.5	6.3	43.2	17.2	25.2	13.0	35.4	17.7

Note: Instrument used was the Woodcock-Johnson III Tests of Cognitive Abilities (Woodcock et al., 2001). All analyses were on weighted data; Ns are unweighted. Reported Ns vary slightly across analyses because of missing data in some variable categories. Pearson χ^2 tests for cluster samples were used for significance tests. Asterisks indicate statistical significance (*$p < .05$, **$p < .01$, ***$p < .001$). Asterisks in a column apply to the subsequent results for the covariate.

[a] When Calculation scores 2 SD below the normative mean were compared with those in the normative range, 11- to 12-year-olds were found to be significantly less likely than 13- to 14-year-olds and 15- to 17-year-olds to have scores 2 SD or more below the mean ($p < .05$).

[b] When Applied problems scores 2 SD below the normative mean were compared with those in the normative range, 11- to 12-year-olds were found to be significantly less likely than 13- to 14-year-olds and 15- to 17-year-olds to have scores 2 SD or more below the mean ($p < .05$).

[c] When Passage Comprehension scores one to 1.99 SD below the normative mean were compared with those in the normative range, 15- to 17-year-olds were found to be significantly more likely than 13- to 14-year-olds to have scores falling between −1 and −1.99 SD ($p < .01$).

[d] When Calculation scores one to 1.99 SD below the normative mean were compared with those in the normative range, 15- to 17-year-olds were found to be significantly more likely than 11- to 12-year-olds and 13- to 14-year-olds to have scores falling between −1 and −1.99 SD ($p < .01$).

[e] When Applied Problems scores one to 1.99 SD below the normative mean were compared with those in the normative range, 15- to 17-year-olds were found to be significantly more likely than 11- to 12-year-olds and 13- to 14-year-olds to have scores falling between —1 and —1.99 SD (p < .0 1).

[f] When Letter Identification scores one to1 .99 SD below the normative mean were compared with those in the normative range, Black adolescents were found to be significantly more likely than White and Hispanic adolescents to have scores falling between —1 and —1.99 SD (p < .0 1).

[g] When Letter Identification scores one to 1.99 SD below the normative mean were compared with those 2 or more SD below the mean, Black adolescents were found to be significantly less likely than White adolescents to have scores 2 SD or more below the mean (p < .05).

[h] When Calculation scores one to 1.99 SD below the normative mean were compared with those in the normative range, Black adolescents were found to be significantly more likely than White and Hispanic adolescents to have scores between –1 and –1.99 SD (p < .01).

[I] When Calculation scores one to 1.99 SD below the normative mean were compared with those 2 SD or more below the mean, Black adolescents were found to be significantly less likely than White adolescents to have scores 2 SD or more below the mean (p < .05).

[j] When Applied Problem scores one to 1.99 SD below the normative mean were compared with those within the normative range, Black adolescents were found to be significantly more likely than white and Hispanic adolescents to have scores falling between –1 and –1.99 SD (p < .0 1).

[k] When Applied Problem scores one to 1.99 SD below the normative mean were compared with those 2 SD or more below the mean, Black adolescents were found to be significantly less likely than White and Hispanic adolescents to have scores 2 SD or more below the mean (p < .05).

[l] When Calculation scores 2 SD or more below the normative mean were compared with those in the normative range, Hispanic adolescents were found to be significantly less likely than White and Black adolescents to have scores 2 SD or more below the mean (p < .05).

[m] When Letter Identification scores one to 1.99 SD below the normative mean were compared with those in the normative range, adolescents living with their biological parents were found to be significantly more likely than adolescents living with adoptive or foster caregivers to have scores between –1 and –1.99 SD (p < .01).

[n] When Letter Identification scores one to 1.99 SD below the normative mean were compared with those in the normative range, adolescents living with kin were found to be significantly more likely than adolescents living with foster caregivers to have scores between –1 and –1.99 SD (p < .01).

Exhibit 24. Caregiver-Reported Social Competence of Adolescents, by Characteristics of the Adolescent Population at Wave 5

	N	Total		Social skills ratings [a]					
				Fewer skills		Average skills		More skills	
		M	*SE*	%	*SE*	%	*SE*	%	*SE*
Total	1,469	96.5	1.1	20.6	2.2	66.8	2.4	12.6	1.9
Gender	1,469								
Male	724	97.6	1.5	16.2	2.8	70.0	3.3	13.8	2.4
Female	745	95.4	1.1	25.1	3.0	63.5	3.3	11.4	2.3
Age (years)	1,469								
11–12	432	95.4	1.5	20.1	3.5	69.4	4.2	10.6	2.8
13–14	422	96.3	2.0	21.6	4.6	68.5	4.5	9.9	2.2
15–17	615	97.5	1.4	20.2	2.8	63.5	3.8	16.3	3.3
Race/ethnicity	1,468								

Exhibit 24. (Continued)

	N	Total		Social skills ratings [a] Fewer skills		Average skills		More skills	
		M	*SE*	%	*SE*	%	*SE*	%	*SE*
Black	447	96.1	1.5	21.1	3.8	68.2	4.6	10.7	3.1
White	675	97.3	1.3	19.7	3.1	63.5	3.7	16.8	3.3
Hispanic	263	94.6	3.0	24.5	6.2	69.2	5.0	6.3	3.1
Other	83	97.8	2.6	13.6	4.8	79.9	6.3	6.5	3.3
Placement at Wave 5	1,467	***		**					
In home biological parents	1,011	97.2 [b]	1.2	19.7 [c]	2.5	65.7	2.6	14.6	2.3
In home adoptive parents	100	93.0 [d]	1.6	18.3 [e]	7.1	74.7	8.8	7.0	3.4
Kin care	267	96.7 [f]	2.2	21.0 [g]	4.9	72.1	5.3	7.0	2.6
Foster care	57	88.8 [h]	3.0	24.7	10.7	75.3	10.7	0.0	0.0
Group home or residential program	32	78.4	3.8	58.3	16.9	41.7	16.9	0.0	0.0

Note: Instrument used was the Social Skills Rating System (SSRS; Gresham & Elliott, 1990). All analyses were on weighted data; Ns are unweighted. Reported Ns vary slightly across analyses because of missing data in some variable categories. Pearson χ^2 tests for cluster samples were used for significance tests. Asterisks indicate statistical significance (**$p < .01$, ***$p < .00$ 1). Asterisks in a column apply to the subsequent results for the covariate.

[a] The SSRS standardized scores are based on a mean of 100 with an SD of 15. Total scores were categorized as suggested in the SSRS manual (Gresham & Elliott, 1990): fewer social skills (<85), average social skills (85 to 115), or more social skills (>115). The proportion showing "more" skills in the normative sample was 16%.

[b] Adolescents in home with biological parents had a significantly higher mean score than adolescents in home with adoptive parents ($p < .05$), adolescents in foster care ($p < .01$), or adolescents in group homes or residential programs ($p < .001$).

[c] Adolescents in home with biological parents were significantly less likely than adolescents in foster care ($p < .01$) or adolescents in group homes or residential programs ($p < .05$) to be rated as having fewer social skills.

[d] Adolescents in home with adoptive parents had a significantly higher mean score than adolescents in group homes or residential programs ($p < .00$ 1).

[e] Adolescents in home with adoptive caregivers were significantly less likely than adolescents in group homes or residential programs ($p < .05$) to be rated as having fewer social skills.

[f] Adolescents in kin care had a significantly higher mean score than adolescents in foster care ($p < .05$) or adolescents in group homes or residential programs ($p < .001$).

[g] Adolescents in kin care were significantly less likely than adolescents in group homes or residential programs ($p < .05$) to be rated as having fewer social skills.

[h] Adolescents in foster care had a significantly higher mean score than adolescents in group homes or residential programs ($p < .05$).

Exhibit 25a. Adolescents' Self-Reported Loneliness and Social Dissatisfaction at Wave 5

		Never		Hardly ever		Sometimes		Most of the time		Always	
Items	*N*	**%**	*SE*	**%**	*SE*	**%**	*SE*	**%**	*SE*	**%**	*SE*
It's easy for me to make new friends at school.	1,321	3.9	1.0	4.5	0.9	16.7	2.1	36.7	2.8	38.3	2.9
I have nobody to talk to at school.	1,319	70.8	2.4	16.6	2.1	8.1	1.3	1.9	0.5	2.6	0.8
I'm good at working with other kids at school.	1,320	3.7	1.1	5.5	1.1	21.2	2.3	37.1	2.6	32.4	2.6
It's hard for me to make friends at school.	1,321	62.0	2.7	21.1	3.0	10.6	1.7	3.4	1.0	2.9	0.8
I have lots of friends at school.	1,320	2.3	0.8	3.9	0.9	11.0	1.6	19.5	2.0	63.3	2.4
I feel alone at school.	1,321	73.0	2.3	14.3	1.9	7.9	1.6	2.1	0.7	2.7	0.9
I can find a friend when I need one.	1,320	4.9	1.2	4.5	1.3	12.1	1.7	21.2	2.5	57.3	2.6
It's hard to get kids in school to like me.	1,321	60.7	2.5	17.6	1.9	11.8	1.5	5.6	1.4	4.4	1.1
I don't have anyone to play with at school.	1,318	74.8	2.3	9.8	1.5	8.8	1.9	2.0	0.7	4.7	1.1
I get along with other kids at school.	1,319	3.1	0.9	4.2	1.2	18.5	2.4	28.0	2.4	46.3	2.6
I feel left out of things at school.	1,319	59.6	2.5	23.8	2.5	10.8	1.7	3.7	1.1	2.1	0.8
There are no kids at school that I can go to when I need help.	1,312	66.0	2.7	15.8	2.0	7.4	1.2	4.5	1.2	6.4	2.0
I don't get along with other kids at school.	1,314	48.8	2.7	19.5	2.3	22.2	2.1	4.7	1.1	4.9	1.2
I'm lonely at school.	1,317	73.4	2.6	15.6	2.1	7.9	1.6	1.3	0.3	1.8	0.6
I am well liked by the kids at school.	1,316	3.2	0.9	6.1	1.2	15.1	1.9	36.9	2.7	38.7	2.4
I don't have any friends at school.	1,314	81.5	1.5	8.4	1.1	5.6	1.2	0.9	0.3	3.7	0.9

Note: Instrument used was the Loneliness and Social Dissatisfaction Scale (Asher & Wheeler, 1985). All analyses were on weighted data; Ns are unweighted. Reported Ns vary slightly across analyses because of missing data in some variable categories.

Exhibit 25b. Adolescents' Self-Reported Loneliness and Social Dissatisfaction by Characteristics of the Adolescent Population at Wave 5

		Loneliness	
	N	*M*	*SE*
Total	1,321	27.3	0.5
Gender	1,321		
Female	683	27.5	0.5
Age (years)	1,321		
11–12	414	28.0	0.7
13–14	399	27.8	1.2
15–17	508	26.4	1.0
Race/ethnicity	1,320		
Black	404	24.7 [a]	0.6
White	603	28.3	0.6
Hispanic	241	28.2	1.5
Other	72	29.3	2.2
Placement at Wave 5	1,320		
In home biological parents	909	27.5	0.6
In home adoptive parents	87	26.9	2.1
Kin care	240	25.2 [b]	1.1
Foster care	56	34.6	4.5
Group home or residential program	28	34.3	8.0

Note: Instrument used was the Loneliness and Social Dissatisfaction Scale (Asher & Wheeler, 1985). All analyses were on weighted data; *N*s are unweighted. Because of lack of normal distribution of the loneliness score, a square root transformation of the variable was completed before T tests were performed for cluster samples.

[a] Black adolescents had a significantly lower mean score than White adolescents ($p < .001$), Hispanic adolescents ($p < .05$), or those of "other" race/ethnicity ($p < .05$).

[b] Adolescents in kin care had a significantly lower mean score than adolescents in foster care ($p < .05$).

Exhibit 26. Adolescents' Self-Reported School Engagement at Wave 5

		Never		Sometimes		Often		Almost always	
Items	*N*	%	*SE*	%	*SE*	%	*SE*	%	*SE*
How often do you enjoy being in school?	1,322	6.6	1.5	38.6	2.8	32.5	2.8	22.3	2.3
How often do you hate being in school?	1,321	24.8	2.5	51.6	2.6	17.3	2.0	6.2	1.2
How often do you try to do your best work in school?	1,322	1.5	0.8	12.1	1.8	32.5	3.3	54.0	3.0
How often do you find the school work too hard to understand?	1,322	10.7	1.7	66.7	2.3	16.0	1.8	6.7	1.6
How often do you find your classes interesting?	1,322	10.4	1.8	34.0	3.2	36.8	3.1	18.8	2.1
How often do you fail to complete or turn in your assignments?	1,320	18.6	2.3	59.9	2.9	14.3	2.0	7.2	1.8

Exhibit 26. (Continued)

		Never		Sometimes		Often		Almost always	
Items	*N*	%	*SE*	%	*SE*	%	*SE*	%	*SE*
How often do you get sent to the office or have to stay after school because you misbehaved?	1,322	61.1	2.7	27.9	2.8	6.8	1.7	4.2	1.3
How often do you get along with your teachers?	1,321	5.2	1.7	19.6	2.1	26.7	2.6	48.6	3.1
How often do you listen carefully or pay attention in school?	1,321	3.3	1.3	20.7	2.2	39.1	3.0	36.9	2.5
How often do you get your homework done?	1,316	5.4	1.6	21.5	1.9	29.3	2.5	43.8	2.9
How often do you get along with other students?	1,320	2.3	0.8	17.8	2.0	33.1	2.4	46.8	2.4

Note: Instrument used was the School Engagement scale from the Safe and Drug Free Schools survey (Sylvia et al., 1997). All analyses were on weighted data; *N*s are unweighted. Reported Ns vary slightly across analyses because of missing data in some variable categories.

Exhibit 27. Adolescent-Reported Parental Monitoring at Wave 5

Items	***N***	**Never**		**Almost never**		**Once in a while**		**Pretty often**		**Very often**	
		%	***SE***	**%**	***SE***	**%**	***SE***	**%**	***SE***	**%**	***SE***
How often do you leave the house without telling your caregiver or without leaving a note?	1,397	54.0	2.7	17.4	2.1	17.7	1.8	6.2	1.2	4.7	1.1
How often does your caregiver know where you are when you are away from home?	1,392	2.8	0.8	2.5	1.0	6.3	1.5	23.5	2.2	64.9	2.8
How often does your caregiver know whom you are with when you are away from home?	1,393	3.9	1.0	2.9	0.8	9.3	1.7	21.9	2.4	62.1	2.3
How often does your caregiver tell you what time to be home?	1,393	7.2	1.3	3.3	1.0	7.9	1.2	21.0	3.0	60.6	2.9
How often do you tell your caregiver when you expect to be back?	1,388	10.4	1.6	2.9	0.6	20.0	1.8	27.2	2.6	39.5	2.3

Note: Instrument used was the Parental Monitoring Scale (Dishion et al., 1991). All analyses were on weighted data; Ns are unweighted. Reported Ns vary slightly across analyses because of missing data in some variable categories.

Exhibit 28. Insurance Status of Adolescents for the Adolescent Population by Characteristics of the Adolescent Population at Wave 5

	N	Medicaid/State funded		Private insurance		CHAMPUS		No insurance	
		%	*SE*	%	*SE*	%	*SE*	%	*SE*
Total	1,466	64.4	2.6	26.2	2.4	0.9	0.4	8.6	1.5
Gender	1,466								
Male	723	64.5	3.5	26.5	3.3	0.8	0.4	8.2	2.0
Female	743	64.3	4.1	25.8	3.6	0.9	0.5	8.9	2.0
Age (years)	1,466								
11–12	432	61.6	4.3	29.0	4.6	0.9	0.6	8.5	2.7
13–14	419	60.0	5.1	29.8	5.7	1.4	0.9	8.9	3.3
15–17	615	70.0	3.7	21.1	3.2	0.4	0.2	8.5	2.4
Race/ethnicity	1,465								
Black	446	70.3	4.6	23.2	3.9	0.3	0.2	6.2	2.2
White	675	62.4	3.9	26.0	3.9	1.1	0.5	10.4	2.3
Hispanic	262	59.8	6.0	31.0	4.9	1.1	1.1	8.1	3.4
Other	82	68.5	8.6	25.6	8.7	0.1	0.1	5.8	2.4
Placement at Wave 5	1,464	***							
In home biological parents	1,009	60.0 [a]	3.4	30.5	2.9	1.0	0.6	8.5	1.7
In home adoptive parents	100	88.4	4.6	9.8	4.0	1.8	1.4	0.0	0.0
Kin care	266	75.3	4.7	14.2	3.9	0.4	0.2	10.1	3.9
Foster care	57	79.1	17.1	0.0	0.0	0.0	0.0	20.9	17.1
Group home or residential program	32	99.0	0.8	1.0	0.8	0.0	0.0	0.0	0.0

All analyses were on weighted data; *N*s are unweighted. Reported *N*s vary slightly across analyses because of missing data in some variable categories. Pearson χ^2 tests for cluster samples were used for significance tests. Asterisks indicate statistical significance (***$p < .001$). Asterisks in the column apply to the subsequent results for the covariate.

[a] Adolescents in home with biological parents were significantly less likely to have Medicaid than those living with kin ($p < 0.5$) or in foster care ($p < 0.5$).

Exhibit 29. Adolescents' Preventive and Routine Health Services for the Adolescent Population by Characteristics of the Adolescent Population at Wave 5

	N	All preventive services[a]		Usual health care location		Dental care since last interview		Vision testing since last interview[a]		Hearing testing since last interview		Well-child checkup past 12 months		Up-to-date immunizations	
		%	*SE*	%	*SE*	%	*SE*	%	*SE*	%	*SE*	%	*SE*	%	*SE*
Total	1,463	34.3	3.0	92.3	1.7	72.2	2.8	71.9	2.1	59.9	2.6	75.7	2.4	99.2	0.4
Gender	1,463														
Male	723	36.8	4.1	91.1	2.8	72.2	4.1	74.1	3.2	59.8	3.3	76.3	2.8	98.6	0.8
Female	745	31.7	3.7	94.2	1.8	72.2	4.1	69.7	2.9	59.9	3.3	75.2	3.4	99.9	0.1
Age (years)	1,468							**		**					
11–12	432	43.4	4.9	93.2	3.0	75.8	4.3	81.3[b]	3.4	69.0	4.1	79.7	3.5	99.8	0.1
13–14	422	32.0	5.3	91.6	3.8	70.5	5.1	71.2	3.9	65.3	4.8	71.3	5.0	98.5	1.3
15–17	614	28.8	4.0	93.0	2.0	70.7	3.9	64.8	3.6	48.4[c]	4.6	75.9	3.2	99.2	0.4
Race/ethnicity	1,467									*		***			
Black	446	44.7	6.5	88.5	3.8	70.8	5.0	70.9	5.6	66.8	4.7	89.9[d]	1.9	98.1	1.5
White	675	26.2	2.7	94.2	2.1	71.1	3.8	68.3	2.8	53.4[e]	2.9	70.3	3.3	99.7	0.2
Hispanic	263	38.9	9.7	96.8	1.3	78.3	4.5	80.7	5.3	68.5	6.7	71.4	5.4	99.9	0.1
Other	83	38.4	10.6	86.2	10.0	68.7	10.7	77.1	6.0	53.9	10.9	68.5	11.0	98.1	2.0
Placement at Wave 5	1,466	**				***		***		**		**			
In home biological parents	1,011	32.7	3.1	91.3	2.2	69.4[f]	3.1	73.9	2.5	61.7	2.8	74.7	2.6	99.0	0.6
In home adoptive parents	100	29.9	9.6	97.0	2.4	93.7	3.2	43.4	12.9	50.0	13.9	73.3	15.6	100.0	0.0
Kin care	266	33.0	7.3	97.2	1.1	76.2[g]	5.5	62.6	6.8	45.7	7.6	76.1	4.9	99.8	0.2
Foster care	57	87.7[h]	5.4	96.3	2.5	98.3	1.8	96.8[i]	2.0	92.8[j]	3.8	96.6[k]	2.2	100.0	0.0
Group home or residential program	32	97.5[l]	1.6	99.6	0.5	99.4	0.7	99.0[m]	0.8	97.5[n]	1.6	100.0[o]	0.0	100.0	0.0
Insurance	1,460	**				*									
Medicaid	1,009	36.6	3.4	93.2	1.8	76.6	3.3	72.0	2.8	60.9	3.1	79.9	2.3	99.4	0.3
Private or CHAMPUS	343	37.3	5.5	94.3	2.6	73.1	3.9	74.7	3.5	63.8	4.9	74.4	5.0	100.0	0.0
None	108	10.7[p]	5.7	89.8	4.4	43.8[q]	10.4	59.9	9.8	43.0	10.0	55.5	9.4	95.0	4.4

Note: All analyses were on weighted data; Ns are unweighted. Reported *N*s vary slightly across analyses because of missing data in some variable categories. Pearson χ^2 tests for cluster samples were used for all significance tests. All preventive and routine health care was reported by caregivers. Asterisks indicate statistical significance (*$p < .05$, **$p < .01$, ***$p < .001$). Asterisks in a column apply to the subsequent results for the covariate.

[a] Includes having had up-to-date immunizations and recent dental, vision, hearing, and well-child checkups.

[b] The 11- to 12-year-olds were significantly more likely to have had vision testing than the 15- to 17-year-olds ($p < .00\ 1$).

c The 15- to 17-year-olds were significantly less likely to have had hearing testing than the 11- to 12-year-olds ($p < .01$) or 13- to 14-year-olds ($p < .01$).

[d] Black adolescents were significantly more likely to have had a well-child checkup than White ($p < .001$) and Hispanic adolescents ($p < .01$).

[e] White adolescents were significantly less likely to have had hearing testing than Black adolescents ($p < 0.5$) and Hispanic adolescents ($p < 0.5$).

[f] Adolescents in home with biological parents were significantly less likely to have had dental care than adolescents in home with adoptive caregivers ($p < .05$), those in foster care ($p < .00\ 1$), or those in group homes or residential programs ($p < .0\ 1$).

[g] Adolescents in kin care were significantly less likely to have had dental care than adolescents in home with adoptive parents ($p < .05$), those in group homes or residential programs ($p < .05$), or those in foster care ($p < .0\ 1$).

[h] Adolescents in foster care were significantly more likely to have had all preventive services than adolescents in home with biological parents ($p < .0\ 1$), those in home with adopted parents ($p < .0\ 1$), or those in kin care ($p < .0\ 1$).

[i] Adolescents in foster care were significantly more likely to have had vision testing than adolescents in home with biological parents ($p < .0\ 1$), those in home with adoptive parents ($p < .01$), or those in kin care ($p < .01$).

[j] Adolescents in foster care were significantly more likely to have had hearing testing than adolescents in home with biological parents ($p < .0\ 1$), those in kin care ($p < .0\ 1$), or those in home with adoptive parents ($p < .05$).

[k] Adolescents in foster care were significantly more likely to have had a well-child checkup than adolescents in home with biological parents ($p < .01$) or those in kin care ($p < .01$).

[l] Adolescents in group homes or residential programs were significantly more likely to have had all preventive services than adolescents in home with biological parents ($p < .0\ 1$), those with adoptive parents ($p < .0\ 1$), or those in kin care ($p < .01$).

[m] Adolescents in group homes or residential programs were significantly more likely to have had vision testing than adolescents in home with biological parents ($p < .0\ 1$), those with adoptive parents ($p < .0\ 1$), or those in kin care ($p < .05$).

[n] Adolescents in group homes or residential programs were significantly more likely to have had hearing testing than adolescents in home with biological parents ($p < .0\ 1$), those with adoptive parents ($p < .05$), or those in kin care ($p < .05$).

[o] Adolescents in group homes or residential programs were significantly more likely to have had a well-child checkup than adolescents in home with biological parents ($p < .01$) or those in kin care ($p < .05$).

[p] Adolescents without insurance were significantly less likely to receive all preventive services than adolescents with Medicaid ($p < .01$) or those with private insurance ($p < .01$).

[q] Adolescents without insurance were significantly less likely to have had dental care than adolescents with Medicaid ($p < .01$) or those with private insurance ($p < .05$).

Exhibit 30. Adolescents' Urgent Medical Care in the Previous 12 Months by Characteristics of the Adolescent Population at Wave 5

		ER or urgent care for illness or injury		Overnight hospital admission for illness or injury		Care from doctor or nurse for serious injury, accident, or poisoning	
	N	%	*SE*	%	*SE*	%	*SE*
Total	1,465	27.0	1.8	5.1	1.3	11.6	1.5
Gender	1,465						
Male	723	25.8	3.1	3.9	1.5	13.6	2.5
Female	742	28.2	2.7	6.4	2.1	9.5	1.6
Age (years)	1,465	**		*		**	
11–12	431	18.4[a]	2.6	2.2	1.5	5.5[b]	1.4
13–14	422	30.3	4.3	1.9	0.8	13.8	3.1
15–17	612	31.3	3.3	10.0[c]	2.9	14.8	3.0
Race/ethnicity	1,464					**	
Black	446	27.2	4.1	7.3	3.2	13.4	3.5
White	673	29.3	2.6	4.9	1.8	13.1	2.2
Hispanic	262	17.6	5.4	1.6	1.1	3.0[d]	1.1
Other	83	36.3	10.5	8.6	6.7	18.6	9.9
Placement at Wave 5	1,463						
In home biological parents	1,011	26.5	2.2	5.0	1.6	11.6	1.7
In home adoptive parents	99	17.4	7.3	1.9	1.1	5.1	2.7
Kin care	266	31.4	5.7	6.5	4.4	12.2	4.9
Foster care	55	22.1	9.8	2.7	1.9	3.6	2.0
Group home or residential program	32	30.1	17.3	5.2	4.5	27.2	16.6
Insurance	1,462			*			
Medicaid	1,009	30.7	2.8	7.5[e]	2.1	11.1	2.0
Private or CHAMPUS	343	22.7	3.0	0.8	0.6	14.2	3.3
None	110	15.7	4.9	1.8	1.3	8.5	6.0

Note: All analyses were on weighted data; Ns are unweighted. Reported Ns vary slightly across analyses because of missing data in some variable categories. Pearson χ^2 tests for cluster samples were used for initial significance tests. No significant differences in use of urgent services were found by type of maltreatment at baseline or by number of types of maltreatment. Asterisks indicate statistical significance (*$p < .05$, **$p < .01$). Asterisks in column apply to the subsequent results for the covariate. ER = emergency room.

[a] The 11- to 12-year-olds were significantly less likely to receive ER or urgent care than the 13- to 14-year-olds ($p < .05$) or 15- to 17-year-olds ($p < .01$).

[b] The 11- to 12-year-olds were significantly less likely to receive care from a doctor or nurse for serious injury than the 13- to 14-year-olds ($p < .05$) and 15- to 17-year-olds ($p < .01$).

[c] The 15- to 17-year-olds were significantly more likely to have an overnight hospital admission than the 11- to 12- year-olds and 13- to 14-year-olds ($p < .01$).

[d] Hispanic adolescents were significantly less likely to receive care from a doctor or nurse for serious injury than Black adolescents ($p < .05$) or White adolescents ($p < .001$).

[e] Adolescents with Medicaid were significantly more likely to have an overnight hospital admission than adolescents with private insurance ($p < .0 1$).

Exhibit 31. Special Education Services for the Adolescent Population by Characteristics of the Adolescent Population at Wave 5

		Total		Adolescents with IEPs [a]	
	N	%	*SE*	%	*SE*
Total	1,464			25.9	2.2
Gender	1,464			***	
Male	722	51.0	3.0	33.2	3.7
Female	742	49.0	3.0	18.2	2.3
Age (year)	1,464				
11–12	431	31.2	2.7	24.5	3.9
13–14	421	30.1	2.9	29.0	4.5
15–17	612	38.8	2.5	24.6	3.1
Race/ethnicity	1,463				
Black	446	27.1	3.1	21.7	4.0
White	672	48.3	4.0	29.7	3.1
Hispanic	263	18.7	2.7	19.6	3.5
Other	82	6.0	1.2	33.8	10.3
Placement at Wave 5	1,462			*	
In home biological parents	1,009	77.2	1.9	26.2	2.9
In home adoptive parents	99	3.1	0.9	39.4	14.3
Kin care	267	16.2	1.9	15.8	4.2

Exhibit 31. (Continued)

	Total			Adolescents with IEPs [a]	
	N	%	*SE*	%	*SE*
Foster care	56	1.9	0.6	26.3	9.4
Group home or residential program	31	1.6	0.5	85.0 [b]	8.7
Special need [c]	1,394			***	
Cognitive	128	7.3	1.6	41.2	9.3
Behavioral	507	35.4	3.1	21.2	4.3
Both cognitive and behavioral	201	13.7	2.0	69.6 [d]	7.5
None	558	43.6	3.1	12.2 [e]	2.6

Note: All analyses were on weighted data; Ns are unweighted. Pearson χ^2 tests for cluster samples were used to test statistical significance. Statistical significance is noted by asterisks in the column above the statistically significant result (*$p < .05$, ***$p < .001$). IEP = Individualized Education Plan.

[a] Presence of an active IEP was determined by either teacher or caregiver report (i.e., by teacher interview, if available; by caregiver interview if teacher's input was missing).

[b] Adolescents in group homes or residential programs were significantly more likely to have IEPs than adolescents in home with biological parents ($p < .05$), those with adoptive parents ($p < .05$), or those in kin or foster care ($p < .05$).

[c] Adolescents were considered to be in need of a referral for special education services if (1) they had a score in the clinical range for the Child Behavior Checklist (Achenbach, 1991), Teacher's Report Form (Achenbach & Rescorla, 2001), or Youth Self-Report (Achenbach, 1991), or (2) they have scores 2 SD or more below the mean for the Kaufman Brief Intelligence Test (Kaufman & Kaufman, 1990) or Woodcock-Johnson III Tests of Cognitive Abilities (Woodcock et al., 2001).

[d] Adolescents with cognitive and behavioral needs were significantly more likely to have IEPs than adolescents with only cognitive needs ($p < .05$) or those with only behavioral needs ($p < .001$).

[e] Adolescents with no cognitive or behavioral needs were significantly less likely to have IEPs than adolescents with only cognitive needs ($p < .05$) or those with both behavioral and cognitive needs ($p < .00 1$).

Exhibit 32. Caregiver-Reported Utilization of Adolescents' Mental Health Services by Characteristics of the Adolescent Population at Wave 5

	N	Total		Any services [a]		Specialty outpatient services [b]		Inpatient services [c]		Family doctor		School-based services [d]		Current use of psychotropic medication	
		%	*SE*	%	*SE*	%	*SE*	%	*SE*	%	*SE*	%	*SE*	%	*SE*
Total	1,466	100.0	0.0	30.1	2.7	18.9	2.1	6.3	1.2	8.6	1.6	17.9	2.1	16.5	2.1
Gender	1,466					*								***	
Male	721	51.0	3.0	33.0	4.0	23.6	3.7	7.3	2.0	10.4	2.4	20.1	2.9	23.7	3.5
Female	745	49.0	3.0	27.1	3.6	14.0	2.3	5.3	1.5	6.8	1.7	15.7	2.5	8.9	1.6
Age (years)	1,466							***							
11–12	432	31.2	2.7	26.0	3.1	14.3	2.4	0.6 [e]	0.2	6.6	1.8	17.4	3.2	15.5	2.4
13–14	422	30.0	2.9	28.3	5.1	18.7	4.2	4.5 [f]	1.9	5.2	1.8	17.3	3.7	19.4	4.2
15–17	612	38.8	2.5	34.8	4.3	22.5	3.5	12.2	2.7	12.9	3.0	18.8	3.5	14.9	3.1
Race/ethnicity	1,465					**								**	
Black	447	27.1	3.1	27.9	4.0	15.0	3.5	8.3	3.1	10.5	3.1	15.6	3.3	12.3	3.2
White	674	48.3	4.0	36.2	3.7	24.1 [g]	2.8	6.8	1.5	7.8	1.6	20.1	3.0	22.7 [h]	2.9
Hispanic	262	18.7	2.7	16.1	4.4	8.1	2.9	2.7	1.5	4.7	2.2	13.6	4.1	6.1	3.0
Other	82	6.0	1.2	34.0	9.8	27.2	9.5	4.1	1.8	18.6	10.0	24.3	9.6	17.6	9.7
Placement at Wave 5	1,464			* *		* * *								* * *	
In home biological parents	1,009	77.2	1.9	26.4	2.8	14.9	2.1	4.4	1.3	8.0	1.7	15.7	2.2	13.4	2.1
In home adoptive parents	100	3.1	0.9	38.0	12.2	33.9 [i]	11.3	5.1	2.9	9.0	3.7	22.0	8.2	44.2	14.4
Kin care	266	16.2	1.9	32.8	6.2	21.0	5.0	5.9	3.6	5.2	2.7	19.6	5.6	13.2	3.6
Foster care	57	2.0	0.6	86.6 [j]	7.5	82.0 [k]	8.2	16.4	8.5	33.8	14.3	62.2	12.5	61.7 [l]	15.6
Group home or residential program	32	1.6	0.5	95.1 [m]	3.6	79.3 [n]	10.3	92.8	4.3	49.4	18.1	45.1	17.3	88.4 [o]	8.1
Insurance	1,463			**		***		***		***				***	

Exhibit 32. (Continued)

	N	Total		Any services [a]		Specialty outpatient services [b]		Inpatient services [c]		Family doctor		School-based services [d]		Current use of psychotropic medication	
		%	*SE*	%	*SE*	%	*SE*	%	*SE*	%	*SE*	%	*SE*	%	*SE*
Medicaid	1,011	64.4	2.6	36.5 [p]	3.5	24.6 [q]	2.9	9.2 [r]	1.8	11.6 [s]	2.2	20.8	2.7	22.5 [t]	3.0
Private or	343	27.0	2.5	18.9	3.7	9.8	2.7	1.1	0.5	4.3	1.4	11.6	2.8	7.7[u]	2.1
CHAMPUS															
None	109	8.6	1.5	20.9	8.2	6.9	4.8	1.4	1.1	1.5	0.9	18.5	8.3	0.6	0.5
Mental health need	1,466			***		***		***		***		***		***	
Yes	759	49.4	3.5	44.6	3.8	28.9	3.8	11.9	2.3	14.5	2.9	27.1	3.4	25.1	3.7
No	707	50.6	3.5	15.9	2.7	9.1	2.1	0.9	0.3	2.9	1.0	8.9	2.0	8.0	2.1

Note: Mental health services were reported by caregivers and measured with an adapted version of the Child and Adolescent Services Assessment (Burns, Angold, Magruder-Habib, Costello, & Patrick, 1994). All analyses were on weighted data; Ns are unweighted. Pearson χ^2 tests for cluster samples were used for initial significance tests. Asterisks indicate statistical significance (*$p < .05$, **$p < .01$, ***$p < .001$). Asterisks in a column apply to the subsequent results for the covariate. Caregiver report of mental health service utilization represents services received since most recent previous interview.

[a] Includes use of specialty outpatient services, inpatient services, family doctor, and school based services for emotional/behavioral problems.

[b] Includes day treatment for emotional and substance abuse problems, outpatient drug or alcohol unit, mental health center, and private professional help for emotional and substance abuse problems.

[c] Includes use of psychiatric hospital, hospital for emotional and substance abuse problems, residential treatment, emergency shelter for emotional and substance abuse problems, and emergency room for emotional and substance abuse problems.

[d] Includes services from a school guidance counselor, social worker, or psychologist.

[e] The 11- to 12-year-olds were significantly less likely to use inpatient mental health services than the 13- to 14-year-olds ($p < .05$) or 15- to 17-year-olds ($p < .001$).

[f] The 13- to 14-year-olds were significantly less likely to use inpatient mental health services than the 15- to 17-year-olds ($p < .05$).

[g] White adolescents were significantly more likely to use specialty outpatient services than Hispanic adolescents ($p < .01$).

[h] White adolescents were significantly more likely to use psychotropic medication than Black ($p < .05$) and Hispanic adolescents ($p < .001$).

[i] Adolescents with adoptive parents were significantly more likely to use specialty outpatient services than those in home with biological parents ($p < .05$).

[j] Adolescents in foster care were significantly more likely to use any mental health services than those in home with biological parents ($p < .01$), those living with kin ($p < .01$), and those with adoptive parents ($p < .05$).

[k] Adolescents living with foster caregivers were significantly more likely to use specialty outpatient services than those in home with biological parents ($p < .01$), those living with kin ($p < .0 1$), or those with adoptive parents ($p < .05$).

[l] Adolescents in foster care were significantly more likely to use psychotropic medication than those in home with biological parents ($p < .01$) or those living with kin ($p < .01$).

[m] Adolescents living in group homes or residential programs were significantly more likely to use any mental health services than those in home with biological parents ($p < .0 1$), those with adoptive parents ($p < .0 1$), or those living with kin ($p < .0 1$).

[n] Adolescents living in group homes or residential programs were significantly more likely to use specialty outpatient services than those in home with biological parents ($p < .05$), those with adoptive parents ($p < .05$), or those living with kin ($p < .05$).

[o] Adolescents living in group homes or residential programs were significantly more likely to use psychotropic medication than those in home with biological parents ($p < .05$), those with adoptive parents ($p < .05$), or those living with kin ($p < .0 1$).

[p] Adolescents with Medicaid were significantly more likely to use any mental health services than adolescents with private insurance ($p < .001$).

[q] Adolescents with Medicaid were significantly more likely to use any specialty outpatient services than adolescents with private insurance ($p < .00 1$) or those with no insurance ($p < .0 1$).

[r] Adolescents with Medicaid were significantly more likely to use inpatient mental health services than adolescents with private insurance ($p < .00 1$) or those with no insurance ($p < .01$).

[s] Adolescents with Medicaid were significantly more likely to use mental health services from a family doctor than adolescents with private insurance ($p < .01$) or those with no insurance ($p < .00 1$).

[t] Adolescents with Medicaid were significantly more likely to use psychotropic medication than adolescents with private and no insurance ($p < .00 1$).

[u] Adolescents with private insurance were significantly more likely to use psychotropic medication than adolescents with no insurance ($p < .01$)

Exhibit 33. Adolescents' Self-Reported Independent-Living Skills, by Characteristics of the Adolescent Population by Characteristics of the Adolescent Population at Wave 5

		Knows how to interview for a job		Knows how to apply to a college		Knows how to shop and prepare meals		Has taken drivers education		Knows how to use public transportation		Knows how to obtain family planning		Knows how to obtain medical or dental care	
	N	%	*SE*	%	*SE*	%	*SE*	%	*SE*	%	*SE*	%	*SE*	%	*SE*
Total	787	65.5	3.7	29.5	3.2	92.9	2.0	14.6	2.4	79.5	3.5	51.7	4.0	46.0	3.3
Gender	787											**		**	
Male	389	67.2	4.7	26.4	5.4	90.5	3.1	13.7	3.0	82.6	3.7	42.9	5.5	37.4	5.2
Female	398	63.3	4.7	33.0	5.5	95.7	2.3	15.7	3.7	76.1	5.0	61.5	4.4	55.6	3.6
Age (years)	787							***				**			
14	214	56.3	7.3	23.7	8.1	88.1	5.3	1.3 [a]	0.9	64.7	6.8	28.3[b]	5.6	34.7	7.9
15	209	57.9	7.9	28.4	5.8	93.2	3.2	7.6 [c]	2.5	83.2	4.9	57.5	6.7	46.4	7.5
16	199	76.8	5.6	33.8	5.8	97.8	1.4	22.6	6.3	85.9	6.1	59.0	7.3	48.1	7.1
17	165	74.8	7.4	33.5	7.6	93.3	3.5	31.8	5.3	86.9	4.9	66.7	8.5	57.6	8.1
Race/ethnicity	787														
Black	260	71.1	6.4	37.7	6.5	97.6	1.1	14.2	3.6	81.0	5.5	61.1	6.0	48.4	6.3
White	351	61.9	4.7	27.3	5.3	91.3	3.1	14.9	3.2	74.5	5.0	51.0	4.7	48.6	4.9
Hispanic	126	70.7	8.5	14.4	5.5	94.1	4.6	10.8	5.5	86.6	7.3	42.7	9.4	41.6	8.0
Other	50	57.1	13.8	39.7	13.4	83.5	12.7	21.2	9.9	88.1	5.4	38.4	13.5	32.3	11.3
Placement at Wave 5	786														
In home biological parents	545	66.4	4.0	30.3	4.1	92.4	2.5	16.3	2.8	81.0	3.6	52.9	4.8	43.5	4.3
In home adoptive parents	49	78.7	9.9	27.3	13.8	94.6	3.1	9.6	6.6	43.9	18.3	26.9	13.7	67.4	14.0
Kin care	129	59.8	10.2	28.7	7.6	96.9	1.6	10.9	3.9	80.4	8.2	52.8	8.9	50.6	8.3
Foster care	39	49.4	18.1	27.3	13.0	98.7	1.2	2.6	1.9	85.9	10.5	35.6	14.8	43.8	17.0
Group home or residential program	24	86.4	7.4	12.9	8.0	66.0	20.7	6.5	4.2	64.4	21.3	56.4	20.4	69.6	13.9

Note: All analyses were on weighted data; Ns are unweighted. Reported *N*s vary slightly across analyses because of missing data in some variable categories. Pearson χ^2 tests for cluster samples were used for initial significance tests. Asterisks indicate statistical significance (**$p < .01$, ***$p < .001$). Asterisks in a column apply to the subsequent results for the covariate.

[a] The 14-year-olds were significantly less likely to report having taken drivers education than the 15-year-olds ($p < 0.5$) or 16- and 17-year-olds ($p < .001$).

[b] The 14-year-olds were significantly less likely to report knowing how to obtain family planning than 15-year-olds ($p < 0.1$) or 16- and 17-year-olds ($p < .001$).

[c] The 15-year-olds were significantly less likely to report having taken drivers education than the 16-year-olds ($p < 0.5$) or 17-year-olds ($p < .001$).

Exhibit 34. Caregivers' Self-Reported Health, by Caregivers' Characteristics of the Adolescent Population at Wave 5

		In good health	
	N	%	*SE*
Total	1,462	73.4	2.5
Race/ethnicity	1,434		
Black	403	69.2	4.1
White	740	74.8	3.5
Hispanic	210	74.2	5.8
Other	81	70.1	10.4
Caregiver	1,462	**	
Biological	1,009	74.4	2.7
Adoptive	100	73.0	15.2
Kin	267	64.0	6.4
Foster	57	96.9 [a]	2.2
Group home or residential program	29	100.0 [b]	0.0

Note: All analyses were on weighted data; Ns are unweighted. Reported *N*s vary slightly across analyses because of missing data in some variable categories. Pearson χ^2 tests for cluster samples were used for initial significance tests. Asterisks indicate statistical significance (**$p < .01$). Asterisks in the column apply to the subsequent results for the covariate.

[a] Foster caregivers rated themselves significantly healthier than biological parents ($p < .01$) or kin caregivers rated themselves ($p < .0 1$).

[b] Group home or residential program caregivers rated themselves significantly healthier than biological parents ($p < .01$) or kin caregivers rated themselves ($p < .01$).

Exhibit 35. Caregivers' Physical and Mental Health Status, by Caregiver's Characteristics for the Adolescents at Wave 5

	N	Physical		Mental	
		M	*SE*	*M*	*SE*
Total	1,460	45.6	0.7	49.4	0.7
Race/ethnicity	1,459				
Black	446	45.8	1.1	49.3	0.7
White	669	45.5	0.9	50.2	1.2
Hispanic	262	46.6	1.6	48.9	0.9
Other	82	40.9	2.7	49.4	1.2
Caregiver	1,458	**		***	
Biological	1,005	46.1 [a]	0.8	48.6 [b]	0.8
Adoptive	100	43.2	4.6	54.5	1.3
Kin	267	42.1	1.8	51.1	1.4
Foster	57	52.8 [c]	1.8	53.8	2.0
Group home or residential program	29	54.4 [d]	0.6	54.9	1.2

Note: Instrument used was the 12-Item Short-Form Health Survey (Ware, Kosinski, & Keller, 1996). All analyses were on weighted data; Ns are unweighted. *T* tests for cluster samples were used to test statistical significance. Asterisks indicate statistical significance (**$p < .01$, ***$p < .001$). Asterisks in a column apply to the subsequent results for the covariate.

[a] Biological parents described themselves as significantly more healthy than kin caregivers described themselves ($p < .05$).

[b] Biological parents described themselves as in significantly worse mental health than adoptive parents ($p < .001$), foster caregivers ($p < .001$), or group home caregivers ($p < .001$) described themselves.

[c] Foster caregivers described themselves as significantly more healthy than biological parents ($p < .01$), adoptive parents ($p < .01$), or kin caregivers ($p < .01$) described themselves.

[d] Group home caregivers described themselves as significantly more healthy than biological parents ($p < .01$), adoptive parents ($p < .01$), or kin caregivers ($p < .01$) described themselves.

Exhibit 36. Permanent Caregivers' Major Depression, by Caregiver's Characteristics of the Adolescent Population at Wave 5

	N	%	*SE*
Total	1,354	20.9	1.9
Race/ethnicity			
Black	371	15.4	3.4
White	706	24.4	2.7
Hispanic	202	18.8	4.4
Other	75	18.8	8.1
Caregiver	1,354		
Biological	1,009	20.8	2.3
Adoptive	99	16.1	7.3
Kin	246	22.5	5.5

Note: Instrument used was the Composite International Diagnostic Interview Form (CIDI-SF; Kessler et al., 1998). All analyses were on weighted data; Ns are unweighted. Pearson χ^2tests for cluster samples were used for initial significance tests. No significant differences by race or type of caregiver were found. Foster and group home caregivers were not evaluated for major depression.

Exhibit 37. Intimate-Partner Violence Against Female Permanent Caregivers for the Adolescent Population at Wave 5

	N	At least one incident of IPV suffered in past 12 months		Ever suffered IPV	
		%	*SE*	%	*SE*
Total (any violence—less severe or severe)	1,193	8.9	1.4	24.0	2.6
Any less severe violence	1,192	8.3	1.4	22.3	2.6
Had something thrown at her	1,192	5.7	1.2	16.4	2.1
Was pushed, grabbed, or shoved	1,192	5.7	1.1	18.5	2.3
Was slapped	1,192	2.8	0.7	14.1	2.1
Any severe violence	1,193	4.8	1.1	17.6	2.3
Was kicked, bitten, or hit with fist	1,192	2.6	0.9	12.8	1.9
Was hit with something (or such hitting was attempted)	1,192	3.1	0.6	14.4	2.0

Exhibit 37. (Continued)

	N	At least one incident of IPV suffered in past 12 months		Ever suffered IPV	
		%	*SE*	%	*SE*
Was beaten up	1,192	1.0	0.4	10.9	1.7
Was choked	1,192	1.2	0.6	9.8	1.6
Was threatened with knife or gun	1,193	0.4	0.2	6.7	1.4
Knife or gun was used against her	1,193	0.3	0.2	1.9	0.6

Note: Instrument used was the Conflict Tactics Scale (Straus, 1979). All analyses were on weighted data; Ns are unweighted. Reported *N*s vary slightly across analyses because of missing data in some variable categories. Only female permanent caregivers were asked about intimate partner violence. IPV = intimate-partner violence.

Exhibit 38. Permanent Caregivers' Involvement with the Law in the Previous 12 Months, by Caregivers' Characteristics of the Adolescent Population at Wave 5

	N	Arrested in past 12 months		Convicted in past 12 months		On probation in past 12 months	
		%	*SE*	%	*SE*	%	*SE*
Total		3.3	0.9	1.2	0.5	0.9	0.5
Race/ethnicity	1,344	*					
Black	368	3.3	0.9	3.1	1.9	2.7	1.9
White	700	3.4	1.2	0.7	0.2	0.4	0.2
Hispanic	200	0.2 [a]	0.1	0.2	0.1	0.2	0.1
Other	76	1.6	1.0	0.3	0.3	0.3	0.3
Caregiver	1,344	*					
Biological	1,001	3.6[b]	1.0	1.4	0.6	1.1	0.6
Adoptive	100	0.0	0.0	0.0	0.0	0.0	0.0
Kin	243	2.7	1.4	0.3	0.2	0.0	0.0

Note: All analyses were on weighted data; Ns are unweighted. Pearson χ^2 tests for cluster samples were used for significance tests. Asterisks indicate statistical significance (*$p < .05$). An asterisk in a column applies to the subsequent results for the covariate. Only permanent caregivers were asked about involvement with the law; foster and group home caregivers were not queried.

[a] Hispanic caregivers were significantly less likely to have been arrested in the 12 months before the interview than Black ($p < .05$) caregivers or White caregivers ($p < .05$).

[b] Biological parents were significantly more likely to have been arrested in the 12 months before the interview than adoptive parents ($p < .05$).

Exhibit 39. Permanent Caregivers' Reported Service Receipt to Address Family Needs for the Adolescents at Wave 5

		Received service	
Service	*N*	%	*SE*
Received legal aid	1,354	4.6	1.1
Received food from a community source	1,356	19.2	2.2
Received emergency shelter or housing	1,355	0.8	0.4
Received job-related services	1,353	4.9	1.1
Attended any organized support group (caregiver)	1,355	8.6	1.7
Received child care on a regular basis	1,354	7.8	1.4
Received any home management training	1,355	1.9	0.7
Received in-home cleaning or repair help	1,355	5.2	1.1
Received any help with transportation	1,355	10.1	1.6
Received financial help (not TANF or SSI)	1,355	10.7	1.9

Note: All analyses were on weighted data; *N*s are unweighted. Reported Ns vary slightly across analyses because of missing data in some variable categories. Only permanent caregivers were asked if they had received these services to address family needs. TANF = Temporary Assistance for Needy Families. SSI = Supplemental Security Income.

Exhibit 40. Caregivers' Reported Receipt of Federal or State-Supported Services, by Caregivers' Characteristics of the Adolescent Population at Wave 5

	N	TANF		WIC		Food stamps			SSI	Housing support		Any federal service	
		%	*SE*	%	*SE*	%	*SE*	%	*SE*	%	*SE*	%	*SE*
Total	1,466	10.5	1.5	14.0	2.0	38.8	3.2	28.5	2.7	9.5	1.5	60.9	2.6
Race/ethnicity	1,436			*		**				**			
Black	404	14.9	4.4	18.1	3.9	45.1	3.8	33.0	4.3	21.7 [a]	4.0	67.3	4.8
White	741	7.6	1.7	8.8 [b]	1.9	31.4 [c]	2.6	27.9	3.9	4.7	1.3	54.3	3.6
Hispanic	210	12.5	3.2	25.8	5.9	51.3	11.0	23.3	5.0	6.8	3.7	70.8	7.5
Other	81	9.6	5.6	12.7	10.0	52.6	10.4	34.2	8.6	10.9	7.0	71.4	10.0

Exhibit 40. (Continued)

	N	TANF		WIC		Food stamps			SSI	Housing support		Any federal service	
		%	*SE*	%	*SE*	%	*SE*	%	*SE*	%	*SE*	%	*SE*
Caregiver	1,466	**				***				***		**	
Biological	1,010	8.6 [d]	1.6	12.8	2.0	40.7 [e]	3.3	27.4	3.1	9.3 [f]	1.5	62.1 [g]	2.8
Adoptive	100	1.1	0.6	4.4	2.6	6.8	3.8	20.8	8.0	0.2	0.2	26.8	9.1
Kin	267	22.0 [h]	5.6	23.6	8.4	44.2 [i]	7.6	39.0	6.7	14.2 [j]	5.6	69.8 [k]	5.7
Foster	57	0.6	0.5	9.2	6.7	1.0	0.8	9.0	4.6	0.0	0.0	17.9	8.2
Group home or residential program	32	19.1	16.5	0.0	0.0	0.0	0.0	16.2	14.3	0.0	0.0	35.3	18.2

Note: All analyses were on weighted data; Ns are unweighted. Reported *N*s vary slightly across analyses because of missing data in some variable categories. Pearson ÷2 tests for cluster samples were used for initial significance tests. Asterisks indicate statistical significance (*$p < .05$, **$p < .01$, ***$p < .00 1$) for the covariate. TANF = Temporary Assistance for Needy Families. WIC = Special Supplemental Nutritional Program for Women, Infants, and Children. SSI = Supplemental Security Income.

[a] Among those households with a member receiving SSI (n = 431, or 28.5%), caregivers reported that the disability check (SSI) was to provide for the child and other household member for 37.1% (SE = 4.1), for the child only for 25.7% (SE = 3.3), and for other household members and not the child for 37.1% (SE = 4.0). No statistically significant differences by caregivers' race/ethnicity or type of caregiver were found.

[b] Black caregivers were significantly more likely to receive housing support than White caregivers ($p < .00 1$) or Hispanic caregivers ($p < .05$).

[c] White caregivers were significantly less likely to receive WIC than Black caregivers ($p = .05$) or Hispanic caregivers ($p < .0 1$).

[d] White caregivers were significantly less likely to receive food stamps than Black caregivers ($p < .00 1$).

[e] Biological parents were significantly more likely to receive TANF than adoptive parents ($p < .05$) or foster caregivers ($p < .05$).

[f] Biological parents were significantly more likely to receive food stamps than adoptive parents ($p < .00 1$), foster caregivers ($p < .001$), or group caregivers ($p < .001$).

[g] Biological parents were significantly more likely to receive housing support than adoptive parents, foster, and group caregivers ($p < .0 1$).

[h] Biological parents were significantly more likely to receive any federal service than adoptive parents ($p < .05$) or foster caregivers ($p < .05$).

[i] Kin caregivers were significantly more likely to receive TANF than adoptive parents ($p < .01$) or foster caregivers ($p < .0 1$).

j Kin caregivers were significantly more likely to receive food stamps than adoptive parents ($p < .0 1$), foster and group caregivers ($p < .00 1$).

[k] Kin caregivers were significantly more likely to receive housing support than biological parents, adoptive parents, foster caregivers and group home caregivers ($p < .05$).

[l] Kin caregivers were significantly more likely to receive any federal service than adoptive parents ($p < .05$) or foster caregivers ($p < .01$).

Exhibit 41. Permanent Caregivers' Mental Health and Substance Abuse Services Need and Service Receipt, by Caregivers' Characteristics of the Adolescent Population at Wave 5

	N	Total		Received mental health service	
		%	*SE*	%	*SE*
Total	1,356			5.5	1.4
Race/ethnicity	1,356				
Black	371	23.8	3.4	6.0	2.6
White	707	52.8	3.9	4.2	1.6
Hispanic	202	17.5	3.3	6.0	3.2
Other	76	5.9	1.4	14.4	10.6
Caregiver	1,356			**	
Biological	1,010	81.5	2.0	6.7 [a]	1.7
Adoptive	100	3.3	1.0	0.2	0.2
Kin	246	15.2	2.0	0.7	0.5
Insurance	1,353			*	
Medicaid	903	62.8	2.7	6.1 [b]	1.9
Private or CHAMPUS	341	28.5	2.6	1.2	0.7
None	109	8.6	1.5	16.8	8.4
Need for services	1,356				
Mental health [c]	382	26.6	2.1	9.5	2.8
Substance abuse services [d]	53	3.8	1.0	25.2	12.2

Note: All analyses were on weighted data; Ns are unweighted. Pearson χ^2 tests for cluster samples were used to test statistical significance. Asterisks indicate statistical significance (*$p < .05$, **$p < .01$). Asterisks in a column apply to the subsequent results for the covariate. Only permanent caregivers were asked about mental health service receipt.

[a] Biological parents were significantly more likely to have received mental health services than adoptive parents ($p < .05$) or kin caregivers ($p < .00$ 1).

[b] Caregivers with Medicaid were significantly more likely to have received mental health services than caregivers with private insurance ($p < .05$).

[c] Caregivers were determined to be "in need of mental health services" when they met any one of four criteria: (1) caregiver self-reported need for "a lot" or "some" help for a mental health problem, (2) caseworker report of a caregiver's need for a mental health services, (3) self-reported scores in the clinical range on the major depression scale of the Composite International Diagnostic Interview Short Form (CIDI-SF; Kessler et al., 1998), or (4) a score exceeding 1.5 SD below the norm (i.e., a score <35) on the Mental Health component of the 12-Item Short Form Health Survey (Ware et al., 1996).

[d] Caregivers were determined to be in need of substance abuse services when they met any one of three criteria: (1) caregiver self-reported need for "a lot" or "some" help for an alcohol or drug problem, or (2) scores in the clinical range on either the Alcohol Dependence or Drug Dependence scale of the CIDI-SF.

Exhibit 42. Characteristics of Adolescents with an Open Child Welfare System Case at Wave 5

	N	%	*SE*
Total	214	100.0	0.0
Gender	214		
Male	120	46.6	7.1
Female	94	53.4	7.1
Age (years)	214		
11–12	53	38.1	6.8
13–14	71	29.7	5.2
15–17	90	32.2	6.1
Race/ethnicity	214		
Black	63	18.2	5.0
White	90	51.0	6.7
Hispanic	49	26.8	5.8
Other	12	4.0	2.0
Placement at Wave 5	213		
In home biological parents	82	51.3	6.4
In home adoptive parents	15	6.4	5.0
Kin care	34	15.0	6.0
Foster care	54	16.7	5.0
Group home or residential program	28	10.7	4.0

Note: All analyses were on weighted data; *N*s are unweighted. Reported *N*s vary slightly across analyses because of missing data in some variable categories.

Exhibit 43. Caseworkers' Reported Service Receipt Among Those with an Open Child Welfare System Case for the Adolescent Population at Wave 5

Service	*N*	%	*SE*
Total	214	100.0	0.0
Help with identifying and gaining access to other services	196	43.2	6.9
Parents' individual counseling	197	38.1	7.0
Family counseling	186	39.8	8.3
Other nonintensive home-based services	203	26.9	5.0
Parenting training	194	35.8	6.6
Services to prevent out-of-home placement	199	32.5	6.4
Children's in-home counseling	196	15.2	5.3
Family preservation or reunification service	198	17.5	4.9
Household management training	193	11.9	3.6
Agency's provision of emergency financial help	192	10.2	3.9
Parent aid services	193	11.5	4.0
Help with child care through agency	206	8.8	3.3
Respite care for child	199	4.2	1.6
Home management services (cleaning or repairs)	194	5.7	2.6
Help with job training or job search	196	3.8	2.4

Note: All analyses were on weighted data; Ns are unweighted. Reported *N*s vary slightly across analyses because of missing data in some variable categories.

Technical Appendix

Scales. Following is a descriptive list of the instruments used as measures for the adolescent population of NSCAW.

- *Child and Adolescent Services Assessment (CASA).* Data on the use of mental health services were based on an adapted version of CASA (Ascher, Farmer, Burns, & Angold, 1996; Burns et al., 1995; Farmer, Angold, Burns, & Costello, 1994). This instrument gathers information from caregivers and children about an array of child-focused services for emotional or behavioral problems, including outpatient and residential care. Outpatient services include (1) clinic-based specialty mental health services; (2) private practice professionals, including psychiatrists, psychologists, social workers, and psychiatric nurses and drug or alcohol clinics; (3) in-home mental health services (e.g., family preservation); and (4) therapeutic nursery/day treatment. Residential services include (1) hospitalization in a psychiatric hospital or psychiatric unit of a general hospital, (2) hospitalization in a medical inpatient unit for emotional or behavioral problems, and (3) inpatient drug or alcohol detoxification.
- *Child Behavior Checklist (CBCL).* The CBCL was designed to assess children's social competencies and problem behaviors on the basis of "standardized descriptions of behavior rather than diagnostic inferences" (Achenbach, 1991, p. iii). Two versions of the checklist have been developed: one for children aged 11/2 to 5 years and another for those aged 6 to 18. In this wave of data collection, the version for children aged 6 to 18 was used. The checklist consists of 118 items related to behavioral problems. For each item, the child's caregiver indicates how well the behavior describes the child, either now or within the past 6 months, on a 3-point scale: 0, *not true* of the child; 1, *somewhat/sometimes true*; or 2, *very/often true*. The caregiver also reports on 20 social competency items, such as the amount and quality of the child's participation in sports, hobbies, jobs and chores, and organizations; friendships; and school functioning. For this report, the CBCL *Total Problem*, *Internalizing*, and *Externalizing* behavior standardized (*T*) score was used to measure the behavioral well-being of children. In keeping with recommended procedures for classifying the *Total Problems*, *Internalizing*, and *Externalizing* scales (Achenbach, 1991; Achenbach & Rescorla, 2001), behavior ratings were considered clinically significant if scale *T* scores were at or above 64.
- *Children's Depression Inventory (CDI).* The CDI measures depression by asking various questions of children aged 7 to 17 years about their engagement in certain activities or their experience of certain feelings (e.g., sad, enjoyment around other people). CDI contains 27 items, each with a 3-point Likert-type scale (0 = *absence of symptom*, 1 = *mild symptom*, 2 = *definite symptom*) that addresses a range of depressive symptoms as indicated by five factors: Negative Mood, Interpersonal Problems, Ineffectiveness, Anhedonia, and Negative Self-Esteem. The normative sample consisted of 1,266 Florida public school students aged 7 to 16 (Kovacs, 1992). Children were determined to have a clinically significant total score on CDI if the total depression standard *T* score was greater than or equal to 65. This clinical

cutoff is based on the CDI normative sample's rates of depression in the CDI manual (Kovacs, 1992); it corresponds to a raw score of 19 for girls and 24 for boys.

- *Composite International Diagnostic Interview Short Form (CIDI-SF).* The CIDISF is a highly standardized interview that screens for mental health and substance use disorders, using the criteria established in the *Diagnostic and Statistical Manual of Mental Disorders* (American Psychiatric Association, 1987). The full instrument evaluates the presence of eight disorders: major depression, generalized anxiety, specific phobia, social phobia, agoraphobia, panic attack, alcohol dependence, and drug dependence (World Health Organization, 1990). For this study, only the sections on major depression, alcohol dependence, and drug dependence were administered. Questions are scripted to ask about the previous 12-month period (Kessler et al., 1998); the section on depression was administered by in-person interview, while the sections on alcohol and drug dependence were administered by means of audio computer-assisted self- interviewing. The CIDI-SF version used in NSCAW does not indicate comorbidity with other disorders, nor does it differentiate between depression occurring as a primary diagnosis or in the context of other disorders, such as bipolar disorder or schizoaffective disorder.
- *Conflict Tactics Scale (CTS1).* The CTS 1 is a self-report measure designed to assess the overt means by which family members respond to conflicts (Straus, 1979). In NSCAW, the CTS1 's Physical Violence scale was used to assess female young adults' experiences with intimate-partner violence. This measure is divided into minor and severe subscales based on the severity of the violent act. The *minor* violence items include being pushed, grabbed, shoved, or slapped, whereas the *severe* violence items inquire about experiences that include being choked, beaten, and threatened with a knife or gun. Response categories range from 0 (*never*) to 6 (*more than 20 times*), indicating the frequency of occurrence of the violent acts in the preceding 12 months. For events that did not occur in the previous 12 months, the respondent was asked to indicate if they had ever happened. The CTS1 has been used in national surveys of intimate-partner violence and is the most frequently employed and thoroughly validated measure of intimate-partner violence. The reliability (α = .88) and validity of the physical violence section of CTS1 have been well documented (Straus, 1979).
- *Conflict Tactics Scale, Parent-Child Version (CTS-PC).* The CTS-PC was developed to measure psychological and physical maltreatment and neglect by parents, as well as nonviolent modes of discipline CTS-PC scales include nonviolent discipline (e.g., putting a child in "time out"), psychological aggression (e.g., shouting, yelling, or screaming at a child), physical assault, and neglect (Straus et al., 1998). Because items in the physical assault scale range widely in severity, from spanking to burning a child on purpose, the scale may be divided into subscales for minor, severe, and very severe physical assault. In NSCAW, parental report on the CTS-PC measures were obtained from both adolescents and permanent caregivers, including biological parents, adoptive parents, and other in-home caregivers, but excluded foster parents and other outof-home caregivers. This report presents findings from the nonviolent discipline, psychological aggression, and neglect scales, as well as the physical assault subscales. Measures shown are annual prevalence for each scale.

- *Kaufman Brief Intelligence Test (K-BIT).* The Kaufman Brief Intelligence Test is a brief, individually administered screener of verbal and nonverbal intelligence; it is designed for individuals 4 years old or older (Kaufman & Kaufman, 1990). It includes two subtests: Vocabulary (expressive vocabulary and definitions) and Matrices (ability to perceive relationships and complete analogies). NSCAW used the standard score for Vocabulary, Matrices, and Total IQ Composite. Each is normed to have a mean of 100 and standard deviation of 15. This report provides the percentage of adolescents with low (defined as scores between −1 and −1.99 standard deviations below the mean) and very low scores (defined as scores −2 standard deviations or more below the mean) on the Composite, Vocabulary, and Matrices.
- *Loneliness and Social Dissatisfaction Scale.* The Loneliness and Social Dissatisfaction Scale assesses adolescents' feelings of loneliness and dissatisfaction with peer support at school, using a self-report questionnaire (Cassidy & Asher, 1992). This instrument is a modification of the version used for older elementary school children. The adolescents rate on a 3-point scale 16 items, such as "Can you find a friend at school when you need one?" This report presents item-specific responses.
- *Parental Monitoring Scale.* The Parental Monitoring Scale assesses an adolescents' report on the extent to which the caregiver monitors the adolescent's activities (Dishion et al., 1991). It consists of 6 questions asking how often the parent provides the child with a type of parental monitoring, using a 5-point scale: 1 (*never*), 2 (*almost never*), 3 (*once in awhile*), 4 (*pretty often*), or 5 (*very often*). This report presents item-specific responses.
- *School Engagement.* By means of a self-rating scale, this measure assesses adolescents' "connection" to the school experience (U.S. Department of Education, 1995). It was designed for children in elementary and middle school. The scale includes 11 items that measure both the behavioral component (participation) and psychological component (identification) of school engagement. Items are measured on a 4-point scale from 1 (*never*) to 4 (*almost always*). This report presents item-specific responses.
- *Self-Report Delinquency Scale.* Adolescents reported any illegal activity, using the Self-Report Delinquency Scale developed for the National Youth Survey (Elliott et al., 1985). Respondents were asked if they had committed several illegal acts in the 6 months prior to interview. According to type of crime and level of severity, illegal activities were divided into the following categories (Elliott et al., 1985): Status Offense (ran away, skipped school, or lied about age for movie admittance), Public Disorder (hitchhiked; was loud, rowdy, or unruly in a public place; begged for money or things; was drunk in a public place; carried a hidden weapon; or paid for having sex), Damaged Property, Minor Theft (stole things worth $50 or less; went joyriding; avoided paying for things such as movies, bus or subway rides, food, or clothing; shoplifted; or pickpocketed), Serious Property Crime (arson; stole things worth over $50; burglary or attempted burglary; motor vehicle theft or attempted motor vehicle theft; or fraud), Simple Assault (threw objects such as rocks or bottles at people; or hit someone, with the intention of hurting him or her), and Felony Assault (attacked someone with a weapon, with the intention of seriously hurting or

killing him or her; was involved in a gang fight; or had or tried to have sexual relations with someone against his or her will).

- *Short Form Health Survey (SF-12).* The SF-12 is a standardized survey instrument designed to provide an indicator of physical and mental health status (Ware et al., 1996). It includes 12 items selected from the Medical Outcomes Study 36-Item Short Form Health Survey (SF-36). The SF-12 is collapsed into two summary scales—a physical health component summary and a mental health component summary. Average scores for the two summary scales have been shown to closely reflect those from the original 36-item form. Furthermore, the SF-12 has demonstrated adequate reliability and validity (Ware et al., 1996).
- *Social Skills Rating System.* The Social Skills Rating System (SSRS) measures caregiver and teacher perception of the social skills of children between the ages of 3 and 18. Separate versions have been developed for preschool, elementary school, and secondary school (Gresham & Elliott, 1990). The scores used in this report are based on the caregiver report. The SSRS assesses social skills in four domains—cooperation, assertion, responsibility, and self-control—and provides standard scores and competence categories for the total, as well as competence categories for the individual domains. The SSRS standardized scores are based on a mean of 100, with a standard deviation of 15. Total scores were categorized as suggested in the SSRS manual (Gresham & Elliott, 1990): Fewer Social Skills (standard scores < 85), Average Social Skills (standard scores 85 to 115), or More Social Skills (standard scores > 115).
- *Teacher Report Form (TRF).*The TRF, from the Achenbach System of Empirically Based Assessment, uses the same constructs as the CBCL to evaluate a child's behavioral problems (Achenbach, 1991; Achenbach & Rescorla, 2001). The TRF is different in that it is completed by the child's teacher, rather than a caregiver, and it includes some items specifically related to behaviors displayed in school. As with the CBCL, two versions of the form have been developed: one for children aged 1 1/2 to 5 and another for those aged 6 to 18. In this wave of data collection, the version for children aged 6 to 18 was used. Each item on the Problem Section of the TRF contains a statement about a child's behavior. The teacher selects the response that assesses how well each statement describes the child, either currently or within the previous 2 months. Response options include *not true (0)*, *somewhat or sometimes true (1)*, and *very true or often true* (2). For this report, the TRF Total Problem, Internalizing, and Externalizing behavior standardized (*T*) scores were used. In keeping with recommended procedures for classifying the Total Problems, Internalizing, and Externalizing scales, behavioral ratings were considered clinically significant if scale *T* scores were at or higher than 64.
- *Trauma Symptom Inventory (TSI).* The TSI is used in the evaluation of acute and chronic posttraumatic symptomatology, including the effects of rape, spouse abuse, physical assault, combat experiences, major accidents, and natural disasters—and the lasting sequelae of childhood abuse and other early traumatic events (Briere, 1996). The various scales of the TSI assess a wide range of psychological effects. These effects include not only symptoms typically associated with posttraumatic stress disorder or acute stress disorder, but also those intra- and interpersonal difficulties often associated with more chronic psychological trauma. Each symptom item is

rated according to its frequency of occurrence, using a 4-point scale ranging from 0 (*never*) to 3 (*often*). All clinical scales yield gender- and age-normed *T* scores. One clinical scale was used: Post Traumatic Stress (PTS). Clinically significant scores on the PTSD subscale were defined as those standardized scale scores at or higher than 65.

- *Violence Exposure Scale (VEX-R).* The VEX-R was used to assess frequency of exposure to violent and criminal events in children aged 5 or older (Fox & Leavitt, 1995). The VEX-R is a 23-item child self-report measure in a cartoon format that has been previously administered to minority, inner-city children and elementary school children in Israel (Raviv et al., 2001; Raviv, Raviv, Shimoni, Fox, & Leavitt, 1999; Shahinfar, Fox, & Leavitt, 2000). Children are shown cards depicting violent and criminal acts and are asked to respond on a 4-point scale (*never*, *once*, *a few times*, *lots of times*) about their experiences. VEX-R inquires about being a victim or witness to 13 types of violent and criminal events. A recent factor analysis of VEX-R on a sample of 134 children indicated two dimensions falling into *mild* and *severe* violence categories (Raviv et al., 2001). This factor analysis was consistent with another factor analytic study of this instrument (Raviv et al., 1999), which found alpha reliabilities to be .84 and .85 for mild and severe violence.
- *Woodcock-Johnson III Tests of Cognitive Abilities.* Four subtests were used from the Woodcock Johnson III Tests of Cognitive Abilities (Woodcock et al., 2001). *Letter-Word Identification* is a basic reading skill involving naming letters and reading words aloud from a list. *Calculation* is a test of math achievement measuring the ability to perform arithmetic computation with paper and pencil. *Passage Comprehension* is a measure of reading comprehension in which the individual has to orally supply the missing word removed from each sentence or very brief paragraph. *Applied Problems* is a test of math reasoning requiring the individual to solve oral word-problems. Standardized scores are based on a mean of 100, with a standard deviation of 15. This report provides the percentage of adolescents with low (defined as scores between −1 and −1.99 standard deviations below the mean) and very low scores (defined as scores −2 standard deviations or more below the mean) on all scales.
- *Youth Self-Report (YSR).* The YSR was designed to assess self-reported feelings and behavior for comparison to normative groups of 11- to 18-year-olds (Achenbach, 1991; Achenbach & Rescorla, 2001). The YSR is almost identical to the CBCL in content and structure, including the competence scales, problem syndromes, and other problems. The normative sample was drawn from a group of 1,719 children who completed the YSR. The normative sample is nationally representative and consisted of those children who were 11 to 18 years old when they completed YSR and who had not received mental health services or special remedial school classes in the past 12 months (Achenbach, 1991; Achenbach & Rescorla, 2001). For this report, the YSR Total Problem, Internalizing, and Externalizing behavior standardized (*T*) scores were used to measure adolescent behavioral well-being. In keeping with recommended procedures for classifying the Total Problems, Internalizing and Externalizing scales (Achenbach, 1991; Achenbach & Rescorla, 2001), behavioral ratings were considered clinically significant if scale *T* scores were at or higher than 64.

Derived Variables. Following is a descriptive list of the variables derived for the adolescent population in NSCAW.

- *Any Mental Health Service.* This service use category included an adolescents' use of specialty outpatient services, inpatient services, visits to a family doctor, and school-based services for emotional or behavioral problems.
- *Chronic Health Condition.* At Wave 5, caregivers were asked whether their child had any health problems that "last a long time or come back again and again." If the response was "yes," caregivers were asked to name them. Conditions classified as chronic health conditions included AIDS, anemia, arthritis, asthma, brain tumor, cerebral palsy, chronic health condition, diabetes, eczema, epilepsy, fetal alcohol syndrome, hernia, high blood pressure, birth defect, blood disorders, respiratory problems, persistent bowel problems, physical deformities, repeated ear infections, severe allergies, sickle cell anemia, and spina bifida.
- *Ever Out of Home.* Adolescent placement history was examined across Waves 1 to 4. *Placement history* refers to the adolescent's current living situation (in home versus out of home) at Wave 1, 2, 3, or 4. *Ever out of home* indicates that an adolescent was not living in a home with a biological caregiver at the time of at least one of the interviews. An out-of-home placement could include foster care, kinship care, or group home or other residential treatment facility.
- *Good Health (adolescents and caregivers).* Adolescents of caregivers who reported that their adolescents' health was *good*, *very good*, or *excellent* were classified as being in good health. Caregivers who reported their own health as *good*, *very good*, or *excellent* were classified as being in good health.
- *Household Poverty Status.* This variable represents the percentage of adolescent households at Wave 5 with household incomes below the federal poverty level. *Household income* represents caregiver-reported combined income for all members of the adolescents' household. To calculate poverty status, this household income figure was divided by the total number of household members dependent on that income.
- *Inpatient Services.* This service use category included an adolescents' use of a psychiatric hospital, a hospital for emotional and substance abuse problems, a residential treatment, an emergency shelter for emotional and substance abuse problems, and an emergency room for emotional and substance abuse problems.
- *Need for Mental Health Services (Caregivers).* Caregivers were determined to be "in need of mental health services" when they met any one of four criteria: (1) caregiver self-reported need for "a lot" or "some" help for a mental health problem, (2) caseworker-reported caregiver's need for a mental health services, (3) self-reported scores in the clinical range on the Major Depression scale of the Composite International Diagnostic Interview Short Form (Kessler et al., 1998), or (4) a score exceeding 1.5 standard deviations below the norm (i.e., a score <35) on the Mental Health component of the 12-Item Short Form Health Survey (Ware et al., 1996).
- *Need for Mental Health Services (Adolescents).* Adolescents were defined as "in need of mental health services" if either (1) a caregiver reported an elevated score (>1.5 standard deviations above the mean) on the Total Problems, Internalizing, or

Externalizing scales of the CBCL (Achenbach & Rescorla, 2001); (2) an adolescent reported an elevated score (>1.5 standard deviations above the mean) on the Total Problems, Internalizing, or Externalizing scales of the YSR (Achenbach & Rescorla, 2001); (3) a teacher reported an elevated score (>1.5 standard deviations above the mean) on the Total Problems, Internalizing, or Externalizing scales of the TRF (Achenbach & Rescorla, 2001); (4) a clinically significant score on the CDI (Kovacs, 1992), or (5) a clinically significant score on the PTSD scale of the Trauma Symptoms Checklist (Briere, 1996).

- *Need for Special Education.* Adolescents were considered to be in need of a referral for special education services if (1) they had a Total Problems, Internalizing, or Externalizing score in the clinical range for the CBCL, TRF, or YSR (considered a behavioral need) (Achenbach & Rescorla, 2001), or (2) they had a score 2 standard deviations or more below the mean for the K-BIT or Woodcock-Johnson III (considered a cognitive need) (Kaufman & Kaufman, 2004; Woodcock et al., 2001).
- *Need for Substance Abuse Services (Caregivers).* Caregivers were determined to be in need of substance abuse services when they met one of two criteria: (1) caregiver self-reported need for "a lot" or "some" help for an alcohol or drug problem, or (2) scores in the clinical range on either the Alcohol Dependence or Drug Dependence scale of the CIDI-SF (Kessler et al., 1998).
- *Special Education Services.* Teachers were asked if the adolescent had an Individualized Education Plan (IEP). Caregivers were asked whether they had been told that the child had a learning/developmental problem and, if so, whether the child had an Individualized Education Plan (or IEP) or had received special education services. This report relied on teacher report of an IEP to determine the presence of special education services. Where teacher report data were missing, the caregiver report was used to positively identify IEP receipt. If teacher data were missing and the caregiver report was negative, a case was coded as *missing*.
- *Specialty Outpatient Services.* This service use category refers to an adolescents' use of services received from a private mental health clinician (i.e., psychiatrist, psychologist, social worker, or psychiatric nurse not working in a community health center), a community mental health center, day treatment for emotional and substance abuse problems, or an outpatient drug or alcohol unit.

References

[1] Achenbach, T. M. (1991). *Integrative guide for the 1991 CBCL/4-18, YSR, and TRF profiles*. Burlington, VT: University of Vermont, Department of Psychiatry.

[2] Achenbach, T. M. (1991). *Manual for the Child Behavior Checklist/4-18 and 1991 profile*. Burlington, VT: University of Vermont, Department of Psychiatry.

[3] Achenbach, T. M. (1991). *Manual of the Teacher's Report Form and 1991 Profile*. Burlington, VT: University of Vermont, Department of Psychiatry.

[4] Achenbach, T. M. & Rescorla, L. A. (2001). *Manual for the ASEBA School-Age Forms and Profiles* Burlington, VT: University of Vermont, Research Center for Children, Youth & Families.

[5] Adams, P. F., Barnes, P. M. & Vickerie, J. L. (2008). Summary health statistics for the U.S. population: National Health Interview Survey, 2007. In *Vital and Health Statistics* (Vol. 10, pp. 1-113). Atlanta, GA: National Center for Health Statistics.

[6] Administration for Children and Families (2005). *National Survey of Child and Adolescent Well- Being (NSCA W): CPS sample component, Wave 1 data analysis report.* Retrieved January 7, 2009, from http://www.acf.hhs.gov/programs/opre/abuse_neglect/nscaw/reports/cps_sample/cps_rep ort revised 090105.pdf

[7] Administration for Children and Families (2008). *Indicators of welfare dependence: Annual report to congress 2008.* Retrieved March 10, 2009, from http://aspe.hhs.gov/hsp/indicators08/index.shtml

[8] American Psychiatric Association (1987). *Diagnostic and statistical manual of mental disorders* (3rd rev. ed.). Washington, DC: Author.

[9] Artiles, A. J., Harry, B., Reschly, D. J. & Chinn, P. C. (2002). Over-identification of students of color in special education: A Critical overview. *Multicultural Perspectives, 4*, 3-10.

[10] Ascher, B. H., Farmer, E. M. Z., Burns, B. J. & Angold, A. (1996). The Child and Adolescent Services Assessment (CASA): Description and psychometrics. *Journal of Emotional and Behavioral Disorders*, *4(1)*, 12-20.

[11] Asher, S. R. & Wheeler, V. A. (1985). Children's loneliness: A comparison of rejected and neglected peer status. *Journal of Consulting and Clinical Psychology*, *53(4)*, 500-505.

[12] Bloom, B. & Cohen, R. A. (2007). Summary health statistic for U.S. children: National Health Interview Survey, 2006. In *Vital and Health Statistics* (Vol. 10, pp. 1-87). Atlanta, GA: National Center for Health Statistics.

[13] Briere, J. (1996). *Trauma Symptom Checklist for Children: Professional manual.* Lutz, FL: Psychological Assessment Resources.

[14] Briere, J. (1996). *Trauma Symptom Inventory (TSI) professional manual.* Lutz, FL: Psychological Assessment Resources.

[15] Burns, B. J., Angold, A., Magruder-Habib, K., Costello, E. J. & Patrick, M. K. S. (1994). *The Child and Adolescent Services Assessment (CASA), parent interview and child interview.* Durham, NC: Developmental Epidemiology Program, Department of Psychiatry, Duke University Medical Center.

[16] Burns, B. J., Costello, E. J., Angold, A., Tweed, D., Stangl, D., Farmer, E. M. Z. & Erkanli, A. (1995). Children's mental health service use across service sectors. *Health Affairs*, *14(3)*, 147-159.

[17] Burns, B. J., Phillips, S. D., Wagner, H. R., Barth, R. P., Kolko, D. J., Campbell, Y. & Landsverk, J. (2004). Mental health need and access to mental health services by youth involved with child welfare: A national survey. *Journal of the American Academy of Child and Adolescent Psychiatry*, *43(8)*, 960-970.

[18] Cassidy, J. & Asher, S. R. (1992). Loneliness and peer relations in young children. *Child Development*, *63(2)*, 350-365.

[19] Center on the Developing Child at Harvard University (2007). *A science-based framework for early childhood policy: Using evidence to improve outcomes in learning, behavior, and health for vulnerable children.* Retrieved March 9, 2009, from http://www.developingchild.net/pubs/persp/pdf/Policy Framework.pdf

[20] Centers for Disease Control and Prevention (1999). *YRBSS: Youth Risk Behavior Surveillance System*. Retrieved October 2007, from http://www.cdc.gov/Healthy Youth/yrbs/

[21] Centers for Disease Control and Prevention (2008). Youth Risk Behavior Surveillance--United States, 2007. *Surveillance Summaries*, *57*(SS-4), 1-136.

[22] Christ, S. & Biemer, P. (2005). *National Survey of Child and Adolescent Well-Being (NSCA W) statistical users' manual.* Washington, DC: Administration for Children and Families.

[23] DeNavas-Walt, C., Proctor, B. D., Smith, J. C. & U.S. Census Bureau (2008). Income, poverty, and health insurance coverage in the United States: 2007. In *Current population reports.* (pp. 1-7 1). Washington, DC: U.S. Government Printing Office.

[24] Dishion, T. J., Patterson, G. R., Stoolmiller, M. & Skinner, M. L. (1991). Family, school, and behavioral antecedents to early adolescent involvement with antisocial peers. *Developmental Psychology*, *27(1)*, 172-180.

[25] Eccles, J. S. (1999). The development of children ages 6 to 14. *Future of Children*, *9(2)*, 30-44.

[26] Elliott, D. S., Huizinga, D. & Ageton, S. (1985). *Explaining delinquency and drug use.* Beverly Hills, CA: Sage Publications.

[27] Farmer, E. M. Z., Angold, A., Burns, B. J. & Costello, E. J. (1994). Reliability of self-reported service use: Test-retest consistency of children's responses to the Child and Adolescent Services Assessment (CASA): Description and psychometrics. *Journal of Child and Family Studies*, *3*, 307-325.

[28] Fox, N. A. & Leavitt, L. A. (1995). *The Violence Exposure Scale for Children—Revised (VEX- R).* College Park, MD: University of Maryland.

[29] Fuligni, A. J. & Hardway, C. (2004). Preparing diverse adolescents for the transition to adulthood. *Future of Children*, *14(2)*, 99-119.

[30] Gresham, F. M. & Elliott, S. N. (1990). *Social Skills Rating System manual.* Circle Pines, MN: American Guidance Service.

[31] Hodapp, R. M. & Fidler, D. J. (1999). Special education and genetics: Connections for the 21st century *Journal of Special Education*, *33(3)*, 130-137.

[32] Hosp, J. L. & Reschly, D. J. (2003). Referral rates for intervention or assessment: A meta-analysis of racial differences. *Journal of Special Education*, *37(2)*, 67-80.

[33] Johnston, L. D., O'Malley, P. M., Bachman, J. G. & Schulenberg, J. E. (2007). *Monitoring the Future national results on adolescent drug use: Overview of key findings, 2006. (NIH Publication No. 07-6202).* Bethesda, MD: National Institute on Drug Abuse.

[34] Kataoka, S. H., Zhang, L. & Wells, K. B. (2002). Unmet need for mental health care among U.S. children: Variation by ethnicity and insurance status. *American Journal of Psychiatry*, *159(9)*, 1548-1555.

[35] Kaufman, A. & Kaufman, N. (1990). *Kaufman Brief Intelligence Test (K-BIT).* Circle Pines, MN: American Guidance Service.

[36] Kaufman, A. S. & Kaufman, N. L. (2004). *Kaufman Assessment Battery for Children manual* (2nd ed.). Circle Pines, MN: American Guidance Service.

[37] Kessler, R. C., Andrews, G., Mroczek, D., Ustun, T. B. & Wittchen, H.-U. (1998). The World Health Organization Composite International Diagnostic Interview Short Form (CIDISF). *International Journal of Methods in Psychiatric Research*, *7*, 171-185.

[38] Kessler, R. C., Chiu, W. T., Demler, O. & Walters, E. E. (2005). Prevalence, severity, and comorbidity of 12-Month *DSM-IV* disorders in the National Comorbidity Survey Replication. *Archives of General Psychiatry, 62(6)*, 617-709.

[39] Kortenkamp, K. & Ehrle, J. (2002). *The well-being of children involved with the child welfare system: A national overview*. Washington, DC: Urban Institute.

[40] Kovacs, M. (1992). *Children's Depression Inventory*. North Tonawanda, NY: Multi-Health Systems.

[41] Kovacs, M. (1992). *The Children's Depression Inventory (CDI) manual*. Toronto: Multi-Health Systems.

[42] McCurley, C. (2006). *Self-reported law violating behavior from adolescence to early adulthood in a modern cohort*. Retrieved January 8, 2008, from http://www.ncjrs.gov/pdffiles1/nij/grants/217588.pdf

[43] NSCAW Research Group (2002). Methodological lessons from the National Survey of Child and Adolescent Well-Being: The first three years of the USA's first national probability study of children and families investigated for abuse and neglect. *Children and Youth Services Review*, *24*(6/7), 513-541.

[44] Office of Applied Studies (2008). *Results from the 2007 National Survey on Drug Use and Health: National Findings*. Rockville, MD: Substance Abuse and Mental Health Services Administration, NSDUH Series H-34, DHHS Publication No. SMA 08-4343.

[45] Olfson, M., Marcus, S. C., Tedeschi, M. & Wan, G. J. (2006). Continuity of antidepressant treatment for adults with depression in the United States. *American Journal of Psychiatry*, *163(1)*, 101-108.

[46] Pickett, W., Molcho, M., Simpson, K., Janssen, I., Kuntsche, E., Mazur, J., Harel, Y. & Boyce, W. F. (2005). Cross national study of injury and social determinants in adolescents. *Injury Prevention, 11(4)*, 213-218.

[47] Raviv, A., Erel, O., Fox, N., Leavitt, L., Raviv, A., Dar, I., Shahinfar, A. & Greenbaum, C. (2001). Individual measurement of exposure to everyday violence among elementary schoolchildren across various settings. *Journal of Community Psychology*, *29(2)*, 117-140.

[48] Raviv, A., Raviv, A., Shimoni, H., Fox, N. & Leavitt, L. (1999). Children's self-report of exposure to violence and its relation to emotional distress. *Journal of Applied Developmental Psychology.*, *20(2)*, 337-353.

[49] Shahinfar, A., Fox, N. & Leavitt, L. (2000). Preschool children's exposure to violence: Relation of behavior problems to parent and child reports. *American Journal of Orthopsychiatry*, *70(1)*, 115-125.

[50] Simpson, G. A., Cohen, R. A., Pastor, P. N. & Reuben, C. A. (2008). *Use of mental health services in the past 12 months by children aged 4-1 7 years: United States 2005-2006. NCHS data brief, N. 8.* Retrieved January 15, 2009, from http://www.cdc.gov/nchs/data/databriefs/db08.pdf.

[51] Straus, M. A. (1979). Measuring intrafamily conflict and violence: The Conflict Tactics (CT) Scale. *Journal of Marriage and the Family*, *41*, 75-88.

[52] Straus, M. A., Hamby, S. L., Finkelhor, D., Moore, D. W. & Runyan, D. (1998). Identification of child maltreatment with the Parent-Child Conflict Tactics Scales: Development and psychometric data for a national sample of American parents. *Child Abuse & Neglect*, *22(4)*, 249-270.

[53] Sylvia, S. E., Thorne, J. & Tashjian, C. A. (1997). *School based drug prevention programs: A longitudinal study in selected school districts.* Retrieved March 20, 1009, from http://eric.ed.gov/ERICDocs/data/ericdocs2sql/content_storage_01/0000019b/80/15/38/2 0.pdf

[54] Tjaden, P. & Thoennes, N. (2000). *Extent, nature and consequences of intimate partner violence: Findings from the National Violence Against Women Survey.* Washington, DC: U.S. Department of Justice. U.S. Department of Education (1995). *Drug Free Schools (DFSCA) Outcome Study Questions.* Washington, DC: Author.

[55] Wang, P. S., Lane, M., Olfson, M., Pincus, H. A., Wells, K. B. & Kessler, R. C. (2005). Twelve-month use of mental health services in the United States: Results from the National Comorbidity Survey Replication. *Archives of General Psychiatry, 62(6)*, 629-640.

[56] Ware, J., Jr., Kosinski, M. & Keller, S. D. (1996). A 12-Item Short-Form Health Survey: Construction of scales and preliminary tests of reliability and validity. *Medical Care, 34(3)*, 220-233.

[57] Woodcock, R. W., McGrew, K. S. & Mather, N. (2001). *Examiner's manual: Woodcock- Johnson III Tests of Cognitive Abilities.* Itasca, IL: Riverside.

[58] World Health Organization (1990). *Composite International Diagnostic Interview (CIDI), Version 1.0.* Geneva, Switzerland: Author.

End Notes

[1] *Substantiation* is the child welfare system's official decision that allegations of child maltreatment are valid.

[2] Caregivers were repeatedly warned in the informed consent process that abusive or neglectful behaviors would be reported to CWS because of mandated reporting laws; these reminders may have made caregivers reluctant to disclose aggressive tactics.

[3] Teacher data were collected for 70.0% of the adolescents whose caregivers gave authorization for contacting the teacher at this wave (authorized by 1,125 caregivers, or 75.8%).

[4] Adolescents were considered to be in need of a referral for special education services if they met any of the following criteria: (1) Behavioral problems: Total Problem, Internalizing, or Externalizing *T* scores were equal or greater than 64 on either the CBCL, Teacher's Report Form, or Youth Self-Report; (2) Cognitive problems: an overall score on the composite Kaufman Brief Intelligence Test or on any of the subscales of the Woodcock- Johnson III Tests of Cognitive Abilities of 2 or more standard deviations below the mean. See the Technical Appendix for a detailed description of these measures.

In: Child Welfare System: Transitions
Editors: Aubrey D. Wilson and Sally G. Ryan
ISBN: 978-1-61324-713-6

Chapter 3

ADOLESCENTS INVOLVED WITH CHILD WELFARE: A TRANSITION TO ADULTHOOD

United States Department of Health and Human Services

EXECUTIVE SUMMARY

In 1999 the Administration on Children, Youth and Families, U.S. Department of Health and Human Services, undertook the National Survey of Child and Adolescent Well-Being (NSCAW) to learn about children and families coming in contact with the child welfare system (CWS). The sample, which represents the population of children and families who entered CWS services within a 15-month period (October 1999 through December 2000), included 5,501 children (aged 0 to 14 at the time of sampling) from 92 child welfare agencies nationwide. The first national longitudinal survey of its kind, NSCAW gathers information about children's safety, living-situation permanency, well-being, and services after a maltreatment investigation by child protective services. Baseline data were collected approximately 4 months after the completion of the index CWS maltreatment investigation; follow-up data were collected 1 year (Wave 2), 1 1/2 years (Wave 3), 3 years (Wave 4), and 6 to 7 years later (Wave 5). Wave 5 data for young adults were collected in 2006 and 2007.

Purpose of the Report

This is the first report to focus on adolescents transitioning to young adulthood, presenting findings from the NSCAW Wave 5 follow-up. It provides information about 620 young adults who were adolescents (12 to 15 years old) at baseline. Some adolescents' cases were closed after investigation; others had a case opened to CWS services. Although the majority remained at home after investigation, a small proportion were removed from their homes. At Wave 5, 6 to 7 years after the child protective services investigation, these young adults are 18 to 21 years old.

Young adults who were the focus of maltreatment in adolescence are at a critical transition as they age into early adulthood. They are making decisions that may shape the rest of their lives. They are learning to take care of themselves, independent of their caregivers. Furthermore, many are doing so while learning how to be parents themselves. They face many critical risks to their well-being that are related not only to the experimentation that characterizes their newly acquired independence, but also to having been involved with a family investigated for child maltreatment. Important health issues for these young adults include reproductive health, obesity, mental health, substance abuse, violence, and access to services within a changing system. In addition to health issues, these young adults are in the midst of establishing their own places of residence, finding employment, and forming lasting adult relationships. This report provides information to enhance our understanding of the needs of young adults by addressing the following questions:

- Who are the young adults who had contact with the CWS during adolescence? What types of maltreatment did they experience as adolescents? What risks did they face? What environments are these young adults living in by the time they are 18 to 21 years old?
- How well are these young adults doing in terms of their physical, psychosocial, and emotional development? How does this development compare with that of young adults in the general population?
- How are they transitioning to adulthood and integrating into society? How many have a job, and what types of work are they doing? For those who are parents, how are they doing in this new role?
- What services do young adults need? What have they received?

Who Are the Young Adults Who Have Had Contact with the CWS during Adolescence?

Young Adults' Age, Sex, and Race/Ethnicity

At the Wave 5 follow-up 6 to 7 years after the baseline survey, the largest age group (making up 39.9%) of young adults were 20 years old, 30.2% were 19, 19.8% were 18, and 10.2% were 21. Almost 60% (59.7%) were female and 40.3% were male. White young adults made up the largest group (52.4%), followed by Blacks (26.5%), Hispanics (14.1%), and Other races/ethnicities (7.1%).

Type of Abuse

At the time of the index maltreatment report of child abuse or neglect, caseworkers reported that almost a third (31.9%) of the adolescents came to the attention of the CWS because of physical abuse. Failure to supervise was reported for 29.1%, sexual abuse for 14.5%, failure to provide for 9.5%, emotional abuse for 7.2%, and moral/legal or educational abuse for 6.3%. Slightly more than a quarter of these maltreatment investigations were substantiated.

Out-of-Home Placement History during Adolescence

Almost a fifth (17.2%) of young adults had ever lived in an out-of-home placement at some point during their adolescence (across Waves 1 to 4). Over the course of the study period, most adolescents remained at home with their biological parents.

Living Situation.

At Wave 5, 48.7% were living with a caregiver, and 6.7% were living with a caregiver and a spouse or partner; thus, more than half (55.4%) of young adults were living with a caregiver, such as a biological parent, adoptive parent, foster parent, grandparent, aunt or uncle, or stepparent. A small percentage (9.5%) were married and living with their spouse, and 17.2% were cohabiting with a boyfriend or girlfriend. An additional 11.8% of young adults reported living alone, and 6.3% reported living with one or more adults over the age of 18 who were not relatives. On average, young adults reported moving households 1.4 times within the previous 12 months; 19.0% reported having moved 3 or more times during this period.

What Risks Did these Young Adults Face at the CWS Investigation?

Prior CWS Involvement

Caseworkers reported that 57.6% of families had been reported for child maltreatment prior to the index investigation. Almost two thirds of the families previously reported for child maltreatment had substantiated incidents of abuse or neglect.

Caseworker Risk Assessment at Investigation

At the first interview, when the young adults were 12 to 15 years old, caseworkers were asked about their perceptions of caregiver risk factors. Caseworkers reported that 7.4% of caregivers were abusing alcohol, 7.6% were abusing drugs, and 9.3% had recently been arrested. Nearly one fifth (17.8%) had a serious mental health problem, and 7.0% had a cognitive impairment. Caseworkers estimated that nearly half (40.8%) of caregivers had poor parenting skills, and 21.5% had unrealistic expectations of their adolescent. Among caregivers, 15.3% had a history of abuse and neglect themselves, and 35.7% had been victims of domestic violence. At the time of the first interview, there was active domestic violence against 9.9% of caregivers.

How Well Are these Young Adults doing in Terms of Their Physical, Psychosocial, Cognitive, and Behavioral Development?

Physical Well-being

At Wave 5 the majority of young adults (83.7%) reported being in good, very good, or excellent health. Females (78.4%) were less likely than males (91.5%) to report that they were in good, very good, or excellent health. About a third of all young adults reported that a health condition currently somehow limited their activities. Weight problems were the most prevalent health issue among young adults: 27.7% were overweight and 28.9% were obese.

Young adults reported a low consumption of fruits and vegetables and limited physical activity. Approximately a third had experienced some type of injury, accident, or poisoning during the 12 months prior to interview. The injuries themselves were most commonly bad cuts or scrapes (24.3%) and bad sprains or torn ligaments (14.0%).

Mental Health

Young adults' mean mental health score as measured with the 12-Item Short-Form Health Survey (SF-12)[1] was 47.3, which is slightly below the mean for the U.S. adult population. Mean mental health scores were significantly lower for female young adults (44.8) than for male young adults (50.9). Standardized assessments across several indicators showed that 27.5% of young adults were in the clinical range for major depression, 10.2% reported clinically high levels of experiencing intrusive thoughts associated with past trauma, and 6.2% showed significant dissociative symptoms (indicators of psychosocial stress reactions to a traumatic event). Young adults had higher rates of reported internalizing (e.g., depression and anxiety) and externalizing (e.g., aggression and inattention) behavior problems than the normative sample. On the Achenbach Adult Symptom Checklist, 16.0% had scores within the clinical range for Internalizing problems, 18.9% for Externalizing problems, and 13.4% for Total Problems. Another 6.6% reported symptoms consistent with alcohol dependence, and 6.5% reported symptoms consistent with drug dependence.

Academic Achievement

Overall, young adults displayed scores substantially lower than norms on standardized measures of academic achievement. The young adults' average score on the Woodcock-Johnson III Tests of Cognitive Abilities was one standard deviation below the average for the general population in each subscale. The proportion that scored more than 1.5 standard deviations below the mean was 15.0% for applied problems, 25.3% for passage comprehension, 29.7% for word-letter identification, and 43.6% for calculation.

Sexual Behavior

Three fourths of young adults were sexually active. Less than half of sexually active young adults used a condom at last sex, and 15.3% used no contraception in the year prior to interview.

Illegal Activity and Victimization

In the year prior to interview, 16.7% of young adults were arrested and 9.0% were convicted. Males were much more likely to have been involved with the law than females. Sixteen percent of young adults were victims of violent crimes in the year prior to interview. More than one fourth of females experienced intimate-partner violence in the 12 months prior to interview, including 15.5% of the sample who experienced severe violence.

How Are Young Adults Transitioning to Adulthood and Integrating into Society?

Cohabitation/Marital Status

At Wave 5 more than a quarter of young adults (2 6.7%) were either married and living with their spouse, or living with a boyfriend or girlfriend. Females were significantly more likely to be living with a spouse or partner (37.2%) than males (11.1%). When compared with young adults of other races, Hispanic young adults most frequently reported living with a spouse or partner (40.8%) and were significantly more likely than Black young adults (11.4%) to report this living arrangement.

Parenting Status

More than a third (3 7.4%) of young adults reported having had children, and 29.0% were raising their child in their home. Females (44.9%) were more likely to have had a child than males (26.3%). Among those raising a child, 87.3% were females. Almost all of the females (94.5%) with a child and 34.7% of the males with a child were raising their child in their own homes. Young adults reported having from 1 to 5 children. On the average, young adult parents at Wave 5 had 1.3 children. Older young adults (20 to 21 years) were more likely than younger adults (18 to 19 years) to report having had children. Young adults living in poverty (54.8%) were also more likely than those not living in poverty (3 5.5%) to have had children.

Young Adult Parents' Well-being

Among young adult mothers, 61.8% were living in poverty. Young adult mothers demonstrated many behavioral health risks: 24.1% reported signs of clinical depression, 6.7% reported clinically significant dissociative symptoms, and 18.5% reported intrusive experiences associated with past trauma. Another 6.3% of mothers reported having experienced an incident of severe physical domestic violence in the 12 months prior to interview. Among young adult fathers, 9.0% reported signs of clinical depression, and none of them reported symptoms associated with past trauma. Clinically significant reports of depressive and interpersonal violence reported among young adult parents were lower than those reported for all young adults at Wave 5.

Young Adult Parents' Disciplinary Techniques

About half of young adults raising children reported having used psychologically aggressive discipline tactics (e.g., shouting or screaming at a child) in the year prior to interview, and 55.6% reported having used corporal punishment. Much lower proportions reported any type of severe physical assault (5.2%). In the year prior to interview, 16.5% reported some form of neglect.

Financial Resources

More than half (5 9%) of young adults were living at Wave 5 in households with incomes below the federal poverty level. Females (48.8%) were more likely to be living in poverty than were males (30.6%). The average young adult at Wave 5 was living in a household that earned on the average \$551.30 per week. Male young adults were living in households that earned significantly more money per week (\$711.20) than females (\$446.40).

Those living with caregivers were also living in households with significantly higher weekly income ($635.90) than those living without caregivers ($469.50).

Employment

More than half of young adults (58.1%) reported being employed either full or part time. Among those who reported working, the average number of hours worked per week was 34.4. More than half (57.4%) of young adults not currently working reported that they had worked in the 12 months prior to interview.

Social Support and Contact with Biological Family Members

The great majority of young adults (88.6%) had contact with their mothers; 47.1% had daily contact and 22.7% had weekly contact. More than a third had daily contact with their siblings. Many (76.6%) reported that they had contact with other relatives. Few young adults reported having no contact with a living biological mother (7.2%) or siblings (4.6%); 17.6% reported having no contact with fathers.

What Services do Young Adults Need? What Have They Received?

Health Services

Almost two thirds (62.1%) of young adults reported having a usual source of medical care at Wave 5. Half of young adults had received a medical checkup (52.2%); the same percentage had had dental care in the year prior to interview. Females were significantly more likely than males to have a usual source of care, to have received dental care, to have received a medical checkup, and to have seen a doctor in the 12 months prior to interview. Among young adults, 15.7% reported having had contact with a physician or nurse for serious accidents, injuries, or poisonings in the 12 months prior to interview. Medicaid or other state-funded coverage was the most common type of health insurance among young adults (43.5%); more than a third (36.7%) did not have any type of insurance coverage. Females (75.1%) were more likely than males (45.6%) to have insurance. Young adults with insurance were more likely than uninsured young adults to have a usual source of care, to have had dental care in the 12 months prior to interview, and to have received all types of preventive health care.

Mental Health Services

Overall, 45.4% of young adults were assessed by the survey to be in need of mental health services, and 9.3% were in need of substance abuse services. Among those in need of mental health services, 22.0% received specialty outpatient services, and 17.5% received nonspecialty mental health services (in-home counseling or family doctor). A small group among those in need of mental health services received inpatient psychiatric services (13.3%), and 20.7% were currently using psychotropic medication. The large majority of young adults found to be in need of mental health services received none (67.1%). In contrast, although only a small number of young adults were in need of substance abuse services, more than half (56.2%) received at least one service.

Domestic Violence Services

Of those females who were victims of intimate-partner violence (26.4%), only 4.5% received a referral to domestic violence services, and only 0.9% received a domestic violence service.

Independent Living, Education, and Job-Related Services

Young adults reported receiving help with independent living, education, and job-related services in the following proportions: 63.9% received help with education, 65.5% with jobs, 57.1% with managing finances, 23.7% with housing, and 57.1% with daily living. Overall, 91.7% reported having received help with at least one of the areas. The main sources of assistance were biological parents or other original family members, teachers or schools, and "others."

Services to Address Basic Needs

Young adults were asked about several services to address basic needs in the 12 months prior to interview. More than a third of young adults were receiving some type of service to help meet their basic needs. Among those with children, only females received Temporary Assistance for Needy Families (TANF), or "welfare" (26.6%), and 70.7% of females with children received benefits from the Special Supplemental Nutrition Program for Women, Infants, and Children (WIC). Other services not restricted to persons having children of their own were still more likely to be provided to females. Thus, 35.5% of females received food stamps, compared with 4.8% of males; 10.3% of females received Supplemental Security Income (SSI), compared with 2.7% of males; and, overall, 5 1.9% of females received any federal service, compared with 9.0% of males.

Conclusion

This report summarizes the well-being, young adult milestones, and service use of young adults who were involved with the child welfare system during adolescence. Two critical contextual factors put young adults who were reported for abuse or neglect as adolescents in a highly vulnerable position. The first relates to the demands of becoming a young adult in today's society. The transition to adulthood is a critical time during which young adults need to juggle several developmental tasks. They are learning to live independently and support themselves financially, and many are also learning to raise their own children. For the young adults in this sample, having come from high-risk environments adds to the normal challenges of negotiating these developmental tasks. The second critical factor relates to changes in the infrastructure of the available service systems as an individual ages from adolescence to adulthood. Unlike the many children's services, adult service systems are not intrinsically developed to support individuals with histories of maltreatment. Health services and other systems (e.g., correctional facilities, federal programs) are very different in the adult system than in their counterparts for children. By virtue of becoming adults, individuals lose the potential safety net that was represented by the school system, the CWS, or pediatric health services. They may be largely on their own now, navigating a confusing social services system, with diminished access to services to address their risks for negative developmental outcomes. As many of these young adults become parents, a new generation may be exposed to less than optimal environments. Consequently, the challenges faced by young adults with a history of CWS involvement are of special interest to caseworkers, policy makers, service providers, and members of the general public.

In some ways these young adults appeared quite similar to their peers across the United States. Many reported themselves to be in good physical health, although the percentage in good health (83.7%) was lower than in the general population of young adults (94.1%; Pleis & Lethbridge-Cejku, 2006). Many reported having established significant romantic relationships and being generally satisfied with the degree of social support available to them. Consistent with their same-age peers, many (55.5%) reported living with a caregiver, an estimate similar to the estimates for the general population of 18- to 24-year-olds living with a caregiver, where 55% of males and 46% of females report this living arrangement (U.S. Census Bureau, 2003). Almost all young adults had relatively consistent contact with their biological families. Many had joined the workforce and were working almost full time, with the percentage of young adults currently employed full or part time (58.1%) being similar to the percentage of working young adults across the country (36.7% among 16-year-olds to 19-year-olds, and 67.6% among 20-year-olds to 24-year-olds; U.S. Census Bureau, 2005).

Despite these similarities, these young adults fared worse than their counterparts in the general population in several ways. More than a fifth (21.6%) of young adult females reported being in fair or poor health, a rate higher than that of females in fair or poor health in the general U.S. population aged 18 years or older (12.9%) and higher than that of adults of both sexes aged 18 to 44 years (5.9%; Pleis & Lethbridge-Cejku, 2006). A disproportionate number of them were reported to be overweight or obese (28.9% were obese, compared with 13.6% of young adults in the general population; CDC, 2007a), which could further jeopardize their physical health. Young adult scores on standardized measures of academic achievement were significantly below national norms, which could limit educational and vocational aspirations. More than a third (34.3%) of young adult females had been in an intimate relationship that involved physical violence, a rate substantially higher than the national 22.1% lifetime prevalence for intimate- partner violence among adult females (Tjaden & Thoennes, 2000). Furthermore, mental health problems were very common and compounded by ongoing unmet mental health services needs.

An alarming number of these young adults were living in households below the federal poverty level, especially young adult mothers raising children: 61.8% of young adult mothers were raising their children in poverty, compared with 3 7.2% of female young adults living in poverty without children. Among all young adults, 41.8% were living in poverty, which is far more than young adults nationally (3 0%; Rumbaut, 2004). Another key difference between these young adults and their peers was the number reported to have had children and the number actively parenting those offspring. Young adults who were parents did not appear to have substantially more risks to their well-being (e.g., mental health problems, domestic violence) when compared with other young adults who were in the NSCAW sample at Wave 5. However, young adult parents reported substantially more mental health problems, traumatic stress, and histories of domestic violence than are reported for the general population of adults.

Very few young adults reported having received services for emotional, behavioral, learning, or attentional problems. Half of those with symptoms consistent with alcohol or drug dependence were receiving substance abuse services, but half were not. These levels of unmet service needs illustrate a missed opportunity to facilitate the transition of these at-risk young adults into a successful adulthood. Facilitating young adults' access to preventive services, mental health services, and vocation-oriented services may be particularly critical for adolescents with a history of past CWS involvement.

1. ADOLESCENTS INVOLVED WITH CHILD WELFARE — A TRANSITION TO ADULTHOOD

For the past 50 years, young adulthood has been conceived of as a challenging period, full of major risks and opportunities as young people acquire greater autonomy. During this period, young adults may be completing school, establishing independent households, and finding employment. This time also coincides with heightened expectations that young adults will form and maintain significant interpersonal relationships and become increasingly active participants in society (Erikson, 1950; Masten et al., 2004). For young adults who were reported for child abuse or neglect, the legacy of maltreatment can have a direct impact on their ability to adapt and comply with society's expectations (Arias, 2004). This report focuses on the wellbeing and transition to adulthood among young adults who were involved with the child welfare system (CWS) as adolescents.

This report uses data from the National Survey of Child and Adolescent Well-Being (NSCAW), a longitudinal study of a national probability sample of children involved with child welfare. NSCAW originated in the Personal Responsibility and Work Opportunity Reconciliation Act of 1996, which directed the U.S. Department of Health and Human Services to carry out a national study of children who were at risk for maltreatment or were otherwise involved with the CWS (Administration for Children, Youth and Families [ACYF], 2005; NSCAW Research Group, 2002). NSCAW gathered data on children's safety, permanency of living situation, well-being, and services at five points in time. Data for the current report are from Wave 5, collected 6 to 7 years after baseline.

This report is the first to focus on adolescents transitioning to young adulthood, presenting findings from the NSCAW Wave 5 follow-up. It provides information about 620 young adults (aged 18 to 21) who were adolescents (12 to 15 years old) at baseline. Research questions were as follows:

- Who are the young adults who had contact with the CWS during adolescence? What types of maltreatment did they experience as adolescents? What risks did they face? What environments are these young adults living in by the time they are 18 to 21 years old?
- How well are these young adults doing in terms of their physical, psychosocial, and emotional development? How does this development compare with that of other young adults in the general population?
- How are they transitioning to adulthood and integrating into society? How many have a job, and what types of work are they doing? For those who are parents, how are they doing in this new role?
- What services do young adults need? What have they received?

Background

In 2005 the national rate of victimization among children aged 12 to 15 was 10.2 per 1,000 same-aged children (Administration for Children and Families [ACF], 2007). Among 12- to 15-year-olds, the main types of reported maltreatment were neglect (53.8%) and physical abuse (21.3%). Although sexual abuse was not the most common type of abuse, the rate of sexual abuse in this age group (17.3%) was higher than that for any other age group (ACF, 2007).

The effects of maltreatment can extend well beyond childhood. For young adults, child maltreatment can affect all aspects of life, including physical health, mental health, behavior, academic performance, interpersonal relationships, and self-perception. Furthermore, childhood maltreatment is a critical risk factor for subsequent victimization in adulthood, which can further compromise any physical or mental health problems (Arias, 2004; Brown, Cohen, Johnson, & Smailes, 1999; Danielson, de Arellano, Kilpatrick, Saunders, & Resnick, 2005; Hillis, Anda, Felitti, Nordenberg, & Marchbanks, 2000; Kaplan et al., 1998; Lansford et al., 2002; Molnar, Buka, & Kessler, 2001; Riggs, Alario, & McHorney, 1990; Thompson, Arias, Basile, & Desai, 2002; Walker et al., 1999; Wolfe, Scott, Wekerle, & Pittman, 2001; Wonderlich, Wilsnack, Wilsnack, & Harris, 1996).

Not all adolescents reported for maltreatment necessarily experienced maltreatment: less than one third of CWS investigations lead to a substantiation of the allegation of abuse or neglect (ACF, 2007). However, research suggests that even children in unsubstantiated cases have disproportionate exposure to risks, have disproportionate rates of developmental deficits and mental health problems, and, in some cases, experience family violence at home and disruptions in caregiving (Hussey et al., 2005; Leiter, Myers, & Zingraff, 1994). Thus, there is reason to believe that all children with a past report to the CWS may be at risk for negative developmental outcomes.

The period of young adulthood is a critical juncture in life. For youth in the United States, the transition to adulthood brings expectations of emotional and economic independence from caregivers and increased societal roles and responsibilities. For instance, it is during this developmental period that young adults might be expected to complete school, find a job, establish significant romantic relationships, and even have children of their own. However, the expectations for a young adult in today's society have changed from those of even a decade ago. In particular, the period of transition into adulthood has lengthened and become more complex. There is greater diversity in the order and way in which young adults go about achieving the traditional milestones of early adulthood. There are also an increasing number of different and more complicated paths through marriage and parenting than were seen in the past. One reason for this prolonged and increasingly complex transition to adulthood is the increased education and job training required to find employment sufficient to support a family (Furstenberg, Kennedy, McLoyd, Rumbaut, & Settersten, 2004). As a result, many young adults rely on support from their parents for longer periods of time and delay marriage and children while they work to meet increased job training needs. Young adults who cannot prolong their reliance on their families of origin, however, may not be able to pursue extensive job training and are likely to have a more compressed transition to adulthood. Research findings demonstrate that young adults living in poverty tend to leave home, obtain full-time employment, and have children at younger ages than those who are financially better off (Furstenberg et al., 2004).

The transition to adulthood is also marked by significant changes in health insurance coverage. Many young adults lose parental insurance coverage when they turn 18 if they are no longer in school, and the types of jobs held by many young adults generally do not provide insurance coverage (Callahan & Cooper, 2004; Lyons & Melton, 2005; Park, Mulye, Adams, Brindis, & Irwin, 2006). Access to health services may be affected in other ways, as well. For example, even if young adults qualify for the same services that they received as children, many mental health services are age based, and the transitions are not seamless. Waiting periods or lack of access to needed services may result because of difficulties in navigating a complex system (Callahan & Cooper, 2004; Lyons & Melton, 2005; Park et al., 2006).

Given the significant challenges posed by the transition to adulthood and the critical developmental tasks to be accomplished, it is crucial to understand how well young adults who were involved with the CWS as adolescents navigate this stage of life. Much of what we know about the transition to adulthood among adolescents involved with the CWS has come from research focused on young adults with a history of foster care placement. A substantial amount of research suggests that the transition-to-adulthood period is especially difficult for maltreated youth who are "aging out" of the foster care system (Courtney & Heuring, 2005). For example, former foster youth have been found to have higher rates of out-of-wedlock births than their peers (Cook, Fleischman, & Grimes, 1991), high rates of unemployment (George et al., 2002), and substantial housing instability in adulthood (Courtney, Piliavin, Grogan-Kaylor, & Nesmith, 2001). Adolescents placed in foster care, however, represent a small minority of the adolescents investigated by the CWS, and no research to date has examined how adolescents investigated by the CWS fared during the transition to adulthood, including both those adolescents who were placed out-of-home and those who remained with their original, biological families.

Purpose of the Report

The purpose of this report is to describe the well-being, early adulthood developmental milestones, and service needs of young adults who were involved with the CWS in adolescence. We provide an overview of their status at 18 to 21 years of age. Using their self-reports, we describe young adults' physical and emotional well-being, current living situation, social relationships, and service utilization.

Definitions

Young Adult

We use the term *young adult* to describe the developmental stage of this report's target population. In the research literature, it has been recently argued that the transition-to-adulthood period is lengthening for young adults in the United States and that this developmental stage may begin at age 18 and extend into a young person's 30s (Furstenberg, Rumbaut, & Settersten, 2004). The population described in this report, however, ranges in age from 18 to 21 years, with approximately 70% being 19 to 20 years old. Thus, they are in the early stages of young adulthood, just beginning the transition.

Wave 5

We use the term *Wave 5* to describe the NSCAW follow-up interview period on which the data in this report are based. For most individuals in this report, the interview occurred 6 to 7 years after the original, baseline interview, which occurred about 4 months after the index report of maltreatment.

Involved with the CWS in Adolescence

We describe this target population as having been "involved with child welfare system (or CWS) in adolescence." At baseline, this target population was between 12 and 15 years of age. Thus, their "index maltreatment report," or the maltreatment report on which their participation in NSCAW was based, occurred in early adolescence. We do not wish to imply that these young adults were not involved with the CWS prior to adolescence; in fact, we have reason to believe that many of them were involved (see Exhibit 1-3). However, we do not have detailed information about their families or their experiences with the CWS prior to adolescence, so the conclusions and references in this report are based on our knowledge of their involvement with the CWS during adolescence.

NSCAW Methods

The methodology of NSCAW provides a number of advantages for this analysis, while also entailing some limitations. We give a brief overview of the methodology in this section; detailed explanations of methods are presented in several available documents (NSCAW Research Group, 2002; Christ & Biemer, 2005; Administration for Children and Families, 2005).

The NSCAW survey included 5,501 children aged 0 to 14 (at the time of sampling—by the time they were reached for the first interview, some of them had turned 15) who had contact with the CWS within a 15-month period beginning in October 1999. These children were selected from 92 primary sampling units in 92 counties nationwide. The sample of investigated/assessed cases included cases that received ongoing services, as well as those that did not receive services, either because they were not substantiated or because it was determined that services were not required.

This sample design required oversampling of infants (to ensure enough cases for permanency planning), sexual abuse cases (to ensure sufficient statistical power to analyze this kind of abuse alone), and cases receiving ongoing services after investigation (to ensure adequate power to understand the process of services). This approach allowed for generation of national estimates for the full population of children and families entering the system, with power to consider key subgroups of the child welfare population.

Weighted percentages were used to provide the most accurate population estimates possible (Christ & Biemer, 2005). Specific weights were developed for the sample of young adults at Wave 5. These young adult Wave 5 weights were based on the sampling frames just described: whether the child's Wave 3 and Wave 4 caregivers were the same, whether there was a history of domestic violence against the Wave 1 caregiver, level of severity of risk to the child, and the caregiver's education level. Significant predictors of Wave 5 nonresponse were also taken into consideration in the development of these weights: caregiver age, whether the Wave 4 caregiver was permanent or temporary, type of maltreatment, child's race/ethnicity, substantiated versus unsubstantiated status after investigation, indicators for whether the child was incarcerated at Wave 5, whether the child had any delinquent behaviors at the time of the Wave 1 interview, and the interaction between gender and delinquent behaviors.[2]

Exhibit 1-1 gives an overview of how and from whom data have been collected in NSCAW. NSCAW provides the widest range of informants of any major study of child welfare: data were collected from children or young adults (Wave 5 only) reported for maltreatment, current caregivers (primarily biological parents, foster parents, or kin), caseworkers, and teachers. Questionnaires used standardized instruments measuring safety, child development, child well-being, service delivery, and other constructs, as well as items specially designed for this study. For children, young adults, and caregivers, data were collected in face-to-face interviews conducted in their homes. To help ensure their privacy and comfort while reporting personal information, sensitive data (e.g., substance use or victimization) were collected through an audio computer-assisted self-interview (ACASI) system, in which respondents enter data directly into laptop computers and follow voiced instructions given to them through headphones attached to the laptop.

Data for Waves 1 through 4 were collected for the entire sample according to the time interval since the investigation of maltreatment was closed (2 to 6 months, 12 months, 18 months, and 36 months after the investigation). In contrast, data for Wave 5 were collected by age cohort. Data collection for Wave 5 began in September 2005 for children younger than 12 months old at the time of sampling. Wave 5 data collection continues for other age cohorts (e.g., adolescents). This report focuses on 620 young adults who turned 18 years old by April 30, 2006. Data collection for this age group was conducted between July 2006 and January 2007. An additional 337 young adults who turned 18 after April 30, 2006, are being surveyed between March and November 2007. Because the data on this group of young adults were not available at the time this report was written, they were not included in the analyses.

Exhibit 1-1. Time Line of NSCAW Data Collection

	Wave				
	1	**2**	**3**	**4**	**5a**
Start and end dates	11/15/99–04/30/01	10/01/00–03/31/02	04/01/01–09/30/02	08/01/02–02/28/04	09/05/05–present
Months after close of investigation	2–6	12	18	36	57 87[b]
Respondent					
Child	X		X	X	X
Current caregiver	X	X	X	X	X
Investigator/services caseworker	X	X	X	X	X
Teacher	X		X	X	X
Young adult					X

[a] Interviews were conducted with children, current caregivers, services caseworkers, and teachers at Wave 5 for children younger than 18 at the time of the Wave 5 interview. For those aged 18 or older at Wave 5, only a young adult interview was conducted.

[b] This interval refers to the time period for the infant, young child, and young adult cohorts at Wave 5. Young adults at Wave 5 were interviewed between 31 and 51 months after the close of the CWS investigation.

NSCAW is available to all qualified researchers through the National Data Archive on Child Abuse and Neglect (NDACAN) at Cornell University (2007). The data analyzed in this report will be released through NDACAN in NSCAW data version 5.2. The data on all young adults, including those analyzed in this report and the 337 interviewed in 2007, will be released for public use through NDACAN in NSCAW data version 5.3.

This report focuses on Wave 5 data collected directly from the young adults who turned 18 years old by April 30, 2006. Baseline data for this young adult cohort were collected 1 to 10 months after the close of the index CWS investigation (with a median time of 4 months). Baseline data included interviews with permanent or nonpermanent caregivers, caseworkers, and children. Data collection at Wave 3 (1 1/2 years later) and Wave 4 (3 years later) included the majority of the same variables as the baseline set. Data collection at Wave 2 included only caseworker and caregiver interviews. At Wave 5, only a young adult interview was conducted. The mean time between Wave 5 and Wave 4 (when young adults were between 14 and 18 years old) was 41 months, with a range of 31 to 51 months. Thus, at Wave 5 young adults were between 18 and 21 years old.

It is noteworthy, as shown in the following sections of this chapter, that most of the adolescents at baseline had been reported for maltreatment prior to the index report; thus, the types of maltreatment recorded at baseline and placement history after baseline capture only part of their lifetime experience. Finally, data on the types of maltreatment are based on the caseworkers' limited knowledge about the case and the specific crisis that triggered the report and may not accurately reflect the young adults' actual experiences.

Wave 5 for Young Adults Who Were Adolescents at Baseline

All results described for young adults at Wave 5 came exclusively from a young adult interview. No caregiver, caseworker, or teacher interviews were conducted at Wave 5 for young adult cases. The young adult interview addressed a wide range of constructs relevant to the young adults' well-being and service receipt. Below is a partial list of the constructs measured:

- physical and mental health
- academic achievement
- illegal activity
- living situation and household status
- employment and financial resources
- family formation
- young adult parenting
- utilization of health and mental health services

A detailed description of the instruments used is provided in the baseline report (ACYF, 2005). The Technical Appendix at the end of this report provides a brief overview.

This report focuses on data collected from a target population of 800 young adults who turned 18 years old by April 30, 2006; however, the final Wave 5 young adult sample included 620 cases. Twenty-one young adults at Wave 5 could not be interviewed because of their placement in correctional or other restrictive settings (e.g., jail, prison, or a juvenile corrections center). These restrictive settings did not allow the participants to be interviewed while incarcerated. There were 8 deceased children among those who were adolescents at baseline. Thus, the eligible young adult sample for the purpose of calculating response rates was 800 (800 original sample minus 8 deceased). The overall weighted response rate was 81%.

Young Adult Characteristics

Exhibit 1-2 gives an overview of some key characteristics of young adults who were involved with the CWS at baseline. These characteristics are analyzed in further detail in the following chapters. More than half of the sample were females (59.7%). Half (52.4%) were White, 26.5% were Black, 14.1% were Hispanic, and 7.1% described their race/ethnicity as "Other." Slightly more than 40% were living in households where the combined income was below the federal poverty level. About 3 6.7% did not report having any health insurance. On average, the young adults were 19.4 years old (SE = 0.1). The majority (39.9%) were 20 years old, 30.2% were 19, 19.8% were 18, and 10.2% were 21. Most young adults (55.5%) reported living with a caregiver in their household at Wave 5. About 9.5% were married, and 17.2% were cohabitating.

More than a third of these young adults (37.4%) had children: 29.0% were currently living with at least one of their biological children, and 8.4% had children but were not living with them. An examination of out-of-home placement history during adolescence revealed that 17.2% had been placed outside of their home at some point between baseline and the Wave 4 interview.

Young Adults at NSCAW Baseline and Previous Waves

Data collected between baseline and Wave 4 provide useful background information on the young adults. This section presents selected findings from baseline to Wave 4, including the following: results of the caseworker baseline risk assessment, adolescent out-of-home placement history, and well-being at Wave 4.

Baseline Risk Assessment

Exhibit 1-3 provides data from the caseworker report on maltreatment and risk variables for these young adults at the baseline interview. Regarding the most serious type of maltreatment, 3 1.9% of cases were reported for physical abuse; 29.1% for failure to supervise; 14.5% for sexual abuse; 9.5% for failure to provide; 7.2% for emotional abuse; 6.3% for moral/legal, educational, or other maltreatment; and 1.6% for abandonment. Slightly over one quarter of the cases (26.3%) were substantiated. Another 4.9% of the cases were "indicated," a category used in some jurisdictions for cases in which some evidence exists for maltreatment but not enough for substantiation. A substantial percentage (5 7.6%) were not substantiated.

Exhibit 1-2. Characteristics of Young Adults at Wave 5

	N	% (SE)
Sex		
Male	233	40.3 (4.2)
Female	387	59.7 (4.2)
Age		
18 years	130	19.8 (2.8)
19 years	198	30.2 (3.8)
20 years	217	39.9 (3.5)
21 years	75	10.2 (2.2)
Race/ethnicity		
Black	184	26.5 (4.6)
White	294	52.4 (4.4)
Hispanic	84	14.1 (3.0)
Other	54	7.1 (1.7)
Percentage of federal poverty level at Wave 5		
<50%	80	16.1 (3.0)
50% to <100%	121	25.7 (3.8)
100% to 200%	147	29.2 (3.7)
>200%	149	29.0 (4.0)
Insurance status at Wave 5		
Insured	406	63.3 (4.1)
Uninsured	196	36.7 (4.1)
Current living situation at Wave 5[a]		
Living with a caregiver	326	55.5 (3.6)
Not living with a caregiver	294	44.5 (3.6)
Cohabitation status at Wave 5		
Married and living with spouse	45	9.5 (2.7)
Cohabitating	122	17.2 (3.3)
Separated, divorced, never married, or not cohabitating	453	73.3 (3.8)
Parenting status at Wave 5		
Has a child living in the home	176	29.0 (3.4)
Has a child not living in the home	49	8.4 (2.4)
Does not have a child	395	62.6 (3.7)
Out-of-home placement history (Waves 1–4)		
Ever placed out of home in adolescence	223	17.2 (2.3)
Never placed out of home in adolescence	316	82.8 (2.3)

Note: All analyses are on weighted data; Ns are unweighted. Reported Ns vary slightly across analyses because of missing data in some variable categories.

[a] "Current living situation" is a derived variable based on a young adult's report of who was living in his or her household at the time of the Wave 5 interview. "Living with caregiver" indicates that a young adult reported living with at least one of the following: biological parent, adoptive parent, foster parent, grandparent, aunt/uncle, or stepparent.

Exhibit 1-3. Caseworker Report on Baseline Maltreatment and Risk for Young Adults Involved with the Child Welfare System as Adolescents

	N (Min)	% (SE)
Most serious maltreatment type	571	
Physical abuse		31.9 (3.7)
Sexual abuse		14.5 (3.0)
Failure to supervise		29.1 (4.1)
Failure to provide		9.5 (2.1)
Emotional abuse		7.2 (1.9)
Moral/legal, educational maltreatment, or other		6.3 (1.8)
Abandonment		1.6 (1.0)
CWS outcome[a]	569	
Substantiated		26.3 (3.3)
Indicated		4.9 (1.4)
Unsubstantiated		57.6 (4.1)
Level of harm	566	
None		43.3 (4.2)
Mild		27.9 (3.3)
Moderate		22.8 (3.2)
Severe		6.0 (1.3)
Level of risk	515	
None		28.4 (3.7)
Mild		44.5 (4.5)
Moderate		18.9 (2.7)
Severe		8.2 (1.7)
Risk factors		
Prior reports of child maltreatment	566	57.6 (4.5)
Prior child welfare service history	545	34.8 (4.3)
Child has major special needs or behavioral problems	566	36.4 (3.7)
Active alcohol abuse by primary caregiver	526	7.4 (1.5)
Active alcohol abuse by secondary caregiver	530	12.3 (2.5)
Active drug abuse by primary caregiver	529	7.6 (2.1)
Primary caregiver has serious mental health problem	536	17.8 (2.7)
Primary caregiver has recent history of arrests	528	9.3 (2.1)
Primary caregiver has intellectual or cognitive impairments	550	7.0 (2.1)
Primary caregiver has physical impairments	553	10.4 (2.6)
Primary caregiver has poor parenting skills	560	40.8 (4.7)
Parent has unrealistic expectations of child	551	21.5 (3.2)
History of domestic violence against caregiver	515	35.7 (4.2)
Active domestic violence against caregiver	551	9.9 (2.0)
Primary caregiver uses inappropriate or excessive discipline	553	13.2 (2.5)
History of abuse or neglect of primary caregiver	436	15.3 (3.1)

Note: All analyses are on weighted data; Ns are unweighted. Reported Ns vary slightly across analyses because of missing data in some variable categories. Only young adult cases with Wave 5 follow-up data were analyzed.

[a] Data on CWS outcome do not represent all possible responses. Not included here are those cases for whom a substantiation decision was not made but for whom a level of risk was determined (e.g., high risk, medium risk, low risk).

During a baseline risk assessment, caseworkers indicated the level of harm that they believed had occurred and the kinds of risks that were present in the adolescents' homes. For 43.3% of cases, the caseworker assessed that no harm had occurred; the level of harm was judged to be mild for 27.9% of cases, moderate for 22.8%, and severe for 6.0%. The most common risk factor (57.6% of families) was having prior CWS reports of maltreatment. The majority (94.1%) of these cases were investigated, and, of those, 64.2% were substantiated (not shown). It should be noted that these prior reports were not necessarily related to the caregiver report at baseline and may or may not have been related to the index adolescent. Other risks that were present in a substantial percentage of the cases included poor parenting skills (40.8%), the adolescent's having major special needs or behavioral problems (36.4%), a history of domestic violence against the primary caregiver (3 5.7%), a primary caregiver mental health problem (17.8%), and a history of abuse or neglect to the primary caregiver (15.3%).

Out-of-Home Placement History

We examined adolescent placement history across Waves 1 through 4 to obtain a comprehensive picture of young adult living situations throughout adolescence. Placement history refers to the adolescent's current living situation (in-home versus out-of-home) at Waves 1, 2, 3, or 4. *Out-of-home* indicates that an adolescent was not living in a home with a biological caregiver at the time of the interview. An out-of-home placement could include being in foster care, being in kinship care, or living in a group home or other residential treatment facility. As presented in Exhibit 1-2, 17.2% of young adults had ever lived out of home at some point across Waves 1 through 4 (corresponding to the period of their adolescence). So, over the course of the study period, most adolescents remained at home with their biological parents. At each wave of data collection from baseline to Wave 4, 82.7% were living at home with their biological parents. Others were at in-home settings with adoptive parents (0.56% to 1.1%, depending on wave) or other caregivers (3.7% to 6.0%). Depending on the wave, 10.9% to 14.0% were in out-of-home settings, including foster care (3.1% to 4.4%), kinship care (2.7% to 6.4%), group home or residential treatment (2.6% to 3.3%), and other out-of-home settings (0.54% to 2.2%). Considered over time, 81.9% of youths were at home both at Wave 1 and at Wave 4, and 5% were out of home at both time points. In terms of transitions, 5.4% of youth went from in-home settings at Wave 1 to out-of-home settings at Wave 4, and 7.1% went from out-of-home to in-home settings. A large majority of youth never experienced a placement.

Mental Health in Late Adolescence

Exhibit 1-4 describes mental health indicators to give some sense of how these young adults fared during late adolescence. Depression was measured with the Children Depression Inventory (CDI); children were classified as depressed if they fell at or above the 91st percentile for their age and sex group on the CDI (Kovacs, 1992). More than a quarter (29.8%) of adolescents had a score in the clinical range for depression. Scores on the Child Behavior Checklist (CBCL) developed by Achenbach and colleagues were used as indicators of adolescents' mental health and behavioral and emotional functioning. Externalizing, Internalizing, and Total Problems were measured using the CBCL (Achenbach, 1991). The proportion of adolescents in the borderline/clinical range (at or over the 92nd percentile) of scores from the caregiver reports on the CBCL was 34.5% on Externalizing behaviors, 17.6%

on Internalizing behaviors, and 3 1.3% on the Total Problems scale. Only one result across all measures of mental health was different by sex: females (40.9%) were more likely to be described by their caregiver as having externalizing behaviors than were males (25.0%).

Delinquency in Late Adolescence

Delinquency during the 6 months prior to the Wave 4 interview was assessed via ACASI using the Self-Report Delinquency Scale developed for the National Youth Survey (Elliott, Huizinga, & Ageton, 1985; see Technical Appendix). Just over 40% of adolescents had engaged in some delinquent activity, primarily public disorder, in the 6 months prior to interview. Males were significantly more likely than females to have engaged in delinquent activity (51.0% versus 34.2%). Five percent of adolescents had been arrested in the 12 months prior to Wave 4, with no significant difference between males and females (Exhibit 1-5).

Guide to the Report

Chapter 2 reviews data on child well-being in terms of health, mental health, sexual behavior, delinquency, and academic achievement. Chapter 3 discusses results regarding developmental milestones related to the transition-to-adulthood period. Chapter 4 discusses the services that young adults received and whether these services met their needs. Chapter 5 describes key characteristics of young adult parents who were living with their children at Wave 5. Chapter 6 draws overall conclusions about the status of young adults who were involved with the CWS during adolescence. References are provided, and the Technical Appendix explains the measures and specially derived variables used.

2. Young Adult Well-being

A notable proportion of young adults who were reported for maltreatment as adolescents were already showing risks to their social and emotional well-being at Wave 4. As noted in Chapter 1, more than a quarter of young adults showed signs of mental health problems at Wave 4, and slightly more than 40% had engaged in some type of delinquent activity in the 6 months before the Wave 4 interview. This chapter will examine these and other indicators of well-being for young adults at Wave 5. Estimates of well-being are compared with estimates based on the general population of young adults in the United States; if no estimates are available, then comparisons are made against the general adult population.

We should begin by noting some patterns of typical well-being of young adults from the general population, particularly as they progress from adolescence to adulthood. For instance, indicators of well-being related to mental health problems and exposure to violence have been found to improve between adolescence and young adulthood (Harris, Gordon-Larsen, Chantala, & Udry, 2006; Schulenberg, O'Malley, Bachman, & Johnston, 2005). Other indicators, such as those related to physical health and substance use, appear to worsen (Harris et al., 2006; Schulenberg et al., 2005).

Exhibit 1-4. Young Adults' Mental Health at Wave 4

	N (Min)	Depression[a] % (SE)	Problem Behaviors (Caregiver Report)[b]		
			Total Problems % (SE)	Externalizing % (SE)	Internalizing % (SE)
Total	400	29.8 (3.9)	31.3 (4.2)	34.5 (4.3)	17.6 (3.2)
Sex				*	
Male	148	39.3 (7.7)	27.3 (6.4)	25.0 (6.0)	17.0 (5.1)
Female	252	23.9 (4.5)	33.9 (5.0)	40.9 (5.2)	18.0 (3.7)

Note: All analyses are on weighted data; Ns are unweighted. Reported Ns vary slightly across analyses because of missing data in some variable categories. Pearson ÷2 tests for cluster samples were used for significance tests. Asterisks indicate statistical significance (*p < .05). Asterisks in column apply to the subsequent results for the covariate.

[a] Depression was assessed at Wave 4 with the Children's Depression Inventory (CDI). The CDI measures depression by asking various questions of children aged 7 to 17 about their engagement in certain activities or their experience of certain feelings (e.g., sadness or enjoyment in being around other people). CDI contains 27 items, each with a 3-point Likert-type scale (0 = *absence of symptom, 1 = mild symptom, 2 = definite symptom*) that addresses a range of depressive symptoms as indicated by five factors: negative mood, interpersonal problems, ineffectiveness, anhedonia, and negative self-esteem. Children were classified as depressed if they fell at or above the 91st percentile for their age and sex group. This clinical cutoff is based on the CDI normative sample's rates of depression in the CDI manual (Kovacs, 1992).

[b] Externalizing and internalizing behaviors were measured at Wave 4 with the Child Behavior Checklist (Achenbach, 1991 a).

Exhibit 1-5. Young Adult Delinquency at Wave 4

	N (Min)	Any Delinquency in Past 6 Months % (SE)	Arrested in Past 12 Months % (SE)
Total	**522**	**41.1 (4.3)**	**5.0 (2.0)**
Sex		**	
Male	194	51.0 (7.1)	5.2 (3.8)
Female	328	34.2 (4.9)	4.8 (2.2)

Note: All analyses are on weighted data; Ns are unweighted. Reported Ns vary slightly across analyses because of missing data in some variable categories. Pearson $\div^2$ tests for cluster samples were used for significance tests. Asterisks indicate statistical significance (***p* < .01). Asterisks in column apply to subsequent results for the covariate.

A history of maltreatment may well alter the typical profile of a young adult's well-being. Maltreatment during childhood or adolescence has been found potentially to affect well-being long term, into adulthood. For example, physical abuse during childhood has been found to be associated with an increase in both physical and mental health problems in adulthood (Thompson, Kingree, & Desai, 2004), and physical abuse during adolescence has been found to be associated with an increase in antisocial behavior during young adulthood, including both general offending and violent offending (Smith, Ireland, & Thornberry, 2005). Some evidence suggests that sexual abuse is associated with high rates of sexual risk taking, placing young adults at high risk for unintended pregnancy or sexually transmitted diseases, including HIV/AIDS (Blinn-Pike, Berger, Dixon, Kuschel, & Kaplan, 2002; Malow, Dévieux, & Lucenko, 2006).

The purpose of this chapter is to assess the well-being of young adults along various dimensions and to identify any differences in well-being across groups. The analyses within this chapter examine the following issues:

1. overall physical health;
2. prevalence of specific health conditions;
3. nutrition, exercise, and obesity;
4. overall mental health;
5. depression;
6. trauma;
7. externalizing and internalizing behaviors;
8. substance dependence;
9. academic achievement;
10. sexual behavior;
11. illegal activity; and
12. victimization, including intimate partner violence.

Well-being outcomes likely vary across individual characteristics. We assessed indicators of well-being according to six different characteristics: sex, race/ethnicity, age, whether respondents were ever placed out of home, number of types of maltreatment, and types of maltreatment. Key results for young adults' well-being were as follows:

- Key physical health results:
  - A full 83.7% reported that they were in good, very good, or excellent health.
  - Male young adults experienced better overall health than females, according to both self-report and the 12-Item Short-Form Health Survey (SF-12) physical health measure.
  - A third experienced some type of injury or accident during the 12 months prior to survey, primarily bad cuts or scrapes (24.3%) and bad sprains or torn ligaments (14.0%).
  - 4.4% of young adults were underweight, 39.1% had a normal weight, 27.7% were overweight, and 28.9% were obese.
  - Reported consumption of fruits and vegetables and reported physical activity were both low
- Key mental health results:
  - Using the SF-12 mental health measure, we found the mean score for overall mental health was 47.3, only slightly lower than the national norm of 50.0. Female young adults scored significantly lower (44.8) than male young adults (50.9).
  - More than one fourth of young adults were in the clinical range for major depression.
  - In relation to trauma, 10.2% reported intrusive symptoms associated with post-traumatic stress (flashbacks, nightmares, intrusive thoughts), and 6.2% reported traumatic dissociation symptoms (depersonalization, derealization, out-of-body experiences, and psychic numbing).

- Based on self-report, 18.9% of young adults were in the clinical range on the externalizing behaviors scale (behaviors such as aggression, hyperactivity, and oppositional behavior.)
- For internalizing behaviors (behaviors signaling anxiety, depression, and fears), 16.0% were in the clinical range.
- Using the Composite International Diagnostic Interview Short Form (CIDI-SF), we found that 6.5% were dependent on alcohol, and 6.5% were dependent on drugs.

- Key results related to academic achievement, sexual behavior, illegal activity, and victimization:
  - Mean scores for academic achievement were substantially lower than norms.
  - Three fourths of young adults were found to be sexually active; half have had more than one sexual partner in the year prior to interview. Fewer than half of sexually active young adults used a condom during last sex, and 15.3% used no contraception in the year prior to interview.
  - Nearly half of young adults had engaged in some illegal activity in the 6 months prior to interview, primarily public disorder. Male young adults were significantly more likely to have committed a crime than female young adults.
  - In the year prior to survey, 16.7% of young adults were arrested, and 9.0% were convicted of a crime. Male young adults were much more likely to have been involved with the law than female young adults: 28.9% of male young adults were arrested in the year prior to interview, and 19.1% were convicted of a crime.
  - In the year prior to survey, 16.0% of young adults were victims of violent crimes.
  - More than one fourth of female young adults experienced intimate-partner violence in the 12 months before survey, including 15.5% who experienced severe violence.

Physical Health

According to their own self-report, the majority of young adults (83.7%) were in good health (either *good, very good,* or *excellent;* Exhibit 2-1). This percentage is lower than that for other age groups in the National Survey of Child and Adolescent Well-Being (NSCAW) at Wave 5 (e.g., 93.5% of children aged 5 to 6 years and 96.9% of children aged 6 to 9 years were reported to be in good, very good, or excellent health). It is also lower than the proportion of adults (aged 18 to 44 years) nationally who report being in good health (94.1%) in the National Health Interview Survey [NHIS]; Pleis & Lethbridge-Cejku, 2006). Another measure of overall health, the SF-12 (see the Technical Appendix), suggests that young adults' physical health was comparable to that of the U.S. adult population. Both the self-report measure and the SF-12 indicate that the overall physical health of female young adults is not as good as that of male young adults, and that of 18-year-olds is not as good as that of those 19 years of age or older.

Exhibit 2-1. Overall Physical Health of Young Adults at Wave 5

	N (Min)	Self-Reported Good Health[a] % (SE)	SF-12 Physical Health Score Mean (SE)
Total	619	83.7 (2.4)	50.0 (0.6)
Sex	619	**	*
Male	232	91.5 (2.3)	51.7 (0.8)
Female	387	78.4 (3.7)	48.9 (0.8)
Race/ethnicity	615		
Black	183	91.6 (2.1)	50.4 (1.1)
White	294	86.7 (2.9)	50.9 (0.8)
Hispanic	84	76.0 (9.5)	48.9 (2.3)
Other	54	62.6 (13.2)	47.6 (1.9)
Age		*	**
18 years	130	68.2 (8.7)[b]	46.0 (2.2)[c]
19 years	198	91.3 (2.6)	52.4 (0.8)
20 years	216	82.9 (4.7)	50.5 (0.8)
21 years	75	94.0 (3.6)	49.8 (2.1)

Note: All analyses are on weighted data; Ns are unweighted. Reported Ns vary slightly across analyses because of missing data in some variable categories. Pearson $\div^2$ tests for cluster samples were used for initial significance tests. No significant differences in the self-report of good health or the SF-12 physical health score were found by types of abuse at baseline, by number of types of maltreatment, or by ever out-of-home placement. Asterisks indicate statistical significance (*$p < .05$, **$p < .01$). Asterisks in column apply to the subsequent results for the covariate. SF-12 = 12-Item Short-Form Health Survey.

[a] *Good health* was defined as young adults' self-report that their health was good, very good, or excellent.

[b] Age 18 is significantly different from age 19 ($p < .05$).

[c] Age 18 is significantly different from age 19 ($p < .01$).

Because of their health, a relatively large proportion of young adults experienced limitations in their activities. For example, slightly more than a quarter reported that their health limited them either *a little* (19.3%) or *a lot* (6.7%) in moderate activities; 15% declared that they were limited in their ability to walk, run, or play; and 11.8% declared that, during the 4 weeks prior to interview, pain interfered *quite a bit* or *extremely* with their normal work.

Nearly a third (30.3%) of young adults reported that they had a health condition that currently limited them in some way. Exhibit 2-2 lists the conditions that young adults were ever told by a doctor that they had and, for those who had the condition, the percentage for which that condition currently limited activities in any way. Vision problems were the most common condition (41.6%), followed by back or neck problems (29.9%), migraine (22.9%), asthma (22.3%), dental problems (18.1%), weight problems (15.6%), hypertension (11.9%), chronic bronchitis (10.1%), and sinusitis (9.5%). Although the proportion of young adults with reported health conditions might appear high, it should be noted that, for many of these conditions, recent NHIS findings indicate similar prevalence rates for adults aged 18 to 44 years nationally. For example, rates of neck and lower back pain in the past 3 months (13% and 18%, respectively), migraine or severe headache (18%), and sinusitis (12%) were all similar. Rates of some conditions, however, were more prevalent among the young adults in NSCAW than they are nationally. In particular, the proportion of young adults who reported being told they have asthma (22.3%) is double that of adults nationwide (11%). Rates of hypertension were also higher among the young adults (11.9%), compared with adults aged 18 to 44 years nationally (7.3%; Pleis & Lethbridge-Cejku, 2006).

Among those who had ever been told they had a health condition, many were not currently limited by that condition. The conditions most likely to currently limit activities *a lot* were weight problems (25.1% of those who had ever been told they a weight problem), migraine (22.1%), back or neck problems (19.0%), and asthma (17.5%).

Slightly more than a third (34.6%) of young adults reported having experienced some type of injury or accident during the 12 months before the interview; 20.3% saw a doctor or nurse for an injury or accident. The most common injuries were a bad cut or scrape and bad sprain or torn ligament (Exhibit 2-3). Fewer than half of the bad cuts or scrapes were treated by a doctor or nurse. In contrast, the great majority of those who suffered a bad sprain or torn ligament (73.2%); a broken bone, dislocated joint, or broken nose (76.2%); or a head injury or concussion (93.7%) saw a doctor or nurse for that injury. Because national injury data are based on emergency room visits and most injuries reported by the NSCAW young adults were not treated by a doctor, no national comparisons are possible.

Exhibit 2-2. Most Common Health Conditions for Young Adults at Wave 5

Condition Name	*N*	Ever Told by a Doctor Had Condition % (SE)	Currently Limited by Condition (Among Those Ever Told Had Condition)		
			Not Limited % (SE)	Limited a Little % (SE)	Limited a Lot % (SE)
Vision	619	41.6 (3.3)	57.8 (5.0)	36.3 (4.7)	6.0 (2.4)
Back or neck	618	29.9 (4.0)	41.6 (7.8)	39.3 (18.0)	19.0 (5.8)
Migraine	618	22.9 (3.2)	38.3 (8.1)	39.7 (7.6)	22.1 (6.8)
Asthma	618	22.3 (3.4)	42.8 (8.0)	39.6 (8.0)	17.5 (6.4)
Dental	617	18.1 (3.0)	57.2 (9.2)	32.1 (8.3)	10.8 (6.5)
Weight	618	15.6 (2.5)	40.1 (9.1)	34.8 (9.0)	25.1 (9.7)
Hypertension	618	11.9 (2.7)	52.8 (13.5)	47.2 (13.5)	0.03 (0.1)
Chronic bronchitis	618	10.1 (2.4)	34.7 (12.5)	58.9 (12.7)	6.5 (4.6)
Anemia	618	9.6 (2.2)	80.4 (7.3)	11.7 (6.3)	7.8 (4.3)
Sinusitis	618	9.5 (2.3)	59.2 (12.1)	24.9 (9.4)	15.9 (8.1)
Repeated ear infections	618	9.1 (2.4)	73.3 (11.6)	23.0 (11.4)	3.7 (2.3)
Eczema or other skin disorder	618	6.9 (1.8)	61.2 (15.1)	37.2 (14.9)	1.6 (1.1)
Fracture, bone, or joint injury	619	25.9 (3.7)	63.3 (7.7)	35.5 (7.7)	1.2 (0.6)

Note: All analyses are on weighted data; *Ns* are unweighted.

Exhibit 2-3. Serious Injury, Accident, or Poisoning of Young Adults at Wave 5

	N (Min)	Serious Injury, Accident, or Poisoning in Past 12 Months % (SE)	Saw Doctor for This Injury % (SE)
Bad cuts or scrapes	615	24.3 (2.9)	43.2 (7.9)
Bad sprain or torn ligament	615	14.0 (2.8)	73.2 (8.1)
Broken bone, dislocated joint, broken nose	615	9.8 (2.6)	76.2 (23.8)
Bite from person or animal	615	4.6 (1.6)	1.5 (1.0)
Bad burn	615	3.8 (1.3)	1.9 (1.0)
Head injury or concussion	615	2.6 (1.3)	93.7 (6.4)
Gunshot wound or stab wound	615	2.3 (1.5)	1.0 (0.9)

Note: All analyses are on weighted data; *Ns* are unweighted.

Young adults' body mass index (BMI) was calculated on the basis of their self-report of height and weight. The Centers for Disease Control and Prevention (CDC) considers an adult with a BMI between 25 and 29.9 to be overweight and considers an adult with a BMI of 30 or more to be obese (CDC, 2007a). By these criteria, more than half (56.6%) of young adults were either overweight (27.7%) or obese (28.9%; Exhibit 2-4). Among adults aged 18 to 24 years nationally, the percentage who are overweight (26.1%) is similar to the percentage of young adults in NSCAW, but the percentage who are obese (13.6%) is less than half that of the young adults in NSCAW. No significant differences were found by sex, race, or age. Young adults who were ever placed out of home were more likely than those who were never out of home to be in the normal range for BMI: those who were never out of home were more likely to be overweight or obese.

The proportion of young adults who were overweight or obese (56.6%) according to BMI calculations was substantially higher than the proportion who considered themselves overweight (36.6%) or the proportion who reported they had been told by a doctor that they had a weight problem (15.6%). Among obese young adults, 65.7% reported that they had tried to lose weight during the 12 months before the interviews—similar to the proportion of obese adults aged 18 to 24 years nationwide (67.2%) that were currently trying to lose weight (McCracken, Jiles, & Blanck, 2007). Among overweight young adults, fewer than a third (31.5%) were trying to lose weight.

The federal government recommends that all adults eat five servings of fruits and vegetables per day (U.S. Department of Agriculture and U.S. Department of Health and Human Services, 1990). However, only 36.5% of young adults reported eating at least some fruit or green vegetables every day, and 9.1% reported never eating fruits or vegetables. National data indicate that the proportion of adults aged 18 to 24 years who do not eat any fruits or vegetables is slightly lower (8.2%). In terms of exercise, CDC recommends that adults engage in moderate- intensity physical activities for at least 30 minutes on 5 or more days of the week (CDC, 2007d). Only 30.8% of young adults exercised at least 30 minutes 5 or more days a week. Thus, more than two thirds (69.2%) of young adults were exercising less than what is recommended, and nearly a third (32.3%) never exercised 30 minutes or more. Nationally, the proportion of adults aged 18 to 24 years nationwide who reported insufficient or no physical activity (41.8%) is substantially lower (McCracken et al., 2007).

Exhibit 2-4 Body Mass Index of Young Adults at Wave 5

	N (Min)	Underweight % (SE)		Normal Weight % (SE)	Overweight % (SE)		Obese % (SE)
Total	554	4.4	(1.5)	39.1 (4.3)	27.7	(3.7)	28.9 (3.1)
Sex							
Male	204	7.1	(3.5)	36.4 (6.4)	32.8	(5.0)	23.8 (4.9)
Female	350	2.7	(1.1)	40.8 (5.1)	24.3	(4.7)	32.2 (4.2)
Race/ethnicity	550						
Black	163	6.8	(5.0)	34.1 (5.1)	29.6	(5.9)	29.4 (6.1)
White	266	3.3	(1.3)	40.7 (5.7)	25.2	(5.3)	30.8 (4.3)
Hispanic	70	4.0	(4.0)	27.7 (8.7)	32.9	(10.8)	35.5 (10.2)
Other	51	6.2	(3.6)	52.9 (12.2)	34.2	(11.0)	6.7 (4.5)
Age	554						
18 years	111	4.1	(2.7)	51.4 (8.2)	14.5	(5.1)	29.9 (7.9)
19 years	174	1.8	(0.9)	34.9 (6.2)	29.9	(7.2)	33.4 (7.1)
20 years	198	1.9	(0.8)	39.3 (7.1)	33.7	(5.9)	25.1 (5.3)
21 years	71	21.5	(11.3)	27.9 (10.6)	22.1	(7.3)	28.9 (10.3)
Ever placed out of home[a]							
Yes	215	2.5	(1.1)	48.7 (7.2)	36.7	(6.6)	12.1 (2.9)
No	316	5.1	(2.0)	37.0 (5.1)	25.1	(3.8)	32.9 (4.0)

Note: All analyses are on weighted data; Ns are unweighted. Reported Ns vary slightly across analyses because of missing data in some variable categories. Pearson $\div^2$ tests for cluster samples were used for initial significance tests. No significant differences in BMI were found by types of abuse at baseline or by number of types of maltreatment.

[a] "Ever placed out of home" is significantly different from "never out of home" at $p < .01$.

Mental Health

According to the SF-12 for mental health, young adults' mean mental health score was 47.3—which is 0.3 standard deviations below the mean for the U.S. adult population (Exhibit 2-5). Mean mental health scores were significantly lower for female young adults (44.8) than for male young adults (50.9), and significantly lower for Hispanic young adults (42.0) than for White young adults (48.8).

Depression in young adults was assessed with the screening scale of the World Health Organization CIDI-SF (Kessler, Andrews, Mroczek, Ustun, & Wittchen, 1998; see Technical Appendix). More than a quarter (27.5%) of young adults had a score in the clinical range for major depression in the previous 12 months (Exhibit 2-6). National data for adults aged 18 years or older that used the CIDI to assess depression (Kessler, Chiu, Demler & Walters, 2005) indicate much lower rates of depression: both the proportion who had a major depressive episode (MDE) in the year prior to interview (6.7%) and the proportion of adults 18 years old or older who had any mood disorder in the previous 12 months (9.5%) were about one third the proportion of young adults in NSCAW who were depressed.[3]

Exhibit 2-5. Young Adults' Mental Health Status (SF-12) at Wave 5

	N	Mean (SE)
Total	612	47.3 (1.0)
Sex		***
Male	229	50.9 (0.9)
Female	383	44.8 (1.3)
Race/Ethnicity		*
Black	181	48.0 (1.8)
White	291	48.8 (1.2)
Hispanic	82	42.0 (2.9)[a]
Other	54	46.8 (1.8)
Age		
18 years	129	46.0 (1.7)
19 years	195	47.9 (1.5)
20 years	215	47.0 (1.6)
21 years	73	49.2 (2.5)

Note: All analyses are on weighted data; Ns are unweighted. The t tests for cluster samples were used for initial significance tests. No significant differences in the SF-12 mental health score were found by types of abuse at baseline, by types of maltreatment, or by ever out-of-home placement. Asterisks indicate statistical significance (*$p < .05$, ***$p < .001$). Asterisks in columns apply to the subsequent results for the covariate. SF-12 = 12-Item Short-Form Health Survey.

[a] Hispanic is significantly different from White at $p < .05$.

No significant differences were found by sex, race/ethnicity, or age. Rates of depression were very high for both sexes as compared with national data. Depression among female young adults (31.5%) was almost three times the national past-year prevalence among females aged 18 to 25 years (12.9%), while depression among male young adults (21.3%) was more than three times the national past-year prevalence among males aged 18 to 25 years (6.6%, Substance Abuse and Mental Health Services Administration [SAMHSA], Office of Applied Studies [OAS], 2005).

Trauma was measured with two clinical scales from the Trauma Symptom Inventory (Briere, 1996; see Technical Appendix). The Intrusive Experiences Scale measures intrusive symptoms associated with post-traumatic stress (flashbacks, nightmares, intrusive thoughts); the Dissociation Scale measures dissociative symptomatology such as depersonalization, derealization, out-of-body experiences, and psychic numbing. The proportion of young adults who reported having intrusive experiences was 10.2%, and the proportion who reported experiencing dissociation was 6.2%; no significant differences were found by sex, race/ethnicity, or age. Although the proportions of young adults reporting trauma were relatively low, these estimates were substantially higher than national rates: a national study of English-speaking respondents aged 18 years or older found that the rate of post-traumatic stress disorder in the previous 12 months was 3.5% (Kessler et al., 2005). A caveat to this comparison is that the scales used in NSCAW were not designed to capture diagnoses; most of the scales capture symptoms, without all the criteria required for diagnosis. Thus, it is possible that the differences in measures across the two studies account for some or all of the differences in rates.

Exhibit 2-6. Depression and Trauma Among Young Adults at Wave 5

	N (Min)	Depression % (SE)	Trauma	
			Intrusive Experiences % (SE)	Dissociation % (SE)
Total	616	27.5 (3.5)	10.2 (2.5)	6.2 (1.9)
Sex				
Male	230	21.3 (4.8)	7.4 (3.7)	5.5 (3.3)
Female	386	31.5 (4.8)	12.1 (3.6)	6.7 (2.3)
Race/Ethnicity				
Black	182	19.7 (5.8)	11.9 (5.6)	4.4 (1.9)
White	292	27.7 (4.9)	12.4 (4.2)	7.8 (3.5)
Hispanic	84	26.1 (9.6)	1.3 (1.0)	3.6 (2.2)
Other	54	43.9 (12.9)	7.1 (4.9)	8.3 (4.2)
Age			*	
18 years	130	34.0 (9.5)	17.2 (7.4)	17.0 (7.2)
19 years	197	22.4 (4.8)	6.2 (1.0)	2.4 (0.8)
20 years	215	28.0 (5.8)	11.1 (4.5)	2.2 (0.9)
21 years	74	24.0 (10.1)	17.1 (8.9)	12.5 (8.7)

Note: All analyses are on weighted data; Ns are unweighted. Reported *Ns* vary slightly across analyses because of missing data in some variable categories. Pearson $\div^2$ tests for cluster samples were used for initial significance tests. No significant differences in depression, intrusive experiences, and dissociation were found by type of abuse at baseline, by number of types of maltreatment, or by ever out-of-home placement. Asterisks indicate statistical significance (*$p < .05$). Asterisks in column apply to the subsequent results for the covariate.

Young Adult Behavior

Scores on the behavior checklists developed by Achenbach and colleagues were used as indicators of young adults' mental health and behavioral and emotional functioning. Externalizing, Internalizing, Total Problem Behaviors, and *DSM*-oriented scales were measured with use of the Adult Self-Report (ASR; Achenbach & Rescorla, 2003; see Technical Appendix).

The proportion of young adults in the borderline or clinical range of scores was 18.9% on externalizing behaviors, 16.0% on internalizing behaviors, and 13.4% on the Total Problems Scale (Exhibit 2-7). These proportions are higher than those found in the normative sample for each of these scales (8%; Achenbach & Rescorla, 2003). No significant differences were found by sex, race, or age.

At baseline, when the young adults were between 12 and 15 years old, the estimates of behavioral problems based on the Youth Self-Report (YSR, Achenbach, 1991b) were much higher. At that time, the percentage in the borderline or clinical range was 3 3.0% on externalizing behaviors, 24.6% on internalizing behaviors, and 36.3% on the Total Problems scale (Administration for Children and Families, 2005). In order to explain the decrease in behavioral problems between baseline and Wave 5, further exploration would be necessary to determine the influence of the change in measure from the YSR to the ASR, maturational issues, use of mental health services during adolescence, living situation, stability, and other contextual influences. Those analyses are beyond the scope of this report.

Exhibit 2-7. Young Adults' Report of Behavior Problems at Wave 5

	N	Percent in Clinical Range		
		Total Problems Score	**Internalizing Score**	**Externalizing Score**
Total	619	13.4 (2.5)	16.0 (2.8)	18.9 (2.8)
Sex				
Male	233	13.9 (4.1)	10.7 (2.9)	19.8 (4.8)
Female	386	13.4 (3.1)	19.5 (4.3)	18.2 (3.4)
Race/Ethnicity				
Black	184	12.4 (3.8)	18.5 (6.2)	18.3 (4.2)
White	293	13.5 (3.7)	13.8 (3.5)	20.0 (4.5)
Hispanic	84	9.7 (4.7)	18.4 (9.8)	15.3 (6.1)
Other	54	31.3 (10.0)	20.4 (8.0)	23.0 (9.4)
Age				
18 years	130	19.3 (5.8)	23.8 (7.1)	26.6 (8.0)
19 years	198	10.3 (3.5)	14.4 (4.6)	15.0 (3.8)
20 years	216	12.3 (4.4)	13.8 (4.6)	15.7 (4.7)
21 years	75	19.3 (9.3)	13.8 (8.7)	27.6 (9.9)

Note: All analyses are on weighted data; Ns are unweighted. Reported Ns vary slightly across analyses because of missing data in some variable categories. Pearson ÷2 tests for cluster samples were used for significance tests. No significant differences in Total Problems, Internalizing, and Externalizing clinical scores were found by types of abuse at baseline, number of types of maltreatment, or ever out-of-home placement.

On the *DSM-IV*–oriented scales, around 10% of young adults responded positively to items consistent with diagnostic criteria for anxiety disorders (including generalized anxiety disorder, separation anxiety disorder, and specific phobia), somatic disorders (including somatization disorder and undifferentiated somatoform disorder), and avoidant personality disorder (Exhibit 2-8). Anxiety Problems and Somatic Problems were significantly more likely among young female than among young male adults; Avoidant Personality Disorder was significantly more likely among 18-year-olds than among 19- to 21-year-olds. Given that the ASR *DSM-I V* scales are fairly new, it was not possible to find equivalent national data based on the ASR for comparison. National comparison data using the CIDI are available from a national study of English speakers aged 18 years or older. The estimate for anxiety problems in young adults (10.6%) was lower than national estimates (18.1% for any anxiety disorder), while the percentage for avoidant personality problems (11.6%) was higher than the national estimate of 6.8% for social phobia (which would be the most serious disorder associated with avoidant personality).

In the area of impulse control, 24.5% of young adults responded positively to items consistent with attention-deficit/hyperactivity disorder (ADHD), which is sixfold the national estimates (4.1%). ADHD problems were significantly less likely among Blacks (12.0%) than among Whites (28.0%) or the group classified as "Other" race/ethnicity (55.3%); they were less likely among those who were reported for sexual abuse (10.8%) than among those who were not reported for sexual abuse (26.7%). More than a fifth (22%) of young adults responded positively to items consistent with antisocial personality, which is higher than national estimates based on the National Epidemiologic Survey on Alcohol and Related

Conditions, which uses *DSM-IV* criteria to estimate lifetime prevalence of antisocial personality disorders (3.6%), conduct disorder (1.1%), and adult antisocial behavior (12.3%; Compton, Conway, Stinson, Colliver, & Grant, 2005).

Exhibit 2-8. Young Adults' Report of Behavior Problems Following *DSM-IV* Classification at Wave 5

	N	Percent in Clinical Range					
		Anxiety Disorders			Impulse Control Problems		
		Anxiety Problems	Somatic Problems	Avoidant Personality Problems	ADHD Problems	Antisocial Personality Problems	
Total	619	10.6 (2.3)	9.1 (2.5)	11.6 (2.3)	24.5 (3.3)	22.0	(2.9)
Sex		*	*				
Male	233	5.8 (2.1)	2.7 (1.1)	12.4 (3.5)	25.9 (5.3)	24.3	(5.0)
Female	386	13.8 (3.3)	13.4 (4.1)	11.1 (3.2)	23.5 (4.1)	20.4	(3.7)
Race/ethnicity					**		
Black	184	12.3 (4.8)	8.7 (3.9)	17.7 (6.2)	12.0 (3.9)[a]	21.7	(4.4)
White	293	10.0 (3.1)	6.3 (2.6)	10.1 (2.8)	28.0 (4.8)	21.4	(4.7)
Hispanic	84	7.1 (4.5)	9.4 (7.8)	7.8 (5.2)	21.7 (7.3)	19.3	(7.5)
Other	54	17.2 (7.3)	31.7 (14.4)	10.1 (4.6)	55.3 (11.6)	18.1	(7.0)
Age				*			
18 years	130	17.2 (6.3)	17.3 (7.3)	22.3 (6.0)	36.0 (8.0)	32.8	(8.9)
19 years	198	14.1 (4.8)	6.7 (3.6)	11.5 (4.3)	22.9 (5.3)	20.0	(4.5)
20 years	216	4.4 (1.8)	6.4 (3.3)	9.1 (3.4)	19.0 (5.6)	13.2	(3.9)
21 years	75	11.2 (8.7)	10.6 (8.7)	1.0 (0.9)	28.0 (9.9)	41.2	(12.3)
Sexual abuse					*		
Yes	135	10.3 (4.0)	3.3 (1.7)	14.6 (8.8)	10.8 (3.8)	11.3	(3.8)
No	437	9.8 (2.4)	9.3 (2.9)	11.0 (2.3)	26.7 (3.6)	21.3	(3.2)

Note: All analyses are on weighted data; Ns are unweighted. Reported Ns vary slightly across analyses because of missing data in some variable categories. Pearson $\div^2$ tests for cluster samples were used for significance tests. No significant differences in DSM-IV classification were found by physical abuse, by failure to provide and lack of supervision at baseline, by number of types of maltreatment, or by ever out-of-home placement. Asterisks indicate statistical significance (*$p <$ .05, **$p < .01$). Asterisks in column apply to the subsequent results for the covariate.

[a] Black is significantly different from White and "Other" at $p < 0.5$.

Exhibit 2-9. Young Adults' Report of Substance Dependence at Wave 5

	N (Min)	Alcohol Dependence % (SE)	Drug Dependence % (SE)	Any Alcohol or Drug Dependence % (SE)
Total	613	6.5 (2.0)	6.5 (1.9)	9.0 (2.3)
Sex				
Male	230	10.4 (4.1)	7.3 (3.5)	11.3 (4.1)
Female	385	3.8 (1.7)	5.9 (2.1)	7.4 (2.2)
Race/ethnicity				
Black	181	7.1 (4.0)	5.6 (3.4)	8.9 (4.0)
White	292	5.8 (2.7)	6.3 (2.7)	7.9 (2.8)
Hispanic	84	10.7 (6.2)	9.6 (5.6)	15.7 (10.3)
Other	54	1.5 (1.5)	5.7 (3.2)	5.8 (3.2)
Age				
18 years	129	3.2 (2.6)	3.3 (2.7)	3.5 (2.6)
19 years	196	8.7 (4.4)	5.0 (3.0)	10.2 (4.4)
20 years	214	5.9 (3.6)	10.6 (4.0)	10.8 (4.0)
21 years	74	8.8 (4.5)	1.1 (1.0)	8.7 (4.4)

Note: All analyses are on weighted data; *Ns* are unweighted. Reported *Ns* vary slightly across analyses because of missing data in some variable categories. Pearson $\div^2$ tests for cluster samples were used for significance tests. No significant differences in alcohol or drug dependence were found by types of abuse at baseline, number of types of maltreatment, or ever out-of-home placement.

Substance Dependence

Alcohol and drug dependence were measured by self-report using the CIDI-SF, a measure that identifies substance dependence but not substance abuse; thus, estimates reported here do not necessarily include substance users and abusers (Kessler et al., 1998; see Technical Appendix). The proportion of young adults scoring in the dependence range was 6.5% for alcohol and 6.5% for drugs (Exhibit 2-9). A total of 9.3% of young adults were dependent on alcohol, drugs, or both. National statistics for adults between the ages of 18 and 25 are roughly similar: 7.2% dependent on alcohol, 5.8% dependent on drugs, and 11.5% dependent on either (SAMHSA, OAS, 2006). There were no significant differences among young adults in either alcohol or drug dependence by sex, race/ethnicity, or age.

When findings from all sources of information were combined, 45.7% of young adults were determined to have at least one mental health or substance dependence problem.

Academic Achievement

The Woodcock-Johnson III Tests of Cognitive Abilities (Woodcock, McGrew, & Mather, 2001) were used to assess academic achievement (see Technical Appendix). On average, young adults scored substantially below the normative mean of 100 in all categories (Exhibit 2-10). The proportion who scored more than 1.5 standard deviations below the mean was 15.0% for Applied Problems, 25.3% for Passage Comprehension, 29.7% for Word-Letter

Identification, and 43.6% for Calculation (not shown). Female young adults scored significantly lower than male young adults on Applied Problems, and Blacks scored significantly lower than Whites on Word-Letter Identification, Passage Comprehension, and Applied Problems. There were no significant differences in test scores by age.

Sexual Behavior

Young adults reported on sexual behaviors by means of audio computer-assisted self-interviewing (ACASI). The large majority of young adults (85.2%) reported ever having had sexual intercourse, and more than three fourths were currently sexually active (Exhibit 2-11), with no significant differences by sex or race/ethnicity. These proportions are very similar to those reported nationally for males and females between the ages of 20 and 24 (Chandra, Martinez, Mosher, Abma, & Jones, 2005; Martinez, Chandra, Abma, Jones, & Mosher, 2006). Young adults differ from the general population, however, in that a large proportion of them began sexual activity at an early age: 32.4% of male young adults and 19.7% of female young adults reported having sexual intercourse for the first time before age 14. In contrast, among males and females aged 20 to 24 years nationally, only 9% of males and 7% of females report having sex before the age of 14.

Exhibit 2-10. Academic Achievement (Woodcock-Johnson Tests of Cognitive Abilities) of Young Adults at Wave 5

	N (Min)	Word-Letter Identification Mean (SE)	Passage Comprehension Mean (SE)	Calculation Mean (SE)	Applied Problems Mean (SE)
Total	614	83.1 (1.6)	85.0 (1.4)	78.5 (1.2)	84.5 (0.9)
Sex					*
Male	231	82.2 (2.7)	86.8 (1.4)	78.2 (1.3)	86.9 (0.9)
Female	383	83.6 (2.0)	83.9 (2.1)	78.8 (1.9)	83.0 (1.3)
Race/ethnicity					
Black	181	76.3 (3.4)[a]	80.8 (2.5)[a]	79.8 (2.8)	81.7 (1.8)[a]
White	292	86.3 (3.4)	87.6 (1.6)	78.1 (1.5)	86.2 (1.0)
Hispanic	82	83.7 (2.0)	84.4 (3.6)	78.5 (2.8)	85.7 (1.4)
Other	53	80.0 (5.6)	80.1 (6.4)	74.1 (3.7)	79.7 (4.1)
Age					
18 years	130	84.1 (3.0)	83.8 (3.2)	76.7 (3.0)	83.2 (2.1)
19 years	195	84.7 (3.8)	86.4 (2.6)	81.0 (1.3)	85.8 (1.6)
20 years	215	81.8 (2.5)	83.7 (2.1)	77.6 (2.1)	84.7 (1.2)
21 years	73	81.2 (2.7)	88.6 (2.7)	78.9 (2.1)	83.1 (1.9)

Note: All analyses are on weighted data; *Ns* are unweighted. Reported *Ns* vary slightly across analyses because of missing data in some variable categories. Pearson $\div^2$ tests for cluster samples were used for significance tests. For the total, differences in means were tested against means of the standardization sample. Instruments used are the Woodcock-Johnson III Tests of Cognitive Abilities. No significant differences in academic achievement were found by types of abuse at baseline, by number of types of maltreatment, or by ever out-of-home placement. Asterisks indicate statistical significance (*$p < .05$). Asterisks in column apply to the subsequent results for the covariate.

[a] Black is significantly different from White at $p < .05$.

Exhibit 2-11. Sexual Experience of Young Adults at Wave 5

	N (Min)	Ever Had Sex % (SE)	Had Sex in Past Year % (SE)	First Sex before Age 14 % (SE)	Ever Forced to Have Sex % (SE)	More than one Sexual Partner in Past 12 Months % (SE)
Total	580	85.2 (2.9)	76.8 (3.0)	24.8 (3.5)	13.0 (2.3)	32.2 (3.8)
Sex					**	
Male	209	86.1 (4.3)	74.4 (5.6)	32.4 (6.1)	1.8 (1.0)	39.7 (6.7)
Female	371	84.5 (3.7)	78.5 (3.5)	19.7 (3.8)	20.7 (3.7)	27.7 (4.2)
Race/ethnicity						
Black	171	84.1 (5.8)	76.5 (5.6)	34.7 (7.6)	17.2 (6.2)	39.7 (6.6)
White	278	88.8 (3.6)	78.6 (4.9)	22.4 (5.2)	8.4 (2.2)	31.6 (5.9)
Hispanic	79	91.6 (4.9)	86.4 (6.5)	15.9 (5.9)	15.7 (6.2)	29.1 (8.2)
Other	48	65.3 (14.1)	60.7 (13.2)	28.4 (9.6)	28.1 (9.2)	23.5 (7.9)
Sexual abuse		**				
Yes	125	98.5 (0.9)	86.9 (9.9)	26.9 (9.7)	29.6 (9.2)	21.5 (6.3)
No	412	83.6 (3.4)	75.3 (3.3)	25.2 (3.6)	11.0 (2.3)	34.0 (4.4)
Age						
18 years	124	75.7 (8.3)	65.5 (9.0)	20.2 (7.5)	14.4 (5.2)	33.7 (7.0)
19 years	187	80.1 (6.0)	68.8 (6.2)	10.9 (3.9)	11.7 (3.9)	24.6 (5.1)
20 years	201	91.2 (3.2)	85.9 (3.6)	34.3 (7.1)	15.4 (3.8)	34.0 (6.6)
21 years	68	94.8 (3.4)	87.2 (5.1)	37.7 (12.5)	4.7 (1.8)	45.8 (11.5)

Note: All analyses are on weighted data; Ns are unweighted. Reported Ns vary slightly across analyses because of missing data in some variable categories. Pearson ÷ tests for cluster samples were used for significance tests. No significant differences in sexual experience were found by number of types of maltreatment or by ever out-of home placement. Asterisks indicate statistical significance (**$p < .0$ 1). Asterisks in column apply to the subsequent results for the covariate.

Thirteen percent of young adults reported ever being forced to have sex (intercourse, oral sex, or anal sex) against their will. Among female young adults, the proportion ever forced to have sex was 20.7%, which is comparable to national rates (19% of females between the ages of 20 and 24). Nearly a third (32.2%) of young adults had more than one sexual partner in the year prior to interview (39.7% of male young adults and 27.7% of female young adults), and 5.1% reported having five partners or more (not shown). Nationally, the proportion of young adults aged 18 to 24 years who report having more than one sexual partner in the year prior to interview is slightly lower among both male young adults (33.5%) and female young adults (24.3%; Park et al., 2006). No measures of sexual experience differed by sex, race/ethnicity, or age. Those who had been reported for sexual abuse, however, were significantly more likely to have ever had sex than those not reported for sexual abuse. Other types of abuse at baseline had no significant association with sexual experience.

Exhibit 2-12. Young Adults' Contraceptive Use, among Those Who Had Sex in Past Year at Wave 5

	N (min)	Used Condom at Last Sex % (SE)	Used No Contraception in Past Year % (SE)
Total	494	49.1 (3.8)	15.3 (2.9)
Sex		**	
Male	167	64.7 (6.5)	9.9 (3.5)
Female	327	39.1 (4.7)	18.8 (3.8)
Race/ethnicity			
Black	143	52.5 (7.9)	12.6 (4.5)
White	235	49.3 (5.3)	13.5 (3.3)
Hispanic	71	48.0 (12.5)	20.5 (10.6)
Other	43	38.8 (9.7)	30.7 (11.3)
Age			
18 years	101	42.1 (8.5)	11.8 (4.8)
19 years	155	57.0 (6.4)	14.6 (3.5)
20 years	178	47.5 (6.0)	19.0 (5.1)
21 years	61	47.6 (12.7)	8.0 (4.5)

Note: All analyses are on weighted data; Ns are unweighted. Reported Ns vary slightly across analyses because of missing data in some variable categories. Pearson $÷^2$ tests for cluster samples were used for significance tests. No significant differences in contraceptive use were found by types of abuse at baseline, by number of types of maltreatment, by or ever out-of-home placement. Asterisks indicate statistical significance (**p < .0 1). Asterisks in column apply to the subsequent results for the covariate.

Among young adults who had sex in the year before interview, fewer than half (49.1%) reported using a condom the last time they had sex (Exhibit 2-12). Condom use was significantly higher among male young adults (64.7%) than among female young adults (39.1%). Condom use at last sex among male young adults was comparable to national rates (72% among those aged 15 to 19 years, and 47% among those aged 20 to 24), but condom use among female young adults was somewhat lower than national rates (56% among those aged 15 to 19 years, and 42% among those aged 20 to 24; Chandra et al., 2005; Martinez et al., 2006). Fifteen percent of sexually active young adults reported not using any contraception at all in the year prior to survey. There were no significant differences in contraceptive nonuse by sex, race/ethnicity, or age.

Illegal Activity

Young adults reported any illegal activity via ACASI, using the Self-Report Delinquency Scale developed for the National Youth Survey (Elliott, Huizinga, & Ageton, 1985; see Technical Appendix). Nearly half (48.5%) of young adults reported engaging in some kind of illegal activity in the 6 months before interview (Exhibit 2-13). By far, the most common type of illegal activity was public disorder (3 9.2%), followed by simple assault (10.9%) and minor theft (10.8%). Under 10% had damaged property, sold drugs, or committed either serious property crime or felony assault. Male young adults were significantly more likely than female young adults to have been involved in any illegal activity, to have engaged in public disorder, or to have sold drugs. Young adults reported for sexual abuse were significantly *less* likely to have damaged property, to have committed felony assault, or to have sold drugs than those who had not been sexually abused. This finding may be in part because most reported for sexual abuse are female and because females are less likely than males to be involved in illegal activity. This association does not entirely explain the finding, however, because the association between sexual abuse and illegal activity is stronger than the association between sex and illegal activity. There were no significant differences in illegal activity by other types of maltreatment at baseline, by race/ethnicity, or by age.

National-level data on self-reported illegal activity are not available for young adults. Typically, levels of illegal activity drop off sharply between late adolescence and young adulthood (Howard & Sickman, 2006). It is therefore striking that in this population the incidence of nearly all types of illegal activity either remained steady or increased between Wave 4 (when the young adults were aged 14 to 18 years) and Wave 5.

Nearly 16.7% of young adults had been arrested at least once in the 12 months prior to interview, 9.0% had been convicted of a crime, and 5.9% had been on probation (Exhibit 2-14). The annual arrest rate (counting all arrests, including multiple arrests of the same person) is 480 per 1,000, (not shown); this is more than four times the national rate for 18- to 24-year-olds, (118.5 per 1,000; Fox, Connolly, & Snyder, 2005). Note, too, that the sample at Wave 5 excludes 21 young adults who were incarcerated, so these estimates of involvement with the law are biased downward. The proportions involved with the law were much higher for male young adults than for female young adults. For example, 28.9% of male young adults had been arrested in the previous 12 months, compared with just 8.5% of female young adults. Figures on involvement with the law at Wave 4 were presented in Chapter 1. For male young adults, the proportion arrested in the 12 months prior to interview increased sharply between Wave 4 and Wave 5 (from 5.2% to 28.9%); for female young adults, the increase was less pronounced (from 4.8% to 8.5%).

Interpersonal Safety

Sixteen percent of young adults reported that they had been victimized in some way in the 12 months prior to interview: 10.6% had been robbed, 5.1% had been attacked or beaten up, and 2.5% had been victimized sexually (Exhibit 2-15). There were no significant differences in victimization by sex, by race/ethnicity, or by age. These rates were substantially higher than those reported nationally. In 2005, 4.4% of 16- to 19-year-olds reported that they had been a victim of any crime, including 0.7% robbed, 3.4% assaulted, and 0.3% sexually victimized; rates were similar for those aged 20 to 24 years (U.S. Bureau of Justice Statistics, 2006).

Exhibit 2-13. Young Adults' Illegal Activity in the Past 6 Months at Wave 5

	N (Min)	Any Illegal Activity % (SE)	Public Disorder % (SE)	Damaged Property % (SE)	Minor Theft % (SE)	Serious Property Crime % (SE)	Simple Assault % (SE)	Felony Assault % (SE)	Sold Drugs % (SE)
Total	611	48.5 (3.9)	39.2 (3.8)	7.3 (2.0)	10.8 (2.3)	7.0 (1.8)	10.9 (2.2)	8.6 (2.0)	9.1 (2.3)
Sex		*	*						*
Male	228	57.7 (4.7)	47.5 (5.1)	8.7 (3.5)	11.9 (3.9)	9.7 (3.2)	14.8 (3.8)	12.5 (3.5)	16.9 (4.9)
Female	383	42.4 (5.2)	33.6 (4.7)	6.4 (2.5)	10.0 (2.8)	5.2 (2.2)	8.2 (2.6)	5.9 (2.3)	3.9 (1.5)
Race/ethnicity									
Black	182	52.8 (6.0)	43.7 (5.6)	7.4 (3.3)	13.4 (5.4)	4.2 (6.5)	17.7 (4.7)	11.2 (3.6)	10.6 (5.2)
White	292	47.2 (5.9)	39.0 (6.0)	5.7 (3.0)	8.3 (2.9)	6.5 (2.6)	9.6 (3.2)	9.5 (3.4)	10.7 (3.5)
Hispanic	84	41.4 (11.7)	32.8 (11.1)	14.8 (7.3)	3.8 (3.0)	5.1 (3.8)	5.5 (3.8)	3.7 (2.9)	3.6 (2.7)
Other	53	47.5 (13.1)	44.4 (13.5)	5.5 (2.9)	16.6 (7.8)	7.8 (3.5)	7.3 (3.4)	3.2 (2.5)	4.8 (3.0)
Sexual maltreatment				*				*	*
Yes	135	42.7 (11.7)	40.6 (12.1)	0.8 (0.7)	9.1 (4.5)	3.1 (1.8)	3.6 (1.7)	1.7 (1.0)	1.3 (0.5)
No	430	47.4 (4.3)	39.5 (4.5)	8.0 (2.3)	9.7 (2.6)	6.7 (2.0)	10.6 (2.4)	9.4 (2.3)	10.9 (2.9)
Age									
18 years	129	57.6 (9.3)	39.1 (8.4)	8.8 (4.3)	8.7 (6.2)	15.3 (7.1)	12.5 (4.8)	9.0 (4.4)	6.4 (3.6)
19 years	196	41.9 (4.8)	32.5 (5.3)	7.0 (3.3)	13.0 (4.9)	3.9 (1.4)	8.8 (3.2)	5.4 (3.0)	7.5 (3.6)
20 years	213	44.0 (4.7)	37.5 (6.1)	4.7 (3.2)	11.6 (4.0)	6.8 (3.4)	10.5 (3.9)	8.8 (3.7)	6.4 (3.3)
21 years	73	68.3 (4.1)	66.4 (9.1)	15.9 (9.4)	5.3 (4.3)	1.0 (1.2)	15.0 (9.3)	16.1 (9.4)	30.1 (13.0)

Note: All analyses are on weighted data; Ns are unweighted. Reported *Ns* vary slightly across analyses because of missing data in some variable categories. Pearson $\div^2$ tests for cluster samples were used for significance tests. No significant differences in illegal activity were found by number of types of maltreatment or by ever out-of-home placement. Asterisks indicate statistical significance (*$p < .05$). Asterisks in column apply to the subsequent results for the covariate.

Exhibit 2-14. Young Adults' Involvement with the Law in the Past 12 Months at Wave 5

	N (min)	Arrested in Past 12 Months % (SE)	Convicted in Past 12 Months % (SE)	On Probation in Past 12 Months % (SE)
Total	614	16.7 (3.9)	9.0 (3.3)	5.9 (2.4)
Sex		*	*	*
Male	230	28.9 (7.4)	19.1 (7.1)	14.0 (5.2)
Female	384	8.5 (2.6)	2.2 (1.1)	0.4 (0.3)
Race/ethnicity				
Black	180	21.1 (6.6)	14.0 (5.8)	10.4 (5.7)
White	292	18.8 (6.4)	8.6 (5.2)	5.6 (3.3)
Hispanic	84	6.7 (4.1)	5.7 (4.0)	2.0 (1.6)
Other	54	8.0 (5.5)	1.4 (1.5)	0.0 (0.0)
Age				
18 years	129	16.3 (7.4)	4.4 (2.8)	0.5 (0.4)
19 years	196	14.9 (5.6)	9.0 (5.0)	3.4 (2.9)
20 years	215	14.2 (4.9)	9.7 (4.5)	8.1 (4.4)
21 years	74	32.5 (12.6)	14.9 (10.7)	14.9 (10.7)

Note: All analyses are on weighted data; *Ns* are unweighted. Reported *Ns* vary slightly across analyses because of missing data in some variable categories. Pearson $\div^2$ tests for cluster samples were used for significance tests. No significant differences were found for race/ethnicity or age. Asterisks indicate statistical significance (*$p < .05$). Asterisks in column apply to the subsequent results for the covariate.

Exhibit 2-15. Young Adults' Victimization in Past 12 Months at Wave 5

	N (Min)	Any Victimization % (SE)	Robbed % (SE)	Attacked or Beaten Up % (SE)	Victimized Sexually % (SE)
Total	615	16.0 (2.9)	10.6 (89.4)	5.1 (1.8)	2.5 (1.3)
Sex					
Male	230	18.8 (4.9)	14.0 (4.9)	7.4 (3.5)	2.3 (2.2)
Female	385	14.1 (3.7)	8.2 (2.8)	3.6 (1.8)	2.7 (1.5)
Race/ethnicity					
Black	181	17.1 (6.0)	13.9 (5.7)	7.1 (3.4)	3.7 (3.3)
White	292	14.3 (4.1)	7.3 (2.6)	5.6 (3.0)	1.7 (1.3)
Hispanic	84	15.8 (6.8)	10.3 (5.7)	1.6 (0.9)	3.9 (3.7)
Other	54	9.3 (5.1)	6.3 (4.0)	2.2 (1.6)	1.9 (1.3)
Age					
18 years	130	22.9 (7.8)	13.1 (7.1)	4.1 (1.7)	6.8 (4.3)
19 years	196	12.2 (4.5)	11.4 (4.5)	3.8 (2.9)	3.0 (2.9)
20 years	215	12.4 (4.0)	7.3 (2.8)	5.4 (3.2)	0.5 (0.3)
21 years	74	27.6 (12.5)	16.5 (11.1)	10.3 (8.7)	0.9 (0.9)

Note: All analyses are on weighted data; *Ns* are unweighted. Reported *Ns* vary slightly across analyses because of missing data in some variable categories. Pearson $\div^2$ tests for cluster samples were used for significance tests.

Almost half (46.2%) of young adults reported that they had been intentionally physically hurt in the 12 months prior to interview, and 10.8% of all young adults received medical treatment from a doctor or nurse for an intentional injury (not shown). Among those that were hurt by someone, 41.3% knew the people who hurt them. At the national level, the percentage of adults aged 18 to 21 who received emergency care for an intentional injury in the year prior to interview (any type of assault) was 1.6% (CDC, 2007c), several times lower than the 10.8% of young adults who received medical treatment for an intentional injury. Because the medical care received by the young adults included care received both in emergency rooms and in other settings, however, it is not directly comparable to the national figure.

Female young adults reported on their experiences of severe and less severe physical intimate-partner violence, using the Conflict Tactics Scale (Straus, 1979; Exhibit 2-16; see Technical Appendix). More than a quarter of female young adults (26.4%) were victims of intimate-partner violence during the 12 months before the interview: 24.6% suffered acts of less severe physical violence, and 15.5% suffered severe physical violence. Although, nationally, the annual prevalence of intimate-partner violence reported for females of all ages is much lower (1.3%; Tjaden & Thoennes, 2000), younger adult females experience higher rates of such violence than older adult females (Tjaden & Thoennes, 2000). Females who were not cohabiting with their partners were significantly more likely to have ever experienced severe violence (25.8%) than females who were married or cohabiting (11.4%).

More than a third (34.3%) of female young adults had been victims of intimate-partner violence at some point in their lives. This finding is substantially higher than the national 22.1% lifetime prevalence for intimate-partner violence among adult females (Tjaden & Thoennes, 2000).

Conclusion

Young adults at Wave 5 were significantly worse off than young adults nationally for nearly all indicators of well-being. Although the proportion reporting that their physical health was good or better was high (84%), it was substantially lower than the proportion of young adults nationally (94%), and about a third reported that a health condition currently limited their activities. In addition, the young adults' high rates of obesity, poor nutrition, and low levels of exercise suggest that they may be at high risk for chronic health disease later in life. The slightly elevated numbers of sexual partners and (among female young adults) relatively low rates of condom use place young adults at increased risk of sexually transmitted infections. Mental health problems, including depression, trauma, and problem behaviors, were also found to be prevalent, and academic achievement was substantially below national norms. Finally, relatively high proportions were involved in illegal activity, were victims of violent crime, or suffered from intimate-partner violence. Substance dependence was the only indicator of well-being for which young adults in NSCAW did not fare substantially worse than young adults nationally.

Female young adults generally were found to have worse physical and mental health than male young adults, whereas male young adults were more likely than female young adults to engage in illegal activity or be involved with the law. Blacks had lower scores on tests of achievement than Whites. In general, few other differences in levels of well-being were found by sex, race/ethnicity, or age.

Exhibit 2-16. Intimate-Partner Violence Against Female Young Adults at Wave 5

	N	1 ≤ Incident in Past 12 Months					Ever Suffered IPV				
		Total % (SE)	Married or Cohabiting % (SE)		Not married or cohabiting % (SE)		Total % (SE)	Married or Cohabiting % (SE)		Not married or cohabiting % (SE)	
Total	380	100 (0.0)	37.5	(4.9)	62.5	(4.9)	100 (0.0)	37.5	(4.9)	62.5	(4.9)
Any less severe violence	380	24.6 (4.7)	26.4	(7.3)	23.5	(5.0)	33.5 (4.6)	36.0	(6.9)	32.0	(5.8)
Had something thrown	379	16.7 (4.3)	16.9	(5.9)	16.5	(4.5)	23.3 (4.0)	26.5	(6.1)	21.3	(4.5)
Pushed, grabbed, shoved	380	19.8 (4.5)	18.3	(5.7)	20.6	(5.0)	26.7 (4.4)	27.9	(6.2)	25.9	(5.4)
Slapped	380	12.9 (3.5)	15.6	(6.2)	11.3	(4.3)	16.3 (3.9)	16.0	(6.2)	16.6	(5.3)
Any severe violence	380	15.5 (3.3)	9.0	(3.5)	19.3	(5.0)	20.4 (3.8)	11.4	(4.0)[a]	25.8	(5.5)[a]
Kicked, bitten, or hit with fist	380	10.2 (3.0)	5.8	(3.1)	12.9	(4.6)	14.6 (3.7)	5.8	(3.0)[b]	19.8	(5.5)[b]
Hit or tried to hit with something	380	11.1 (3.0)	7.7	(3.5)	13.1	(4.5)	14.8 (3.6)	8.1	(3.5)	18.8	(5.3)
Beaten up	380	8.5 (2.8)	5.3	3.1()	10.5	(4.2)	11.2 (3.4)	5.7	(3.1)	14.4	(5.2)
Choked	380	9.1 (2.9)	6.1	(3.1)	10.9	(4.3)	13.0 (3.5)	8.5	(3.6)	15.8	(5.3)
Threatened with knife or gun	380	5.0 (2.3)	4.1	(3.0)	5.5	(3.2)	7.4 (3.0)	4.2	(3.0)	9.4	(4.5)
Knife or gun used	380	1.8 (1.2)	4.1	(3.0)	0.5	(0.4)	4.6 (2.5)	4.3	(3.0)	4.8	(3.5)
Any violence—less severe or severe	380	26.4 (4.8)	26.4	(7.3)	26.4	(5.1)	34.3 (4.6)	36.1	(6.9)	33.3	(5.7)

Note: All analyses are on weighted data; *Ns* are unweighted. IPV = intimate-partner violence.

[a] Married or cohabiting is significantly different from not married or cohabitating at $p < .05$ on any severe violence.

[b] Married or cohabiting is significantly different from not married or cohabiting at $p < .05$ on having been kicked, bitten, or hit.

Placement history, number of types of maltreatment, and types of maltreatment were generally not significantly associated with well-being. Exceptions were that young adults who had been placed out of home were less likely to be obese than those who remained in home, and those who were reported for sexual abuse were less likely to experience ADHD problems or to be involved in illegal activity than those who were not reported for sexual abuse. The lack of observed association between these variables and other measures of well-being may accurately reflect underlying relationships, or it may be attributable to a variety of misclassification issues, including the fact that, as described in Chapter 1, most of the young adults had been reported for maltreatment prior to the index report; but no information is available about those experiences.

Clearly, young adults at Wave 5 demonstrate many risks to their social, emotional, and cognitive well-being. These results merit further attention and examination. Future research should be directed at investigating the extent to which the low levels of well-being among young adults are associated with the experience of maltreatment, or whether they are more accurately a function of other environmental factors, such as living in poverty. In addition, it would be important to assess comorbidities across areas of well-being—for example, the extent to which mental illness is associated with illegal activity or sexual risk taking, the association between depression and substance abuse, or the association between substance abuse and poor impulse control.

3. The Transition to Adulthood

Chapter 2 described physical health, mental health, academic, and other social outcomes for young adults reported for maltreatment during adolescence. Results indicated that such young adults show substantial risks across many indicators of general health and well-being. This chapter is meant to supplement findings from Chapter 2 by expanding our description of relevant young adult characteristics. Specifically, this chapter examines a series of developmental milestones uniquely relevant to the transition to adulthood.

The developmental period marking transition to adulthood involves establishing an emotional and economic independence from caregivers. Important economic milestones include completing school, establishing an independent household, and finding employment—all facilitating a young person's ability to support a family. Important socioemotional milestones include establishing significant relationships, marrying, and having children, traditionally in that order (Furstenburg et al., 2005). However, the expectations for a young adult in today's society have changed from the expectations of even a decade ago. In particular, the transition to the adulthood developmental period has become longer and more complex (Furstenburg et al., 2005; Mouw, 2005). In particular, greater diversity appears in the order and ways in which young adults achieve the "traditional" milestones of early adulthood. Moreover, the percentage of young adults who by age 20 to 30 have completed the major traditionally defined young adult milestones has largely declined (Furstenburg et al., 2005).

For instance, increasing numbers of young people move back and forth between work and school, do both at the same time, or do neither at all. There are also an increasing number of different and more complicated paths through marriage and parenting than were seen in the past (Fussell & Furstenberg, 2005). Furthermore, young adults appear to be relying economically and socially upon their families of origin for an increasingly longer period of time. However, these early adulthood experiences differ by sex, race/ethnicity, and social class. Young adults living in poverty, for instance, show an earlier entry into the workforce and parenthood than young adults from more economically advantaged households (Furstenberg et al., 2005). Although it is clear that these transitions to adulthood have become increasingly complicated, it is not clear these differences in the sequencing or timing of young adult outcomes in and of themselves ultimately affect other key outcomes in young adulthood (e.g., income, self-reported happiness; Mouw, 2005).

How the transition to adulthood plays out for young adults who have a history of maltreatment, or of involvement with the child welfare system (CWS), is largely unknown. Maltreatment during adolescence does appear to be linked to an increased likelihood of teen pregnancy (e.g., Thornberry, Ireland, & Smith, 2001); however, apart from this link, the potential relationship between adolescent maltreatment and other "traditional" young adult milestones is not well understood. Most research related to children involved with the CWS during adolescence has focused on those in foster care. This research suggests that the transition to adulthood is especially difficult for maltreated youth who are "aging out" of the foster care system (see Courtney & Heuring, 2005). For example, youth formerly in foster care have been found to have higher rates of out-of-wedlock births than their peers (e.g., Cook, Fleischman, & Grimes, 1991), high rates of unemployment (e.g., George et al., 2002), and substantial housing instability in adulthood (e.g., Courtney, Piliavin, Grogan-Kaylor, & Nesmith, 2001).

The literature on youth formerly in foster care is only partially relevant to the young adults discussed in this chapter. Most young adults described here remained with their biological families; only a small portion (17.1%) ever lived out of home during adolescence. The unique degree of influence that involvement with the CWS or out-of-home placement during adolescence might have on a youth's transition to adulthood therefore remains largely unknown. Furthermore, questions remain as to whether young adults who came in contact with the CWS as adolescents will achieve traditional young adult developmental milestones much as young adults do within the general U.S. population.

In this chapter, we describe outcomes specifically relevant to the transition-to-adulthood developmental period. These outcomes were intentionally separated from the indicators of general well-being described in Chapter 2. This measure was taken to distinguish young adult milestones from indicators analyzed in previous National Survey of Child and Adolescent Well- Being (NSCAW) waves and reports. The NSCAW Wave 5 for those reported for maltreatment in adolescence represents the first opportunity to describe the achievement of young adult milestones. Analyses in Chapter 3 examine the following issues:

1. household living situation and neighborhood characteristics;
2. family formation, including marriage, cohabitation and parenting status;
3. financial resources and employment; and
4. social support and contact with biological family members.

Key outcomes of interest during the transition to adulthood have been shown to vary across individual characteristics. To aid examination of these differences, findings in this chapter are often analyzed across a variety of factors, including sex, race/ethnicity, age, living situation, poverty, index maltreatment type, and history of out-of-home placement.

Being in an "early transition" period (18 to 19 years old) may entail developmental objectives that differ from those of a young adult in his or her early 20s. Being from a racial or ethnic minority group often shapes a young person's path to early adulthood (e.g., see Mollenkopf, Waters, Holdaway, & Kasinitz, 2005). In this chapter we examine how the accomplishment of young adult milestones is related to the young adult's sex, race/ethnicity, and age at Wave 5. Typically, findings related to sex, race/ethnicity, and age are included in Chapter 3 exhibits. In a few cases, findings are presented in relationship to poverty or other variables conceptually better related to the topic of the exhibit.

Research suggests that a young adult's living situation also may influence outcomes in young adulthood. In particular, research suggests that the onset of some key young adult transitions, particularly first employment, marriage, and having a child, tend to be earlier for young adults from impoverished backgrounds than for those from more socioeconomically advantaged households (e.g., Furstenberg et al., 2005); therefore, outcomes in Chapter 3 will also be analyzed by characteristics of a young adult's living situation, such as household poverty status and whether or not he or she reported living with a caregiver at Wave 5.

We examined the degree to which the young adult milestones summarized in this chapter may have been influenced by the type of baseline maltreatment report (e.g., physical maltreatment, neglect, or sexual abuse); however, we found no consistent significant differences. Consequently, key outcomes of young adulthood by type of baseline maltreatment report are not presented in Chapter 3 exhibits. We also explored the influence of ever having been placed in out-of-home care during adolescence (i.e., having been in out-of-home placement at any of the Waves 1 through 4) on young adult milestones. We found differences based upon out-of-home placement history for only one outcome—contact with biological family members. Only the Chapter 3 exhibit illustrating contact with biological family members shows results separately for those with and without out-of-home placement histories.

As already mentioned, this chapter describes outcomes unique to the young adult developmental period. Wherever possible, these outcomes are compared with U.S. Census data for similarly aged young adults from the general population. Key findings about the developmental milestones of young adulthood are as follows:

- Slightly more than half of young adults were living with a caregiver at Wave 5. Most of those not living with a caregiver indicated they were living with a boyfriend or girlfriend.
- On average, young adults reported moving households approximately 1.4 times within the 12 months prior to interview; 19.0% reported having moved 3 or more times in the 12 months prior to interview.
- Young adults reported having lived in a variety of places, but predominantly with friends or relatives. Only 1.3% of young adults reported having stayed in their car, truck, or other vehicle, and of these persons almost all (98.5%) stayed less than 2 weeks. Almost no young adults reported having stayed in an abandoned building, a shelter for battered women, or a shelter for homeless persons.
- Ten percent of young adults reported being married. Twenty-two percent reported living with a boyfriend or girlfriend.
- Thirty-seven percent of the young adults reported having at least one child. Seventy-eight percent of those who had a child were living with their children at Wave 5.
- A substantial number of young adults (41.8%) were living in households with incomes below the federal poverty line. On average, young adult households were living on an income of $551.30 per week. The average household size was 3.9 persons.
- The majority of young adults (58.1%) reported working full or part time. On average, those working reported working 34.4 hours per week.

- Most young adults were in contact with biological parents and siblings. Young adults with a history of out-of-home placement had significantly less contact with their biological mothers and biological siblings than those without out-of-home histories.
- Young adults were fairly satisfied with the level of social support available to them. They reported, on average, 2 to 7 people who were a support to them across a variety of roles (e.g., giving advice, going out for activities, offering to help with childcare).

Living Situation

The period from adolescence to adulthood means transition. In part, this transition involves a young adult's residential independence. Historically, part of a young adult's independence after turning 18 years old stemmed from his or her ability to live independently, apart from caregivers. In today's society, however, it is increasingly common that young adults live at home with a caregiver into their 20s or even 30s (e.g., Schoeni & Ross, 2005). According to the U.S. Census Bureau (2003), many 18- to 24-year-old U.S. young adults report living "at home" with a caregiver (55% of males, 46% of females). A young adult's living situation is intrinsically tied to economic resources, contact with family members, and social and community connections. Consequently, some of the elements of young adult living situation described here will be used to examine other types of young adult milestones later in the chapter.

In this section, we examine the characteristics of young adults' living situations at the Wave 5 interview. The section offers a description of young adult living arrangements, as well as the environmental context. Findings characterize typical household members, housing arrangements, the stability of these arrangements, and young adults' perceptions of their neighborhood or community environment.

Household Members and Housing Status

At Wave 5, slightly more than half of the young adults (55.5%) reported living with a caregiver. Caregivers included biological parents, adoptive parents, foster parents, grandparents, aunts and uncles, or stepparents. Those not living with a caregiver reported a variety of living situations. Usually, young adults not living with a caregiver indicated living with a spouse or a boyfriend or girlfriend (19.6% of all young adults). An additional 11.8% of young adults reported living alone, and approximately 6% reported living with one or more adults (aged 18 years or older) who were not relatives. A few reported living alone with one or more of their children (3.2%), living with a child and a noncaregiver relative (1.9%), or living with another relative (1.7%).

In terms of sex, race/ethnicity, age, and poverty status (e.g., living above or below the federal poverty level), young adults living with a caregiver did not differ substantially from those living without a caregiver.

When asked about the place where they were currently living, young adults reported whether they owned their place, rented, were "just staying there," or had "some other type of arrangement." Very few young adults reported owning a place of residence (3.6%). Most reported renting (40.7%), "just staying there" (39.0%), or some other type of arrangement (16.7%). Young adults living without caregivers most commonly indicated they were renting

(55.9% of those living without a caregiver); 57.5% of those living with caregivers responded that they were "just staying there." Fifteen percent of all young adults at Wave 5 reported currently living in public housing.

Living Stability

The stability of young adults' reported living arrangements during the 12 months preceding the Wave 5 interview was mixed. On average, young adults reported moving households approximately 1.4 times within the previous 12 months. Although most young adults moved 0 to 2 times, a sizable proportion (19.0%) reported having moved 3 or more times in the 12 months prior to interview. Young adults living with a caregiver moved on average significantly less often than those living without a caregiver (1.0 versus 1.7 times in 12 months, respectively). There were no differences in numbers of times moved over 12 months by sex, race/ethnicity, or age.

Young adults also reported having lived in a variety of places, but predominantly with friends or relatives. At Wave 5, young adults were asked about the types of places they had stayed over the 12 months prior to interview and for how long they had stayed there. A full 62.2% reported having stayed in the house of a relative, 20.1% of these for at least a month and 25.7% for at least 6 months. Slightly more than one fifth (21.3%) had stayed in the home of a friend, 46.1% of these for at least a month and 8.3% for at least 6 months. Another 13.9 % reported having stayed in a hotel, motel, or single-occupancy dwelling, 47.0% of these for less than 2 weeks, 35.2% for at least a month, and 9.1% for at least 6 months. Only 1.3% of young adults reported having stayed in their car, truck, or other vehicle, and of these almost all (98.5%) stayed less than 2 weeks. Very few young adults (all less than 4.0%) reported having stayed in an abandoned building, shelter for battered women, or shelter for homeless persons.

Neighborhood Environment

Young adults' perceptions of their neighborhood characteristics were assessed with an adaptation of a measure of neighborhood context used in the Philadelphia Family Management Project (Furstenberg, Cook, Eccles, Elder, & Sameroff, 1999). Young adults were asked to describe their neighborhood and community by indicating the degree to which some potential community problems (e.g., open drug use or drug dealing) were *not a problem at all*, *somewhat of a problem*, or *a big problem.* Exhibit 3-1 summarizes the percentage of young adults who described a series of neighborhood characteristics as "somewhat of a problem" or "a big problem."

Young adults described a number of neighborhood characteristics as problematic. Open drug use or drug dealing was described by 20.0% of young adults as a "big problem" and by 26.4% as "somewhat of a problem." Teenagers "hanging out" in public places and making a nuisance was described by 19.3% as a "big problem" and by 30.1% as "somewhat of a problem." Assaults and muggings were not seen as often as other characteristics, but 7.1% of young adults nonetheless described them as "a big problem," and 19.0% described them as "somewhat of a problem." Neighborhood characteristics did not differ by a young adult's sex, age, or poverty status. There were also no neighborhood differences noted between those living with and those living without a caregiver. When comparisons based on race/ethnicity were made, only perceptions surrounding the presence of neighborhood gangs differed. White

Exhibit 3-1 Neighborhood Characteristics of Young Adults at Wave 5

	N (Min)	Assaults and Muggings		Delinquent Gangs or Drug Gangs		Open Drug Use or Drug Dealing		Unsupervised Children		Teenagers Hanging Out and Making a Nuisance	
		Somewhat of a Problem % (SE)	A Big Problem % (SE)	Somewhat of a Problem % (SE)	A Big Problem % (SE)	Somewhat of a Problem % (SE)	A Big Problem % (SE)	Somewhat of a Problem % (SE)	A Big Problem % (SE)	Somewhat of a Problem % (SE)	A Big Problem % (SE)
Total	620	19.0 (2.7)	7.1 (2.0)	21.6 (3.2)	12.8 (2.7)	26.4 (3.2)	20.0 (3.4)	38.9 (4.4)	13.1 (2.7)	30.1 (4.2)	19.3 (3.6)
Race/ethnicity				**							
Black	181	25.6 (5.0)	11.6 (4.2)	40.8 (8.0)	16.2 (4.9)	22.3 (6.2)	30.3 (5.1)	39.2 (5.8)	20.4 (5.9)	23.9 (5.7)	30.1 (6.8)
White	293	13.9 (3.4)	5.6 (3.1)	11.7 (3.7)	11.1 (3.9)	24.2 (3.8)	17.3 (5.8)	34.6 (6.4)	10.8 (3.9)	29.5 (4.7)	14.3 (4.1)
Hispanic	84	28.3 (10.3)	4.4 (3.7)	30.8 (8.9)	16.0 (8.9)	23.7 (8.6)	15.1 (9.0)	50.8 (11.9)	10.1 (5.1)	31.7 (10.0)	17.5 (8.3)
Other	52	16.9 (7.4)	8.1 (6.9)	10.3 (4.2)	8.9 (7.0)	51.9 (12.8)	15.9 (8.3)	33.5 (10.6)	12.0 (7.7)	41.9 (13.2)	23.4 (9.0)
Poverty											
< Federal level	199	20.8 (4.4)	11.1 (4.5)	28.3 (6.1)	12.2 (4.2)	31.4 (5.9)	24.7 (6.5)	43.5 (5.8)	13.8 (4.3)	27.0 (5.8)	21.9 (7.0)
> Federal level	296	18.9 (4.2)	4.7 (2.1)	16.9 (3.8)	14.1 (4.2)	25.7 (4.5)	17.6 (4.5)	34.6 (6.5)	11.0 (3.6)	31.4 (5.8)	17.6 (4.5)

Note: All analyses are on weighted data; *Ns* are unweighted. Reported *Ns* vary slightly across analyses because of missing data in some variable categories. Pearson $\div^2$ tests for cluster samples were used for initial significance tests. There were no statistically significant differences in neighborhood characteristics by sex, by age, by type of maltreatment at baseline, or by out-of-home placement history. Asterisks indicate statistical significance (**$p <$ .01). Asterisks in column apply to the subsequent results for the covariate.

young adults were significantly less likely than Black or Hispanic young adults to live in neighborhoods where they perceived gangs to be "somewhat of a problem" or "a big problem." Despite describing their neighborhood as harboring some degree of risky activities, young adults reported their neighborhood as feeling safer (40.7%) or "about the same" (46.6%) as other neighborhoods. Similarly, they typically indicated that their neighborhood was "about the same" as other neighborhoods (53.0%) or "a better place to live" than other neighborhoods (36.7%).

Findings from other studies about the influence of neighborhood characteristics on adolescent and young adult well-being have been mixed. In fact, findings from the Philadelphia Family Management Project suggest that family relationships and support may be more influential than neighborhood context in determining successful young adult outcomes (Furstenberg et al., 1999). The combination of poor family support with problematic neighborhood context, however, was detrimental. Consequently, it is important to supplement a discussion of young adult neighborhood context with a consideration of family relationships and support.

Family Formation

Young adulthood is the time during which we expect long-lasting significant relationships to begin to be established. For instance, the transition from teenager to adult is, for some, marked by marriage. It is estimated that only 2.6% of 18- to 19-year-olds are married, whereas 15.5% of 20- to 24-year-olds report being married (U.S. Census Bureau, 2006). This is also the time for many young adults to begin establishing their own family, separate from their biological family of origin.

Cohabitation/Marital Status

At Wave 5, 9.5% of young adults reported being married; an additional 2.0% of young adults reported themselves to be "separated" from a spouse. This rate of marriage closely parallels that for all U.S. young adults aged 18 to 20 years (2.6% 18- to 19-year-olds married and with spouses present, 15.5% 20- to 24-year-olds married and with spouses present; U.S. Census Bureau, 2006). The rate of cohabitation among young adults 18 to 21 years old is slightly higher (22.0%) than the Current Population Survey rate of 19% for all U.S. young adults aged 24 years or younger (U.S. Census Bureau, 2006).

In total, 26.7% of young adults were either married and living with their spouse or living with a boyfriend or girlfriend. Females were significantly more likely to be living with a spouse or partner (37.2%) than males (11.1%). When compared with young adults of other races, Black young adults were less likely to report living with a spouse or partner (11.4%) than White (30.0%) or Hispanic young adults (40.8%). Living with a spouse or partner did not vary by young adult age or by household poverty status.

Parenting Status

Thirty-seven percent of the young adults reported having at least one child. Young adults with children reported from 1 to 5 children, but on average reported 1.3 births. Female young adults (44.9%) were significantly more likely to report having children than male young adults (26.3%). Older young adults (20 to 21 years) were more likely than younger adults (18 to 19 years) to report having children. Young adults living in poverty (54.8%) were also more likely than those not living in poverty (35.5%) to have children. Having a child did not vary by young adult race/ethnicity (Exhibit 3-2).

Exhibit 3-2. Young Adult Family Formation at Wave 5

	N (Min)	Married, Living with Spouse, or Living with Boyfriend or Girlfriend % (SE)	Had a Child % (SE)
Total	620	26.7 (3.8)	37.4 (3.7)
Sex		***	*
Male	233	11.1 (3.7)	26.3 (6.0)
Female	387	37.2 (5.0)	44.9 (4.6)
Race/ethnicity		*	
Black	184	11.4 (4.3)[a]	34.6 (7.3)
White	294	30.0 (5.4)	35.3 (5.2)
Hispanic	84	40.8 (11.2)	59.3 (8.7)
Other	54	35.9 (13.8)	26.8 (9.4)
Age			***
18 years	130	22.4 (7.7)	18.4 (7.3)[b]
19 years	198	22.9 (4.1)	18.9 (4.3)[c]
20 years	217	29.5 (7.1)	57.1 (6.2)
21 years	75	35.0 (11.3)	52.1 (11.3)
Household poverty			*
<Federal level	201	27.8 (6.3)	54.8 (6.7)
>Federal level	296	30.1 (4.6)	35.5 (5.3)

Note: All analyses are on weighted data; *Ns* are unweighted. Reported *Ns* vary slightly across analyses because of missing data in some variable categories. Pearson $\div^{2}$ tests for cluster samples were used for initial significance tests and for subsequent pairwise contrasts when warranted. There were no statistically significant differences in family formation by type of maltreatment at baseline or by history of out-of-home placement. Asterisks indicate statistical significance (*$p < .05$, ***$p < .001$). Asterisks in column apply to the subsequent results for the covariate.

[a] Black < White ($p < .01$); Black < Hispanic ($p < .05$).

[b] 18 years < 20 years ($p < .001$), 18 years < 21 years ($p < .05$).

[c] 19 years < 20 years ($p < .001$), 19 years < 21 years ($p < .05$).

Seventy-eight percent of young adults who reported having children were living with their children at Wave 5. Most young adults who reported not living with their children were male (85.6%). More than a third (34.7%) of young adult males who had children were living with them, and 94.5% of young adult females who had children were living with them. In most cases (94.6%), young adult parents not living with their children reported having some degree of contact with at least one of their children; however, none of the female young adults not living with their children paid child support, and slightly fewer than half of males not living with their children (49.2%) reported paying child support for at least one child. It should be noted that no way exists to determine from NSCAW data why young adult parents might not be living with their children, so we do not know, for instance, the number of young adults who may have given up their children for adoption.

The rate of NSCAW young adults who are living with their children (29%) is substantially higher than the percentage of adults within the general U.S. population who are living with children (not necessarily their own). A recent Child Trends report (2006) indicates that 6.6% of all U.S. young adults between the ages of 18 and 20 were living with children (7.9% males, 19.8% females). Because of the number of young adults actively parenting their children, Chapter 5 will describe the characteristics of young adults raising children, their discipline techniques, their behavioral health risks, and their federal service use.

Financial Resources and Employment

A critical component of young adults' ability to live independently is their ability to financially support both themselves and their families. Evidence suggests that gaining this financial independence has become increasingly difficult for young adults in today's society (see Corcoran & Matsudaira, 2005). In fact, one study that compared young adults in the 1970s and 1980s to young adults in the 1990s found that young adults in the 1990s were making less money and had lost occupational prestige (Smith, 2005). In this section, we describe the household poverty status, weekly household income, employment status, and hours worked per week among young adults at Wave 5.

Household Poverty

Household poverty indicators were calculated with consideration of both household income (including the earnings of all household members) and the number of individuals dependent on this income. The households had a mean of 1 child and 2.8 adults; the total mean number of persons living in the household was 3.9. As shown in Exhibit 3-3, 41.8% of young adults were living at Wave 5 in households with incomes below 100% of the federal poverty level, compared with an estimated 30% of all 18- to 24-year-old young adults living below the federal poverty level (Rumbaut, 2004). The percentage of NSCAW young adults living in poverty did not differ according to race/ethnicity or age, or by whether the young adult was living with or without his or her caregiver. Household poverty status did differ by sex, however: females (48.8%) were more likely to be living in poverty than males (30.6%).

Weekly Household Income

To provide an alternative description of young adults' financial resources, weekly household incomes were calculated on the basis of young adults' report of household members' incomes. Based on this information, the estimated average young adult at Wave 5 was living in a household that earned $551.3 per week. Male young adults ($711.2) were living in households that earned significantly more money per week than females' households did ($446.4). Those young adults living with caregivers were also living in households with a significantly higher weekly household income ($635.9) than those living without caregivers ($469.5). Weekly household income did not differ by young adults' sex, race/ethnicity, or age. It should be noted that weekly household income, unlike household poverty status, does not take into account the number of individuals dependent on these financial resources to live.

Exhibit 3-3. Young Adults' Job Status and Financial Resources at Wave 5

	Household Poverty Status Below 100% of the Federal Poverty Level[a]		Weekly Household Income[b]		Currently Employed Full or Part Time		Number of Hours Worked per Week[c]	
	N	% (SE)	*N*	Mean (SE)	*N*	% (SE)	*N*	Mean (SE)
Total	497	41.8 (3.7)	502	$551.3 (38.2)	617	58.1 (4.2)	326	34.4 (1.7)
Sex		**		***				
Male	171	30.6 (5.7)	175	$711.2 (69.7)	139	63.6 (6.5)	138	35.9 (2.8)
Female	326	48.8 (4.5)	327	$446.4 (29.8)	189	54.4 (4.9)	188	33.3 (1.8)
Race/ethnicity								*
Black	129	42.3 (8.8)	132	$527.3 (75.1)	182	53.3 (8.0)	89	31.8 (2.6)
White	246	37.0 (5.1)	248	$603.2 (59.0)	293	64.4 (5.8)	166	37.8 (2.1)[d]
Hispanic	71	60.7 (10.4)	71	$442.5 (69.5)	84	42.9 (11.9)	40	27.6 (4.5)
Other	47	45.1 (10.3)	47	$464.7 (63.9)	54	51.4 (12.4)	28	34.8 (2.7)
Age								
18 years	101	53.0 (9.7)	102	$472.5 (77.1)	130	59.2 (8.7)	65	27.6 (3.6)
19 years	155	37.1 (7.4)	156	$539.9 (59.7)	198	53.6 (7.8)	94	34.0 (2.8)
20 years	179	44.4 (7.0)	181	$578.7 (71.8)	215	62.4 (6.7)	129	36.4 (2.8)
21 years	62	26.7 (10.4)	63	$600.3 (128.9)	74	52.3 (11.9)	38	39.8 (2.6)
Living situation				*				
Living with caregiver	239	36.6 (5.7)	241	$635.9 (54.9)	324	62.5 (5.1)	171	32.3 (2.4)
Living without caregiver	258	46.6 (5.3)	261	$469.5 (55.3)	293	52.6 (5.4)	155	37.8 (2.0)

Note: All analyses are on weighted data; *Ns* are unweighted. Reported *Ns* vary slightly across analyses because of missing data in some variable categories. Pearson $\div^2$ tests for cluster samples were used for initial significance tests and pairwise comparisons for household poverty status and current employment. The t-test or regression comparisons and contrasts were used to examine significant group differences for household weekly income and hours worked per week. There were no statistically significant differences in job status and financial resources by type of maltreatment at baseline or history of out-of-home placement. Asterisks indicate statistical significance (*$p < .05$, ** $p < .01$, ***$p < .001$). Asterisks in column apply to the subsequent results for the covariate.

[a] "Household poverty status" represents the percentage of young adult households living below 100% of the federal poverty level. Household income is based upon the combined income for all members of any given household, divided by the number of individuals dependent on that income.

[b] "Weekly household income" is a derived variable that represents the approximate dollars earned by a young adult's household per week across the course of the 12 months prior to interview. Young adults were asked to estimate the total combined income of their household over the 12 months prior to interview. Young adults could answer with estimates of income daily, weekly, or annually across 11 income ranges. Respondents cited the range and did not provide an exact dollar amount. Based on this response, a midpoint of the weekly salary range was assigned for each of the wage categories.

[c] "Number of hours worked per week" was calculated only for those who reported they were currently employed full or part time.

[d] White > Black ($p < .05$); White > Hispanic ($p < .05$).

Employment

Fifty-eight percent of young adults reported currently being employed either full or part time. The percentage of young adults working appears similar to the percentage of working young adults across the country. For instance, the American Community Survey (U.S. Census Bureau, 2005) indicates that 36.7% of older U.S. adolescents (16- to 19-year-olds) and 67.6% of young adults (20- to 24-year-olds) are employed at any given time.

Among those who reported working, the average number of hours worked per week was 34.4. There were no differences in a young adult's likelihood to work by sex, race/ethnicity, age, or living situation. There were differences in the numbers of hours worked per week by race/ethnicity. White young adults reported working significantly more hours per week than Black young adults and Hispanic young adults. There were no differences in hours worked per week by sex, age, or living situation.

More than half (5 7.4%) of young adults not currently working reported that they had worked in the past 12 months. Many young adults had worked more than one job over the course of the 12-month period. Forty-nine percent of all young adults reported that their current job had not been their only job during the previous 12 months. Young adults working more than 1 job reported, on average, having worked 1.7 other jobs (with most working between 1 and 4 different places).

Young adults were asked about their primary type of work and their satisfaction with this job. The most commonly reported occupations included laborer (26.8%), "other" (25.1%), service worker (15.2%), sales (12.0%), and office worker (7.7%). Young adults were also fairly satisfied with their current job. Most indicated that they liked it "very much" (34.5%), liked it "fairly much" (15.6%), or thought it was "okay" (34.3%).

Social Support

The transition to adulthood usually happens as a gradual process whereby young adults increasingly take on new responsibilities. In this process, then, it is not unusual that young adults remain at least partially connected to and often dependent on their biological family members. Families may provide financial support, food, or shelter but may also provide social or emotional support to facilitate the young adult's goals. For young adults disconnected from their families, the role of external social support becomes especially important.

Contact with Biological Family

Young adults were well connected to their biological family members. Almost all young adults reported that they knew their biological mother (98.7%), knew their biological father (91.1%), and have biological siblings (96.6%). Of those who knew their biological parents, 4% reported that their mother had died; 15% reported that their father had died (Exhibit 3-4). Many reported that they had contact with other biological relatives (76.6%). Few young adults reported having no contact with a living biological mother (7.2%) or siblings (4.6%); more reported having no contact with their father (17.6%). Young adults had the most frequent contact with their mothers; 47.1% had daily contact. More than a third had daily contact with their siblings. Exhibit 3-4 presents young adults' contact with biological mother, father, and siblings by frequency of contact (*none*, *monthly*, *weekly*, *daily*).

Contact with biological family members differed between those young adults with a history of out-of-home placement during adolescence and those without (at any one of the Waves 1 through 4). For instance, while there were no differences for knowing the identity of biological mothers, young adults with a history of out-of-home placement were significantly less likely to know their biological fathers (81.6%) than those with no history of out-of-home placement (92.8%). Furthermore, young adults with a history of out-of-home placement had significantly less contact with their biological mothers and biological siblings than those without out-of-home histories. There were no differences for contact with biological mothers, fathers, or siblings by sex, race/ethnicity, age, or living situation (living with or without caregiver).

Exhibit 3-4. Young Adults' Contact with Biological Family at Wave 5

	N (Min)	None/ Deceased % (SE)	None/No Contact % (SE)	Monthly % (SE)	Weekly % (SE)	Daily % (SE)
Total						
Contact with biological mother	607	4.2 (1.3)	7.2 (2.3)	18.9 (3.0)	22.7 (2.9)	47.1 (3.9)
Contact with biological father	533	14.5 (2.7)	17.6 (2.6)	19.9 (2.8)	22.1 (3.5)	25.9 (3.8)
Contact with biological siblings	584	NA	4.6 (1.5)	24.7 (3.5)	31.4 (4.0)	39.2 (3.2)
History of at least one out-of-home placement during adolescence						
Contact with biological mother[a]	232	13.6 (4.5)	11.7 (4.9)	25.7 (4.6)	22.9 (5.2)	26.1 (4.9)
Contact with biological father	186	26.4 (6.5)	12.4 (5.2)	22.6 (6.3)	23.7 (6.0)	15.0 (6.0)
Contact with biological siblings[a]	232	NA	8.9 (2.6)	26.0 (5.4)	42.4 (6.3)	22.7 (4.2)
No history of out-of-home placement during adolescence						
Contact with biological mother	349	6.0 (2.8)	2.7 (1.1)	16.7 (3.7)	21.7 (3.7)	52.9 (4.5)
Contact with biological father	325	16.2 (3.1)	13.7 (3.3)	20.2 (3.5)	22.2 (4.0)	27.7 (4.7)
Contact with biological siblings	337	NA	3.9 (1.8)	24.1 (3.9)	28.7 (4.3)	43.2 (3.9)

Note: All analyses are on weighted data; *Ns* are unweighted. Reported *Ns* vary slightly across analyses because of missing data in some variable categories. Contact with biological mother, father, and siblings was gathered only from those young adults who knew the identity of the particular biological family member. There were no statistically significant differences in contact with biological family by sex, race/ethnicity, age, or type of maltreatment at baseline. NA = not applicable.

[a] History of out-of-home placement < no history of out-of-home placement for contact with mother and siblings at $p < .01$.

Social Support

Young adults were asked about the number of people available to offer them confidant support (i.e., inviting them out for activities or offering advice about money or about "important things in life") or instrumental support (i.e., helping to take care of their children, helping with transportation, helping during illness, or helping with cooking and housework).

Young adults were also asked about their degree of satisfaction with this support (across a 4-point scale from 1 [*very dissatisfied*] to 4 [*very satisfied*]).[4] Young adults reported feeling moderately satisfied with the degree of social support that they received from individuals to help with a variety of activities (Exhibit 3-5). Their degree of satisfaction across types of social support did not vary extensively, from 3.1 to 3.5 on the 4-point scale. Young adults reported the most people to invite them out for activities (6.9 persons on average) or give them "useful advice about important things" (6.8 persons on average). They reported the fewest people available to them to help with cooking and housework (1.7 persons on average) or to help them when they were sick (2.3 persons on average).

Exhibit 3-5. Social Support among Young Adults at Wave 5

	N (Min)	None % (SE)	1 to 3 Persons % (SE)	4 or More Persons % (SE)	Average Number Persons Mean (SD)	Average Satisfaction Mean (SD)
Confidant support						
People who invite you out to do things	617	4.2 (1.4)	33.3 (3.5)	62.5 (3.6)	6.9 (0.4)	3.3 (0.1)
People who offer chances to talk about money/ budgeting	616	19.0 (3.4)	58.1 (4.0)	22.9 (3.1)	2.6 (0.2)	3.2 (0.1)
People who give you useful advice about important things in life	615	5.5 (2.0)	34.2 (3.6)	60.3 (3.5)	6.8 (0.6)	3.4 (0.1)
Instrumental support						
People who help you take care of your children (can be rated "not applicable")	290	25.4 (6.3)	35.4 (5.8)	39.3 (6.3)	3.5 (0.5)	3.5 (0.1)
People who offer help with transportation	614	8.3 (2.0)	64.0 (3.5)	27.7 (2.7)	3.4 (0.3)	3.3 (0.1)
People who give you help when you're sick in bed	615	14.0 (2.6)	70.5 (3.7)	15.5 (2.7)	2.3 (0.2)	3.4 (0.1)
People who give you help with cooking and housework	614	20.8 (3.3)	68.6 (3.9)	10.6 (2.5)	1.7 (0.2)	3.2 (0.1)

Note: All analyses are on weighted data; *Ns* are unweighted. Reported *Ns* vary slightly across analyses because of missing data in some variable categories. There were no statistically significant differences in contact with biological family by sex, by race/ethnicity, by age, by type of maltreatment at baseline, or by history of out-of-home placement.

Conclusion

In many ways, these young adults who had contact with the CWS in adolescence resemble their normative U.S. peers. Most remained living with their biological families through adolescence and were still living with a caregiver in early adulthood. About one fifth were married or cohabiting with a partner. Most have also entered the workforce.

Furthermore, the key young adult milestones described in this chapter also reflect growing national trends for young people in this age group. Few young adults at Wave 5 are living independently, most are unmarried, and many show a substantial amount of contact with their families of origin. Young adults with a history of CWS involvement are also not making the transition to adulthood alone. Many have weekly or daily contact with their biological mothers, fathers, siblings—or with a combination of these family members. Even many young adults with a history of out-of-home placement in adolescence have relatively consistent contact with some members of their biological families. Young adults also indicate moderate satisfaction with their self-reported levels of social support.

As noted at the beginning of this chapter, diversity is increasing in the order in which U.S. young adults pursue certain traditional developmental milestones, such as marriage or parenting (e.g., Furstenberg et al., 2005). This diversity appears in the young adults described here. There were a few critical ways in which they differed from their normative U.S. peers. The primary difference relates to the percentage of young adults who had a child and who were actively parenting. It is estimated that 6.6% of all U.S. young adults between the ages of 18 and 20 are living with their own children (7.9% male, 19.8% female; Child Trends, 2006). Here, 29.0% of young adults reported currently living with one of their own children. Almost all young adult mothers were living with at least one of their biological children.

The second major difference from other U.S. young adults relates to living in poverty: 41.8% of all young adults and 59.1% of young adult parents were living below the federal poverty level at Wave 5. This rate is substantially more than the 30% of all young adults living in poverty in the United States aged 18 to 24 years (Rumbaut, 2007). So, while young adults with a history of CWS involvement may be progressing along the milestones to adulthood in relative tandem to their national counterparts, they are doing so with substantially fewer financial resources at their disposal. Furthermore, many are beginning this transition to adulthood after having already begun one of the most complicated young adult roles and responsibilities: being a parent.

Chapter 2 illustrated that young adults were faring worse than their peers on a number of well-being indicators. It is beyond the scope of this report to examine relationships between well-being and traditional young adult developmental milestones, although undoubtedly these relationships exist. For instance, a young adult's physical limitations, mental illness, or criminal activity may seriously impact his or her ability to parent, work, or maintain effective social relationships. Future research should examine relationships between well-being and traditional young adult developmental milestones, as well as the potential mediating influence of service access upon these trajectories.

4. Young Adult Services

Maltreatment during childhood is associated in adolescents and young adults with a variety of health problems (Arias, 2004; Hillis, Anda, Felitti, Nordenberg, & Marchbanks, 2000). When compared with children who have not been maltreated, maltreated children show higher rates of adolescent or adult depression, suicidal behavior, aggression, anxiety, dissociation, post- traumatic stress disorder symptoms, social problems, thought problems, conduct disorder, substance abuse, sexually transmitted diseases, eating disorders, perceived poorer overall health, functional disability, and increased numbers of distressing physical symptoms (Brown, Cohen, Johnson, & Smailes, 1999; Danielson, de Arellano, Kilpatrick, Saunders, & Resnick, 2005; Hillis et al., 2000; Kaplan et al., 1998; Lansford et al., 2002; Molnar, Buka, & Kessler, 2001; Riggs, Alario, & McHorney, 1990; Thompson, Arias, Basile, & Desai, 2002; Walker et al., 1999; Wolfe, Scott, Wekerle, & Pittman, 2001; Wonderlich, Wilsnack, Wilsnack, & Harris, 1996).

As presented in Chapter 2, a number of young adults had mental health problems, and some of them had substance dependence problems at Wave 5. Although it is not uncommon that young adults experience reactive, transient, or situational disorders, it is likely that many of these disorders will not completely resolve with no or little intervention. Moreover, as presented in Chapter 1, some of these young adults showed signs of mental health and behavioral problems at Wave 4. Consequently, one concern is that behavioral health issues may evolve into chronic problems that not only challenge a successful transition to adulthood, but also interfere with the ability to parent effectively. Thus, the receipt of services at this age comes at a critical time, when young adults need to negotiate several developmental tasks while learning to live independently and raise their children (Osgood, Foster, Flanagan, & Ruth, 2005). These services may represent the difference between making a successful transition to adulthood and being left in a downward spiral.

The transition to adulthood is marked by significant changes in access to health services and health insurance coverage for all young adults, changes which have been described as a "significant weakening of the safety net, as well as supportive institutions, organizations and networks that serve adolescents" (Park, Mulye, Adams, Brindis, & Irwin, 2006, p. 306). For those aged 18 years, insurance access and eligibility vary by a number of factors. For instance, only young adult students are eligible for parental insurance coverage. Medicaid eligibility ends at age 18 for many young people; however, other young adults may still qualify for Medicaid because of income level and number of dependents. Some young adults may be working, but nearly half of employed young adults nationwide hold employment positions that do not offer health insurance coverage (Callahan & Cooper, 2004).

Similarly, admission into independent-living programs and eligibility for federal and state help through programs like Temporary Assistance for Needy Families (TANF), Special Supplemental Nutrition Program for Women, Infants, and Children (WIC), and Supplemental Security Income (SSI), may be reduced for some young adults, and expanded for others if they have children of their own. Even if after age 18 young adults qualify for the same services that they received as children, many mental health interventions are age based, and transitions even within one mental health system may not be seamless (Lyons & Melton, 2005). In the transition from child to adult services, young adults face many barriers, including poor communication between providers, lack of service continuity and coordination, confusion about procedures to access adult services, and other problems associated with navigating a complex service system while trying to learn to function as an adult (Davis, Geller, & Hunt, 2006; Davis & Sondheimer, 2005; Vostanis, 2005).

The purpose of this chapter is to examine what services young adults received, which young adults were more likely to receive different services, and whether the service was sufficient to meet needs. Analyses examine the following issues:

1. insurance status,
2. preventive and urgent health care services,

3. accidents and injuries and associated use of emergency room (ER) or urgent care,
4. mental health and substance dependence services,
5. independent-living skills services, and
6. services to address basic needs.

For most services, we examined the degree to which need for a particular service matched actual service receipt. We were also interested in which types of young adults were more likely to receive different kinds of services. Consequently, we analyzed findings in relation to a young adult's sex, race, age, insurance status, living situation (living with a caregiver or not), number of types of abuse at baseline, types of maltreatment, and whether he or she had any history of out-of-home placement. When other characteristics of young adults were deemed relevant, we also examined their impact on service delivery; these characteristics included function-limiting health problems, need for mental health services, need for substance dependence services, and the like.

It was beyond the scope of this report to examine the impact of services on young adult outcomes such as employment, interpersonal relationships, parenthood, parenting skills, or crime. Also outside the scope of this work was comparison of the influence of various predictors of service use rates and patterns. This chapter describes the services received by young adults during the 12 months prior to interview. Key results were as follows:

- Medicaid or other state-funded coverage was the most common type of health insurance among young adults (43.5%); more than a third (3 6.7%) did not have any type of insurance coverage. Female young adults (75.1%) were more likely than males (45.6%) to have insurance.
- Almost two thirds (62.1%) of young adults reported having a usual place for health services. Half had recently participated in a checkup (51.9%), recent dental visit (52.2%), or both. Female young adults were significantly more likely than males to have a usual health care place and to have received dental care, to have received a medical checkup, and to have seen a physician in the previous 12 months. Young adults with insurance were more likely than uninsured young adults to have a consistent place to receive medical services, to have received dental care in the previous 12 months, and to have received all types of preventive health care.
- A limited percentage (15.7%) of young adults reported contact with a physician or nurse for serious accidents, injuries, or poisonings.
- Overall, based on clinically significant scores on several measures related to mental health, 45.7% of young adults were determined to be in need of mental health services or in need of substance dependence services.
- In the 12 months prior to interview, a limited percentage (17.5%) received outpatient mental health services or inpatient services (8.4%). Among those with clinically significant mental health scores and considered in need of mental health services, inpatient mental health services were received by 13.3%, a rate almost three times higher than national estimates (4.6%; Substance Abuse and Mental Health Services [SAMHSA], Office of Applied Studies [OAS], 2005)
- Among young adults with clinically significant mental health scores and considered in need of mental health services, 27.6% received outpatient mental health services, and 13.3% received inpatient mental health services (some received both services).

The large majority of young adults determined to be in need of mental health services received none (67.1%). In contrast, although only a small number of young adults were in need due to substance abuse problems, more than half (56.2%) received a substance abuse or a mental health service.

- More than a quarter of female young adults had been victims of physical intimate-partner violence in the previous 12 months, but few received any domestic violence service.
- Almost two thirds (63.9%) of young adults received help with education, 65.5% with jobs, 57.1% with managing finances, 23.7 % with housing, and 57.1 % with daily living. Overall, 91.7% reported receiving help in at least one of these areas. The main sources of assistance were biological parents or other original family members, teachers or schools, or "others." Very few identified independent-living skills training or a caseworker as a source of assistance (between 0% and 6.8%).
- More than a third of young adults were receiving some type of service to address basic needs. Among those with children, only females received TANF, or "welfare," (26.6%); 70.7% of females with children received WIC. Other services not restricted to persons having children were even more likely to be provided to females as opposed to males: 35.5% of females received food stamps, compared with 4.8% of males; 10.3% of females received SSI, compared with 2.7% of males; and, overall, 51.9% of females received any federal service, compared with 9.0% of males.

Insurance Status

Given its critical role in financing health services for the young adult population, insurance coverage—or the lack of it—among this population can determine use of and access to needed physical and behavioral health care. Young adults were asked their current insurance status, with reference to the following categories: (1) Medicaid or another state-funded program, (2) private insurance (including health maintenance organizations, preferred provider organizations, independent practice associations, fee for service, Blue Cross Blue Shield, or employer plan), (3) Civilian Health and Medical Program of the Uniformed Services (CHAMPUS; military insurance), or (4) no insurance of any kind (uninsured). Medicaid or state- funded insurance was the most commonly held type of health insurance among young adults (43.5%). Only 17.4% had private insurance, and 2.4% had CHAMPUS. A full 3 6.7% did not have any insurance coverage. No significant differences in insurance status were found by poverty level, with those below and above the federal poverty level having similar rates of insurance coverage (66.2% and 61%, respectively).

Exhibit 4-1 shows variations in insurance status by sex, race, and age. Female young adults (75.1%) were significantly more likely than males (45.6%) to have insurance. Among young adults, 36.7% were uninsured, a rate that exceeds the national rate for 19- to 24-year-olds (30.6%) according to the Annual Social and Economic Supplement to the Current Population Survey (CPS) of the U.S. Census Bureau (DeNavas-Walt, Proctor, & Lee, 2006). Nevertheless, fewer young adults were uninsured when compared with national data based on the CPS for adults aged 19 to 24 years who live 200% beneath the federal poverty level (44.3% uninsured nationally, as compared with 30.6% in the Wave 5 sample). Differences among young adults by sex were also consistent with national estimates showing that males aged 19 to 34 years are more likely to be uninsured (32.8%) than female young adults aged 19 to 34 (25.2%; Kaiser Commission on Medicaid and the Uninsured, 2006).

Exhibit 4-1. Insurance Status of Young Adults at Wave 5

	N (Min)	Medicaid/State Funded % (SE)	Private Insurance % (SE)	No Insurance % (SE)
Total	602	43.5 (3.8)	17.4 (2.9)	36.7 (4.1)
Sex		***	*	***
Male	221	25.1 (5.5)	19.4 (5.1)	54.4 (7.3)
Female	381	55.9 (4.5)	16.1 (3.6)	24.9 (4.7)
Race/ethnicity				
Black	175	56.3 (7.4)	9.4 (3.8)	29.3 (7.8)
White	286	33.2 (5.0)	23.0 (4.9)	42.2 (6.4)
Hispanic	83	59.8 (9.3)	10.9 (5.3)	27.9 (9.9)
Other	54	47.2 (12.9)	22.0 (9.0)	29.7 (9.1)
Age				
18 years	125	62.2 (8.7)	14.0 (4.3)	22.0 (8.6)
19 years	192	38.7 (5.7)	20.6 (5.3)	35.0 (6.0)
20 years	211	39.7 (6.2)	16.7 (5.4)	42.9 (6.3)
21 years	74	35.7 (10.6)	17.9 (6.1)	46.3 (11.4)

Note: All analyses are on weighted data; *Ns* are unweighted. Reported *Ns* vary slightly across analyses because of missing data in some variable categories. Pearson $\div^2$ tests for cluster samples were used for initial significance tests. CHAMPUS (military insurance) was reported by only 2.4% (SE = 1.3); as a consequence, all analysis of CHAMPUS by sex, race, and age had cells with very small n. No significant differences in insurance status were found by types of abuse at baseline, number of types of maltreatment, ever out-of-home placement, or poverty level. Asterisks indicate statistical significance (*$p < .05$, ***$p < .001$). Asterisks in column apply to the subsequent results for the covariate. CHAMPUS = Civilian Health and Medical Program of the Uniformed Services.

Preventive and Urgent Health Services

Preventive Health Services

About half of young adults reported that they had received preventive and routine health services in the 12 months prior to interview (Exhibit 4-2). Almost two thirds (62.1%) of young adults reported having a usual source of care, compared with approximately 69% of adults 18 to 24 years old nationally (Centers for Disease Control and Prevention [CDC], 2006; Pleis & Lethbridge-Cejku, 2006). Approximately half of the young adults had recently participated in a checkup (51.9%) or dental care (5 2.2%). During the previous 12 months, some young adults also received vision testing (40.6%), hearing testing (24.0%), or both. A small percentage of young adults (11.3%) had received all of these preventive health care services (dental care, vision and hearing testing, and checkup) in the 12 months before the interview.

Exhibit 4-2. Preventive and Routine Health Services for Young Adults at Wave 5

	N (Min)	All Preventive Services[a] % (SE)	Usual Source of Care % (SE)	Dental Care Past 12 Months % (SE)	Vision Testing Past 12 Months % (SE)	Hearing Testing Past 12 Months % (SE)	Checkup Past 12 Months % (SE)	Saw a Doctor in Past 12 Months % (SE)
Total	617	11.3 (2.1)	62.1 (4.0)	52.2 (3.4)	40.6 (3.5)	24.0 (3.1)	51.9 (3.8)	55.3 (3.9)
Sex			*	*			**	**
Male	232	10.3 (2.7)	50.3 (6.7)	42.1 (5.4)	39.9 (6.5)	26.2 (5.5)	38.7 (6.4)	44.7 (5.5)
Female	386	12.0 (3.1)	70.1 (5.0)	59.1 (4.6)	41.0 (4.6)	22.4 (3.6)	60.9 (4.5)	62.5 (4.8)
Race/ethnicity							*	
Black	183	14.3 (3.3)	60.1 (6.5)	63.9 (6.9)	41.6 (7.0)	27.3 (5.1)	70.2 (5.1)[b]	54.8 (7.3)
White	293	11.9 (3.3)	65.9 (5.8)	48.9 (5.2)	38.0 (5.1)	23.1 (4.6)	48.1 (5.9)	50.3 (5.2)
Hispanic	84	7.7 (4.1)	53.5 (11.9)	53.4 (9.7)	47.8 (10.8)	22.5 (9.7)	46.1 (12.2)	58.9 (12.1)
Other	54	5.6 (3.1)	70.0 (9.2)	39.8 (10.7)	30.3 (9.4)	25.5 (9.0)	31.8 (10.4)	79.0 (7.4)
Age					*			
18 years	130	23.2 (6.7)	63.9 (8.1)	59.2 (9.1)	63.7 (8.1)[c]	40.8 (7.7)	56.9 (8.6)	67.4 (7.6)
19 years	198	7.2 (2.1)	68.2 (5.1)	49.7 (6.2)	29.1 (5.6)	18.8 (4.9)	46.9 (6.5)	52.8 (7.2)
20 years	214	10.1 (3.4)	55.7 (7.2)	52.4 (6.4)	39.8 (6.4)	20.2 (5.3)	58.1 (6.5)	56.2 (7.1)
21 years	75		65.3 (12.1)	45.3 (10.9)	32.6 (9.9)	21.1 (6.7)	32.3 (9.6)	36.1 (10.2)
Insurance		***	**	***				
Yes	406	16.1 (3.2)	72.5 (4.8)	64.4 (4.4)	44.0 (4.9)	26.1 (3.5)	58.2 (4.4)	59.2 (5.1)
No	196	1.9 (0.9)	44.1 (5.9)	29.7 (6.2)	34.0 (7.6)	19.1 (6.5)	41.4 (7.6)	50.7 (5.8)
Health problem that currently limits activities								
Yes	179	15.3 (5.4)	64.6 (5.9)	47.6 (6.8)	41.8 (7.2)	27.2 (6.3)	51.1 (7.1)	66.9 (7.9)
No	438	9.6 (2.1)	61.0 (4.8)	54.2 (4.0)	40.0 (4.0)	22.5 (3.6)	52.2 (4.4)	50.3 (4.9)
Sexual abuse		**					*	
Yes	135	3.1 (1.4)	67.7 (10.9)	39.2 (10.1)	55.9 (11.4)	20.2 (9.5)	72.0 (10.0)	59.9 (11.3)

Exhibit 4-2.(Continued)

	N (Min)	All Preventive Services[a] % (SE)	Usual Source of Care % (SE)	Dental Care Past 12 Months % (SE)	Vision Testing Past 12 Months % (SE)	Hearing Testing Past 12 Months % (SE)	Checkup Past 12 Months % (SE)	Saw a Doctor in Past 12 Months % (SE)
No	436	12.5 (2.2)	61.2 (4.0)	54.5 (3.8)	34.4 (3.5)	24.8 (3.0)	49.1 (4.0)	54.2 (4.3)
Ever placed out of home								
Yes	238	16.2(4.3)	66.7(5.5)	51.6(6.5)	51.4(6.6)	31.9(6.3)	67.0 (6.0)	53.9(6.3)
No	355	10.8(2.7)	62.5(4.3)	51.8(4.0)	39.2(4.2)	23.6(3.6)	49.2 (4.5)	55.2(4.6)

Note: All analyses are on weighted data; *Ns* are unweighted. Reported *Ns* vary slightly across analyses because of missing data in some variable categories. Pearson $\div^2$ tests for cluster samples were used for all significance tests. All preventive and routine health care was reported by young adults for the 12 months prior to interview. No significant differences in use of preventive services were found by physical abuse, physical neglect and lack of supervision at baseline, or number of types of maltreatment. Asterisks indicate statistical significance (*$p < .05$, **$p < .01$, ***$p < .00$ 1). Asterisks in column apply to the subsequent results for the covariate.

[a] Includes having had recent dental, vision, and hearing checkups.

[b] Black is significantly different from White at $p < .01$,and from Other at $p < .05$.

[c] Age 18 is significantly different from age 19 ($p < .01$), 20 ($p < .05$), and 21 ($p < .05$).

Exhibit 4-3. Young Adults' Urgent Medical Care in the Past 12 Months at Wave 5

	N (Min)	ER or Urgent Care for Illness or Injury % (SE)	Hospital Admission for Illness or Injury % (SE)	Care from Doctor or Nurse for Serious Injury, Accident, or Poisoning % (SE)
Total	602	37.0 (3.4)	13.0 (2.4)	15.7 (2.9)
Sex		*	**	
Male	232	28.7 (5.3)	5.5 (2.6)	17.1 (4.7)
Female	386	42.9 (4.5)	18.0 (3.4)	14.8 (3.6)
Race/ethnicity				
Black	183	32.2 (6.2)	13.9 (5.0)	5.7 (2.5)
White	292	37.2 (4.2)	12.0 (3.2)	18.6 (4.1)
Hispanic	84	30.0 (9.5)	10.5 (5.9)	10.3 (5.8)
Other	54	54.8 (11.8)	5.5 (3.3)	26.5 (14.4)
Age				
18 years	130	50.1 (7.6)	16.2 (7.8)	27.9 (8.3)
19 years	198	31.9 (5.8)	11.0 (3.6)	7.3 (2.5)
20 years	215	37.1 (6.5)	13.0 (3.8)	17.3 (5.4)
21 years	75	25.9 (9.8)	12.4 (8.6)	10.8 (8.7)
Insurance	602			
Yes	196	40.8 (4.5)	16.6 (3.3)	15.2 (3.3)
No	406	33.0 (5.3)	7.7 (4.1)	17.8 (5.5)
Ever placed out of home				*
Yes	237	48.2 (7.5)	16.6 (5.4)	7.4 (2.9)
No	345	39.3 (3.7)	12.9 (7.8)	18.1 (3.7)

Note: All analyses are on weighted data; *Ns* are unweighted. Reported *Ns* vary slightly across analyses because of missing data in some variable categories. Pearson $\div^2$ tests for cluster samples were used for initial significance tests. No significant differences in use of urgent services were found by type of maltreatment at baseline or by number of types of maltreatment. Asterisks indicate statistical significance (*$p < .05$, **$p < .01$). Asterisks in column apply to the subsequent results for the covariate.

The percentage of young adults receiving these preventive health services varied significantly according to sex, race/ethnicity, insurance status, sexual abuse at baseline, and whether they were ever out of home. Female young adults were significantly more likely than males to have a usual source of care, to have received recent dental care or medical checkup, and to have seen a physician in the past 12 months. As might be expected, young adults with insurance were more likely than uninsured young adults to have a usual source of care, to have had dental care in the 12 months prior to interview, and to have received all preventive services. Only one preventive service, vision testing in the previous 12 months, was more likely to be received by 18-year-olds than by other age groups. Young adults who were reported for sexual abuse at baseline were more likely than those who were not reported for sexual abuse to have received a checkup during the previous 12 months, but were less likely to have received all preventive services. Similarly, young adults who were ever out of home between baseline and Wave 4 were more likely to have received a checkup in the previous 12 months than those who were never out of home.

Between a quarter and a third (30.5%) of young adults reported experiencing some or much limitation due to a health condition. Access to preventive and routine health services would be particularly important for this population. No significant differences were found in the receipt of preventive and routine health services between young adults with a health limitation and young adults without health limitations.

Accidents, Injuries, and Associated Use of ER or Urgent Care

Young adults reported on their use of urgent-care services for illnesses or injuries in the 12 months prior to interview (Exhibit 4-3). Slightly more than a third (37.0%) of young adults reported having used the ER or urgent-care services for an illness or an injury in that time frame. Overnight hospital admissions for illnesses and injuries were less common (13.0%). About 15.7% of young adults reported contact with a physician or nurse for serious accidents, injuries, or poisonings. Nationally, the percentage of young adults aged 18 to 21 years who were treated for all causes of nonfatal injuries in 2005 was similar to these findings (14.9%; CDC, 2007).

Although young adults' race, age, and insurance status had no significant association with the likelihood of receiving urgent-care health services, the young adults' sex did have a significant association. Female young adults (42.9%) were more likely than males (28.7%) to have used the ER or urgent-care services for an illness or an injury in the 12 months prior to interview. Additionally, female young adults (18.0%) were more likely than males (5.5%) to have had an overnight hospital admission for an illness or injury. Nevertheless, when young adults' reporting was restricted to serious accidents, injuries, or poisonings that required the care of a nurse or doctor, they followed the expected trend of more cases among males. Here, rates for female young adults (14.8%) and for males (17.1%) are similar to those reported by CDC for all U.S. male young adults (17.2%) and slightly higher than the rates for U.S. female young adults (12.3%) aged 18 to 21 who were treated for all causes of nonfatal injuries in 2005 (CDC, 2007). Young adults who were ever placed in out-of-home care (7.4%) were less likely than those who were never out of home (18.1%) to use the care from a doctor or nurse for a serious injury, accident, or poisoning.

In summary, young adults who were reported to the child welfare system (CWS) for maltreatment in adolescence used fewer preventive health services than other U.S. adults 18 to 24 years old. Female young adults reported more use of preventive health services and greater use of urgent-care services for an injury or illness than male young adults.

Mental Health and Substance Dependence Services

In this section we describe the mental health and substance dependence needs of young adults and compare their need with their use of services in the 12 months preceding their reports. The service use questions were framed so that young adults could respond positively for all service providers or service settings that were applicable; consequently, young adults could report having received services from more than one source. All questions included the following phrasing: "In the past 12 months have you received any (name of service) for emotional, behavioral, learning, attentional, or substance abuse problems?"

Young adults' needs for mental health and substance abuse services were assessed in five ways: (1) young adults' responses to questions about the degree to which they needed help by being admitted to a psychiatric hospital or detox unit; (2) the sections of the Composite International Diagnostic Interview Short Form (CIDI-SF; Kessler, Andrews, Mroczek, Ustun, & Wittchen, 1998) on major depression, alcohol dependence, and drug dependence; (3) the intrusive and dissociation sections of the Trauma Symptom Inventory, (4) Externalizing, Internalizing, and Total Problems subscales of the Adult Self-Report (ASR; Achenbach & Rescorla, 2003); and (5) the mental health section of the 12-Item Short-Form Health Survey (SF- 12; Ware, Kosinski, & Keller, 1996). Scores within the clinical range on any of these standardized measures identified the young adult as at risk for a mental health, alcohol, or drug problem and potentially in need of behavioral health services.

According to the data on young adults, only 2.6% reported that they needed to be admitted to a psychiatric hospital but were not; the same percentage reported that they needed to be admitted to a detox unit but were not. As reported in Chapter 2, more than a quarter (27.5%) of young adults were in the clinical range for major depression; 10.2% had a clinical score for traumatic intrusiveness; 6.2% had a score for traumatic dissociation. According to the ASR, 16.0% had a clinical score for Internalizing, 18.9% for Externalizing, and 13.4% for Total Problems (27.2% had elevated scores in at least one of the three ASR scales). Eleven percent had poor mental health, according to the SF-12; 6.6% had alcohol dependence; and 6.5% had drug dependence. When findings from all sources of information on the need for mental health or substance dependence services were combined, 45.7% of young adults were determined to be in need of mental health services (Exhibit 4-4).

Mental health need among young adults was almost double the national 12-month estimates for English-speaking respondents aged 18 years or older for any mental disorder (26.2%), as measured by the National Comorbidity Survey Replication using the CIDI, including anxiety, mood, impulse control, and substance disorders (Kessler, Chiu, Demier, & Walters, 2005).[5] Comparisons with other young adults who were maltreated in childhood are limited because of other studies' use of local samples, use of self-report to determine childhood maltreatment, or the limited number of disorders evaluated. In one prospective study of major depression among young adults (mean age 28.7 years) who before age 12 had court-substantiated records of abuse or neglect in a metropolitan area in the Midwest, the percentage with major depressive disorder was 25.3% among those who had been neglected, 30.2% among those who had been physically abused, 24.0% among those who had been sexually abused, and 31.4% among those who had experienced multiple types of maltreatment (Spatz Widom, DuMont, & Czaja, 2007); these rates of major depression are similar to those found for young adults in this report (27.5%).

Total mental health problems were somewhat higher when compared with the 12-month prevalence of mental health disorders among adolescents 17 years old in the foster care system in eight of the largest counties of Missouri, where 37% had any disorder, including major depression, attention-deficit/hyperactivity disorder, internalizing or externalizing disorder, or conduct disorder (McMillen et al., 2005). In summary, mental health needs among young adults were higher than national estimates for the general population, but are somewhat similar to previous studies based on young adults with a history of reports or placements in the CWS; although there are previous reports that estimate a higher rate of mental health problems, those studies are based on self-report of maltreatment with local sample that were not representative of the CWS population (Ferguson & Lynskey, 1997; MacMillan et al., 2001; Silverman, Reinherz, & Giaconia, 1996).

Exhibit 4-4. Young Adults' Need for Mental Health and Substance Abuse Services at Wave 5

	N (Min)	Young Adult in Need of Mental Health Services[a] % (SE)	Young Adult in Need of Substance Dependence Services % (SE)
Total	615	45.4 (3.7)	9.3 (2.3)
Sex		**	
Male	230	34.5 (5.5)	11.4 (4.1)
Female	385	52.8 (4.5)	7.9 (2.3)
Race/ethnicity			
Black	181	44.9 (7.2)	8.9 (4.0)
White	292	39.8 (5.2)	8.0 (2.8)
Hispanic	84	52.8 (11.6)	15.7 (10.3)
Other	54	63.9 (10.0)	9.0 (4.3)
Age			
18 years	130	58.1 (9.2)	4.1 (2.7)
19 years	196	32.4 (5.2)	10.7 (4.5)
20 years	215	51.1 (5.8)	11.0 (4.0)
21 years	74	37.0 (10.4)	8.9 (5.2)
Insurance			
Yes	404	48.1 (4.7)	7.8 (2.2)
No	195	42.7 (6.1)	11.8 (4.4)
Living with caregiver			
Yes	324	44.5 (5.1)	9.4 (3.3)
No	291	46.6 (5.7)	9.1 (3.3)

Note: All analyses are on weighted data; *Ns* are unweighted. Reported *Ns* vary slightly across analyses because of missing data in some variable categories. Pearson $\div^2$ tests for cluster samples were used for initial significance tests. No significant differences in need for mental health services or need for substance dependence services were found by types of abuse at baseline, by number of types of maltreatment, or by ever out-of-home placement. Asterisks indicate statistical significance (**p < .0 1). Asterisks in column apply to the subsequent results for the covariate.

[a] Need for mental health services was defined as being positive for any of the following: young adult self-reports of needing to be admitted to a psychiatric hospital or detox unit; clinical range for major depression; clinical score for traumatic intrusiveness or for traumatic dissociation; clinical score for internalizing, externalizing, or total behavioral problems; or poor mental health according to the 12-Item Short-Form Health Survey, alcohol dependence, or drug dependence.

Substance dependence was similar to national estimates for adults between the ages of 18 and 25 (7.2% dependent on alcohol, 5.8% dependent on drugs, and 11.5% dependent on either; Substance Abuse and Mental Health Services Administration, Office of Applied Studies [SAMHSA, OAS], 2006). In the present reporting, there were no significant variations in the need for mental health services by young adults' race/ethnicity, age, insurance status, or living situation; however, there were variations by sex, with female young adults (52.8%) more likely to need mental health services than male young adults (34.5%). No significant differences were found in need for substance dependence services by sex, race/ethnicity, age, insurance status, and living situation.

Exhibit 4-5. Young Adults' Need for Mental Health and Substance Dependence Services and Service Receipt at Wave 5

	N (Min)	Outpatient Mental Health Services[a] % (SE)	Specialty Outpatient Services[b] % (SE)	In-Home Counseling or Family Doctor % (SE)	Inpatient Mental Health Services[c]	Current Use of Psychotropic Medication % (SE)
Total	616	17.5 (3.1)	14.3 (2.8)	9.3 (2.6)	8.4 (2.1)	11.2 (2.5)
Sex						***
Male	230	12.5 (4.2)	8.1 (3.6)	6.9 (3.5)	3.7 (2.2)	2.5 (0.9)
Female	386	20.9 (4.3)	18.5 (3.9)	11.0 (3.5)	11.6 (3.3)	17.1 (4.1)
Race/ethnicity						*
Black	181	7.5 (4.1)	5.9 (3.5)	5.6 (3.5)	11.0 (5.8)	6.7 (4.8)
White	293	23.4 (4.7)	18.1 (4.2)	14.3 (4.5)	6.6 (2.8)	16.3 (4.1)
Hispanic	84	11.1 (5.0)	10.7 (5.0)	1.5 (0.6)	12.1 (6.1)	2.1 (0.8)[d]
Other	54	27.7 (14.3)	27.3 (14.4)	3.9 (2.4)	6.4 (3.4)	10.7 (5.6)
Age						**
18 years	129	28.3 (8.1)	20.0 (7.7)	18.0 (6.8)	6.3 (4.6)	9.2 (5.1)
19 years	198	8.7 (3.3)	8.6 (3.3)	4.1 (2.8)	8.2 (3.5)	2.2 (0.8)[e]
20 years	215	16.3 (4.8)	12.8 (3.8)	8.5 (4.2)	9.1 (3.8)	17.3 (4.9)
21 years	74	27.7 (12.2)	26.6 (12.3)	11.5 (8.8)	10.6 (8.8)	18.7 (10.2)
Insurance						
Yes	405	20.5 (4.3)	18.3 (3.8)	10.4 (3.5)	8.4 (2.7)	14.9 (3.5)
No	196	13.6 (4.9)	8.5 (4.2)	8.0 (4.1)	8.9 (4.6)	5.9 (3.7)
Living with caregiver						
Yes	323	18.3 (4.2)	17.3 (4.2)	9.3 (3.3)	9.0 (3.1)	12.9 (3.7)
No	293	16.6 (4.4)	10.7 (3.3)	9.3 (4.0)	7.8 (3.5)	9.2 (3.5)
Young adult in need of mental health services[f]		**	*	*		**
Yes	265	27.6 (6.1)	22.0 (5.1)	17.4 (5.4)	13.3 (4.1)	20.7 (5.1)
No	351	9.0 (3.0)	7.9 (3.0)	2.5 (1.6)	4.3 (2.0)	3.3 (1.6)
Young adult in need of substance abuse services[g]			*			
Yes	47	54.5 (11.6)	40.4 (11.6)	32.8 (14.5)	20.8 (9.8)	18.3 (9.5)
No	566	13.8 (3.0)	11.7 (2.8)	6.9 (2.1)	6.9 (2.1)	10.5 (2.6)

Note: Young adults' report of mental health or substance abuse service use represents services received in the12 months prior to interview. All analyses are on weighted data; *Ns* are unweighted. Reported *Ns* vary slightly across analyses because of missing data in some variable categories. Pearson $\div^2$ tests for cluster * samples were used for initial significance tests and pairwise contrasts. Mental health services measured through an adapted version of the Child and Adolescent Services Assessment (Child & Adolescent Services Assessment; see Technical Appendix). No significant differences in use of mental and substance dependence services or in use of psychotropic medication were found by types of abuse at baseline, number of types of maltreatment, or ever out-ofhome placement. Asterisks indicate statistical significance (*$p < .05$, **$p < .01$, ***$p < .00$ 1). Asterisks in column apply to the subsequent results for the covariate.

[a] Any outpatient mental health service included use of specialty outpatient (e.g., day treatment for emotional and substance abuse problems, outpatient drug or alcohol unit, mental health center, private professional help for emotional and substance abuse problems) and in-home counseling for emotional and substance abuse problems, family doctor for emotional and substance abuse problems, or both.

[b] Any specialty outpatient service included day treatment for emotional and substance abuse problems, outpatient drug or alcohol unit, mental health center, and private professional help for emotional and substance abuse problems.

[c] Any inpatient mental health service included use of psychiatric hospital, hospital for emotional and substance abuse problems, residential treatment, emergency shelter for emotional and substance abuse problems, and ER for emotional and substance abuse problems.

[d] Hispanic is significantly different from White at $p < .01$.

[e] Age 19 is significantly different from age 21 at $p < .01$.

[f] Young adult was determined to be "in need of mental health services" when he or she met any one of four criteria; (1) young adult self-reported need for "a lot" or "some" help by being admitted to a psychiatric hospital; (2) scores within the clinical range on the depression scale of the Composite International Diagnostic Interview Short Form (CIDI-SF) or a score of 1.5 standard deviations or more below the norm ($t \leq 35$) on the Mental Health scale of the SF-12; (3) a score in the clinical range of the intrusive experiences or dissociation subscales of the Trauma Symptom Inventory; or (4) a score in the clinical range of the Adult Self-Report for Total Problems, Internalizing, and Externalizing subscales.

[g] Young adult was determined to be in need of substance abuse services when he or she met any one of two criteria: (1) young adult self-reported need for "a lot" or "some" help by being admitted to a detox unit or inpatient drug or alcohol unit or to a hospital medical inpatient unit; or (2) he or she had scores within the clinical range on either the Alcohol Dependence or Drug Dependence scales of the CIDI-SF.

The high number of young adults in need of mental health and substance abuse services contrasts with the number that in the 12 months before interview received behavioral health services. As shown in Exhibit 4-5, only 17.5% received any outpatient mental health services. When the analysis of outpatient services was restricted to specialty outpatient services, the percentage that received services was reduced to 14.3%, while 9.3% received nonspecialty mental health services (in-home counseling or family doctor). Inpatient mental health services were received by 8.4%, and 11.2% were currently using psychotropic medication. Among those in need of mental health services, 13.3% received inpatient mental health services. The percentage receiving inpatient mental health services among those in need was almost triple the national rate. In 2005 it was estimated that 24.6 million adults suffered serious psychological distress; among these adults, 45.3% received treatment for a mental health problem in the previous year, but only 4.6% received inpatient treatment (Substance Abuse and Mental Health Services [SAMHSA], Office of Applied Studies [OAS], 2005).

In the present reporting, there were no significant variations in the use of outpatient mental health services, specialty outpatient services, in-home counseling or help from a family doctor, or inpatient mental health services by sex, race/ethnicity, age, insurance status, living situation, type of abuse at baseline, number of types of abuse, or out-of-home placement. As expected, however, young adults in need of mental health services were more likely than those determined not to be in need to receive outpatient mental health. In terms of psychotropic medication use, females were more likely to use such medications than males, Hispanics were less likely than Whites, and 19-year-olds were less likely than 21-year-olds. As expected, those in need of mental health services were more likely than those not in need to use psychotropic medication, outpatient mental health services, specialty outpatient services, and in-home counseling or help from their family doctor. Similarly, young adults in need of substance dependence services were more likely than those not determined to be in need to receive outpatient mental health services and specialty outpatient services.

Although having a mental health need made a young adult's receipt of a mental health service more likely, the large majority of young adults determined to be in need of mental health services received none (67.1%). It should be noted that high levels of unmet mental health needs are not unique to this population: a recent national study found that only 41% of English- speaking adults aged 18 years or older with a diagnosable mental disorder reported having received some treatment within a 12-month period (including help from a general doctor); only 21.7% received specialty treatment (psychiatrist or nonpsychiatrist mental health specialist; Wang et al., 2005).

In contrast to levels of unmet mental health service needs, more young adults with substance dependence needs received substance abuse services. Although only a small number of young adults were in need of these services, more than half (56.2%) received any service, and 40.4% received specialty outpatient treatment, which is four times higher than national estimates that show only 10.0% of persons aged 12 years or older and needing treatment for illicit drug use or alcohol use received treatment at a specialty facility (SAMHSA, OAS, 2005). Given that the substance abuse indicator used with young adults screens for substance dependence rather than abuse, providing a very narrow and high need definition, it is not surprising that the National Survey of Child and Adolescent Well-Being (NSCAW) data show many receiving help and at a higher rate than the national population.

There are some limitations to the ways in which NSCAW assesses young adults' mental health and substance service use. For instance, the NSCAW survey does not ask young adults about group therapy or participation in self-help groups such as Alcoholics Anonymous or Narcotics Anonymous, which is an important limitation because the national rate shows that more than half of those in need of treatment for illicit drug or alcohol use received treatment in the previous 12 months from a self-help group (SAMHSA, OAS, 2005). Consequently, service use rates may be underestimated. Despite these limitations, the data still suggest that receipt of services in this population is not adequate for the level of need. By any measure of need, no more than a third of those in need of mental health services received them, and more than 40% of those in need for substance dependence did not receive any service.

Domestic Violence Services

As reported in Chapter 2, in the 12 months prior to interview, 26.4% of female young adults had been victims of physical intimate-partner violence. Of those who were victims, only 4.5% of female young adults received a referral to domestic violence services; only 0.9% actually received any domestic violence service, although the few that received the service reported that it was very helpful.

Independent-Living, Education, and Job-Related Services

For the past 20 years, federal funds have been provided to states to help adolescents receiving CWS services develop independent-living skills and to support their making the transition to independent living. The goal of independent-living programs is to "increase educational attainment, increase employment rates and job stability, improve interpersonal and relational skills, reduce non-marital pregnancy and births, and reduce delinquency and crime rates" (Urban Institute, 2007). Previous studies at the national and state levels have reported that training in some specific independent-living skills (particularly money management, credit, consumer, education, and employment) is positively associated with reduced criminal activity and a self-concept better than that of young people who do not receive specific training in independent-living skills (Cook, Fleishman, & Grimes, 1992; Georgiades, 2005). It is noteworthy that these services are usually intended for youth in out-of-home placements and may not be particularly applicable to the majority of young adults described in this report, given that only 17% of them were ever in out-of-home placement during adolescence.

Young adults were previously queried about their independent-living skills at Wave 4. At that time they were between 15 and 19 years old. At Wave 4 the great majority reported that they knew how to shop for and prepare meals (95.6%), use public transportation (86.3%), interview for a job (79.5%), obtain family planning (71.1%), obtain medical and dental care (65.9%), and secure community support (60.2). Nevertheless, only 30.0% knew how to apply for college, and only 31.4% knew how to obtain income assistance. The main sources of help for learning these skills were biological parents or other original family members, teachers and schools, and "others." At that time, 3 3.0% had received independent-living skills training. Of those who had participated in some independent-living skills training program, only 11.8% reported that they learned how to interview for a job from the skills training program. For all other skills the percentage reporting that they learned the skill from the independent-living skills training varied between 0% and 8.1%.

At Wave 5, young adults were asked whether they had ever received help in several areas, including education, job, managing finances, housing services, and daily living. Almost two thirds (63.9%) had received help with education; 65.5%, with jobs; 57.1%, with managing finances; 23.7 %, with housing; and 57.1 %, with daily living. Overall, 91.7% reported receiving help with at least one of the areas (Exhibit 4-6). The main sources of assistance were biological parents or other original family members, teachers and schools, and "others." Very few identified independent-living skills training or a caseworker as a source of assistance (between 0% and 6.8%). Thus, the most traditional support systems (relatives and the educational system) helped young adults in the areas of education, job, and daily living, while independent-living programs were rarely mentioned as a source of help. This finding is consistent with information provided in the first chapter: that very few young adults transitioned to adulthood from the foster care system, which is the main population target of independent-living skills programs.

Exhibit 4-6. Number of Young Adults at Wave 5 Who Ever Received Services Related to Education, Job, or Daily-Living Skills

Area of Received Service	*N*	Yes % (SE)
Future education		
General Education Development Diploma preparation	617	32.6 (3.6)
ACT or Scholastic Aptitude Test preparation	617	28.0 (2.9)
Assistance with college applications	618	28.8 (3.3)
Assistance with vocational or career counseling	618	27.2 (3.1)
Any educational help	618	63.9 (3.8)
Job		
Resume writing	617	42.2 (4.0)
Identifying potential employers	617	24.2 (3.2)
Completing job applications	617	43.5 (3.9)
Job interviewing	618	46.4 (4.3)
Job referral or placement	618	32.7 (3.4)
Help securing work permits or Social Security cards	617	24.2 (3.2)
Any job-related help	618	65.5 (3.8)
Management of finances		
Money management	617	33.7 (4.1)
Use of a budget	618	35.0 (3.9)
Opening a checking and savings account	618	43.8 (4.5)
Balancing a checkbook	618	35.7 (3.7)
Any finances-related help	618	57.1 (3.9)
Housing		
Finding an apartment	618	16.9 (2.7)
Completing apartment application	618	13.5 (2.7)
Making a down payment or a security deposit on an apartment	618	12.3 (2.1)
Any housing-related help	618	23.7 (3.1)
Daily living		
Meal planning and preparation	618	27.9 (2.7)
Personal hygiene	618	33.4 (3.5)
Nutritional needs	618	43.9 (3.8)
Obtaining personal health records	617	24.5 (3.7)
Any daily-living–related help	618	57.1 (3.3)
Any education, job, finances, housing, or daily living	618	91.7 (2.3)
Independent-living skills training	618	19.7 (3.4)

Note: All analyses are on weighted data; *Ns* are unweighted. Reported *Ns* vary slightly across analyses because of missing data in some variable categories.

Exhibit 4-7. Young Adults' Use of Independent-Living and Job-Related Services at Wave 5

	N (Min)	Education % (SE)	Job Related % (SE)	Managing Finances % (SE)	Housing % (SE)	Daily Living % (SE)	Any Independent Living % (SE)
Total	618	63.9 (3.8)	65.5 (3.8)	57.1 (3.9)	23.7 (3.1)	57.1 (3.3)	91.7 (2.3)
Sex					**		
Male	231	72.5 (7.0)	70.1 (5.9)	59.6 (5.1)	13.0 (3.3)	49.3 (5.5)	91.7 (3.9)
Female	387	58.1 (4.1)	62.5 (5.4)	55.4 (5.6)	31.0 (4.7)	62.4 (4.3)	91.7 (2.3)
Race/ ethnicity	614						
Black	182	68.6 (6.2)	73.0 (9.1)	56.5 (9.2)	22.5 (4.7)	67.1 (5.7)	95.8 (2.6)
White	294	63.0 (6.2)	64.0 (5.1)	56.5 (4.9)	23.1 (5.0)	51.3 (5.6)	88.7 (4.1)
Hispanic	84	52.6 (11.2)	67.0 (10.6)	53.9 (11.6)	35.5 (11.3)	60.7 (9.4)	96.9 (2.6)
Other	54	68.1 (10.3)	39.6 (10.8)	62.0 (10.6)	13.6 (4.8)	48.4 (12.3)	87.3 (6.3)
Age	618	**					*
18 years	130	84.9 (4.4) [a]	71.8 (7.7)	71.8 (6.8)	25.2 (6.7)	68.0 (8.3)	98.0 (1.0)
19 years	198	61.2 (6.2)	67.7 (7.7)	52.1 (7.1)	13.5 (3.3) [b]	56.1 (5.9)	85.4 (5.5) [c]
20 years	216	52.4 (5.4) [d]	59.3 (6.3)	55.3 (6.8)	26.4 (5.2)	58.2 (6.2)	91.5 (3.7)
21 years	74	76.1 (9.5)	71.5 (10.8)	50.4 (12.1)	41.1 (10.9)	34.7 (10.6)	99.2 (0.8)
Physical abuse							
Yes	213	* 54.6 (6.3)	61.5 (6.2)	* 57.3 (6.3)	25.5 (5.4)	54.6 (6.0)	89.1 (4.9)
No	358	72.0 (4.2)	65.8 (5.4)	56.7 (5.7)	22.9 (3.9)	55.6 (4.8)	93.3 (2.3)
Failure to supervise		*					
Yes	201	74.4 (4.9)	63.5 (7.5)	54.1 (7.2)	21.5 (4.8)	52.3 (6.0)	93.7 (2.6)
No	370	58.2 (5.3)	64.2 (5.4)	58.7 (4.7)	25.6 (4.3)	56.9 (4.3)	90.1 (3.6)
Ever placed out of home			*		**		
Yes	238	63.4 (7.0)	76.9 (5.1)	60.3 (7.0)	41.9 (6.4)	65.3 (5.2)	89.2 (4.1)
No	354	64.1 (4.8)	63.0 (4.4)	54.8 (4.3)	19.0 (3.3)	56.1 (4.0)	91.8 (2.8)

Note: All analyses are on weighted data; *Ns* are unweighted. Reported *Ns* vary slightly across analyses because of missing data in some variable categories. Pearson $\div^2$ tests for cluster samples were used for initial significance tests. No significant differences in the receipt of services were found by reported sexual abuse and failure to provide or by number of types of maltreatment. Asterisks indicate statistical significance (* $p < .05$, ** $p < .01$). Asterisks in column apply to the subsequent results for the covariate.

[a] Age 18 is significantly different from age 19 ($p < .01$) and 20 ($p < .001$).

[b] Age 19 is significantly different from age 20 ($p < .05$) and 21 ($p < .05$).

[c] Age 19 is significantly different from age 18 ($p < .05$) and 21 ($p < .05$).

[d] Age 20 is significantly different from age 21 ($p < .05$).

Exhibit 4-7 shows the receipt of education, independent-living, and job-related services by sex, race/ethnicity, and age. Female young adults (31.0%) were more likely than males

(13.0%) to receive housing services. Because female young adults are more likely than male young adults to be raising children, this finding is not surprising. Several differences were found by age. Eighteen-year-olds were more likely to report receiving support for educational issues than the oldest groups; 21-year-olds were more likely than the youngest groups to have received assistance with housing; and 19-year-olds were slightly less likely than the other age groups to have received any assistance. Young adults who were reported to child protective services (CPS) at baseline for physical abuse (54.6%) were less likely to receive support with educational issues than young adults reported for all other types of abuse (72.0%), while young adults who were reported to CPS at baseline for failure to supervise (74.4%) were more likely to receive help with education than young adults reported for all other types of abuse (58.2%). Young adults who were ever placed out of home between baseline and Wave 4 were more likely to receive assistance with job-related issues and housing (76.9% and 41.9%, respectively) than young adults who were never placed out of home (63.0% and 19.0%, respectively).

Services to Address Basic Needs

The Wave 5 young adults were asked about several services to address basic needs in the 12 months prior to interview. Some of these services include as a criteria for eligibility being a financially poor parent raising a child (TANF, or welfare benefits; WIC benefits), while other services are associated with poverty (food stamp benefits) or disability (SSI benefits). As reported in Chapter 3, 44.9% of female young adults and 26.3% of male young adults had a child. Of those who had a child, more than half were living below the poverty line, making many of them eligible for several federal services to meet basic needs. Most of the services shown in Exhibit 4-8 were more likely to be provided to female young adults, which is not surprising in that more females (87%) were raising a child than males. Among those with children, only female young adults received TANF or Welfare (26.6%), and 70.7% of female young adults received WIC.

Other services not restricted to those having children of their own were still more likely to be provided to female young adults than to males. Thus, 35.5% of female young adults received food stamps, compared with 4.8% of males; 10.3% of female young adults received SSI, compared with 2.7% of males; and, overall, 5 1.9% of female young adults received any federal service, compared with 9.0% of males. There were no significant differences in the receipt of services by age, but young adults of Hispanic ethnicity were more likely to receive any federal services than White young adults, which is consistent with information provided in Chapter 3 (Exhibit 3-2) that 60% of Hispanic young adults had a child. Receipt of federal services among female young adults was higher for all types of services as compared with national data from 2004. Thus, the percentage of female young adults with children and receiving TANF was higher than the national rate of 1.8% for the total U.S. population, and higher than the 14.3% for the population in poverty. The percentage of female young adults receiving food stamps was also higher than the national rate of 8.1%, but it was lower when compared with the receipt of food stamps among those Americans in poverty (64.4%). Receipt of SSI was higher than the national average for both sexes. Female young adults were receiving SSI at an especially high rate, several times higher than the national rate of 2.2% for adults aged 18 to 64 years (Administration on Children, Youth and Families [ACYF], 2006).

Exhibit 4-8. Young Adults' Use of Federal Services to Meet Basic Needs at Wave 5

	N (Min)	TANF or Welfare[a] % (SE)	WIC[a] % (SE)	Food Stamps % (SE)	SSI % (SE)	Any Federal Service
Total	616	19.3 (4.7)	51.7 (5.7)	23.1 (2.6)	7.2 (2.2)	34.6 (3.3)
Sex		***	***	***	*	***
Male	233	1.4 (1.4)	3.0 (1.6)	4.8 (1.8)	2.7 (0.9)	9.0 (2.3)
Female	387	26.6 (6.7)	70.7 (6.1)	35.5 (4.4)	10.3 (3.5)	51.9 (5.0)
Race/ ethnicity						*
Black	184	14.6 (5.3)	36.1 (12.2)	20.2 (5.3)	7.4 (3.8)	31.7 (6.0)
White	294	16.4 (6.2)	47.6 (9.4)	18.4 (3.6)	6.1 (2.4)	27.0 (4.9)
Hispanic	84	34.0 (13.9)	79.3 (14.1)	47.2 (10.2)	5.8 (3.8)	62.5 (9.6)[b]
Other	54	5.8 (4.1)	45.9 (18.1)	24.8 (8.4)	18.6 (15.5)	51.8 (12.2)
Age						
18 years	130	25.5 (7.2)	53.2 (23.0)	17.0 (5.1)	17.0 (7.3)	36.4 (8.2)
19 years	198	28.3 (10.5)	76.3 (7.0)	17.1 (4.1)	5.2 (3.5)	27.7 (5.2)
20 years	215	15.2 (5.5)	44.4 (8.3)	29.0 (5.4)	3.0 (0.9)	38.7 (5.8)
21 years	75	22.9 (15.7)	55.5 (17.2)	29.4 (9.9)	10.8 (8.7)	35.3 (10.1)

Note: All analyses are on weighted data; *Ns* are unweighted. Reported *Ns* vary slightly across analyses because of missing data in some variable categories. Pearson $\div^2$ tests for cluster samples were used for initial significance tests. No significant differences in the receipt of services were found by type of maltreatment at baseline, by number of types of maltreatment, or by ever living out of home during adolescence. Asterisks indicate statistical significance (*$p < .05$, ** $p < .01$, ***$p < .001$). Asterisks in column apply to the subsequent results for the covariate. TANF = Temporary Assistance for Needy Families. WIC = Special Supplemental Nutritional Program for Women, Infants, and Children. SSI = Supplemental Security Income.

[a] Asked only of those who had children, n = 221.

[b] Hispanic is significantly different from White at $p < .01$.

In summary, more than a third of young adults were receiving some type of services to address basic needs. The services most commonly received by young adults in the 12 months preceding the interview were food services (WIC and food stamps). About a quarter of female young adults were receiving TANF, while about 10% of female young adults were receiving SSI.

Conclusion

Young adults who were maltreated during their childhood or adolescence constitute a vulnerable population in need of multiple services. Society demands much of young adults and, to a large degree, makes them legally accountable for their actions after age 18. In the face of these multiple demands, adequate health and behavioral health services, independent-living services, and services to meet basic family needs could only help to facilitate a successful transition to adulthood. As described in Chapter 3, the great majority of young adults are making an effort to integrate into society; many are working or are taking care of their young children (or both) and are learning to take care of themselves.

A positive finding in this chapter is that many young adults are safeguarding their physical health: at least half of young adults had a physical checkup in the 12 months prior to interview, even if they did not have health insurance. A second promising finding in this chapter is that need for services for a serious accident or injury was similar to national rates, indicating that young adults are no more prone than other people the same age to be afflicted by these problems. Lack of health insurance was a barrier for some types of health services. Being uninsured did increase the likelihood that young adults would describe themselves as lacking a usual place to receive health services; being uninsured also decreased the likelihood that they would report having recently received dental care. These services may each play a critical role in the prevention of future health problems.

Many young adults had mental health needs, while few received mental health services. Almost half of the young adults had mental health problems, but only one third of young adults in need of mental health services received some type of service. This percentage was lower than national rates of service receipt among U.S. adults with mental health problems (41%; Wang et al., 2005). Levels of unmet mental health needs are particularly concerning for female young adults, for whom rates of depression (27.5%) and other mental health problems (52.8%) may prove particularly detrimental to raising children. Previous studies have shown that parental depression often manifests as insensitivity and unavailability to the child, which can disrupt bonding, impede quality of care, and escalate negative interactions (yelling, spanking, and showing annoyance with the child) that can ultimately devolve into child maltreatment (Cassell & Coleman, 1995; Cohn, Matias, Tronick, Connell, & Lyons-Ruth, 1986; Lyons-Ruth, Wolfe, & Lyubchik, 2000). Other parental mental health problems have also been associated with child maltreatment, making it especially critical to help young adults access needed services as a means to interrupt the intergenerational transmission of violence and other developmental risks (Barnett, Miller-Perrin, & Perrin, 1997).

More promising in this chapter is the finding that among the few young adults with substance dependence problems, more than half received some services, which is several times higher than national estimates among adults with substance abuse problems (10%; SAMHSA, OAS, 2005). This finding requires further exploration to determine if the severity of the problem explains higher rates of service receipt, given that the measure used in this study identified only those with substance dependence while other national studies may include those with substance abuse behavior but not dependence.

As with history of maltreatment during childhood, young adults are at risk of poor outcomes due to current violence. It is sobering that, although about a quarter of female young adults were victims of physical abuse by an intimate partner in the 12 months preceding the interview, only a few received any domestic violence services. Future research should explore barriers to accessing domestic violence services, as well as barriers to needed mental and physical health care.

Among the positive findings of this chapter is the help that young adults have received in areas that are critical for their transition to adulthood—like education, job, management of personal finances, housing, and daily living. Most of the help in these areas was received from biological parents, or other original family members, and the school system; a small group received them through independent-living skills programs. The high percentage (more than 90%) that received help in at least one area, as well as the fact that most received help from their original families and schools, is a sign that they have maintained a needed level of connectedness with significant adults at least during adolescence and part of young adulthood. As reported in Chapter 3, more than half of young adults were still living with an adult that could be considered a caregiver; family members reportedly provided support or help in many of the areas that are critical for the transition to adulthood. Future research should explore the role that parents, relatives, and others can play in facilitating the transition to adulthood and how they can be involved in case planning or service provision.

Another important finding in this chapter is that young adults were receiving both federal and family support services to help meet their basic needs during this critical developmental period. A relatively high percentage of young adults, especially females with children, were receiving help through federal programs designed to help a family meet its basic needs. Rates of this type of federal service use were higher than rates found for use across the nation (ACYF, 2006). Although this assistance may be considered a negative outcome reflecting lack of autonomy and cost to society (Cook et al., 1992), receiving federal assistance may help this vulnerable population transition to adulthood with less difficulty than it otherwise would. Future research should explore the level of contact of young adults not in foster care with the CWS and should determine what type and level of contact is recommended to facilitate access to services that can help the transition to adulthood.

This Wave 5 follow-up on young adults identified by the CWS for maltreatment when they were adolescents indicates that a substantial proportion of these adults have needs related to physical health, mental health, domestic violence, and daily living. Although some have received necessary services, many have not. There were substantial unmet needs for services, especially for services related to mental health. These unmet needs may be exacerbated by the lack of health insurance coverage for many or generally by the complexities of navigating new service systems targeting adults. Future research should explore how this vulnerable population can be better helped to access needed services.

5. YOUNG ADULT PARENTS RAISING CHILDREN

The previous chapters described the health and well-being, transition to adulthood, and service utilization patterns of young adults reported for maltreatment during adolescence. As noted in Chapter 3, more than a third (37.4%) of the young adults reported having at least one child; 29.0% of young adults reported currently living with one of their children at Wave 5. This chapter is meant to supplement findings from Chapters 2 to 4 by reexamining several core aspects of well-being, young adult developmental milestones, and service use for the subpopulation of young adults reported to be currently living with one of their children at Wave 5. The following section of this chapter describes outcomes for young adult parents across key indicators of well-being (e.g., depression), transition-to-adulthood milestones (e.g., employment), and use of federal services (e.g., food stamps) that might be of particular relevance to young adult parents and their children.

Young adult parents with an adolescent history of child welfare system (CWS) involvement are of particular public health interest. For this report, they are interesting largely because of their especially high prevalence in this population of young adults. In a broader child welfare context, they may be of interest because of public concerns that individuals who were abused as children will be more likely than those without a history of childhood abuse to maltreat their own offspring. However, scientific findings to support this concern are mixed and confounded by poor methodology (Ozturk, Leventhal, & Dobbs, 2000). Research appears to support the concern that the prevalence of environmental or personal risk factors increases the likelihood that this intergenerational transmission of abuse will occur. For instance, one recent study found that becoming a parent before reaching 21 years of age, having a history of mental illness or depression, and living with a violent partner were all positively associated with child maltreatment among parents who were abused as children (Dixon, Browne, & HamiltonGiachritsis, 2005). Consequently, raising a child in environmental or personal stress—for example, poverty or low social support—likely increases personal or family hardships. Such stressors may in themselves increase the potential risk of future child maltreatment. Analyses in Chapter 5 cover the following issues:

1. demographic characteristics of young adult parents raising children;
2. parental mental health, trauma, and experiences of domestic violence;
3. discipline strategies;
4. social support;
5. financial resources and job status; and
6. services to address basic needs.

The chapter's key findings as related to the key characteristics of young adult parents living with their children at Wave 5 are as follows:

- Young adult parents demonstrated many behavioral health risks: – 22.2% reported signs of clinical depression;
    - 5.8% reported clinically significant dissociative symptoms, and 16.2% reported intrusive experiences associated with past trauma; and
    - 16.3% of mothers reported having experienced an incident of severe physical domestic violence in the 12 months prior to interview.
- When asked about disciplinary techniques,
    - 50.6% of young adult parents reported using some form of psychological aggression (e.g., shouting or threatening to spank) with their child;
    - 55.6% reported the use of minor physical assault or corporal punishment (e.g., spanking on the bottom with a bare hand);
    - 5.2% reported some type of severe assault against their child (e.g., kicking, or threatening with a knife or gun); and
    - 16.5% reported some form of neglect in the year prior to interview.
- Nearly 60% (59.1%) of young adult parents were living in households where the income was below 100% of the federal poverty level; 61.8% of young adult mothers were living in poverty.
- Half of young adult parents were currently employed full or part time. These working parents worked, on average, 36 hours per week.
- Many young adult parents reported receiving federal services to meet their family's basic living needs: 66.4% received benefits from the Special Supplemental Nutrition Program for Women, Infants, and Children (WIC), and 57.1% received food stamps;

27.0% of young adult mothers received Temporary Assistance for Needy Families (TANF) or welfare.

Exhibit 5-1. Characteristics of Young Adults Raising Children (*N* = 176) at Wave 5

	N	% (SE)
Sex		
Male	25	12.7 (4.2)
Female	151	87.3 (4.2)
Race/ethnicity		
Black	42	16.8 (5.2)
White	88	50.5 (7.0)
Hispanic	30	27.4 (6.6)
Other	15	5.4 (2.3)
Age		
18 years	21	7.9 (2.6)
19 years	50	18.1 (4.5)
20 years	79	60.9 (7.2)
21 years	26	13.1 (4.1)
Marital status		
Married	30	27.3 (8.1)
Unmarried, divorced, or separated	146	72.7 (8.1)
Living situation[a]		
Living with caregiver[b]	67	38.0 (7.2)
Living with spouse or significant other	74	44.1 (7.7)
Living alone with son or daughter	20	10.7 (5.0)
Other living arrangement	15	7.2 (2.9)
Reported maltreatment at baseline[c]		
Physical maltreatment	57	39.0 (6.1)
Sexual abuse	46	25.6 (6.7)
Neglect—failure to provide	28	10.7 (3.6)
Neglect—failure to supervise	60	33.2 (5.7)
Ever placed out of home in adolescence	70	13.2 (3.0)

Note: All analyses are on weighted data; *Ns* are unweighted.

[a] "Living situation" is a derived variable based on a young adult's report of who is living in his or her household at the time of the Wave 5 interview. Living situation categories are mutually exclusive and hierarchical. For instance, those living with a spouse or significant other are not living with a caregiver.

[b] "Living with caregiver" indicates that a young adult reported living with at least one of the following: biological parent, adoptive parent, foster parent, grandparent, aunt/uncle, or stepparent.

[c] "Reported maltreatment at baseline" refers to the index maltreatment incident recorded at baseline. Types of maltreatment are not independent of one another. An individual could have been reported for multiple types of maltreatment. Type of maltreatment here refers to whether a particular type of maltreatment was reported (e.g., physical maltreatment "yes" or "no").

Demographic Characteristics

Exhibit 5-1 gives an overview of the sociodemographic characteristics of young adults who were currently living with one or more of their children at the Wave 5 interview. Most were females (87.3%). Approximately half were White (50.5%), 27.4% were Hispanic, 16.8% were Black, and 5.4% described their race/ethnicity as "Other." The majority were 20 years old (60.9%) and unmarried (72.7%). Most young adult parents (44.1%) reported that they were living with a spouse or significant other at the Wave 5 interview, 3 8.0% were living with a caregiver at the Wave 5 interview (3 8.0%), and 10.7% were living alone with their child. Only a few, 6.7%, were living with a caregiver and a spouse or partner.

Parental Mental Health, Trauma, and Experiences of Domestic Violence

Symptoms of clinical depression were measured with the Composite International Diagnostic Interview Short Form (CIDI-SF; Kessler, Andrews, Mroczek, Ustun, & Wittchen, 1998) and were analyzed consistently with depression findings from Chapter 2. The proportion of young adult parents with a score in the clinical range for major depression was 22% for all young adult parents and 24% for mothers (Exhibit 5-2). These rates of depression were slightly lower among young adult parents than among all young adults in the NSCAW sample (27.5% of all young adults, 31.5% of all female young adults); however, the rate of depression among young adult parents was higher than that found among all U.S. adults aged 18 to 24 (6.7% depression in past year; Kessler, Chiu, Demler, & Walters, 2005).

Trauma among young adult parents was measured with two scales of the Trauma Symptom Inventory (Briere, 1996). The scales measured intrusive symptoms associated with post-traumatic stress (such as flashbacks or nightmares) and dissociative symptoms (such as depersonalization or out-of-body experiences). Exhibit 5-2 describes levels of traumatic stress symptoms among young adult parents: 16.2% of young adult parents and 18.5% of young adult mothers had experienced intrusive experiences; 5.8% of young adult parents and 6.7% of young adult mothers had experienced dissociation. The percentage of young adult parents reporting intrusive experiences was slightly higher than that for all young adults; 12.1% of all female young adults had experienced intrusive symptoms (see Chapter 2). Rates of dissociation among young adult parents were similar to those for all young adults. Rates of traumatic stress symptoms among young adult parents were substantially higher, however, than national estimates of post-traumatic stress disorder among all U.S. adults aged 18 years or older (Kessler et al., 2005).

Using the Conflict Tactics Scale (Straus, 1979), young adult mothers reported on their experiences of severe and less severe physical intimate-partner violence (see Exhibit 5-2). Among this group, 16.3% reported having experienced any severe physical violence in the 12 months prior to interview. Severe physical violence included reports of being kicked, hit with a fist, beaten up, choked, or threatened with a knife or gun. Although rates of intimate-partner violence in the 12 months prior to interview were lower among young adult mothers than among all female young adults, they were substantially higher than the rates for all U.S. females aged 18 years or older (Tjaden & Thoennes, 2000).

Exhibit 5-2. Depression, Trauma, and Domestic Violence Among Young Adults Raising Children at Wave 5

	N (Min)	Depression[a] % (SE)	Trauma Intrusive Experiences[b] % (SE)	Trauma Dissociation % (SE)	Experienced Any Severe Physical Violence in Past 12 Months[c] % (SE)
Total	176	22.2 (6.1)	16.2 (6.4)	5.8 (3.5)	NA
Sex					
Male	25	9.0 (8.8)	0.0 (NA)	0.0 (NA)	NA
Female	151	24.1 (6.6)	18.5 (7.2)	6.7 (3.9)	16.3 (5.1)

Note: All analyses are on weighted data; *Ns* are unweighted. Pearson $\div^2$ tests for cluster samples were used for initial significance tests related to categorical variables. No significant differences were found for race/ethnicity or age. Because of insignificant findings and small sample sizes across many cells, these results are not presented in the exhibit. NA = not applicable.

[a] Rates of depression were calculated according to young adult responses on the Composite International Diagnostic Interview Short Form (CIDI-SF; Kessler, Andrews, Mroczek, Ustun, & Wittchen, 1998). To meet diagnostic criteria for depression, a young adult needed to report three or more depression symptoms in the 12 months prior to interview and endorse all questions related to any one of the following: having a dysphoric mood, having 2 or more weeks of anhedonia, or using medication for depression.

[b] Intrusive experiences and dissociation related to trauma were measured with use of the Trauma Symptom Inventory (Briere, 1996). Intrusive experiences include flashbacks, nightmares, or intrusive thoughts. Dissociation includes depersonalization, derealization, out-of-body experiences, and psychic numbing.

[c] Domestic violence was measured by the Conflict Tactics Scale. "Any severe physical violence in the 12 months prior to interview" included reports of being kicked or hit with a fist, beaten up, choked, or threatened with a knife or gun. This scale was administered only to female young adults at the Wave 5 interview.

Discipline Strategies

The young adult interview asked parents living with their children to describe disciplinary strategies, particularly their use of aggression toward and neglect of their children, using the Conflict Tactics Scale–Parent-Child Version (CTS-PC; Straus, Hamby, Finkelhor, Moore, & Runyan, 1998; see Technical Appendix). These parents were asked about the tactics they used in their conflicts with their children. Included were both nonviolent disciplinary tactics and tactics that were mildly or seriously aggressive (ranging from spanking to hitting, slapping, and injurious actions). The CTS-PC also asked about neglect.

Exhibit 5-3 presents the proportion of young adult parents who used each type of tactic in the year prior to interview, by selected characteristics. Most (85.6%) reported having used some form of nonviolent discipline. Nonviolent discipline included explaining why something was wrong, putting the child in "time out," or sending the child to his or her room. The use of psychological aggression was reported by 50.6% of young adult parents. Psychological aggression included shouting, yelling, or screaming at the child or threatening to spank the child. Nearly 55.6% of young adult parents reported using minor physical assault or corporal punishment with their child. Minor physical assault included disciplinary techniques such as spanking on the bottom with a bare hand or slapping on the hand, arm, or leg. The proportion of young adult parents reporting any type of severe assault was 5.2%. Approximately 16.5% of young adult parents reported some form of neglect in the year prior to interview—primarily that they were "so caught up with problems" that they were not able to show or tell their child that they loved him or her. Some young adults reported an inability to access needed health care or provide needed food for their child.

Exhibit 5-3. Discipline Strategies Among Young Adult Parents Raising Children at Wave 5

	N (Min)	Nonviolent Discipline % (SE)	Psychological Aggression % (SE)	Minor Assault/ Corporal Punishment % (SE)	Severe Physical Assault % (SE)	Neglect % (SE)
Total	162	85.6 (3.7)	50.6 (6.8)	55.6 (6.7)	5.2 (3.4)	16.5(5.3)
Sex						
Male	23	85.3 (9.4)	35.7 (21.0)	58.8 (18.3)	28.7 (22.2)	7.3(4.9)
Female	139	85.6 (4.0)	52.6 (6.7)	55.1 (7.4)	2.1 (1.1)	17.8(6.0)

Note: All analyses are on weighted data; *Ns* are unweighted. Reported *Ns* vary slightly across analyses because of missing data in some variable categories. Pearson $÷^{2}$ tests for cluster samples were used for initial significance tests and for subsequent pairwise contrasts when warranted. Cells were left empty when sample sizes were too small to be meaningfully reported. There were no differences by age; consequently, results are not presented in the exhibit. Asterisks indicate statistical significance (** $p < .0\ 1$). Asterisks in column apply to the subsequent results for the covariate.

Social Support

Young adults living with their children were asked about the number of people available to them for confidant support (e.g., being invited out for activities, receiving advice about money, or receiving advice about "important things in life") or instrumental support (e.g., being given assistance with child care, transportation, care when sick, cooking, or housework). Young adults were also asked about their degree of satisfaction with this support (across a 4-point scale ranging from 1 for *very dissatisfied* to 4 for *very satisfied*).

Young adult parents reported feeling moderately satisfied with the degree of social support they received from individuals to help with a variety of activities (Exhibit 5-4). Very few differences were found in their ratings of satisfaction with different types of social support. Young adults reported that they had, on average, 4.5 people who offered them chances to talk about money or budgeting. They indicated that they had, on average, 5.1 people available to help them take care of their children, 1.8 people who could give them useful advice about "important things in life," and 1.9 people who could help them when they were sick. Among young adult parents, 23.5% reported that they had no one to offer them opportunities to talk about budgeting, and 19.5% had no one to help them when they were sick.

Exhibit 5-4. Social Support Among Young Adult Parents Raising Children at Wave 5

	None % (SE)	1–3 People % (SE)	4 or More People % (SE)	Average Number of People Mean (SD)	Average Satisfaction Mean (SD)
Confidant support					
People who invite you out to do things	3.7 (2.0)	42.6 (6.9)	53.7 (7.1)	5.7 (0.7)	3.3 (0.1)
People who offer chances to talk about money/budgeting	23.5 (6.6)	66.2 (7.3)	10.3 (4.0)	4.5 (0.6)	3.7 (0.1)
People who give you useful advice about important things in life	12.4 (6.1)	40.4 (6.9)	47.2 (6.9)	1.8 (0.2)	3.0 (0.1)
Instrumental support					
People who help you take care of your children (marked as "not applicable" for those who did not have children)	–	51.0 (6.7)	47.8 (6.8)	5.1 (0.8)	3.1 (0.2)
People who offer help with transportation	6.7 (2.4)	71.1 (5.7)	22.2 (5.4)	2.9 (0.3)	3.2 (0.1)
People who give you help when you're sick in bed	19.5 (5.9)	68.0 (6.0)	12.5 (3.8)	1.9 (0.3)	3.1 (0.1)
People who give you help with cooking and housework	17.7 (5.1)	67.2 (7.3)	15.1 (5.8)	1.7 (0.3)	3.3 (0.1)

Note: All analyses are on weighted data; *Ns* are unweighted. Reported *Ns* vary slightly across analyses because of missing data in some variable categories. There were no statistically significant differences on reports of social support by young adult parents across sex, race/ethnicity, or age.

Financial Resources and Job Status

Many young adults raising children (59.1%) reported living in households with incomes below the federal poverty level. Young adult mothers were significantly more likely to be living in poor households: 61.8% of mothers were raising their children in households below the federal poverty level, compared with 37.2% of female young adults who did not have children. No differences by race/ethnicity were found in the percentage of young adult parents with incomes below the federal poverty level. The average weekly household income for a young adult parent was $394.10 (compared with $551.30 for all young adults at Wave 5).

Approximately half of young adult parents were working either full or part time. On average these working parents worked 36.2 hours per week. These findings were not substantially different from those found for all young adults at Wave 5. There were no differences by sex among young adult parents in job status or number of hours worked (Exhibit 5-5).

Exhibit 5-5. Job Status and Financial Resources of Young Adults Raising Children at Wave 5

	Household Poverty Status[a]		Weekly Household Income[b]		Currently Employed Full or Part Time		Number of Hours Worked per Week[c]	
	N	% (SE)	*N*	Mean (SD)	*N*	% (SE)	*N*	Mean (SD)
Total	163	59.1 (6.1)	163	$394.1 (34.0)	176	50.2 (7.3)	76	36.2 (3.5)
Sex								
Male	25	42.5 (19.0)	25	395.6 (63.8)	25	61.6 (19.1)	18	32.3 (8.3)
Female	138	61.8 (6.0)	138	393.8 (38.3)	151	48.6 (7.4)	58	36.9 (3.6)

Note: All analyses are on weighted data; *Ns* are unweighted. Reported *Ns* vary slightly across analyses because of missing data in some variable categories. There were no differences in variables by age in years at Wave 5; consequently, results are not presented in the exhibit.

[a] "Household poverty status" represents the percentage of young adult households living below the federal poverty level. Household income is based on the combined income for all members of any given household, divided by the number of individuals who depend on that income.

[b] "Weekly household income" is a derived variable that represents the approximate dollars earned by a young adult's household per week across the course of the 12 months prior to interview. Young adults were asked to estimate the total combined income of their household over the 12 months prior to interview. Young adults could answer with estimates of income daily, weekly, or annually across 11 income ranges. Respondents cited the range and did not provide an exact dollar amount. On the basis of this response, a midpoint of the weekly salary range was assigned for each of the wage categories.

[c] "Number of hours worked per week" was calculated only for those who reported themselves to be currently employed on a full- or part-time basis.

Services to Address Basic Needs

Young adult parents were asked about having received several services to assist in meeting basic family needs in the 12 months prior to interview. For some of these services (e.g., TANF, welfare, or WIC benefits), one criterion for eligibility is having low income and raising a child; other services are associated with low income (such as food stamps) or having a disability (such as Supplemental Security Income [SSI] benefits). Most young adult parents had low income and, thus, were eligible for several of these federal services to meet basic needs.

Among young adult mothers, 27.0% received TANF or welfare (Exhibit 5-6), and 70.4% received WIC benefits. More than half (57.1%) of young adult parents and 62.9% of mothers reported receipt of food stamps. About 6.5% of young adult parents and 7.3% of young adult mothers reported having received SSI. Receipt of federal services among female young adults was higher for all types of services as compared with national data from 2004; the percentage of young adult mothers receiving TANF was higher than the national rate of 1.8% for all persons in the U.S. population and higher than the rate of 14.3% for all persons in the U.S. population living in poverty (Administration on Children, Youth and Families, 2006).

Conclusion

This chapter has focused on characteristics of young adult parents because of their importance to child welfare and the added challenges that parenting might bring to the transition to adulthood. Although young adult parents were not typically more likely than other young adults in NSCAW at Wave 5 to suffer symptoms of depression or to experience traumatic stress or domestic violence, they were much more likely to have these experiences than their normative peers. Over 20% reported signs of clinical depression, 5.8% reported clinically significant dissociative symptoms, and 16.2% reported intrusive experiences associated with past trauma. In addition, 6.3% of mothers reported having experienced an incident of severe physical domestic violence in the 12 months prior to interview. Although half of young adult parents were working, they were at particular risk of living in poverty. Among young adult mothers, more than 60% reported living in households below the federal poverty level. Many young adult parents (75.8%) reported receiving some type of federal aid in the year prior to interview to help support the basic needs of their families.

Exhibit 5-6. Use of Federal Services to Meet Basic Needs Among Young Adult Parents Raising Children at Wave 5

	N (Min)	TANF or Welfare % (SE)	WIC % (SE)	Food Stamps % (SE)	SSI % (SE)	Any Federal Service % (SE)
Total	176	24.1 (6.1)	66.4 (6.4)	57.1 (6.5)	6.5 (3.4)	75.8 (6.5)
Sex						
Male	25	3.9 (4.0)	12.1 (8.4)	17.4 (10.5)	0.9 (1.0)	24.8 (12.7)
Female	148	27.0 (7.0)	74.4 (6.5)	62.9 (7.3)	7.3 (3.8)	83.3 (6.7)

Note: All analyses are on weighted data; *Ns* are unweighted. Reported *Ns* vary slightly across analyses because of missing data in some variable categories. Pearson ÷^{2} tests for cluster samples were used for initial significance tests. No differences by race/ethnicity, age, or household poverty status were found; consequently, results are not presented in this exhibit. Cells were left empty when sample sizes were too small to be reported (ii < 9 cases). TANF = Temporary Assistance for Needy Families. WIC = Special Supplemental Nutrition Program for Women, Infants, and Children. SSI = Supplemental Security Income.

At Wave 5 young adult parents did not report substantially high rates of severe physical assault or neglect of their own children. About half of young adults raising children reported having used psychologically aggressive discipline tactics (e.g., shouting, yelling, or screaming at a child) in the year prior to interview, and 55.6% reported having used corporal punishment. Much lower proportions reported any type of severe physical assault (5.2%), while 16.5% reported some form of neglect in the year prior to interview. However, young adult parents were found to have a number of environmental risk factors (e.g., living in poverty) and personal risk factors (e.g., depression), which have been demonstrated to increase the risk of maltreatment (Dixon et al., 2005). The findings from this chapter indicate that some young adults may be at risk for the future maltreatment of their children; therefore, availability of both formal (e.g., federal services) and informal (e.g., continued contact with foster or biological family) supports may help to facilitate healthy child and family development and potentially help mediate future maltreatment.

6. CONCLUSIONS

This report has provided information about a nationally representative sample of 620 young adults who were adolescents (12 to 15 years old) when they became involved in the study's index investigation of child abuse or neglect. Now, 6 to 7 years after the index investigation, these young adults are 18 to 21 years old. The purpose of this report has been to describe the well-being, early-adulthood developmental milestones, and service needs of young adults who were involved with the child welfare system (CWS) in adolescence.

The transition to adulthood is a critical time in life, one in which young adults need to juggle several developmental tasks, including learning to live independently, to support themselves financially, to maintain significant relationships, and, in many cases, to raise their own children. For many of the young adults in this report, successful completion of the developmental milestones of young adulthood may have been complicated by the experience of maltreatment during adolescence. Previous research has found that the effects of experiencing abuse during childhood or adolescence extend over the course of an individual's life. Maltreatment during adolescence can affect many aspects of a young adult's life, including his or her physical health, mental health, behavior, academic performance, interpersonal relationships, and parenting. As these young adults become parents, there is the added concern that a new generation of children are placed in high-risk environments.

Transitioning into young adulthood also brings with it the need to navigate changes in service system infrastructure, which means moving away from a child-oriented system into an adult-oriented one. Unlike many children's services, adult service systems are not intrinsically developed to support individuals with histories of maltreatment. Health services and other adult systems (e.g., correctional facilities, federal programs) are very different from their counterparts in the child system. By entering adulthood, young adults may lose the potential safety net that the school system, CWS, or pediatric health services represent. Independently navigating a different and likely confusing social services system, young adults may be at increased risk for negative developmental outcomes.

Chapter 1 of this report provided background information on the young adults as adolescents at baseline. The most common type of abuse for which adolescents were reported to child protective services was physical abuse (31.9%), followed by failure to supervise (29.1%), sexual abuse (14.5%), failure to provide (9.5%), and emotional abuse (7.2%). Slightly more than a quarter of the cases were substantiated. According to caseworker reports, more than half of the families had prior CWS reports of maltreatment. Caseworkers described many of the families at baseline as confronting a wide range of risks, including poor parenting skills, a history of domestic violence, mental health problems, and a history of abuse or neglect from the primary caregiver. Between baseline and Wave 4, less than a fifth of adolescents were placed in out-ofhome care, and the majority of adolescents remained at home with their biological parents.

Chapter 2 presented information on the well-being of young adults at Wave 5. In general, these young adults were faring more poorly than young adults nationally for nearly all indicators of well-being. Although the majority of young adults reported being in good physical health, the proportion was lower than that of adults nationally who report being in good health (Pleis & Lethbridge-Cejku, 2006). Males reported better health than females. Nearly a third of young adults reported that they had a health condition that currently limited them in some way. The most common such conditions were weight problems, migraine, back or neck problems, and asthma. More than a third of young adults reported having experienced some type of injury or accident during the 12 months prior to interview. The most common injuries were a bad cut or scrape and a bad sprain or torn ligament.

Young adults were particularly at risk for poor health. One critical risk factor for health problems was being overweight or obese, and more than half of young adults were either overweight or obese. The high prevalence of weight problems was consistent with information about low consumption of fruits and vegetables and limited physical activity among young adults, suggesting that they may be at high risk for chronic disease later in life. Additionally, the high number of reported sexual partners also increases the risk of sexually transmitted infections.

Mental health, depression, trauma, and problem behaviors were more prevalent for young adults at Wave 5 than at the national level for young adults of a similar age. More than a quarter of young adults had a score in the clinical range for major depression in the 12 months prior to interview, almost three times as high as national data for adults 18 years or older (Kessler, Chiu, Demler, & Walters, 2005). Trauma symptoms were also much higher than national rates of post- traumatic stress disorder. Substance dependence was the only indicator of well-being for which young adults did not fare substantially worse than young adults nationally. Overall, almost half of young adults were determined to have at least one mental health problem, which is almost double the national 12-month estimates for any mental disorder for adults 18 years or older (Kessler et al., 2005) but somewhat similar to previous studies based on young adults with a history of reports or placements in the CWS (McMillen, 2005; Spatz Widom, DuMont, & Czaja, 2007).

Others areas of well-being also showed troubling results. The assessment of academic achievement found that young adults scored substantially below the normative mean in all categories. Nearly half of young adults had engaged in some illegal activity in the 6 months prior to interview, primarily public disorder. Furthermore, about a fifth of young adults were arrested in the year prior to interview, and about 1 in 10 were convicted of a crime.

Chapter 3 described the young adults' progress in the transition to adulthood. In part, that transition involved a young adult's residential independence, as well as the beginning of emotional and economic independence from caregivers. Young adults who had contact with the CWS in adolescence in many ways resembled all U.S. young adults. More than half remained living with their biological families through adolescence and were still living with a caregiver in early adulthood. About a third were married or cohabitating with a partner. Most had also entered the workforce. In two areas, however, young adults appeared to differ significantly from young adults in the general population: (1) almost a third of the young adults reported living with at least one child, compared with just 7% of all U.S. young adults, and (2) almost half of young adults and 59.1% of young adult parents were living below the federal poverty level, compared with 30% of all young adults in the United States. Thus, although young adults with a history of CWS involvement may have been trying to integrate into society, they were doing so with substantially fewer financial resources at their disposal. Furthermore, many were beginning this transition to adulthood having already begun one of the most complicated of adult roles and responsibilities, being a parent.

Chapter 4 described the services young adults received—an issue of critical importance, given the high level of needs noted in this report. Adequate health and behavioral health services, independent-living services, and services to meet basic family needs could only help to facilitate a successful transition to adulthood. More than a third of young adults who were reported to the CWS for maltreatment in adolescence had no health insurance, and they were less likely to have a usual place to receive health services than were all U.S. young adults. Receipt of mental health services was inadequate to fulfill the need: two thirds of those in need of mental health services did not receive any services. This percentage is even greater than levels of unmet need for mental health services reported nationally. In contrast to levels of unmet mental health service needs, more than half of young adults with substance dependence needs received substance abuse services, a level several times as high as national estimates. The levels of unmet service needs illustrate a missed opportunity to facilitate the transition of these at-risk young adults into a successful adulthood. Facilitating young adults' access to preventive, developmental, mental health, and vocational intervention services may be particularly critical for adolescents with a history of past CWS involvement.

Chapter 5 described some select indicators of well-being among young adult parents at Wave 5. Young adult parents demonstrated many behavioral health risks: 22.2% reported signs of clinical depression, 5.8% reported clinically significant dissociative symptoms (e.g., depersonalization, derealization, out-of-body experiences), and 16.2% reported intrusive experiences associated with past trauma. In addition, 6.3% of young adult mothers reported having experienced an incident of severe physical domestic violence in the 12 months prior to interview. Although young adult parents did not appear to have substantially more risk to their well-being than other young adults with a history of CWS involvement, they had substantially higher rates of mental health problems and traumatic stress than the general population. A particularly important finding was related to young adult parents' financial resources: they were especially likely to be living in poverty. For example, 61.8% of young adult mothers were living in a household whose income was below the federal poverty level. Young adult parents also reported on their own parenting behaviors. More than half of young adult parents reported using psychological aggression against their children; a similar proportion reported using minor physical assault or corporal punishment. Smaller proportions reported using severe assault (5.2%) or neglecting their children (16.5%).

Among the positive findings of this report was the help that young adults have received in areas critical to their transition to adulthood; for example, education, jobs, managing finances, housing, and daily living. Most of the help in these areas came from biological parents or other original family members and the school system, and, for a small group, through independent- living programs. A relatively high percentage of young adults, especially females with children, were also receiving help through federal programs designed to help families meet their basic needs. Rates of this type of federal services use were higher than rates found for use among all people in the U.S. population living in poverty.

Throughout the report, striking differences between males and females were a consistent theme. Six to 7 years after the index report of maltreatment, females were doing significantly worse than males in the areas of physical and mental health, whereas males were more likely than females to engage in criminal activity or be involved with the law and have a greater number of sexual partners. Females were also significantly more likely than males to report having a child, and they were more likely to be living in poverty. Levels of unmet mental health care needs for female young adults were particularly concerning. High rates of depression (24.1%) and other mental health problems among those young adult mothers raising children may prove particularly detrimental. Females were significantly more likely than males, however, to have health insurance, to receive preventive and curative health care, and to receive services to help meet basic needs.

More research on the NSCAW data can help explain and expand the findings in this report. Researchers can obtain NSCAW data from the National Data Archive on Child Abuse and Neglect at Cornell University (2007) to pursue questions that have been raised, particularly from the newly available Wave 5. The findings in this report lead to numerous research topics. The following list is illustrative and by no means exhaustive:

- Explore the effect of multiple family and environmental problems—including parental substance abuse, intimate-partner violence against female caregivers, poor parenting skills, and mental health problems—on adolescents' response to victimization when they reach adulthood.
- Analyze the comorbidity of disorders, particularly comorbidity of substance use and depression (or other symptoms of mental illness), and association between criminal activity and sexual risk taking.
- Examine relationships between well-being and traditional developmental milestones for young adults. For instance, study the effects of emotional and behavioral problems on educational attainment and job stability.
- Investigate the extent to which low levels of well-being among young adults are associated specifically with the experience of maltreatment, or are more a function of other environmental factors, such as living in poverty.
- Examine the potential mediating influence of service access upon trajectories of young adult well-being.
- Explore barriers to accessing needed mental and physical health care, as well as domestic violence services.
- Determine the influence that caregivers, relatives, and caseworkers play in facilitating a successful transition to adulthood.
- Explore the type and level of contact that young adults without histories of out-of-home placement have had with the CWS. Examine the degree to which this contact might differentiate young adult outcomes.

This report has provided a description of young adults who were adolescents when they experienced the index CWS maltreatment investigation. Six to 7 years after the index investigation, these adolescents were entering adulthood and working, and many were raising children. The challenges faced by these young adults were multiple, and the needs, particularly in the area of mental health, substantial. Many were also living in poverty. Other NSCAW reports describe children in other age groups entering the CWS and describe data about services received, well-being, and living stability. These reports, together with previous research, have highlighted that the risks associated with CWS involvement during childhood extend into adolescence and often adulthood. This report supports these previous findings and highlights the continued risks faced by those who experienced the index maltreatment report in adolescence. These risks may influence not only the young adults themselves but also their children. This report has shown the life outcomes and struggles of adolescents who come into contact with the child welfare system. Clearly, their struggles persist and merit the continued attention of researchers, clinicians, service system administrators, and policy makers.

TECHNICAL APPENDIX

Scales

Adult Self-Report

The Adult Self-Report (ASR) is a self-report scale completed by 18- to 59-year-olds to describe their own functioning. The ASR has items that "are designed to tap strengths and problems that are potentially relevant to a person's need for help" (Achenbach & Rescorla, 2003, p. 11). Items are on a 3-point Likert-type scale (0 = *not true,* 1 = *somewhat or sometimes true,* 2 = *very true or often true*). It contains 123 items; the problem scale is composed of eight syndromes (anxious/depressed, withdrawn, somatic complaints, thought problems, attention problems, aggressive behavior, rule-breaking behavior, and intrusive) and an Other Problem Behaviors category. Behaviors are also categorized as externalizing (containing the aggressive behavior, rule-breaking behavior, and intrusive syndromes) or internalizing (containing the anxious/depressed, withdrawn, and somatic complaints syndromes). A Total Problems score may be derived from the total of the syndromes and Other Problems items. The ASR can also be used to derive syndrome scales that are consistent with formal diagnostic systems, such as the fourth edition of the *Diagnostic and Statistical Manual of Mental Disorders* (American Psychiatric Association, 1994). Six *DSM-IV*–oriented scales are derived from the ASR (Depressive Problems, Anxiety Problems, Somatic Problems, Avoidant Personality Problems, ADHD Problems, Antisocial Personality Problems). *DSM* categories were derived from the selections that an international panel of psychiatrists and psychologists rated as being very consistent with particular *DSM-IV* diagnostic categories. A high score on a particular *DSM*oriented scale is suggestive of meeting criteria for any diagnoses that correspond to that scale (Achenbach & Rescorla, 2003).

The problem syndromes were normed by sex and age (18 to 35, or 36 to 59), using a nationally representative sample of 2,020 United States adult residents aged 18 to 59 with no major physical disabilities or mental retardation (Achenbach & Rescorla, 2003). Cronbach's alpha ranged from .78 for Somatic Complaints to .94 for Total Problems.

Young adults classified as having clinical/borderline problem behaviors had scores above 63 on at least 1 of the Externalizing, Internalizing, or Total Problems Scales.

Composite International Diagnostic Interview Short Form (Mental Health)

The Composite International Diagnostic Interview Short Form (CIDI-SF–Mental Health) is a highly standardized interview that screens for mental health and substance use disorders, using the criteria established in the third, revised, edition of the *Diagnostic and Statistical Manual of Mental Disorders* (American Psychiatric Association, 1987). The full instrument evaluates the presence of eight disorders: major depression, generalized anxiety, specific phobia, social phobia, agoraphobia, panic attack, alcohol dependence, and drug dependence. For this study, only the sections on major depression, alcohol dependence, and drug dependence were administered. Questions are scripted to ask about the previous 12-month period (Kessler, Andrews, Mroczek, Ustun, & Wittchen, 1998), the section on depression was administered by in- person interview, whereas the sections on alcohol and drug dependence were administered by audio computer-assisted self-interviewing (ACASI). The CIDI-SF version used in NSCAW does not indicate comorbidity with other disorders, nor does it differentiate between depression occurring as a primary diagnosis or in the context of other disorders such as bipolar disorder or schizoaffective disorder.

For alcohol, respondents scored in the dependence range if (1) they indicated that they had consumed four or more drinks in a single day at least once during the year prior to interview, and (2) they reported at least three of the seven *DSM-III-R* symptoms of dependence. For drugs, respondents scored in the dependence range if (1) they indicated that they had used any of a variety of substances "on their own" (without a doctor's prescription, in larger amounts than prescribed, or for a longer period than prescribed) during the year prior to interview, and (2) they reported at least three of the seven *DSM-III-R* symptoms of dependence.

Conflict Tactics Scale

The Conflict Tactics Scale (CTS1) is a self-report or interview measure designed to assess the overt means by which family members respond to conflicts (Straus, 1979). CTS1 's physical violence scale was used to assess female young adults' experiences with intimate-partner violence. This measure is divided into minor and severe subscales based on the severity of the violent act. The minor violence items include being pushed, grabbed, shoved, or slapped, whereas the severe violence items inquire about experiences that include being choked, beaten, and threatened with a knife or gun. Response categories range from 0 (*never*) to 6 (*more than 20 times*), indicating the frequency of occurrence of the violent acts in the preceding 12 months. For events that did not occur in the previous 12 months, the respondent is asked to indicate if they have ever happened.

CTS1 has been used in national surveys of intimate-partner violence and is the most frequently employed and thoroughly validated measure of intimate-partner violence. The reliability ($\alpha = 0.88$) and validity of the physical violence section of CTS1 have been well documented (Straus, 1979). The violence items have face or content validity because they all describe acts of actual physical force being used by one family member on another.

Parent-Child Conflict Tactics Scales

The Parent-Child Conflict Tactics Scales (CTS- PC) were developed to measure psychological and physical maltreatment and neglect by parents, as well as nonviolent modes of discipline. CTS-PC scales include nonviolent discipline (e.g., putting a child in "time out"), psychological aggression (e.g., shouting, yelling, or screaming at a child; physical assault, and neglect; Straus, Hamby, Finkelhor, Moore, & Runyan,1998). Because items in the physical assault scale range widely in severity, from spanking to burning a child intentionally, the scale may be divided into subscales for minor, severe, and very severe physical assault. In NSCAW, parental reports on the CTS-PC measures were obtained from permanent caregivers, including biological parents, adoptive parents, and other in-home caregivers, but excluding foster parents and other out-of-home caregivers. In this report, we present findings from the nonviolent discipline, psychological aggression, and neglect scales, as well as the physical assault subscales. Measures shown are annual and lifetime prevalence and year chronicity for each scale and each item in each scale. Annual prevalence for each item is the percentage of caregivers who report that they have used the tactic in the year prior to interview; lifetime prevalence is the percentage of caregivers who report that they have ever used the tactic. Prevalence for each scale is the percentage of caregivers who report having used any of the tactics in the scale. Among the subset of caregivers who reported having used a tactic at least once in the year prior to interview, year chronicity is a measure of how often they used it.

Self-Reported Illegal Activity

For each of 32 illegal activities, respondents were asked if they had committed the act in the 6 months prior to interview. According to type of crime and level of severity, illegal activities were divided into the following categories (Elliott, Huizinga, & Ageton, 1985):

- public disorder:
    - hitchhiking where illegal;
    - being loud, rowdy, or unruly in a public place;
    - panhandling;
    - being drunk in a public place;
    - carrying a hidden weapon;
    - prostitution;
    - vandalism; or
    - selling drugs.
- minor theft:
    - stealing or trying to steal things worth $50 or less;
    - joyriding;
    - avoiding paying for things such as movies, bus or subway rides, food, or clothing; – shoplifting; or
    - pickpocketing.
- serious property crime:
    - arson;
    - stealing or trying to steal things worth over $50;
    - burglary or attempted burglary;
    - motor vehicle theft or attempted motor vehicle theft;
    - fencing stolen goods; or
    - fraud (illegal use of checks, bank cards, or counterfeit money; or trying to cheat someone by selling him or her something worthless).
- simple assault:
    - throwing objects such as rocks or bottles at people; or – hitting someone with the idea of hurting him or her.
- felony assault:
    - attacking someone with a weapon with the idea of seriously hurting or killing him or her;
    - being involved in a gang fight; or
    - having or trying to have sexual relations with someone against his or her will.

The 12-Item Short-Form Health Survey

The 12-Item Short-Form Health Survey (SF-12) is a standardized survey instrument designed to provide an indicator of physical and mental health status. It includes 12 items selected from the Medical Outcomes Study 36-Item Short-Form Health Survey. The SF-12 is collapsed into two summary scales: a physical health component summary and a mental health component summary. Average scores for the two summary scales have been shown to closely reflect those from the original 36-item form. Furthermore, the SF-12 has demonstrated adequate reliability and validity (Ware, Kosinski, & Keller, 1996).

Trauma Symptom Inventory

The Trauma Symptom Inventory (TSI) is used in the evaluation of acute and chronic post-traumatic symptomatology, including the effects of rape, spouse abuse, physical assault, combat experiences, major accidents, and natural disasters, as well as the lasting sequelae of childhood abuse and other early traumatic events (Briere, 1996). The various scales of the TSI assess a wide range of psychological impacts. These include not only symptoms typically associated with post-traumatic stress disorder or acute stress disorder, but also those intra- and interpersonal difficulties often associated with more chronic psychological trauma. Each symptom item is rated according to its frequency of occurrence, using a 4-point scale ranging from 0 (*never*) to 3 (*often*). All clinical scales yield sex- and agenormed T scores. Two clinical scales were used: Intrusive Experiences (intrusive symptoms associated with post-traumatic stress, such as flashbacks, nightmares, and intrusive thoughts); and Dissociation (dissociative symptomatology, such as depersonalization, out-of-body experiences, and psychic numbing).

Woodcock-Johnson III Tests of Cognitive Abilities

Four subtests were used from the Woodcock-Johnson III Tests of Cognitive Abilities: (1) Letter-Word Identification is a basic reading skill involving naming letters and reading words aloud from a list. (2) Calculation is a test of math achievement measuring the ability to perform arithmetic computation with paper and pencil. (3) Passage Comprehension is a measure of reading comprehension in which the individual has to orally supply the missing word removed from each sentence or very brief paragraph. (4*)* Applied Problems is a test of math reasoning that requires the individual to solve oral word-problems. Standardized scores are based on a mean of 100, with a standard deviation of 15 (Woodcock, McGrew, & Mather, 2001).

Derived Variables

Body Mass Index

Body Mass Index (BMI) was calculated according to young adults' reports of their height and weight. BMI was estimated by dividing weight in pounds (lbs) by height in inches (in) squared and multiplying by a conversion factor of 703. The Centers for Disease Control and Prevention (CDC) considers an adult with a BMI between 25 and 29.9 to be overweight and one with a BMI of 30 or above to be obese (CDC, 2007).

Ever out of Home

Adolescent placement history was examined across Waves 1 to 4. Placement history refers to the adolescent's current living situation (in home versus out of home) at Wave 1, 2,

3, or 4. "Ever out of home" indicates that an adolescent was not living in a home with a biological caregiver at the time of the interview. An out-of-home placement could include foster care, kinship care, or group home or other residential treatment facility.

Good Health

Young adults who reported that their health was good, very good, or excellent were classified as being in "good health."

Health Limitations

Young adults reported the conditions that a doctor had ever told them that they had. Those who reported a condition were classified as having a health limitation only if that condition currently limited their activities in any way.

Household Poverty Status

Household poverty status represents the percentage of young adult households with household incomes below the federal poverty level. Household income represents the young adult's self-reported combined income for all members of his or her household. To calculate poverty status, this household income figure was then divided by the total number of household members dependent on that income.

Inpatient Mental Health Services

These services include use of a psychiatric hospital, a hospital for emotional-substance abuse problems, a residential treatment facility, an emergency shelter for emotional or substance abuse problems, or an emergency room for emotional or substance abuse problems.

Living with a Caregiver

Young adults were asked to describe all members of their household and how each member was related to them. A young adult was determined to be "living with a caregiver" if he or she described a member of that household as being any one of the following individuals: biological parent, adoptive parent, foster parent, grandparent, aunt or uncle, or stepparent.

Need for Mental Health or Substance Dependence Services

Five different measures were used to assess young adults' need for mental health and substance abuse services: (1) young adult responses to questions about the degree to which they needed help by being admitted to a psychiatric hospital or detox unit; (2) the sections of the CIDI-SF (Kessler et al., 1998) on major depression, alcohol dependence, and drug dependence; (3) the intrusive and dissociation sections of the TSI (Briere 1996); (4) Externalizing, Internalizing, and Total Problems subscales of the ASR (Achenbach and Rescorla 2003); and (5) the mental health section of the SF-12 (Ware, Kosinski, & Keller, 1996). Scores within the clinical range on any of these standardized measures identified the young adult as at risk for a mental health, alcohol, or drug problem and potentially in need of behavioral health services.

Need for Mental Health Services

Young adults were determined to have a need for mental health services if they met one of five criteria: (1) young adult self-reported "a lot" or "some" need to be admitted to a psychiatric hospital; or (2) a score within the clinical range on the depression scale of the CIDI-SF; or (3) a score of 1.5 standard deviations or more below the norm ($t \leq 35$) on the Mental Health scale of the SF- 12; or (4) a score in the clinical range of the intrusive experiences or dissociation subscales of the TSI; or (5) a score in the clinical range of the ASR for Total Problems, Internalizing, or Externalizing subscales.

Need for Substance Dependence Services

Young adults were determined to have a need for services for substance dependence if they met one of two criteria: (1) young adult self- reported "a lot" or "some" need to be admitted to a detox unit or an inpatient drug or alcohol unit or hospital medical inpatient unit; or (2) a score within the clinical range on either the Alcohol Dependence or Drug Dependence scales of the CIDI-SF.

Number of Types of Maltreatment at Baseline

Caseworkers listed at baseline all the types of maltreatment reported for each case. A categorical variable was created with the following categories: (1) only one type of maltreatment and (2) two types of maltreatment or more.

Outpatient Mental Health Services

These services included use of specialty outpatient (e.g., day treatment for emotional or substance abuse problems, outpatient drug or alcohol unit, mental health center, private professional help for emotional or substance abuse problems), and in-home counseling for emotional or substance abuse problems, or family doctor for emotional or substance abuse problems.

Specialty Outpatient Services

These services included day treatment for emotional or substance abuse problems, outpatient drug or alcohol unit, mental health center, and private professional help for emotional or substance abuse problems.

Types of Maltreatment at Baseline

At the baseline interview, caseworkers asked the following question: "Tell me the type or types of abuse or neglect reported on (report date)." They coded all that applied: (1) Physical maltreatment (Yes/No), (2) Sexual Maltreatment (Yes/No), (3) Emotional Maltreatment (Yes/No), (4) Physical Neglect (failure to provide; Yes/No), (5) Neglect (lack of supervision; Yes/No), (6) Abandonment (Yes/No), (7) Moral/Legal Maltreatment (Yes/No), (8) Educational Maltreatment (Yes/No), (9) Exploitation (Yes/No), (10) Other (Yes/No). The four main types of maltreatment (Physical maltreatment, Sexual Maltreatment, Physical Neglect, and Neglect), were analyzed as covariates for this report.

Weekly Household Income

"Weekly household income" represented the approximate dollars earned by a young adult's household per week over the course of the 12 months prior to interview. Young adults were asked to estimate the total combined income of their household over the 12 months prior to interview. Young adults could answer with daily, weekly, or annual estimates of income. If unable to give an exact dollar earning figure, the young adults were asked to describe where their household income fell across 11 income ranges. Often respondents cited an income range and did not provide an exact dollar amount. Consequently, to estimate household income in these cases, we assigned respondents a midpoint of the weekly salary range that they described.

REFERENCES

[1] Achenbach, T. M. (1991a). *Child Behavior Checklist.* Burlington, VT: University Associates in Psychiatry.

[2] Achenbach, T. M. (1991b). *Youth Self-Report.* Burlington, VT: University Associates in Psychiatry.

[3] Achenbach, T. M. & Rescorla, L. A. (2003). *Manual for the ASEBA adult forms and profiles* Burlington, VT: University of Vermont, Research Center for Children, Youth & Families.

[4] Administration for Children and Families (ACF). (2005). *National Survey of Child and Adolescent Well-Being (NSCA W) CPS sample component Wave 1 data analysis.* Retrieved June 19, 2007, from http://www.acf.hhs.gov/programs/opre/abuse_neglect/nscaw/reports/cps _sample/cps _report _revised _090 105 .pdf

[5] Administration for Children and Families (ACF). (2007). *Child maltreatment 2005.* Washington, DC: U.S. Government Printing Office.

[6] Administration for Children, Youth and Families (ACYF). (2005). *National Survey of Child and Adolescent Well-Being (NSCA W): CPS sample component, Wave 1 data analysis report.* Washington, DC: Administration for Children, Youth and Families.

[7] Administration for Children, Youth and Families (ACYF). (2006). *Indicators of welfare dependence: Annual report to congress 2006.* Retrieved June 19, 2007, from http://aspe.hhs.gov/HSP/indicators06/index.htm

[8] American Psychiatric Association. (1987). *Diagnostic and statistical manual of mental disorders* (3rd, Rev. ed.). Washington, DC: Author.

[9] American Psychiatric Association. (1994). *Diagnostic and statistical manual of mental disorders* (4th ed.). Washington, DC: Author.

[10] Arias, I. (2004). Report from the CDC. The legacy of child maltreatment: Long-term health consequences for women. *Journal of Women's Health, 13*(5), 468–473.

[11] Barnett, O., Miller-Perrin, C. & Perrin, R. (1997). *Family violence across the lifespan.* London: SAGE Publications.

[12] Blinn-Pike, L., Berger, T., Dixon, D., Kuschel, D. & Kaplan, M. (2002). Is there a causal link between maltreatment and adolescent pregnancy? A literature review. *Perspectives on Sexual and Reproductive Health, 34*(2), 68–75.

[13] Briere, J. (1989). *Trauma symptom checklist for children.* Lutz, FL: Psychological Assessment Resources, Inc.
[14] Briere, J. (1996). *Trauma symptom inventory (TSI) professional manual.* Lutz, FL: Psychological Assessment Resources, Inc.
[15] Broadhead, W. E., Gehlbach, S. H., de Gruy, F. V. & Kaplan, B. H. (1988). The Duke-UNC functional social support questionnaire: Measurement of social support in family medicine patients. *Medical Care, 26*(7), 709–723.
[16] Brown, J., Cohen, P., Johnson, J. & Smailes, E. (1999). Childhood abuse and neglect: Specificity of effect on adolescent and young depression and suicidality. *Journal of the American Academy of Child & Adolescent Psychiatry, 38*(12), 1490–1496.
[17] Callahan, S. T. & Cooper, W. O. (2004). Gender and uninsurance among young adults in the United States. *Pediatrics, 113*(2), 29 1–297.
[18] Cassell, D. & Coleman, R. (1995). Parents with psychiatric problems. In P. Reder & C. Lucey (Eds.), *Assessment of parenting: Psychiatric and psychological contributions* (pp. 169– 181). New York: Routledge.
[19] Centers for Disease Control and Prevention (CDC). (2006). *Early release of selected estimates based on data from the 2005 National Health Interview Survey.* Retrieved June 19, 2007, from http://www.cdc.gov/nchs/data/nhis/earlyrelease/200606_02.pdf
[20] Centers for Disease Control and Prevention (CDC). (2007a). *About BMI for adults.* Retrieved April 20, 2007, from http://www.cdc.gov/nccdphp/dnpa/bmi/adult_ BMI/about _adult_ BMI.htm#Interpreted
[21] Centers for Disease Control and Prevention (CDC). (2007b). Assault: all injury causes, nonfatal injuries, and rates per 100,000, 2005, United States, all races, both sexes, ages 18 to 21. Retrieved April 20,2007, from http://webappa.cdc.gov/sasweb/ ncipc/nfirates2001.html
[22] Centers for Disease Control and Prevention (CDC). (2007c). Overall: all injury causes nonfatal injuries and rates per 100,000, 2005, United States, all races, both sexes, ages 18 to 21. Retrieved April 20,2007, from http://webappa.cdc.gov/sasweb/ncipc/ nfirates.html
[23] Centers for Disease Control and Prevention (CDC). (2007d). *Physical activity for everyone.* Retrieved April 20, 2007, from http://www.cdc.gov/nccdphp/dnpa/physical/ recommendations/index.htm
[24] Chalk, R. & King, P. (1998). *Violence in families: Assessing prevention and treatment programs.* Washington, DC: National Academy Press.
[25] Chandra, A., Martines, G. M., Mosher, W. D., Abma, J. C. & Jones, J. (2005). Fertility, family planning, and reproductive health of U.S. women: Data from the 2002 National Survey of Family Growth. *Vital Health Statistics, 23*(25), 1–160.
[26] Child Trends. (2006). Facts at a glance. April 2006. Retrieved June 18, 2007, from http://www.childtrendsdatabank.org/index.cfm
[27] Christ, S. & Biemer, P. (2005). *National Survey of Child and Adolescent Well-Being (NSCAW) statistical users' manual.* Washington, DC: Administration for Children and Families.
[28] Cohn, J. F., Matias, R., Tronick, E. Z., Connell, D. & Lyons-Ruth, K. (1986). Face-to-face interactions of depressed mothers and their infants. *New Directions for Child Development, 34,* 31–45.

[29] Compton, W. M., Conway, K. P., Stinson, F. S., Colliver, J. D. & Grant, B. F. (2005). Prevalence, correlates, and comorbidity of *DSM-IV* antisocial personality syndromes and alcohol and specific drug use disorders in the United States: Results from the national epidemiologic survey on alcohol and related conditions. *Journal of Clinical Psychiatry, 66*(6), 677–685

[30] Cook, R., Fleishman, E. & Grimes, V. (1992). *A national evaluation of Title IV-E foster care independent living programs for youth.* Rockville, MA: WESTAT.

[31] Corcoran, M. & Matsudaira, J. (2005). Is it harder to get ahead? Economic attainment in early adulthood for two cohorts. In R. A. Settersten, F. F. Furstenberg, Jr. & R. G. Rumbaut (Eds.), *On the frontier of adulthood: Theory, research and public policy* (pp. 356–395). Chicago: University of Chicago Press.

[32] Cornell University Family Life Development Center, College of Human Ecology. (2007). *National Archive for Child Abuse and Neglect* [Database]. Available at http://www.ndacan.cornell.edu

[33] Courtney, M. E., Piliavin, I., Grogan-Kaylor, A. & Nesmith, A. (2001). Foster youth transitions to adulthood: A longitudinal view of youth leaving foster care. *Child Welfare, 6*, 685– 717.

[34] Courtney, M. E. & Heuring, D. H. (2005). The transition to adulthood for youth "aging out" of the foster care system. In D. W. Osgood, E. M. Foster, C. Flanagan, & G. R. Ruth (Eds.). *On your own without a net* (pp. 27–67). Chicago: University of Chicago Press.

[35] Danielson, C., de Arellano, M., Kilpatrick, D., Saunders, B. & Resnick, H. (2005). Child maltreatment in depressed adolescents: Differences in symptomatology based on history of abuse. *Child Maltreatment, 10*(1), 37–48.

[36] Davis, M. & Sondheimer, D. L. (2005). State child mental health efforts to support youth in transition to adulthood. *Journal of Behavioral Health Services & Research, 32*(1), 27–42.

[37] Davis, M., Geller, J. L. & Hunt, B. (2006). Within-state availability of transition-to-adulthood services for youths with serious mental health conditions. *Psychiatric Services, 57*(11), 1594–1599.

[38] DeNavas-Walt, C., Proctor, B. D. & Lee, C. H. (2006). Income, poverty, and health insurance coverage in the United States: 2005. Retrieved May 14, 2007, from http://www.census.gov/prod/2006pubs/p60–231.pdf

[39] Dixon, L., Browne, K. & Hamilton-Giachritsis, C. (2005). Risk factors of parents abused as children: A mediational analysis of the intergenerational continuity of child maltreatment. *Journal of Child Psychology and Psychiatry and Allied Disciplines, 46*(1), 47–57.

[40] Elliott, D. S., Huizinga, D. & Ageton, S. (1985). *Explaining delinquency and drug use.* Beverly Hills, CA: Sage Publications.

[41] Erikson, E. H. (1950). *Childhood and Society.* New York: Norton.

[42] Fergusson, D. M. & Lynskey, M. T. (1997). Physical punishment/maltreatment during childhood and adjustment in young adulthood. *Journal of Child Abuse & Neglect, 21*(7), 617–630.

[43] Fox, M. A., Connolly, B. A. & Snyder, T. D. (2005). *Youth indicators 2005: Trends in the wellbeing of American youth* (NCES 2005-050). U.S. Department of Education, National

[44] Center for Education Statistics. Washington, DC: U.S. Government Printing Office.
[45] Furstenberg, F. F., Cook, T. D., Eccles, J., Elder, G. H. & Sameroff, A. (1999). *Managing to make it: Urban families and adolescent success.* Chicago: University of Chicago Press.
[46] Furstenberg, F. F., Kennedy, S., McLoyd, V., Rumbaut, R. & Settersten, R. A. (2004). Growing up is harder to do. *Contexts, 3*(3), 33–41.
[47] Furstenburg, F. F., Jr., Rumbaut, R. G. & Settersten, R. A. (2005). On the frontier of adulthood: Emerging themes and new directions. In R. A. Settersten, F. F. Furstenberg, Jr. & R. G. Rumbaut (Eds.), *On the frontier of adulthood: Theory, research and public policy* (pp. 3–25). Chicago: University of Chicago Press.
[48] Fussell, E. & Furstenberg, F. F., Jr. (2005). The transition to adulthood during the twentieth century: Race, nativity and gender. In R. A. Settersten, F. F. Furstenberg, Jr. & R. G. Rumbaut (Eds.), *On the frontier of adulthood: Theory, research and public policy* (pp. 29–75). Chicago: University of Chicago Press.
[49] George, R., Bilaver, L., JooLee, B., Needell, B., Brookhart, A. & Jackman, W. (2002). *Employment outcomes for youth aging out of foster care.* Chicago: Chapin Hall Center for Children at the University of Chicago. Retrieved June 18, 2007, from http://aspe.os.dhhs.gov/hsp/fostercare-agingout02/
[50] Georgiades, S. (2005). A multi-outcome evaluation of an independent living program. *Child and Adolescent Social Work Journal, 22*(5–6), 417–439.
[51] Harris, K. M., Gordon-Larsen, P., Chantala, K. & Udry, J. R. (2006). Longitudinal trends in race/ethnic disparities in leading health indicators from adolescence to young adulthood. *Archives of Pediatric and Adolescent Medicine, 160*, 74–81.
[52] Hillis, S. D., Anda, R. F., Felitti, V. J., Nordenberg, D. & Marchbanks, P. A. (2000). Adverse childhood experiences and sexually transmitted diseases in men and women: A retrospective study. *Pediatrics, 106*(1), e1 1–17.
[53] Hussey, J. M., Marshall, J. M., English, D. J., Knight, E. D., Lau, A. S., Dubowitz, H., et al. (2005). Defining maltreatment according to substantiation: Distinction without a difference? *Child Abuse & Neglect, 29*(5), 479–492.
[54] Kaiser Commission on Medicaid and the Uninsured. (2006). Health insurance coverage in America: 2005 data update. from http://www.kff.org/uninsured/upload/2005DataUpdate.pdf
[55] Kaplan, S., Pelcovitz, D., Salzinger, S., Weiner, M., Mandel, F., Lesser, M., et al. (1998). Adolescent physical abuse: Risk for adolescent psychiatric disorders. *American Journal of Psychiatry, 155*, 954–959.
[56] Kessler, R. C., Andrews, G., Mroczek, D., Ustun, T. B. & Wittchen, H.-U. (1998). The WorldHealth Organization Composite International Diagnostic Interview Short Form (CIDI-SF). *International Journal of Methods in Psychiatric Research, 7*, 171–185.
[57] Kessler, R. C., Chiu, W. T., Demler, O. & Walters, E. E. (2005). Prevalence, severity, and comorbidity of 12-Month *DSM-IV* disorders in the National Comorbidity Survey Replication. *Archives of General Psychiatry, 62*(6), 617–709.
[58] Kovacs, M. (1992). *Children's Depression Inventory.* North Tonawanda, NY: Multi-Health Systems, Inc.
[59] Lansford, J. E., Dodge, K., Pettit, G., Bates, J., Crozier, J. & Kaplow, J. (2002). A 12-Year Prospective Study of the Long-term Effects of Early Child Physical Maltreatment

on Psychological, Behavioral, and Academic Problems in Adolescence. *Archives of Pediatric Adolescent Medicine 156*, 824–830.

[60] Leiter, J., Myers, K. A. & Zingraff, M. T. (1994). Substantiated and unsubstantiated cases of child maltreatment: Do their consequences differ? *Social Work Research 18*(2), 67–82.

[61] Lyons, P. M. & Melton, G. B. (2005). Coping with mental health problems in young adulthood: Diversity of need and uniformity of programs. In D. W. Osgood, M. E. Foster, C. Flanagan & G. R. Ruth (Eds.), *On your own without a net*. Chicago: The University of Chicago Press.

[62] Lyons-Ruth, K., Wolfe, R. & Lyubchik, A. (2000). Depression and the parenting of young children: Making the case for early preventive mental health services. *Harvard Review of Psychiatry, 8*(3), 148–153.

[63] MacMillan, H. L., Fleming, J. E., Streiner, D. L., Lin, E., Boyle, M. H., Jamieson, E., et al. (2001). Childhood abuse and lifetime psychopathology in a community sample. *American Journal of Psychiatry, 158*, 1878–1883.

[64] Malow, R., Dévieux, J. & Lucenko, B. (2006). History of childhood sexual abuse as a risk factor for HIV risk behavior. *Journal of Trauma Practice, 5*(3), 13–32.

[65] Martinez, G. M., Chandra, A., Abma, J. C., Jones, J. & Mosher, W. D. (2006). Fertility, contraception, and fatherhood: Data on men and women from cycle 6 (2002) of the 2002 National Survey of Family Growth. *Vital Health Statistics, 23*(26), 1–142.

[66] Masten, A. S., Burt, K. B., Roisman, G. I., Obradovic, J., Long, J. D. & Tellegen, A. (2004). Resources and resilience in the transition to adulthood: Continuity and change. *Development and psychopathology, 16*(4), 1071–1094.

[67] McAlister, B. (2002). *Children who see too much: Lessons from the child witness to violence project*. Boston: Beacon Press.

[68] McCracken, H. E., Jiles, R. & Blanck, H. M. (2007). Behavioral Risk Factor Surveillance System. Retrieved June 19, 2007, from http://www.cdc.gov/brfss/

[69] McMillen, J. C., Zima, B. T., Scott, L. D., Auslanderm, W. F., Munson, M. R., Ollie, M. T., et al. (2005). Prevalence of psychiatric disorders among older youths in the foster care system. *Journal of the American Academy of Child and Adolescent Psychiatry, 44*(1), 88–95.

[70] Mollenkopf, J., Waters, M. C., Holdaway, J., and Kasinitz, P. (2005). The ever-winding path: Ethnic and racial diversity in the transition to adulthood. In R. A. Settersten, F. F. Furstenberg, Jr. & R. G. Rumbaut (Eds.), *On the frontier of adulthood: Theory, research and public policy* (pp. 454–497). Chicago: University of Chicago Press.

[71] Molnar, B. E., Buka, S. L. & Kessler, R. C. (2001). Child sexual abuse and subsequent psychopathology: Results from the National Comorbidity Survey. *American Journal of Public Health, 91*, 753–760.

[72] Mouw, T. (2005). Sequences of early adult transitions: A look at variability and consequences. In R. A. Settersten, F. F. Furstenberg, Jr. & R. G. Rumbaut (Eds.), *On the frontier of adulthood: Theory, research and public policy* (pp. 256–291). Chicago: University of Chicago Press.

[73] National Survey of Child and Adolescent Well-Being (NSCAW) Research Group (2002). Methodological lessons from the National Survey of Child and Adolescent Well-Being: The first three years of the USA's first national probability study of

children and families investigated for abuse and neglect. *Child and Youth Services Review, 24*(6/7), 5 13–541.

[74] Osgood, D. W., Foster, M. E., Flanagan, C. & Ruth, G. R. (2005). Introduction: why focus on the transition to adulthood for vulnerable populations? In D. W. Osgood, M. E. Foster, C. Flanagan & G. R. Ruth (Eds.), *On your own without a net*. Chicago: The University of Chicago Press.

[75] Ozturk, E. I., Leventhal, J. & Dobbs, S. (2000). Intergenerational continuity of child physical abuse: How good is the evidence? *Lancet, 356*(9232), 814–819.

[76] Park, M., Mulye, T., Adams, S., Brindis, C. & Irwin, C. (2006). The health status of young adults in the United States. *Journal of Adolescent Health, 39*, 305–3 17.

[77] Pleis, J. R. & Lethbridge-Cejku, M. (2006). Summary health statistics for U.S. adults: National Health Interview Survey, 2005. *Vital Health Statistics, 10*(232), 1–163.

[78] Riggs, S., Alario, A. & McHorney, C. (1990). Health risk behaviors and attempted suicide in adolescents who report prior maltreatment. *Pediatrics 116*(5), 815–821.

[79] Rumbaut, R. G. (2007). Young adults in the United States: A profile. Transition to Adulthood Research McArthur Network working paper, retrieved June 18, 2007, from http://www.transad.pop.upenn.edu/downloads/Young%20Adults%20in%20the%20 United%20States%20-%20A%20Profile.pdf

[80] Sarason, I. G., Levine, H. M. & Robert, B. (1983). Assessing social support: The social support questionnaire. *Journal of personality and social psychology 44*, 127–139.

[81] Sarason, I. G., Sarason, B. R., Shearin, E. N. & Pierce, P. R. (1987). A brief measure of social support: Practical and theoretical implications. *Journal of social and personal relationships, 4*(4), 497–510.

[82] Schoeni, R. F. & Ross, K. E. (2005). Material assistance from families during the transition to adulthood. In R. A. Settersten, F. F. Furstenberg, Jr. & R. G. Rumbaut (Eds.), *On the frontier of adulthood: Theory, research and public policy* (pp. 396–416). Chicago: University of Chicago Press.

[83] Schulenberg, J., O'Malley, P. M., Bachman, J. G. & Johnston, L. D. (2005). Early adulthood transitions and their relations to well-being and substance use. In R. A. Settersten, F. F. Furstenberg, Jr. & R. G. Rumbaut (Eds.), *On the frontier of adulthood: Theory, research and public policy* (pp. 417–453). Chicago: University of Chicago Press.

[84] Silverman, A. D., Reinherz, H. Z. & Giaconia, R. M. (1996). The long-term sequelae of child and adolescent abuse: A longitudinal community study. *Child Abuse & Neglect, 20*(8), 709–723.

[85] Smith, C. A., Ireland, T. O. & Thornberry, T. P. (2005). Adolescent maltreatment and its impact on young adult antisocial behavior. *Child Abuse and Neglect, 29*, 1099–1119.

[86] Smith, T. W. (2005). Generation gaps in attitudes and values from the 1970s to the 1990s. In Settersten, R. A., Furstenberg, F. F. Jr. & Rumbaut, R. G. (Eds.), *On the frontier of adulthood: Theory, research and public policy* (pp. 177–221). Chicago: University of Chicago Press.

[87] Snyder, H. N. & Sickmund, M. (2006). *Juvenile offenders and victims: 2006 national report*. Pittsburgh, PA: National Center for Juvenile Justice. Retrieved June 18, 2007, from http://ojjdp.ncjrs.gov/ojstatbb/nr2006/downloads/NR2006.pdf

[88] Spatz Widom, C., DuMont, K. & Czaja, S. J. (2007). A prospective investigation of major depressive disorder and comorbidity in abused and neglected children grown up. *Archives of General Psychiatry, 64*, 49–56.

[89] Straus, M. A. (1979). Measuring intrafamily conflict and violence: The Conflict Tactics (CT) Scale. *Journal of Marriage and the Family, 41*, 75–88.

[90] Straus, M. A., Hamby, S. L., Finkelhor, D., Moore, D. W. & Runyan, D. (1998). Identification of child maltreatment with the Parent-Child Conflict Tactics Scales: Development and psychometric data for a national sample of American parents. *Child Abuse and Neglect, 22*(4), 249–270.

[91] Substance Abuse and Mental Health Services Administration (SAMHSA), Office of Applied Studies (OAS). (2006). Results from the 2005 National Survey on Drug Use and Health: Detailed tables. Retrieved June 18, 2007, from http://www.oas.samhsa.gov/nsduh/ 2k5nsduh/tabs/Sect5peTabs 1 4to25 .pdf

[92] Substance Abuse and Mental Health Services Administration (SAMHSA), Office of Applied Studies (OAS). (2005). *National Survey on Drug Use & Health: National findings.* Retrieved June 18, 2007, from http://oas.samhsa.gov/nsduh/2k5nsduh/ 2k5Results.pdf

[93] Thompson, M. P., Arias, I., Basile, K. C. & Desai, S. (2002). The association between childhood physical and sexual victimization and health problems in adulthood in a nationally representative sample of women. *Journal of Interpersonal Violence, 17*(10), 1115–1129.

[94] Thompson, M. P., Kingree, J. B. & Desai, S. (2004). Gender differences in long-term health consequences of physical abuse of children: Data from a nationally representative survey. *American Journal of Public Health, 94*, 599–604.

[95] Thornberry, T., Ireland, T. & Smith, C. (2001). The importance of timing: The varying impact of childhood and adolescent maltreatment on multiple problem outcomes. *Development and Psychopathology, 13*, 957–979.

[96] Tjaden, P. & Thoennes, N. (2000). *Extent, nature and consequences of intimate partner violence: Findings from the National Violence Against Women Survey.* Washington, DC: U.S. Department of Justice.

[97] U.S. Bureau of Justice Statistics (2006, December). Criminal victimization in the United States, 2005—statistical tables (NCJ 215244). Retrieved May 18, 2007, from http://www.ojp.gov/bjs/pub/pdf/cvus05.pdf

[98] U.S. Census Bureau (2006a). 2005 American Community Survey: subject table S2301 Employment Status. Retrieved June 18, 2007, from http://factfinder.census.gov/ servlet/STTable?_bm=y&-qr_name=ACS_2005_EST_G00_S230 1 &-geo_id= 01 000US&-ds_name=ACS_2005_EST_G00_&-_lang=en&-format=&-CONTEXT=st

[99] U.S. Census Bureau (2006b). America's families and living arrangements: 2006. Retrieved June 18, 2007, from http://www.census.gov/population/www/socdemo/hh-fam/cps2006.html

[100] U.S. Census Bureau. (2000). *Statistical abstract of the United States.* Washington, DC: U.S. Government Printing Office.

[101] U.S. Department of Agriculture and U.S. Department of Health and Human Services (1990). *Nutrition and your health: Dietary guidelines for Americans* (3rd ed.). Washington, DC: Author (Home and Garden Bulletin. No. 232, USDA).

[102] Urban Institute. (2007). *Multi-site evaluation of foster youth programs*. Retrieved June 19, 2007, from http://www.norc.org/projects/Multi-site+Evaluation+of+Foster+Youth+Programs .htm
[103] Vostanis, P. (2005). Patients as parents and young people approaching adulthood: How should we manage the interface between mental health services for young people and adults? *Current Opinion in Psychiatry, 18*, 449–454.
[104] Walker, E. A., Gelfand, A., Katon, W. J., Koss, M. P., Von Korff, M., Bernstein, D., et al. (1999). Adult health status of women with histories of childhood abuse and neglect. *American Journal of Medicine, 107* (4), 332–339.
[105] Wang, P. S., Lane, M., Olfson, M., Pincus, H. A., Wells, K. B. & Kessler, R. C. (2005). Twelve-month use of mental health services in the United States: Results from the National Comorbidity Survey Replication. *Archives of General Psychiatry, 62*(6), 629–640.
[106] Ware, J., Jr., Kosinski, M. & Keller, S. D. (1996). A 12-item short-form health survey: Construction of scales and preliminary tests of reliability and validity. *Medical Care, 34*(3), 220–233.
[107] Whitaker, D. J., Haileyesus, T., Swahn, M. & Saltzman, L. S. (2007). Differences in frequency of violence and reported injury between relationships with reciprocal and nonreciprocal intimate partner violence. *American Journal of Public Health, 97*(5), 941–946.
[108] Wolfe, D., Scott, K., Wekerle, C. & Pittman, A. (2001). Child maltreatment: Risk of adjustment problems and dating violence in adolescence. *Journal of the American Academy of Child & Adolescent Psychiatry, 40*(3), 282–289.
[109] Wonderlich, S. A., Wilsnack, R. W., Wilsnack, S. C. & Harris, T. R. (1996). Childhood sexual abuse and bulimic behavior in a nationally representative sample. *American Journal of Public Health, 86*, 1082–1086.
[110] Woodcock, R. W., McGrew, K. S., and Mather, N. (2001). *Examiner's manual. Woodcock- Johnson III Tests of Cognitive Abilities*. Itasca, IL: Riverside Publishing.

End Notes

[1] The 12-Item Short-Form Health Survey (SF-12) is a standardized survey instrument. It is designed to indicate physical and mental health status. It includes 12 items selected from the Medical Outcomes Study 36-Item Short- Form Health Survey. The SF-12 is collapsed into two summary scales: a physical health component summary and a mental health component summary. Higher scores represent better health, the mean in the general population is 50, and the standard deviation is 10.

[2] Additional information about the procedures used to design the Wave 5 young adult weights is described within the *Data File Users Manual,* Section 7.4.1.

[3] MDE is defined as a period of at least 2 weeks during which a person experiences a depressed mood or loss of interest or pleasure in daily activities and has a majority of the symptoms for depression as described in the fourth edition of the *Diagnostic and Statistical Manual of Mental Disorders* (American Psychiatric Association, 1994).

[4] Questions about social support were modeled after the Duke-UNC Functional Social Support Questionnaire (Broadhead, Gehlbach, de Gruy, & Kaplan, 1988) and the Sarason Social Support Questionnaire (Sarason, Levine, & Robert, 1983; Sarason, Sarason, Shearin, & Pierce, 1987).

[5] It is noteworthy that the Kessler's reports used the long form of the CIDI. Thus, the estimate for need of mental health services among young adults in this report was based on four main sources of information that are not equivalent to what would have been obtained if the complete CIDI had been used as it was with the National Comorbidity Survey Replication. Moreover, the scales used in the present study were not designed to capture

diagnoses, as the CIDI was; instead, most of the scales capture symptoms, without all the CIDI criteria required for diagnosis.

Chapter Sources

Chapter 1 – This is an edited, reformatted and augmented version of a United States Department of Health and Human Services report, dated April 2008.
Chapter 2 – This is an edited, reformatted and augmented version of a United States Department of Health and Human Services report, dated April 2010.
Chapter 3 – This is an edited, reformatted and augmented version of a United States Department of Health and Human Services report, dated April 2008.

INDEX

C

D

I

J

K

L

M

N

O

P

R

S

T

U

V

W

Y